# Lecture Notes in Artificial Intelligence 1572

Subseries of Lecture Notes in Computer Science
Edited by J. G. Carbonell and J. Siekmann

# Lecture Notes in Computer Science

Edited by G. Goos, J. Hartmanis and J. van Leeuwen

## Springer

*Berlin*
*Heidelberg*
*New York*
*Barcelona*
*Hong Kong*
*London*
*Milan*
*Paris*
*Singapore*
*Tokyo*

Paul Fischer   Hans Ulrich Simon (Eds.)

# Computational
# Learning Theory

4th European Conference, EuroCOLT'99
Nordkirchen, Germany, March 29-31, 1999
Proceedings

Springer

Series Editors

Jaime G. Carbonell, Carnegie Mellon University, Pittsburgh, PA, USA
Jörg Siekmann, University of Saarland, Saarbrücken, Germany


Volume Editors

Paul Fischer
Lehrstuhl für Informatik II, Universität Dortmund
D-44221 Dortmund, Germany
E-mail: paulf@ls2.cs.uni-dortmund.de

Hans Ulrich Simon
Fakultät für Mathematik, Ruhr Universität Bochum
D-44780 Bochum, Germany
E-mail: simon@lmi.ruhr-uni-bochum.de

Cataloging-in-Publication data applied for


**Die Deutsche Bibliothek - CIP-Einheitsaufnahme**

**Computational learning theory** : 4th European conference ;
proceedings / EuroCOLT '99, Nordkirchen, Germany, March 29 - 31,
1999. Paul Fischer ; Hans Ulrich Simon (ed.). - Berlin ; Heidelberg ;
New York ; Barcelona ; Hong Kong ; London ; Milan ; Paris ;
Singapore ; Tokyo : Springer, 1999
(Lecture notes in computer science ; 1572 : Lecture notes in artificial
intelligence)
ISBN 3-540-65701-0


CR Subject Classification (1998): I.2.6, I.2.3, F.4.1, F.1.1, F.2


ISBN 3-540-65701-0 Springer-Verlag Berlin Heidelberg New York

© Springer-Verlag Berlin Heidelberg 1999
Printed in Germany

Typesetting: Camera-ready by author
SPIN 10703032   06/3142 – 5 4 3 2 1 0     Printed on acid-free paper

# Preface

This volume contains papers presented at the Fourth European Conference on Computational Learning Theory, which was held at Nordkirchen Castle, in Nordkirchen, NRW, Germany, from March 29 to 31, 1999. This conference is the fourth in a series of bi-annual conferences established in 1993.

The EuroCOLT conferences are focused on the analysis of learning algorithms and the theory of machine learning, and bring together researchers from a wide variety of related fields. Some of the issues and topics that are addressed include the sample and computational complexity of learning specific model classes, frameworks modeling the interaction between the learner, teacher and the environment (such as learning with queries, learning control policies and inductive inference), learning with complex models (such as decision trees, neural networks, and support vector machines), learning with minimal prior assumptions (such as mistake-bound models, universal prediction, and agnostic learning), and the study of model selection techniques. We hope that these conferences stimulate an interdisciplinary scientific interaction that will be fruitful in all represented fields.

Thirty-five papers were submitted to the program committee for consideration, and twenty-one of these were accepted for presentation at the conference and publication in these proceedings. In addition, Robert Schapire (AT & T Labs), and Richard Sutton (AT & T Labs) were invited to give lectures and contribute a written version to these proceedings. There were a number of other joint events including a banquet and an excursion to Münster. The IFIP WG 1.4 Scholarship was awarded to András Antos for his paper "Lower bounds on the rate of convergence of nonparametric pattern recognition".

The EuroCOLT'99 conference was sponsored by the DFG (Deutsche Forschungsgemeinschaft) and by IFIP through WG 1.4.

We want to thank everybody who helped to make this meeting possible: the authors for submitting papers, the Program Committee and referees for their effort in composing the program, the Steering Committee, the sponsors, the local organizers, and Springer-Verlag. Thanks to Norbert Klasner and Karsten Tinnefeld for their help in preparing the proceedings, and thanks to Margret Vaupel for her administrative support. The program committee wishes to thank everybody who acted as subreferee.

January 1999

Paul Fischer and Hans Simon
Conference Chairs
EuroCOLT'99

# Organization

EUROCOLT'99 is organized by the department of Computer Science, University of Dortmund.

## Organizers

Paul Fischer (University of Dortmund, Germany)
Hans Simon (Ruhr-Universität Bochum, Germany)

## Steering Commitee

Shai Ben-David (Chair) Technion, Haifa
Nicolò Cesa-Bianchi, University of Milano
Paul Fischer, University of Dortmund
Gabor Lugosi, Pompeu Fabra University, Barcelona
Arun Sharma, University of New South Wales, Sydney
Hans Simon, Ruhr-Universität Bochum

## Program Commitee

Martin Anthony, London School of Economics
Peter Auer, Technical University of Graz
Shai Ben-David, Technion, Haifa
Nader Bshouty, University of Calgary
John Case, University of Delaware
Nicolò Cesa-Bianchi, University of Milano
Paul Fischer, University of Dortmund
Jyrki Kivinen, University of Helsinki
Nick Littlestone, NEC Research Institute, Princeton
Gábor Lugosi, Pompeu Fabra University, Barcelona
Arun Sharma, University of New South Wales, Sydney
Hans Simon, Ruhr-Universität Bochum (Chair)

# Subreferees

| | | |
|---|---|---|
| Peter Bartlett | Claudio Gentile | Mark Pendrith |
| Gianluca Della Vedova | Tibor Hegedűs | Dale Schuurmans |
| Nadav Eiron | Christian Killin | Frank Stephan |
| Tapio Elomaa | Juha Kärkkäinen | Henry Tirri |
| Ran El-Yaniv | Eric Martin | Jaak Vilo |
| Yoav Freund | Petri Myllymäki | |

# Sponsoring Institutions

Deutsche Forschungsgemeinsschaft (DFG) and IFIP WG 1.4.

# Table of Contents

## Invited Lectures

## Learning from Random Examples

## Learning from Queries and Counterexamples

## Reinforcement Learning

## On-line Learning and Expert Advice

## Teaching and Learning

## Inductive Inference

## Statistical Theory of Learning and Pattern Recognition

## Author Index

# Theoretical Views of Boosting

Robert E. Schapire

AT&T Labs, Shannon Laboratory
180 Park Avenue, Room A279, Florham Park, NJ 07932, USA

**Abstract.** Boosting is a general method for improving the accuracy of any given learning algorithm. Focusing primarily on the AdaBoost algorithm, we briefly survey theoretical work on boosting including analyses of AdaBoost's training error and generalization error, connections between boosting and game theory, methods of estimating probabilities using boosting, and extensions of AdaBoost for multiclass classification problems. We also briefly mention some empirical work.

## Background

Boosting is a general method which attempts to "boost" the accuracy of any given learning algorithm. Kearns and Valiant [21, 22] were the first to pose the question of whether a "weak" learning algorithm which performs just slightly better than random guessing in Valiant's PAC model [34] can be "boosted" into an arbitrarily accurate "strong" learning algorithm. Schapire [28] came up with the first provable polynomial-time boosting algorithm in 1989. A year later, Freund [13] developed a much more efficient boosting algorithm which, although optimal in a certain sense, nevertheless suffered from certain practical drawbacks. The first experiments with these early boosting algorithms were carried out by Drucker, Schapire and Simard [12] on an OCR task.

## AdaBoost

The AdaBoost algorithm, introduced in 1995 by Freund and Schapire [16], solved many of the practical difficulties of the earlier boosting algorithms, and is the focus of this paper. Pseudocode for AdaBoost is given in Fig. 1 in the slightly generalized form given by Schapire and Singer [31]. The algorithm takes as input a training set $(x_1, y_1), \ldots, (x_m, y_m)$ where each $x_i$ belongs to some *domain* or *instance space* $X$, and each *label* $y_i$ is in some label set $Y$. For most of this paper, we assume $Y = \{-1, +1\}$; later, we discuss extensions to the multiclass case. AdaBoost calls a given *weak* or *base learning algorithm* repeatedly in a series of rounds $t = 1, \ldots, T$. One of the main ideas of the algorithm is to maintain a distribution or set of weights over the training set. The weight of this distribution on training example $i$ on round $t$ is denoted $D_t(i)$. Initially, all weights are set equally, but on each round, the weights of incorrectly classified

Given: $(x_1, y_1), \ldots, (x_m, y_m)$ where $x_i \in X$, $y_i \in Y = \{-1, +1\}$
Initialize $D_1(i) = 1/m$.
For $t = 1, \ldots, T$:

- Train weak learner using distribution $D_t$.
- Get weak hypothesis $h_t : X \to \mathbb{R}$.
- Choose $\alpha_t \in \mathbb{R}$.
- Update:

$$D_{t+1}(i) = \frac{D_t(i) \exp(-\alpha_t y_i h_t(x_i))}{Z_t}$$

where $Z_t$ is a normalization factor (chosen so that $D_{t+1}$ will be a distribution).

Output the final hypothesis:

$$H(x) = \text{sign}\left(\sum_{t=1}^{T} \alpha_t h_t(x)\right).$$

**Fig. 1.** The boosting algorithm AdaBoost.

examples are increased so that the weak learner is forced to focus on the hard examples in the training set.

The weak learner's job is to find a *weak hypothesis* $h_t : X \to \mathbb{R}$ appropriate for the distribution $D_t$. In the simplest case, the range of each $h_t$ is binary, i.e., restricted to $\{-1, +1\}$; the weak learner's job then is to minimize the *error*

$$\epsilon_t = \text{Pr}_{i \sim D_t} [h_t(x_i) \neq y_i].$$

Once the weak hypothesis $h_t$ has been received, AdaBoost chooses a parameter $\alpha_t \in \mathbb{R}$ which intuitively measures the importance that it assigns to $h_t$. In the figure, we have deliberately left the choice of $\alpha_t$ unspecified. For binary $h_t$, we typically set

$$\alpha_t = \tfrac{1}{2} \ln \left(\frac{1 - \epsilon_t}{\epsilon_t}\right). \tag{1}$$

More on choosing $\alpha_t$ follows below. The distribution $D_t$ is then updated using the rule shown in the figure. The *final hypothesis* $H$ is a weighted majority vote of the $T$ weak hypotheses where $\alpha_t$ is the weight assigned to $h_t$.

## Analyzing the training error

The most basic theoretical property of AdaBoost concerns its ability to reduce the training error. Specifically, Schapire and Singer [31], in generalizing a theorem of Freund and Schapire [16], show that the training error of the final hypothesis is bounded as follows:

$$\frac{1}{m}|\{i : H(x_i) \neq y_i\}| \leq \frac{1}{m}\sum_i \exp(-y_i f(x_i)) = \prod_t Z_t \qquad (2)$$

where $f(x) = \sum_t \alpha_t h_t(x)$ so that $H(x) = \text{sign}(f(x))$. The inequality follows from the fact that $e^{-y_i f(x_i)} \geq 1$ if $y_i \neq H(x_i)$. The equality can be proved straightforwardly by unraveling the recursive definition of $D_t$.

Eq. (2) suggests that the training error can be reduced most rapidly (in a greedy way) by choosing $\alpha_t$ and $h_t$ on each round to minimize

$$Z_t = \sum_i D_t(i) \exp(-\alpha_t y_i h_t(x_i)).$$

In the case of binary hypotheses, this leads to the choice of $\alpha_t$ given in Eq. (1) and gives a bound on the training error of

$$\prod_t \left[2\sqrt{\epsilon_t(1-\epsilon_t)}\right] = \prod_t \sqrt{1-4\gamma_t^2} \leq \exp\left(-2\sum_t \gamma_t^2\right)$$

where $\epsilon_t = 1/2 - \gamma_t$. This bound was first proved by Freund and Schapire [16]. Thus, if each weak hypothesis is slightly better than random so that $\gamma_t$ is bounded away from zero, then the training error drops exponentially fast. This bound, combined with the bounds on generalization error given below prove that Ada-Boost is indeed a boosting algorithm in the sense that it can efficiently convert a weak learning algorithm (which can always generate a hypothesis with a weak edge for any distribution) into a strong learning algorithm (which can generate a hypothesis with an arbitrarily low error rate, given sufficient data).

Eq. (2) points to the fact that, at heart, AdaBoost is a procedure for finding a linear combination $f$ of weak hypotheses which attempts to minimize

$$\sum_i \exp(-y_i f(x_i)) = \sum_i \exp\left(-y_i \sum_t \alpha_t h_t(x_i)\right). \qquad (3)$$

Essentially, on each round, AdaBoost chooses $h_t$ (by calling the weak learner) and then sets $\alpha_t$ to add one more term to the acculating weighted sum of weak hypotheses in such a way that the sum of exponentials above will be maximally reduced. In other words, AdaBoost is doing a kind of steepest descent search to minimize Eq. (3) where the search is constrained at each step to follow coordinate directions (where we identify coordinates with the weights assigned to weak hypotheses).

Schapire and Singer [31] discuss the choice of $\alpha_t$ and $h_t$ in the case that $h_t$ is real-valued (rather than binary). In this case, $h_t(x)$ can be interpreted as a "confidence-rated prediction" in which the sign of $h_t(x)$ is the predicted label, while the magnitude $|h_t(x)|$ gives a measure of confidence.

## Generalization error

Freund and Schapire [16] showed how to bound the generalization error of the final hypothesis in terms of its training error, the size $m$ of the sample, the VC-dimension $d$ of the weak hypothesis space and the number of rounds $T$ of boosting. Specifically, they used techniques from Baum and Haussler [3] to show that the generalization error, with high probability, is at most

$$\hat{\Pr}\left[H(x) \neq y\right] + \tilde{O}\left(\sqrt{\frac{Td}{m}}\right)$$

where $\hat{\Pr}[\cdot]$ denotes empirical probability on the training sample. This bound suggests that boosting will overfit if run for too many rounds, i.e., as $T$ becomes large. In fact, this sometimes does happen. However, in early experiments, several authors [7, 11, 26] observed empirically that boosting often does *not* overfit, even when run for thousands of rounds. Moreover, it was observed that AdaBoost would sometimes continue to drive down the generalization error long after the training error had reached zero, clearly contradicting the spirit of the bound above. For instance, the left side of Fig. 2 shows the training and test curves of running boosting on top of Quinlan's C4.5 decision-tree learning algorithm [27] on the "letter" dataset.

In response to these empirical findings, Schapire et al. [30], following the work of Bartlett [1], gave an alternative analysis in terms of the *margins* of the training examples. The margin of example $(x, y)$ is defined to be

$$\frac{y \sum_t \alpha_t h_t(x)}{\sum_t |\alpha_t|}.$$

It is a number in $[-1, +1]$ which is positive if and only if $H$ correctly classifies the example. Moreover, as before, the magnitude of the margin can be interpreted as a measure of confidence in the prediction. Schapire et al. proved that larger margins on the training set translate into a superior upper bound on the generalization error. Specifically, the generalization error is at most

$$\hat{\Pr}\left[\text{margin}_f(x, y) \leq \theta\right] + \tilde{O}\left(\sqrt{\frac{d}{m\theta^2}}\right)$$

for any $\theta > 0$ with high probability. Note that this bound is entirely independent of $T$, the number of rounds of boosting. In addition, Schapire et al. proved that boosting is particularly aggressive at reducing the margin (in a quantifiable sense) since it concentrates on the examples with the smallest margins (whether positive or negative). Boosting's effect on the margins can be seen empirically, for instance, on the right side of Fig. 2 which shows the cumulative distribution of margins of the training examples on the "letter" dataset. In this case, even

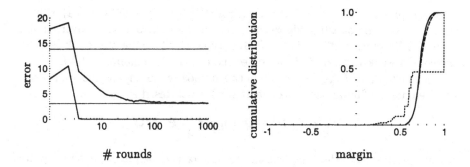

**Fig. 2.** Error curves and the margin distribution graph for boosting C4.5 on the letter dataset as reported by Schapire et al. [30]. *Left*: the training and test error curves (lower and upper curves, respectively) of the combined classifier as a function of the number of rounds of boosting. The horizontal lines indicate the test error rate of the base classifier as well as the test error of the final combined classifier. *Right*: The cumulative distribution of margins of the training examples after 5, 100 and 1000 iterations, indicated by short-dashed, long-dashed (mostly hidden) and solid curves, respectively.

after the training error reaches zero, boosting continues to increase the margins of the training examples effecting a corresponding drop in the test error.

Attempts (not always successful) to use the insights gleaned from the theory of margins have been made by several authors [5, 19, 24]. In addition, the margin theory points to a strong connection between boosting and the support-vector machines of Vapnik and others [4, 8, 35] which explicitly attempt to maximize the minimum margin.

## A connection to game theory

The behavior of AdaBoost can also be understood in a game-theoretic setting as explored by Freund and Schapire [15, 17] (see also Grove and Schuurmans [19] and Breiman [6]). In classical game theory, it is possible to put any two-person, zero-sum game in the form of a matrix $\mathbf{M}$. To play the game, one player chooses a row $i$ and the other player chooses a column $j$. The loss to the row player (which is the same as the payoff to the column player) is $\mathbf{M}_{ij}$. More generally, the two sides may play randomly, choosing distributions $\mathbf{P}$ and $\mathbf{Q}$ over rows or columns, respectively. The expected loss then is $\mathbf{P}^{\mathrm{T}}\mathbf{M}\mathbf{Q}$.

Boosting can be viewed as repeated play of a particular game matrix. Assume that the weak hypotheses are binary, and let $\mathcal{H} = \{h_1, ...h_n\}$ be the entire weak hypothesis space (which we assume for now to be finite). For a fixed training set $(x_1, y_1), \ldots, (x_m, y_m)$, the game matrix $\mathbf{M}$ has $m$ rows and $n$ columns where

$$\mathbf{M}_{ij} = \begin{cases} 1 \text{ if } h_j(x_i) = y_i \\ 0 \text{ otherwise.} \end{cases}$$

The row player now is the boosting algorithm, and the column player is the weak learner. The boosting algorithm's choice of a distribution $D_t$ over training examples becomes a distribution $\mathbf{P}$ over rows of $\mathbf{M}$, while the weak learner's choice of a weak hypothesis $h_t$ becomes the choice of a column $j$ of $\mathbf{M}$.

As an example of the connection between boosting and game theory, consider von Neumann's famous minmax theorem which states that

$$\max_{\mathbf{Q}} \min_{\mathbf{P}} \mathbf{P}^{\mathrm{T}} \mathbf{M} \mathbf{Q} = \min_{\mathbf{P}} \max_{\mathbf{Q}} \mathbf{P}^{\mathrm{T}} \mathbf{M} \mathbf{Q}$$

for any matrix $\mathbf{M}$. When applied to the matrix just defined and reinterpreted in the boosting setting, this can be shown to have the following meaning: If, for any distribution over examples, there exists a weak hypothesis with error at most $1/2 - \gamma$, then there exists a convex combination of weak hypotheses with a margin of at least $2\gamma$ on all training examples. AdaBoost seeks to find such a final hypothesis with high margin on all examples by combining many weak hypotheses; so in a sense, the minmax theorem tells us that AdaBoost at least has the potential for success since, given a "good" weak learner, there must exist a good combination of weak hypotheses. Going much further, Ada-Boost can be shown to be a special case of a more general algorithm for playing repeated games, or for approximately solving matrix games. This shows that, asymptotically, the distribution over training examples as well as the weights over weak hypotheses in the final hypothesis have game-theoretic intepretations as approximate minmax or maxmin strategies.

## Estimating probabilities

Classification generally is the problem of predicting the label $y$ of an example $x$ with the intention of minimizing the probability of an incorrect prediction. However, it is often useful to estimate the *probability* of a particular label. Recently, Friedman, Hastie and Tibshirani [18] suggested a method for using the output of AdaBoost to make reasonable estimates of such probabilities. Specifically, they suggest using a logistic function, and estimating

$$\Pr_f [y = +1 \mid x] = \frac{e^{f(x)}}{e^{f(x)} + e^{-f(x)}} \tag{4}$$

where, as usual, $f(x)$ is the weighted average of weak hypotheses produced by AdaBoost. The rationale for this choice is the close connection between the log loss (negative log likelihood) of such a model, namely,

$$\sum_i \ln \left(1 + e^{-2y_i f(x_i)}\right) \tag{5}$$

and the function which, we have already noted, AdaBoost attempts to minimize:

$$\sum_i e^{-y_i f(x_i)}. \tag{6}$$

Specifically, it can be verified that Eq. (5) is upper bounded by Eq. (6). In addition, if we add the constant $1 - \ln 2$ to Eq. (5) (which does not affect its minimization), then it can be verified that the resulting function and the one in Eq. (6) have identical Taylor expansions around zero up to second order; thus, their behavior near zero is very similar. Finally, it can be shown that, for any distribution over pairs $(x, y)$, the expectations

$$\mathrm{E}\left[\ln\left(1 + e^{-2yf(x)}\right)\right]$$

and

$$\mathrm{E}\left[e^{-yf(x)}\right]$$

are minimized by the same function $f$, namely,

$$f(x) = \tfrac{1}{2}\ln\left(\frac{\Pr\left[y = +1 \mid x\right]}{\Pr\left[y = -1 \mid x\right]}\right).$$

Thus, for all these reasons, minimizing Eq. (6), as is done by AdaBoost, can be viewed as a method of approximately minimizing the negative log likelihood given in Eq. (5). Therefore, we may expect Eq. (4) to give a reasonable probability estimate.

Friedman, Hastie and Tibshirani also make other connnections between Ada-Boost, logistic regression and additive models.

## Multiclass classification

There are several methods of extending AdaBoost to the multiclass case. The most straightforward generalization [16], called AdaBoost.M1, is adequate when the weak learner is strong enough to achieve reasonably high accuracy, even on the hard distributions created by AdaBoost. However, this method fails if the weak learner cannot achieve at least 50% accuracy when run on these hard distributions.

For the latter case, several more sophisticated methods have been developed. These generally work by reducing the multiclass problem to a larger binary problem. Schapire and Singer's [31] algorithm AdaBoost.MH works by creating a set of binary problems, for each example $x$ and each possible label $y$, of the form: "For example $x$, is the correct label $y$ or is it one of the other labels?" Freund and Schapire's [16] algorithm AdaBoost.M2 (which is a special case of Schapire and Singer's [31] AdaBoost.MR algorithm) instead creates binary problems, for each example $x$ with correct label $y$ and each *incorrect* label $y'$ of the form: "For example $x$, is the correct label $y$ or $y'$?"

These methods require additional effort in the design of the weak learning algorithm. A different technique [29], which incorporates Dietterich and Bakiri's [10] method of error-correcting output codes, achieves similar provable bounds to those of AdaBoost.MH and AdaBoost.M2, but can be used with any weak learner which can handle simple, binary labeled data. Schapire and Singer [31] give yet another method of combining boosting with error-correcting output codes.

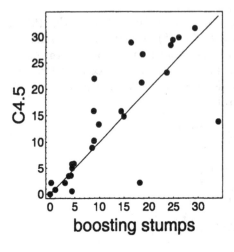
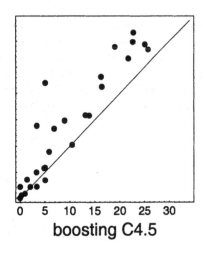

**Fig. 3.** Comparison of C4.5 versus boosting stumps and boosting C4.5 on a set of 27 benchmark problems as reported by Freund and Schapire [14]. Each point in each scatterplot shows the test error rate of the two competing algorithms on a single benchmark. The $y$-coordinate of each point gives the test error rate (in percent) of C4.5 on the given benchmark, and the $x$-coordinate gives the error rate of boosting stumps (left plot) or boosting C4.5 (right plot). All error rates have been averaged over multiple runs.

## Experiments and applications

AdaBoost has been tested empirically by many researchers, including [2, 9, 11, 20, 23, 26, 33]. For instance, Freund and Schapire [14] tested AdaBoost on a set of UCI benchmark datasets [25] using C4.5 [27] as a weak learning algorithm, as well as an algorithm which finds the best "decision stump" or single-test decision tree. Some of the results of these experiments are shown in Fig. 3. As can be seen from this figure, even boosting the weak decision stumps can usually give as good results as C4.5, while boosting C4.5 generally gives the decision-tree algorithm a significant improvement in performance.

In another set of experiments, Schapire and Singer [32] used boosting for text categorization tasks. For this work, weak hypotheses were used which test on the presence or absence of a word or phrase. Some results of these experiments comparing AdaBoost to four other methods are shown in Fig. 4. In nearly all of these experiments and for all of the performance measures tested, boosting performed as well or significantly better than the other methods tested.

## References

1. Peter L. Bartlett. The sample complexity of pattern classification with neural networks: the size of the weights is more important than the size of the network. *IEEE Transactions on Information Theory*, 44(2):525–536, March 1998.

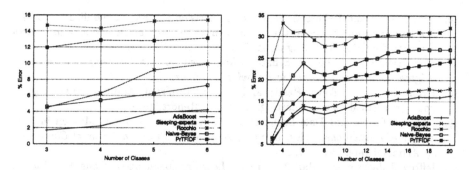

**Fig. 4.** Comparison of error rates for AdaBoost and four other text categorization methods (naive Bayes, probabilistic TF-IDF, Rocchio and sleeping experts) as reported by Schapire and Singer [32]. The algorithms were tested on two text corpora — Reuters newswire articles (left) and AP newswire headlines (right) — and with varying numbers of class labels as indicated on the $x$-axis of each figure.

2. Eric Bauer and Ron Kohavi. An empirical comparison of voting classification algorithms: Bagging, boosting, and variants. *Machine Learning*, to appear.

3. Eric B. Baum and David Haussler. What size net gives valid generalization? *Neural Computation*, 1(1):151–160, 1989.

4. Bernhard E. Boser, Isabelle M. Guyon, and Vladimir N. Vapnik. A training algorithm for optimal margin classifiers. In *Proceedings of the Fifth Annual ACM Workshop on Computational Learning Theory*, pages 144–152, 1992.

5. Leo Breiman. Arcing the edge. Technical Report 486, Statistics Department, University of California at Berkeley, 1997.

6. Leo Breiman. Prediction games and arcing classifiers. Technical Report 504, Statistics Department, University of California at Berkeley, 1997.

7. Leo Breiman. Arcing classifiers. *The Annals of Statistics*, 26(3):801–849, 1998.

8. Corinna Cortes and Vladimir Vapnik. Support-vector networks. *Machine Learning*, 20(3):273–297, September 1995.

9. Thomas G. Dietterich. An experimental comparison of three methods for constructing ensembles of decision trees: Bagging, boosting, and randomization. *Machine Learning*, to appear.

10. Thomas G. Dietterich and Ghulum Bakiri. Solving multiclass learning problems via error-correcting output codes. *Journal of Artificial Intelligence Research*, 2:263–286, January 1995.

11. Harris Drucker and Corinna Cortes. Boosting decision trees. In *Advances in Neural Information Processing Systems 8*, pages 479–485, 1996.

12. Harris Drucker, Robert Schapire, and Patrice Simard. Boosting performance in neural networks. *International Journal of Pattern Recognition and Artificial Intelligence*, 7(4):705–719, 1993.

13. Yoav Freund. Boosting a weak learning algorithm by majority. *Information and Computation*, 121(2):256–285, 1995.

14. Yoav Freund and Robert E. Schapire. Experiments with a new boosting algorithm. In *Machine Learning: Proceedings of the Thirteenth International Conference*, pages 148–156, 1996.

15. Yoav Freund and Robert E. Schapire. Game theory, on-line prediction and boosting. In *Proceedings of the Ninth Annual Conference on Computational Learning Theory*, pages 325–332, 1996.

16. Yoav Freund and Robert E. Schapire. A decision-theoretic generalization of on-line learning and an application to boosting. *Journal of Computer and System Sciences*, 55(1):119–139, August 1997.

17. Yoav Freund and Robert E. Schapire. Adaptive game playing using multiplicative weights. *Games and Economic Behavior*, to appear.

18. Jerome Friedman, Trevor Hastie, and Robert Tibshirani. Additive logistic regression: a statistical view of boosting. Technical Report, 1998.

19. Adam J. Grove and Dale Schuurmans. Boosting in the limit: Maximizing the margin of learned ensembles. In *Proceedings of the Fifteenth National Conference on Artificial Intelligence*, 1998.

20. Jeffrey C. Jackson and Mark W. Craven. Learning sparse perceptrons. In *Advances in Neural Information Processing Systems 8*, pages 654–660, 1996.

21. Michael Kearns and Leslie G. Valiant. Learning Boolean formulae or finite automata is as hard as factoring. Technical Report TR-14-88, Harvard University Aiken Computation Laboratory, August 1988.

22. Michael Kearns and Leslie G. Valiant. Cryptographic limitations on learning Boolean formulae and finite automata. *Journal of the Association for Computing Machinery*, 41(1):67–95, January 1994.

23. Richard Maclin and David Opitz. An empirical evaluation of bagging and boosting. In *Proceedings of the Fourteenth National Conference on Artificial Intelligence*, pages 546–551, 1997.

24. Llew Mason, Peter Bartlett, and Jonathan Baxter. Direct optimization of margins improves generalization in combined classifiers. Technical report, Deparment of Systems Engineering, Australian National University, 1998.

25. C. J. Merz and P. M. Murphy. UCI repository of machine learning databases, 1998. http://www.ics.uci.edu/~mlearn/MLRepository.html.

26. J. R. Quinlan. Bagging, boosting, and C4.5. In *Proceedings of the Thirteenth National Conference on Artificial Intelligence*, pages 725–730, 1996.

27. J. Ross Quinlan. *C4.5: Programs for Machine Learning*. Morgan Kaufmann, 1993.

28. Robert E. Schapire. The strength of weak learnability. *Machine Learning*, 5(2):197–227, 1990.

29. Robert E. Schapire. Using output codes to boost multiclass learning problems. In *Machine Learning: Proceedings of the Fourteenth International Conference*, pages 313–321, 1997.

30. Robert E. Schapire, Yoav Freund, Peter Bartlett, and Wee Sun Lee. Boosting the margin: A new explanation for the effectiveness of voting methods. In *Machine Learning: Proceedings of the Fourteenth International Conference*, pages 322–330, 1997. To appear, *The Annals of Statistics*.

31. Robert E. Schapire and Yoram Singer. Improved boosting algorithms using confidence-rated predictions. In *Proceedings of the Eleventh Annual Conference on Computational Learning Theory*, pages 80–91, 1998.

32. Robert E. Schapire and Yoram Singer. BoosTexter: A system for multiclass multi-label text categorization. *Machine Learning*, to appear.

33. Holger Schwenk and Yoshua Bengio. Training methods for adaptive boosting of neural networks. In *Advances in Neural Information Processing Systems 10*, pages 647–653, 1998.

34. L. G. Valiant. A theory of the learnable. *Communications of the ACM*, 27(11):1134–1142, November 1984.

35. Vladimir N. Vapnik. *The Nature of Statistical Learning Theory*. Springer, 1995.

# Open Theoretical Questions
# in Reinforcement Learning

Richard S. Sutton

AT&T Labs, Florham Park, NJ 07932, USA,
`sutton@research.att.com`, `www.cs.umass.edu/~rich`

Reinforcement learning (RL) concerns the problem of a learning agent inter-
acting with its environment to achieve a goal. Instead of being given examples
of desired behavior, the learning agent must discover by trial and error how to
behave in order to get the most reward. The environment is a Markov decision
process (MDP) with state set, $S$, and action set, $A$. The agent and the environment interact in a sequence of discrete steps, $t = 0, 1, 2, \ldots$ The state and action
at one time step, $s_t \in S$ and $a_t \in A$, determine the probability distribution for
the state at the next time step, $s_{t+1} \in S$, and, jointly, the distribution for the
next reward, $r_{t+1} \in \Re$. The agent's objective is to chose each $a_t$ to maximize the
subsequent *return*:

$$R_t = \sum_{k=0}^{\infty} \gamma^k r_{t+1+k},$$

where the discount rate, $0 \le \gamma \le 1$, determines the relative weighting of immediate and delayed rewards. In some environments, the interaction consists of
a sequence of episodes, each starting in a given state and ending upon arrival
in a terminal state, terminating the series above. In other cases the interaction
is continual, without interruption, and the sum may have an infinite number of
terms (in which case we usually assume $\gamma < 1$). Infinite horizon cases with $\gamma = 1$
are also possible though less common (e.g., see Mahadevan, 1996).

The agent's action choices are a stochastic function of the state, called a
*policy*, $\pi : S \mapsto Pr(A)$. The *value* of a state given a policy is the expected return
starting from that state following the policy:

$$V^\pi(s) = E\{R_t \mid s_t = s, \pi\},$$

and the best that can be done in a state is its optimal value:

$$V^*(s) = \max_\pi V^\pi(s).$$

There is always at least one *optimal policy*, $\pi^*$, that achieves this maximum
at all states $s \in S$. Paralleling the two *state*-value functions defined above are
two *action*-value functions, $Q^\pi(s, a) = E\{R_t \mid s_t = s, a_t = a, \pi\}$ and $Q^*(s, a) =
\max_\pi Q^\pi(s, a)$. ¿From $Q^*$ one can determine an optimal deterministic policy,
$\pi^*(s) = \arg\max_a Q^*(s, a)$. For this reason, many RL algorithms focus on approximating $Q^*$. For example, *one-step tabular Q-learning* (Watkins, 1989) maintains
a table of estimates $Q(s, a)$ for each pair of state and action. Whenever $a$ is taken

in $s$, $Q(s, a)$ is updated based on the resulting next state $s'$, and reward $r$:

$$Q(s, a) \leftarrow (1 - \alpha_{sa})Q(s, a) + \alpha_{sa}[r + \max_{a'} Q(s', a')], \tag{1}$$

where $\alpha_{sa} > 0$ is a time-dependent step-size parameter. Under minimal technical conditions, $Q$ converges asymptotically to $Q^*$, from which an optimal policy can be determined as described above (Watkins and Dayan, 1992).

Modern RL encompasses a wide range of problems and algorithms, of which the above is only the simplest case. For example, all the large applications of RL use not tables but parameterized function approximators such as neural networks (e.g., Tesauro, 1995; Crites and Barto, 1996; Singh and Bertsekas, 1997). It is also commonplace to consider planning—the computation of an optimal policy given a model of the environment—as well as learning (e.g., Moore and Atkeson, 1993; Singh, 1993). RL can also be used when the state is not completely observable (e.g., Loch and Singh, 1998). The methods that are effectively used in practice go far beyond what can be proven reliable or efficient. In this sense, the open theoretical questions in RL are legion. Here I highlight four that seem particularly important, pressing, or opportune. The first three are basic questions in RL that have remained open despite some attention by skilled mathematicians. Solving these is probably not just a simple matter of applying existing results; some new mathematics may be needed. The fourth open question concerns recent progress in extending the theory of uniform convergence and VC dimension to RL. For additional general background on RL, I recommend our recent textbook (Sutton and Barto, 1998).

# 1 Control with Function Approximation

An important subproblem within many RL algorithms is that of approximating $Q^\pi$ or $V^\pi$ for the policy $\pi$ used to generate the training experience. This is called the *prediction* problem to distinguish it from the *control* problem of RL as a whole (finding $Q^*$ or $\pi^*$). For the prediction problem, the use of generalizing function approximators such as neural networks is relatively well understood. In the strongest result in this area, the TD($\lambda$) algorithm with linear function approximation has been proven asymptotically convergent to within a bounded expansion of the minimum possible error (Tsitsiklis and Van Roy, 1997). In contrast, the extension of Q-learning to linear function approximation has been shown to be unstable (divergent) in the prediction case (Baird, 1995). This pair of results has focused attention on Sarsa($\lambda$), the extension of TD($\lambda$) to form a control algorithm.

Empirically, linear Sarsa($\lambda$) seems to perform well despite (in many cases) never converging in the conventional sense. The parameters of the linear function can be shown to have no fixed point in expected value. Yet neither do they diverge; they seem to "chatter" in the neighborhood of a good policy (Bertsekas and Tsitsiklis, 1996). This kind of solution can be completely satisfactory in practice, but can it be characterized theoretically? What can be assured about the quality of the chattering solution? New mathematical tools seem necessary. Linear Sarsa($\lambda$) is thus both critical to the success of the RL enterprise and greatly in need of new learning theory.

## 2 Monte Carlo Control

An important dimension along which RL methods differ is their degree of *bootstrapping*. For example, one-step Q-learning bootstraps its estimate for $Q(s, a)$ upon its estimates for $Q(s', a')$ (see Eq. 1), that is, it builds its estimates upon themselves. Non-bootstrapping methods, also known as Monte Carlo methods, use only actual returns—no estimates—as their basis for updating other estimates. The $\lambda$ in methods such as TD($\lambda$), Q($\lambda$), and Sarsa($\lambda$) refers to this dimension, with $\lambda = 0$ (as in TD(0)) representing the most extreme form of bootstrapping, and $\lambda = 1$ representing no bootstrapping (Monte Carlo methods).

In most respects, the theory of Monte Carlo methods is better developed than that of bootstrapping methods. Without the self reference of bootstrapping, Monte Carlo methods are easier to analyze and closer to classical methods. In linear prediction, for example, Monte Carlo methods have the best asymptotic convergence guarantees. For the control case, however, results exist only for extreme bootstrapping methods, notably tabular Q(0) and tabular Sarsa(0). For any value of $\lambda > 0$ there are no convergence results for the control case. This lacunae is particularly glaring and galling for the simplest Monte Carlo algorithm, *Monte Carlo ES* (Sutton and Barto, 1998). This tabular method maintains $Q(s, a)$ as the average of all completed returns (we assume an episodic interaction) that started with taking action $a$ in state $s$. Actions are selected greedily, $\pi(s) = \arg\max_a Q(s, a)$, while exploration is assured by assuming *exploring starts* (ES)—that is, that episodes start in randomly selected state–action pairs with all pairs having a positive probability of being selected. It is hard to imagine any RL method simpler or more likely to converge than this, yet there remain no proof of asymptotic convergence to $Q^*$. While this simplest case remains open we are unlikely to make progress on any control method for $\lambda > 0$.

## 3 Efficiency of Bootstrapping

Perhaps the single most important new idea in the field of RL is that of temporal-difference (TD) learning with bootstrapping. Bootstrapping TD methods have been shown empirically to learn substantially more efficiently than Monte Carlo methods. For example, Figure 1 presents a collection of empirical results in which $\lambda$ was varied from 0 (pure bootstrapping) to 1 (no bootstrapping, Monte Carlo). In all cases, performance at 0 was better than performance at 1, and the best performance was at an intermediate value of $\lambda$. Similar results have been shown analytically (Singh and Dayan, 1998), but again only for particular tasks and initial settings. Thus, we have a range of results that suggest that bootstrapping

14

TD methods are generally more efficient than Monte Carlo methods, but no definitive proof. While it remains unclear exactly what should or could be proved here, it is clear that this is a key open question at the heart of current and future RL.

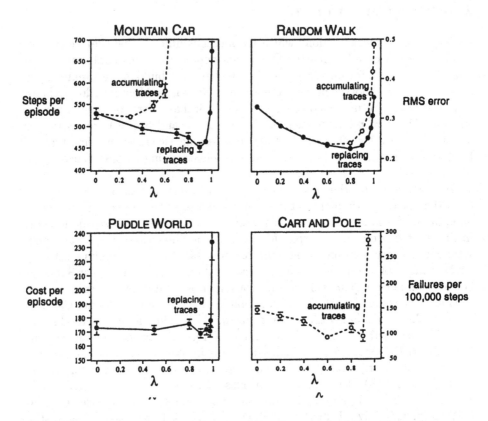

**Fig. 1.** The effect of $\lambda$ on RL performance. In all cases, the better the performance, the *lower* the curve. The two left panels are applications to simple continuous-state control tasks using the Sarsa($\lambda$) algorithm and tile coding, with either replacing or accumulating traces (Sutton, 1996). The upper-right panel is for policy evaluation on a random walk task using TD($\lambda$) (Singh and Sutton, 1996). The lower right panel is unpublished data for a pole-balancing task from an earlier study (Sutton, 1984).

# 4   A VC Dimension for RL

So far we have discussed open theoretical questions at the heart of RL that are distant from those usually considered in computational learning theory (COLT). This should not be surprising; new problems are likely to call for new theory. But it is also worthwhile to try to apply existing theoretical ideas to new problems.

Recently, some progress has been made in this direction by Kearns, Mansour and Ng (in prep.) that seems to open up a whole range of new possibilities for applying COLT ideas to RL.

Recall the classic COLT problem defined by a hypothesis space $\mathcal{H}$ of functions from $\mathcal{X}$ to $\mathcal{Y}$ together with a probability distribution $\mathcal{P}$ on $\mathcal{X} \times \mathcal{Y}$. Given a training set of $x, y$ pairs chosen according to $\mathcal{P}$, the objective is to find a function $\hat{h} \in \mathcal{H}$ that minimizes the generalization error. A basic result establishes the number of examples (on the order of the VC dimension of $\mathcal{H}$) necessary to assure with high probability that the generalization error is approximately the same as the training error.

Kearns, Mansour and Ng consider a closely related planning problem in RL. Corresponding to the set of possible functions $\mathcal{H}$, they consider a set of possible policies $\Pi$. For example, $\Pi$ could be all the greedy policies formed by approximating an action-value function with a neural network of a certain size. Corresponding to the probability distribution $\mathcal{P}$ on $\mathcal{X} \times \mathcal{Y}$, Kearns et al. use a generative or sample model of the MDP. Given any state $s$ and action $a$, the model generates samples of the next state $s'$ and the expected value of the next reward $r$, given $s$ and $a$. They also allow the possibility that the environment is a partially observable (PO) MDP, in which case the model also generates a sample observation $o$, which alone is used by policies to select actions. Corresponding to the classical objective of finding an $\hat{h} \in \mathcal{H}$ that minimizes generalization error, they seek a policy $\hat{\pi} \in \Pi$ that maximizes performance on the (PO)MDP. Performance here is defined as the value, $V^{\hat{\pi}}(s_0)$, of some designated state state, $s_0$ (or, equivalently, on a designated distribution of starting states).

But what corresponds in the RL case to the training set of example $x, y$ pairs? A key property of the conventional training set is that one such set can be *reused* to evaluate the accuracy of *any* hypothesis. But in the RL case different policies give rise to different action choices and thus to different parts of the state space being encountered. How can we construct a training set with a reuse property comparable to the supervised case? Kearns et al.'s answer is the *trajectory tree*, a tree of sample transitions starting at the start state and branching down along all possible action choices. For each action they obtain one sample next state and the expected reward from the generative model. They then recurse from these states, considering for each all possible actions and one sample outcome. They continue in this way for a sufficient depth, or horizon, $H$, such that $\gamma^H$ is sufficiently small with respect to the target regret, $\epsilon$. If there are two possible actions, then one such tree is of size $2^H$, which is independent of the number of states in the (PO)MDP. The reuse property comes about because a single tree specifies a length $H$ sample trajectory for any policy by working down the tree following the actions taken by that policy. A tree corresponds to a single example in the classic supervised problem, and a set of trees corresponds to s training set of examples.

With the trajectory tree construction, Kearns et al. are able to extend basic results of uniform convergence. The conventional definition of VC dimension cannot be directly applied to policy sets $\Pi$, but by going back to the original definitions they establish a natural extension of it. They prove that with (on order of) this number of trajectory trees, with probability $\delta$, one can be assured of finding a policy whose value is within $\epsilon$ of the best policy in $\Pi$.

Kearns, Mansour and Ng's work breaks fertile new ground in the theory of RL, but it is far from finishing the story. Their work could be extended in many different directions just as uniform convergence theory for the supervised case has been elaborated. For example, one could establish the VC dimension on some policy classes of practical import, or extend boosting ideas to the RL case. Alternatively, one could propose replacements for the supervised training examples other than trajectory trees. Kearns et al. consider how trajectories from random policies can be used for this purpose, and there are doubtless other possibilities as well.

## Acknowledgments

The author is grateful for substantial assistance in formulating these ideas from Satinder Singh, Michael Kearns, and Yoav Freund.

## References

Baird, L. C. (1995). Residual algorithms: Reinforcement learning with function approximation. In *Proceedings of the Twelfth International Conference on Machine Learning*, pp. 30–37. Morgan Kaufmann, San Francisco.

Bertsekas, D. P., and Tsitsiklis, J. N. (1996). *Neuro-Dynamic Programming*. Athena Scientific, Belmont, MA.

Crites, R. H., and Barto, A. G. (1996). Improving elevator performance using reinforcement learning. In *Advances in Neural Information Processing Systems: Proceedings of the 1995 Conference*, pp. 1017–1023. MIT Press, Cambridge, MA.

Kearns, M., Mansour, Y., Ng, A. Y. (in prep.). Sparse sampling methods for planning and learning in large and partially observable Markov decision processes.

Loch J., and Singh S. (1998). Using eligibility traces to find the best memoryless policy in partially observable Markov decision processes. In *Proceedings of the Fifteenth International Conference on Machine Learning*. Morgan Kaufmann, San Francisco.

Mahadevan, S. (1996). Average reward reinforcement learning: Foundations, algorithms, and empirical results. *Machine Learning*, 22:159–196.

Moore, A. W., and Atkeson, C. G. (1993). Prioritized sweeping: Reinforcement learning with less data and less real time. *Machine Learning*, 13:103–130.

Singh, S. P. (1993). *Learning to Solve Markovian Decision Processes*. Ph.D. thesis, University of Massachusetts, Amherst. Appeared as CMPSCI Technical Report 93-77.

Singh, S. P., and Bertsekas, D. (1997). Reinforcement learning for dynamic channel allocation in cellular telephone systems. In *Advances in Neural Information Processing Systems: Proceedings of the 1996 Conference*, pp. 974–980. MIT Press, Cambridge, MA.

Singh S., and Dayan P. (1998). Analytical mean squared error curves for temporal difference learning. *Machine Learning*.

Singh, S. P., and Sutton, R. S. (1996). Reinforcement learning with replacing eligibility traces. *Machine Learning*, 22:123–158.

Sutton, R. S. (1984). *Temporal Credit Assignment in Reinforcement Learning*. Ph.D. thesis, University of Massachusetts, Amherst.

Sutton, R. S. (1996). Generalization in reinforcement learning: Successful examples using sparse coarse coding. In *Advances in Neural Information Processing Systems: Proceedings of the 1995 Conference*, pp. 1038–1044. MIT Press, Cambridge, MA.

Sutton, R. S., and Barto, A. G. (1998). *Reinforcement Learning: An Introduction*. MIT Press, Cambridge, MA.

Tesauro, G. J. (1995). Temporal difference learning and TD-Gammon. *Communications of the ACM*, 38:58–68.

Tsitsiklis, J. N., and Van Roy, B. (1997). An analysis of temporal-difference learning with function approximation. *IEEE Transactions on Automatic Control*, 42:674–690.

Watkins, C. J. C. H. (1989). *Learning from Delayed Rewards*. Ph.D. thesis, Cambridge University.

Watkins, C. J. C. H., and Dayan, P. (1992). Q-learning. *Machine Learning*, 8:279–292.

# A Geometric Approach to Leveraging Weak Learners

Nigel Duffy and David Helmbold*

University of California at Santa Cruz
{nigeduff,dph}@cse.ucsc.edu
http://www.ucsc.edu/{~nigeduff,~dph}

**Abstract.** AdaBoost is a popular and effective leveraging procedure for improving the hypotheses generated by weak learning algorithms. AdaBoost and many other leveraging algorithms can be viewed as performing a constrained gradient descent over a potential function. At each iteration the distribution over the sample given to the weak learner is the direction of steepest descent. We introduce a new leveraging algorithm based on a natural potential function. For this potential function, the direction of steepest descent can have negative components. Therefore we provide two transformations for obtaining suitable distributions from these directions of steepest descent. The resulting algorithms have bounds that are incomparable to AdaBoost's, and their empirical performance is similar to AdaBoost's.

## 1 Introduction

Algorithms like AdaBoost [7] that are able to improve the hypotheses generated by weak learning methods have great potential and practical benefits. We call any such algorithm a *leveraging* algorithm, as it leverages the weak learning method. Other examples of leveraging algorithms include bagging [3], arc-x4 [5], and LogitBoost [8].

One class of leveraging algorithms follows the following template to construct master hypotheses from a given sample $(x_1, y_1), \ldots (x_m, y_m)$.

The leveraging algorithm begins with a default master hypothesis $H_0$ and then for $t = 1, 2, \ldots, T$ it:

- Constructs a distribution $D_t$ over the sample (as a function of the sample and the current master hypothesis $H_{t-1}$, and possibly $t$).
- Trains a weak learner using distribution $D_t$ over the sample to obtain a weak hypothesis $h_t$.
- Picks $\alpha_t$ and creates the new master hypothesis,
  $H_t = H_{t-1} + \alpha_t h_t$.

---

* Both authors were supported by NSF Grant CCR 9700201.

This is essentially the Arcing paradigm introduced by Breiman [5, 4] and the skeleton of AdaBoost and other boost-by-resampling algorithms [6, 7]. Although leveraging algorithms include arcing algorithms following this template, leveraging algorithms are more general. In Section 2, we introduce the GeoLev algorithm that changes the examples in the sample as well as the distribution over them.

In this paper we consider 2-class classification problems where each $y_i \in \{-1, +1\}$. However, following Schapire and Singer [15], we allow the weak learner's hypotheses to be "confidence rated," mapping the domain $X$ to the real numbers. The sign of these numbers gives the predicted label, and the magnitude is a measure of confidence. The master hypotheses produced by the above template are interpreted in the same way.

Although the underlying goal is to produce hypotheses that generalize well, we focus on how quickly the leveraging algorithm decreases the sample error. There are a variety of results bounding the generalization error in terms of the performance on the sample [16].

Given a sample $(x_1, y_1), \ldots (x_m, y_m)$, the *margin* of a hypothesis $h$ on instance $x_i$ is $y_i h(x_i)$ and the margin of $h$ on the entire sample is the vector $(y_1 h(x_1), \ldots, y_n h(x_n))$. A hypothesis that correctly labels the sample has a margin vector whose components are all positive. Focusing on these margin vectors provides a geometric intuition about the leveraging problem.

In particular, a potential function on margin space can be used to guide the choices of $D_t$ and $\alpha_t$. The distribution $D_t$ is the direction of steepest descent and $\alpha_t$ is the value that minimizes the potential of $H_{t-1} + \alpha_t h_t$. Leveraging algorithms that can be viewed in this way perform a feasible direction descent on the potential function. An amortized analysis using this potential function can often be used to bound the number of iterations required to achieve zero sample error. These potential functions give insight into the strengths and weaknesses of various leveraging algorithms.

Boosting algorithms have the property that they can convert weak PAC learning algorithms into strong PAC learning algorithms. Although the theory behind the Adaboost algorithm is very elegant, it leads to the somewhat intriguing result that minimizing the normalization factor of a distribution will reduce the training error [14, 15]. Our search for a better understanding of how AdaBoost reduces the sample error led to our geometric algorithms, GeoLev and GeoArc. Although the performance bounds for these algorithms are too poor to show that they have the boosting property, these bounds are incomparable to AdaBoost's in that they are better when the weak hypotheses contain mostly low-confidence predictions.

The main contributions of this paper are as follows:

- We use a natural potential function to derive a new algorithm for leveraging weak learners, called GeoLev (for Geometric Leveraging algorithm).
- We highlight the relationship between AdaBoost, Arcing and feasible direction linear programming [10].

- We use our geometric interpretation to prove convergence bounds on the algorithm GeoLev. These bound the number of iterations taken by GeoLev to achieve $\epsilon$ classification error on the training set.
- We provide a general transformation from GeoLev to an arcing algorithm GeoArc, for which the same bounds hold.
- We summarize some preliminary experiments with GeoLev and GeoArc.

## 2 GeoLev - A Geometric Algorithm

We motivate a novel algorithm, GeoLev, by considering the geometry of "margin space." Since many empirical and analytical results show that good margins on the sample lead to small generalization error [2, 16], it is natural to seek a master hypothesis with large margins. One heuristic is to seek a margin vector with uniformly large margins, i.e. a vector parallel to $\mathbf{1} = (1, 1, \ldots, 1)$. This indicates that the master hypothesis is correct and equally confident on every instance in the sample. The GeoLev algorithm exploits this heuristic by attempting to find hypotheses whose margin vectors are as close as possible to the $\mathbf{1}$ direction.

We now focus on a single iteration of the leveraging process, dropping the time subscripts. Margin vectors will be printed in bold face and often normalized to have Euclidean length one. Thus $\mathbf{H}$ is the margin vector of the master hypothesis $H$, whose $i^{\text{th}}$ component is

$$\mathbf{H}_i = \frac{y_i H(x_i)}{\sqrt{\sum_{j=1}^{n}(y_j H(x_j))^2}} . \tag{1}$$

Let the *goal vector*, $\mathbf{g} = (1/\sqrt{m}, \ldots, 1/\sqrt{m})$, be $\mathbf{1}$ normalized to length one. Recall that $m$ is the sample size, so all margin vectors lie in $\Re^m$, and normalized margin vectors lie on the $m$ dimensional unit sphere. Note that it is easy to re-scale the confidences – multiplying the predictions of any hypothesis $H$ by a constant does not change the direction of $H$'s margin vector. Therefore we can assume the appropriate normalization without loss of generality.

The first decision taken by the leverager is what distribution $D$ to place on the sample. Since distribution $D$ has $m$ components, it can also be viewed as a (non-negative) vector in $\Re^m$.

The situation in margin-space at the start of the iteration is shown in Figure 1. In order to decrease the angle $\theta$ between $\mathbf{H}$ and $\mathbf{g}$ we must move the head of $\mathbf{H}$ towards $\mathbf{g}$. All vectors at angle $\theta$ to the goal vector $\mathbf{g}$ lie on a cone, and their normalizations lie on the "rim" shown in the figure.

If $\mathbf{h}$, the weak hypothesis's margin vector (which need not have unit length), is parallel to $\mathbf{H}$ or tangent to the "rim", then no addition of $\mathbf{h}$ to $\mathbf{H}$ can decrease the angle to $\mathbf{g}$. On the other hand, if the line $\mathbf{H} + \alpha\mathbf{h}$ cuts through the cone, then the angle to the goal vector $\mathbf{g}$ can be reduced by adding some multiple of $\mathbf{h}$ to $\mathbf{H}$. The only time the angle to $\mathbf{g}$ cannot be decreased is when the $\mathbf{h}$ vector lies in the plane $P$ which is tangent to the cone and contains the vector $\mathbf{H}$, as shown in Figure 2.

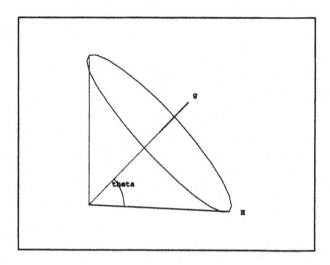

**Fig. 1.** Situation in margin space at the start of an iteration.

If the weak learner learns at all, then its hypothesis $h$ is better than random guessing, so the learners "edge", $\mathbf{E}_{i \sim D}(y_i h(x_i))$, will be positive. This means that $D \cdot \mathbf{h}$ is positive, and if distribution $D$ (viewed as a margin vector) is perpendicular to plane $P$ then $\mathbf{h}$ lies above $P$. Therefore the leverager is able to use $h$ to reduce the angle between $\mathbf{H}$ and $\mathbf{g}$.

As suggested by the figures, the appropriate direction for $D$ is

$$\mathbf{D} = \mathbf{g} - \mathbf{H}(\mathbf{g} \cdot \mathbf{H}). \tag{2}$$

In general neither $\|\mathbf{D}\|_1 = 1$ nor $\|\mathbf{D}\|_2 = 1$.

If all components of $\mathbf{D}$ are positive, it can be normalized to yield a distribution on the sample for the weak learner. However, it is possible for some components of $\mathbf{D}$ to be negative. In this case things are more complicated[1]. If a component of $\mathbf{D}$ is negative, then we flip both the sign of that component and the sign of the corresponding label in the sample. This creates a new direction $\mathbf{D}'$ which can be normalized to a distribution $D'$ and a new sample $S'$ with the same $x_i$'s but (possibly) new labels $y_i'$. The modified sample $S'$ and distribution $D'$ are then used to generate a new weak hypothesis, $h$. Let $\mathbf{h}'$ be the margins of $h$ on the modified sample $S'$, so $\mathbf{h}_i' = y_i' h(x_i)$. Now,

$$\mathbf{D}' \cdot \mathbf{h}' = \sum_{i=1}^{m} \mathbf{D}_i' y_i' h(x_i) = \sum_{i=1}^{m} \mathbf{D}_i y_i h(x_i) = \mathbf{D} \cdot \mathbf{h} \tag{3}$$

---

[1] In fact it is this complication which differentiates GeoLev from Arcing algorithms. Arcing algorithms are not permitted to change the sample in this way. A second transformation avoiding the label flipping is discussed in section 5.

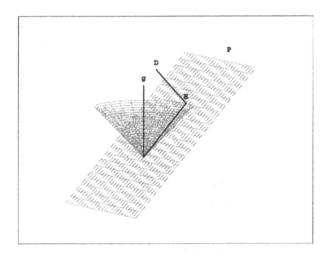

**Fig. 2.** The direction **D** for the distribution used by GeoLev.

as the sign flips cancel.

The second decision taken by the algorithm is how to incorporate the weak hypothesis $h$ into its master hypothesis $H$. Any weak hypothesis with an "edge" on the distribution $D$ described above can be used to decrease $\theta$. Our goal is to find the coefficient $\alpha$ so that $\mathbf{H'} = \frac{\mathbf{H} + \alpha \mathbf{h}}{\|\mathbf{H} + \alpha \mathbf{h}\|_2}$ decreases this angle as much as possible. Taking derivatives shows that $\theta$ is minimized when

$$\alpha = \frac{\mathbf{g} \cdot (\mathbf{h} - \mathbf{H}(\mathbf{H} \cdot \mathbf{h}))}{\mathbf{g} \cdot (\mathbf{H}(\mathbf{h} \cdot \mathbf{h}) - \mathbf{h}(\mathbf{H} \cdot \mathbf{h}))} \quad . \tag{4}$$

¿From this discussion we can see that GeoLev performs a kind of gradient descent. If we consider the angle between $\mathbf{g}$ and the current $\mathbf{H}$ as a potential on margin space, then $\mathbf{D}$ is the direction of steepest descent. Moving in a direction that approximates this gradient takes us towards the goal vector. Since we have only little control over the hypotheses returned by the weak learner, an approximation to this direction is the best we can do. The step size is chosen adaptively to make as much use of the weak hypothesis as possible.

The GeoLev Algorithm is summarized in Figure 3.

## 3 Relation to Previous Work

Breiman [5, 4] defines arcing algorithms using potential functions that can be expressed as component-wise functions of the margins having the form[2] $\sum_i f(\mathbf{H}_i)$.

---

[2] Breiman allows the component-wise potential $f$ to depend on the sum of the $\alpha_i$'s in some arcing algorithms.

---

Input: A sample $S = \{(x_1, y_1), (x_2, y_2), \ldots, (x_m, y_m)\}$, and
a weak learning algorithm.
Initialize master hypothesis $H$ to predict 0 everywhere
Set $\mathbf{g} = (1/\sqrt{m}, \ldots, 1/\sqrt{m})$
Repeat:
    $\mathbf{D} = \mathbf{g} - \mathbf{H}(\mathbf{g} \cdot \mathbf{H})$
    $S' = \emptyset$
    for $i = 1$ to $m$ do
        if $\mathbf{D}_i < 0$ then
            add $(x_i, -y_i)$ to $S'$
            $\mathbf{D}_i = -\mathbf{D}_i / \sum_{i=1}^{m} |\mathbf{D}_i|$
        else
            add $(x_i, y_i)$ to $S'$
            $\mathbf{D}_i = \mathbf{D}_i / \sum_{i=1}^{m} |\mathbf{D}_i|$
    end do
    call weak learner with distribution $D$ over $S'$, obtaining hypothesis $h$
    $\alpha = \frac{\mathbf{g} \cdot (\mathbf{h} - \mathbf{H}(\mathbf{H} \cdot \mathbf{h}))}{\mathbf{g} \cdot (\mathbf{H}(\mathbf{h} \cdot \mathbf{h}) - \mathbf{h}(\mathbf{H} \cdot \mathbf{h}))}$
    $H = (H + \alpha h)/\sqrt{\sum_{i=1}^{m} (\mathbf{H}_i + \alpha \mathbf{h}_i)^2}$

---

**Fig. 3.** The GeoLev Algorithm.

Breiman shows that, under certain conditions on $f$, arcing algorithms converge to good hypotheses in the limit. Furthermore, he shows that AdaBoost is an arcing algorithm with $f(x) = e^x$ and arc-x4 is an arcing algorithm with polynomial $f(x)$.

For completeness, we describe the AdaBoost algorithm and show in our notation how it is performing feasible direction gradient descent on the potential function $\sum_{i=1}^{m} e^{\mathbf{H}_i}$. AdaBoost fits the template outlined in the introduction, choosing the distribution

$$D(x_i) = \frac{\exp(-\mathbf{H}_i)}{Z} \tag{5}$$

where $Z$ is the normalizing factor so that $D$ sums to 1. The master hypothesis is updated by adding in a multiple of the new weak hypothesis. The coefficient $\alpha$ is chosen to minimize

$$\sum_{i=1}^{m} \exp\left(-(\mathbf{H}_i + \alpha \mathbf{h}_i)\right), \tag{6}$$

the next iteration's $Z$ value. Unlike GeoBoost, the margin vectors of AdaBoost's hypotheses are not normalized.

We now show that AdaBoost can be viewed as minimizing the potential

$$\sum_{i} \exp(-\mathbf{H}_i) \tag{7}$$

by approximate gradient descent. The direction of steepest descent (w.r.t. the components of the margin vector) is proportional to (5), the distribution Ada-Boost gives to the weak learner.

Continuing the analogy, the coefficient $\alpha$ given to the new hypothesis should minimize the potential,

$$\sum_i \exp(-(\mathbf{H} + \alpha\mathbf{h})_i), \tag{8}$$

of the updated master hypothesis, which is identical to (6). Thus AdaBoost's behavior is approximate gradient descent of the function defined in (7), where the direction of descent is the weak learner's hypothesis. Furthermore, the bounds on AdaBoost's performance proven by Schapire and Singer are implicitly performing an amortized analysis over the potential function (8).

Arc-x4 also fits the template outlined in the introduction, keeping an unnormalized master hypothesis. In our notation the distribution chosen at trial $t$ is proportional to

$$16 + (t - \mathbf{H}_i)^4. \tag{9}$$

This algorithm can also be viewed as a gradient descent on the potential function

$$\sum_i 16\mathbf{H}_i - \frac{1}{5t}(t - \mathbf{H}_i)^5 \tag{10}$$

at the $t^{th}$ iteration. Rather than computing the coefficient $\alpha$ as a function of the weak hypothesis, arc-x4 always chooses $\alpha = 1$. Thus each $h_t$ has weight $1/t$ in the master hypothesis, as in many gradient descent methods. Unfortunately, the dependence of the potential function on $t$ makes it difficult to use in an amortized analysis.

This connection to gradient descent was hinted at by Freund [6] and noted by Breiman and others [4, 8, 13]. Our interpretation generalizes the previous work by relaxing the constraints on the potential function. In particular, we show how to construct algorithms from potential functions where the direction of steepest descent can have negative components. The potential function view of leveraging algorithms shows their relationship to feasible descent linear programming, and this relationship provides insight into the role of the weak learner.

Feasible direction methods try to move in the direction of steepest descent. However, they must remain in the feasible region described by the constraints. A descent direction is chosen that is closest to the (negative) gradient $-\nabla f$ while satisfying the constraints. For example, in a simplified Zoutendijk method, the chosen direction $d$ satisfies the constraints and maximizes $-\nabla f \cdot d$. Similarly, the leveraging algorithms discussed are constrained to produce master hypotheses lying in the span of the weak learner's hypothesis class. One can view the role of the weak learner as finding a feasible direction close to the given distribution (or negative gradient). In fact the weak learning assumption used in boosting and in the analysis of GeoLev implies that there is always a feasible direction $d$ such that $-\nabla f \cdot \mathbf{d}$ is bounded above zero.

The gradient descent framework outlined above provides a method for deriving the corresponding leveraging algorithm from smooth potential functions over margin space.

The potential functions used by AdaBoost and arc-x4 have the advantage that all the components of their gradients $\mathbf{D}$ are positive, and thus it is easy to convert $\mathbf{D}$ into a distribution. On the other hand, the methods outlined in the previous section and section 5 can be used to handle gradients with negative components. The approach used by Rätsch et al. [13] can similarly be interpreted as a potential function of the margins.

Recently, Friedman et al. [8] have given a maximum likelihood motivation for AdaBoost, and introduced another leveraging algorithm based on the log-likelihood criteria. They indicate that minimizing the square loss potential, $(\mathbf{H} - \mathbf{1})^2$ performed less well in experiments than other monotone potentials, and conjecture that its non-monotonicity (penalizing margins greater than 1) is a contributing factor. Our methods described in section 5 may provide a way to ameliorate this problem.

## 4 Convergence Bound

In this section we examine the number of iterations required by GeoLev to achieve classification error $\epsilon$ on the sample. The key step shows how the sine of the angle between the goal vector $\mathbf{g}$ and the master hypothesis $\mathbf{H}$ is reduced each iteration. Upper bounding the resulting recurrence gives a bound on how rapidly the training error decreases.

We begin by considering a single boosting iteration. The margin space quantities $\mathbf{D}, \mathbf{g}, \mathbf{H}, \mathbf{h}, \theta$ are as previously defined (recall that $\mathbf{g}$ and $\mathbf{H}$ are 2-normed, while $\mathbf{D}$ and $\mathbf{h}$ are not). In addition, let $\mathbf{H}'$ denote the new master hypothesis at the end of the iteration, and $\theta'$ the angle between $\mathbf{H}'$ and $\mathbf{g}$. We assume throughout that the sample is finite.

Define $r = (D \cdot \mathbf{h})$ to be the edge of the weak learner's hypothesis $h$ with respect to the distribution given to the weak learner. Our bound on the decrease in $\theta$ will depend on $h$ only through $r$ and $\|\mathbf{h}\|_2$. Note that $r$ was chosen to maintain consistency with the work of Schapire and Singer [15] and that

$$\mathbf{P}_{i \sim D}[h(x_i) \neq y_i] = \frac{1 - r}{2} \tag{11}$$

At the start of the iteration $\sin(\theta) = \sqrt{1 - \cos^2(\theta)} = \sqrt{1 - (\mathbf{g} \cdot \mathbf{H})^2}$, and at the end of the iteration $\sin(\theta') = \sqrt{1 - \cos^2(\theta')} = \sqrt{1 - (\mathbf{g} \cdot \mathbf{H}')^2}$. Recall that $\mathbf{H}'$ is $\mathbf{H} + \alpha \mathbf{h}$ normalized, and since $\mathbf{H}$ already has unit length,

$$\mathbf{H}' = \frac{\mathbf{H} + \alpha \mathbf{h}}{\sqrt{1 + \alpha^2(\mathbf{h} \cdot \mathbf{h}) + 2\alpha(\mathbf{H} \cdot \mathbf{h})}} . \tag{12}$$

**Lemma 1.** *The value* $\cos^2(\theta')$ *is maximized (and* $\sin(\theta')$ *minimized) when*

$$\alpha = \frac{(\mathbf{g} \cdot \mathbf{h}) - (\mathbf{g} \cdot \mathbf{H})(\mathbf{H} \cdot \mathbf{h})}{(\mathbf{g} \cdot \mathbf{H})(\mathbf{h} \cdot \mathbf{h}) - (\mathbf{g} \cdot \mathbf{h})(\mathbf{H} \cdot \mathbf{h})} . \tag{13}$$

**Proof** The lemma follows from examination of the first and second derivatives of $\cos^2(\theta')$ with respect to $\alpha$. □

Using this value of $\alpha$ a little algebra shows that

$$\cos^2(\theta') = \frac{(\mathbf{H} \cdot \mathbf{h})^2 (\mathbf{g} \cdot \mathbf{H})^2 - ((\mathbf{g} \cdot \mathbf{h}) - (\mathbf{g} \cdot \mathbf{H})(\mathbf{H} \cdot \mathbf{h}))^2 - (\mathbf{h} \cdot \mathbf{h})(\mathbf{g} \cdot \mathbf{H})^2}{((\mathbf{H} \cdot \mathbf{h})^2 - (\mathbf{h} \cdot \mathbf{h}))} \tag{14}$$

$$= \frac{(\mathbf{H} \cdot \mathbf{h})^2 (\mathbf{g} \cdot \mathbf{H})^2 - (\mathbf{D} \cdot \mathbf{h})^2 - (\mathbf{h} \cdot \mathbf{h})(\mathbf{g} \cdot \mathbf{H})^2}{((\mathbf{H} \cdot \mathbf{h})^2 - (\mathbf{h} \cdot \mathbf{h}))} . \tag{15}$$

Although we desire bounds that hold for all $\mathbf{h}$, we find it convenient to first minimize (15) with respect to $(\mathbf{H} \cdot \mathbf{h})$. The remaining dependence on $\mathbf{h}$ will be expressed as a function of $r$ and $||\mathbf{h}||_2$ in the final bound.

**Lemma 2.** *Equation (15) is minimized when* $(\mathbf{H} \cdot \mathbf{h}) = 0$.

**Proof** Again the lemma follows after examining the first and second derivatives with respect to $(\mathbf{H} \cdot \mathbf{h})$. □

This considerably simplifies (15), yielding

$$\cos^2(\theta') \geq (\mathbf{g} \cdot \mathbf{H})^2 + \frac{(\mathbf{D} \cdot \mathbf{h})^2}{(\mathbf{h} \cdot \mathbf{h})} . \tag{16}$$

Recall that

$$r = (D \cdot \mathbf{h}) = \frac{(\mathbf{D} \cdot \mathbf{h})}{||\mathbf{D}||_1} \tag{17}$$

Therefore,

$$\cos^2(\theta') \geq (\mathbf{g} \cdot \mathbf{H})^2 + \frac{r^2}{||\mathbf{h}||_2^2} ||\mathbf{D}||_1^2 . \tag{18}$$

We will bound this in two ways, using different bounds on $||\mathbf{D}||_1$. The first of these bounds is derived by noting that $||\mathbf{D}||_1 \geq ||\mathbf{D}||_2$. Recall that $\mathbf{D} = \mathbf{g} - \mathbf{H}(\mathbf{g} \cdot \mathbf{H})$, so $(\mathbf{D} \cdot \mathbf{D}) = (1 - (\mathbf{g} \cdot \mathbf{H})^2) = \sin^2(\theta)$. Combining this with (18) and the bound on $||\mathbf{D}||_1$ yields

$$\sin^2(\theta') \leq 1 - (\mathbf{g} \cdot \mathbf{H})^2 - \frac{r^2}{||\mathbf{h}||_2^2} \sin^2(\theta) \tag{19}$$

$$\sin(\theta') \leq \sin(\theta)\sqrt{1 - \frac{r^2}{||\mathbf{h}||_2^2}} . \tag{20}$$

Repeated application of this bound yields the following theorem.

**Theorem 1.** *If $r_1, \ldots, r_T$ are the edges of the weak learner's hypotheses during the first $T$ iterations, then the sine of the angle between $\mathbf{g}$ and the margin vector for the master hypothesis computed at iteration $T$ is at most* $\prod_{t=1}^{T} \sqrt{1 - \frac{r_t^2}{||\mathbf{h}_t||_2^2}}.$

We can bound $||\mathbf{D}||_1$ another way to obtain a a bound which is often better. Note that $||\mathbf{D}||_1 \geq (\mathbf{D} \cdot \mathbf{1}) = \sqrt{m}(\mathbf{D} \cdot \mathbf{g}) = \sqrt{m}(1 - (\mathbf{g} \cdot \mathbf{H})^2)$. Substituting this into (18) and continuing as before yields

$$\cos^2(\theta') \geq (\mathbf{g} \cdot \mathbf{H})^2 + \frac{r^2}{||\mathbf{h}||_2^2}m(1 - (\mathbf{g} \cdot \mathbf{H})^2)^2 \tag{21}$$

$$\sin^2(\theta') \leq \sin^2(\theta) - \frac{r^2}{||\mathbf{h}||_2^2}m\,\sin^4(\theta) . \tag{22}$$

Continuing as above results in the following theorem.

**Theorem 2.** *Let* $r_1, \ldots, r_T$ *be the edges of the weak learner's hypotheses and* $\theta_1, \ldots, \theta_T$ *be the angles between* $\mathbf{g}$ *and the margins of the master hypotheses at the start of the first* $T$ *iterations. If* $\theta_{T+1}$ *is the angle between* $\mathbf{g}$ *and the margins of the master hypothesis produced at iteration* $T$ *then*

$$\sin(\theta_{T+1}) \leq \prod_{t=1}^{T} \sqrt{1 - \frac{r_t^2}{||\mathbf{h}_t||_2^2}m\,\sin^2(\theta_t)} . \tag{23}$$

To relate these results to the sample error we use the following lemma.

**Lemma 3.** *If* $\sin(\theta) < \sqrt{\epsilon}$ *where* $\theta$ *is the angle between* $\mathbf{g}$ *and a master hypothesis* $H$, *then the sample error of* $H$ *is less than* $\epsilon$.

**Proof** Assume $\sin(\theta) < \sqrt{R/m}$, so $\cos(\theta) = \mathbf{g} \cdot \mathbf{H} > \sqrt{(m - R)/m}$ and $\sum_i H_i > \sqrt{m - R}$. Since $\mathbf{H}$ is 2-normed, this can only hold if $\mathbf{H}$ has *more* than $m - R$ positive components. Therefore the master hypothesis correctly classifies *more* than $m - R$ examples and the sample error rate is at most $(R - 1)/m$. □

Combining Lemma 3 and Theorem 2 gives the following corollary.

**Corollary 1.** *After iteration* $T$, *the sample error rate of GeoLev's master hypothesis is bounded by*

$$\prod_{t=1}^{T} \left(1 - \frac{r_t^2}{||\mathbf{h}_t||_2^2}m\,\sin^2(\theta_t)\right) . \tag{24}$$

The recurrence of Theorem 2 is somewhat difficult to analyze, but we can apply the following lemma from Abe *et al.* [1].

**Lemma 4.** *Consider a sequence* $\{g_t\}$ *of non-negative numbers satisfying* $g_{t+1} \leq g_t - cg_t^2$, *where* $c > 0$ *is a positive constant. If* $f_t = \dfrac{1}{c\left(t + \frac{1}{g_0 c}\right)}$, *then* $g_t \leq f_t$ *for all* $t \in N$.

Given a lower bound $r$ on the $r_t$ values and an upper bound $\mathcal{H}_2$ on $||\mathbf{h}_t||_2$, then we can apply this lemma to recurrence (22). Setting $g_0 = 1$, $g_t = \sin^2(\theta_t)$ and $c = \frac{r^2}{\mathcal{H}_2^2}m$ shows that

$$sin^2(\theta_{T+1}) \leq \frac{\mathcal{H}_2^2}{r^2mT + \mathcal{H}_2^2} . \tag{25}$$

This, and the previous results lead to the following theorem.

**Theorem 3.** *If the weak learner always returns hypotheses with an edge greater than $r$ and $\mathcal{H}_2$ is an upper bound on $\|h_t\|_2$, then GeoLev's hypothesis will have at most $\epsilon$ training error after*

$$min\left(\frac{1}{2}\frac{\ln(\epsilon)}{\ln\sqrt{1-\frac{r^2}{\mathcal{H}_2^2}}},\frac{\mathcal{H}_2^2(1-\epsilon)}{\epsilon r^2 m}\right) \tag{26}$$

*iterations.*

Similar bounds have been obtained by Freund and Schapire [7] for AdaBoost.

**Theorem 4.** *After $T$ iterations, the sample error rate of AdaBoost's master hypothesis is at most*

$$\prod_{t=1}^{T}\sqrt{1-\frac{r_t^2}{\|h_t\|_\infty^2}} \ . \tag{27}$$

The dependence on $\|h\|_\infty$ is implicit in their bounds and and can be removed when $h_t(x_i) \in [-1,+1]$.

Comparing Corollary 1 and Theorem 4 leads to the following observations. First, the bound on GeoLev does not contain the square-root. If this were the only difference, then it would correspond to a halving of the number of iterations required to reach error rate $\epsilon$ on the sample. This effect can be approximated by a factor of 2 on the $r^2$ terms.

A more important difference is the factors multiplying the $r^2$ terms. With the preceding approximation GeoLev's bound has $2m\sin^2(\theta_t)/\|h_t\|_2^2$, while Adaboost's bound has $1/\|h_t\|_\infty^2$. The larger this factor the better the bound. The dependence on $\sin^2(\theta_t)$ means that GeoLev's progress tapers off as it approaches zero sample error.

If the weak hypotheses are equally confident on all examples, then $\|h_t\|_2^2$ is $m$ times larger than $\|h_t\|_\infty^2$ and the difference in factors is simply $2\sin^2(\theta_t)$. At the start of the boosting process $\theta_t$ is close $\pi/2$ and GeoLev's factor is larger. However, $\sin^2(\theta_t)$ can be as small as $1/m$ before GeoLev predicts perfectly on the sample. Thus GeoLev does not seem to gain as much from later iterations, and this difficulty prevents us from showing that GeoLev is a boosting algorithm.

On the other hand, consider the less likely situation where the weak hypotheses produce a confident prediction for only one sample point, and abstain on the rest. Now $\|h_t\|_2^2 = \|h_t\|_\infty^2$, and GeoLev's bound has an extra factor of about $2m\sin^2(\theta_t)$. GeoLev's bounds are uniformly better[3] than AdaBoost's in this case.

---

[3] We must switch to recurrence (20) rather than recurrence (22) when $\sin^2(\theta_t)$ is very small.

# 5 Conversion to an Arcing Algorithm

The GeoLev algorithm discussed so far does not fit the template for Arcing algorithms because it modifies the labels in the sample given to the weak learner. This also breaks the boosting paradigm as the weak learner may be required to produce a good hypothesis for data that is not consistent with any concept in the underlying concept class. In this section we describe a generic conversion that produces arcing algorithms from leveraging algorithms of this kind without placing an additional burden on the weak learner. Throughout this section we assume that the weak learner's hypotheses produce values in $[-1, +1]$.

The conversion introduces an wrapper between the weak learner and leveraging algorithm that replaces the sign-flip trick of section 2. This wrapper takes the (signed) weighting $D$ from the leveraging algorithm, and creates the distribution $D'$ by setting all negative components to zero and re-normalizing. This modified distribution $D'$ is then given to the weak learner, which returns a hypothesis $h$ with a margin vector $\mathbf{h}$. The margin vector is modified by the wrapper before being passed on to the leveraging algorithm: if $D(x_i)$ is negative then $\mathbf{h}_i$ is set to $-1$. Thus the leveraging algorithm sees a modified margin vector $\mathbf{h}'$ which it uses to compute $\alpha$ and the margins of the new master hypothesis.

The intuition is that the leveraging algorithm is being fooled into thinking that the weak hypothesis is wrong on parts of the sample when it is actually correct. Therefore the margins of the master hypothesis are actually better than those tracked by the leveraging algorithm. Furthermore, the apparent "edge" of the weak learner can only be increased by this wrapping transformation. This intuition is formalized in the following theorems.

**Theorem 5.** *If $r = \sum_i D'(x_i) y_i h(x_i) > 0$ is the edge of the weak learner with respect to the distribution it sees, and $r' = \sum_i D(x_i) y_i h'(x_i)$ is the edge of the modified weak hypothesis with respect to the (signed) weighting $D$ requested by the leveraging algorithm, then $r' \geq r$.*

**Proof** Let $S^+ = \{i : D(x_i) < 0\}$ and $p = \sum_{i \in S^+} D(x_i)$. The construction ensures that both $D'(x_i) = D(x_i)/p$ if $i \in S^+$ and zero otherwise, and $D(x_i) y_i h'(x_i) = |D(x_i)|$ for all $i \notin S^+$. Now,

$$r' = \sum_i D(x_i) y_i h'(x_i) = 1 - p + \sum_{i \in S^+} D(x_i) y_i h(x_i) = 1 - p + pr . \qquad (28)$$

The assumption on $h$ implies $r \leq 1$, so $r'$ is minimized at $p = 1$ where $r' = r$. $\square$

**Theorem 6.** *No component of the master margin vector $\mathbf{H} = \sum_t \alpha_t \mathbf{h}'_t$ used by the wrapped leveraging algorithm is ever greater than the actual margins of the master hypothesis $\sum_t \alpha_t \mathbf{h}_t$.*

**Proof** The theorem follows immediately by noting that each component of $\mathbf{h}'_t$ is no greater than the corresponding component of $\mathbf{h}_t$. $\square$

We call the wrapped version of GeoLev, GeoArc, as it is an Arcing algorithm. It is instructive to examine the potential function associated with GeoArc:

$$\sqrt{1 - \left(\sum_i \frac{1}{\sqrt{m}} \min\left(\mathbf{H}_i, \frac{1}{\sum_i \mathbf{H}_i}\right)\right)^2}. \tag{29}$$

This potential has a similar form to the following potential function which is zero on the entire positive orthant:

$$\sqrt{1 - \left(\sum_i \frac{1}{\sqrt{m}} \min\left(\mathbf{H}_i, 0\right)\right)^2}. \tag{30}$$

The leveraging framework we have described together with this transformation enables the analysis of some undifferentiable potential functions. The full implications of this remain to be explored.

## 6  Preliminary Experiments

We performed experiments comparing GeoLev and GeoArc to AdaBoost on a set of 13 datasets(the 2 class ones used in previous experiments) from the UCI repository. These experiments were run along the same lines as those reported by Quinlan [12]. We ran 10 times 10 fold cross validation on the datasets for two class classification. All leveraging algorithms ran for 25 iterations, and used single node decision trees as implemented in $\mathcal{MLC}$++ [9] for the weak hypotheses. Note that these are $\pm 1$ valued hypotheses, with large 2-norms. It was noticed that the splitting criterion used for the single node had a large impact on the results. Therefore, the results reported for each dataset are those for the better of mutual information ratio and gain ratio. We report only a comparison between AdaBoost and GeoLev, GeoArc performed comparably to GeoLev. The results are illustrated in figure 4. This figure is a scatter plot of the generalization error on each of the datasets. These results appear to indicate that the new algorithms are comparable to AdaBoost.

Further experiments are clearly warranted and we are especially interested in situations where the weak learner produces hypotheses with small 2-norm.

## 7  Conclusions and Directions for Further Study

We have presented the GeoLev and GeoArc algorithms which attempt to form master hypotheses that are correct and equally confident over the sample. We found it convenient to view these algorithms as performing a feasible direction gradient descent constrained by the hypotheses produced by the weak learner. The potential function used by GeoLev is not monotonic: its gradient can have

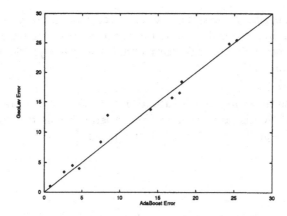

**Fig. 4.** Generalization error of GeoLev versus AdaBoost after 25 rounds.

negative components. Therefore the direction of steepest descent cannot simply be normalized to create a distribution for the weak learner.

We described two ways to solve this problem. The first constructing a modified sample by flipping some of the labels. This solution is mildly unsatisfying as it strengthens the requirements on the weak learner – the weak learner must now deal with a broader class of possible targets. Therefore we also presented a second transformation that does not increase the requirements on the weak learner. In fact, using this second transformation can actually improve the efficiency of the leveraging algorithm. One open issue is whether or not this improvement can be exploited to improve GeoArc's performance bounds. A second open issue is to determine the effectiveness of these transformations when applied to other non-monotonic potential functions, such as those considered by Mason *et al.* [11].

We have upper bounded the sample error rate of the master hypotheses produced by the GeoLev and GeoArc algorithms. These bounds are incomparable with the analogous bounds for AdaBoost. The bounds indicate that GeoLev/GeoArc may perform slightly better at the start of the leveraging process and when the weak hypotheses contain many low-confidence predictions. On the other hand, the bounds indicate that GeoLev/GeoArc may not exploit later iterations as well, and may be less effective when the weak learner produces ±1 valued hypotheses. These disadvantages make it unlikely that the GeoArc algorithm has the boosting property.

One possible explanation is that GeoLev/GeoArc aim at a cone inscribed in the positive orthant in margin space. As the sample size grows, the dimension of the space increases and the volume of the cone becomes a diminishing fraction of the positive orthant. AdaBoost's potential function appears better at navigating into the "corners" of the positive orthant.

However, our preliminary tests indicate that after 25 iterations the generalization errors of GeoArc/GeoLev are similar to AdaBoost's on 13 classification datasets from the UCI repository. These comparisons used 1-node decision tree classifiers as the weak learning method. It would be interesting to compare their relative performances when using a weak learner that produces hypotheses with many low-confidence predictions.

**Acknowledgments**

We would like to thank Manfred Warmuth,Robert Schapire, Yoav Freund, Arun Jagota, Claudio Gentile and the EuroColt program committee for their useful comments on the preliminary version of this paper.

# References

1. N. Abe, J. Takeuchi, and M. K. Warmuth. Polynomial learnability of probabilistic concepts with respect to the Kullback-Leibler divergence. In *Proc. 4th Annu. Workshop on Comput. Learning Theory*, pages 277–289, San Mateo, CA, 1991. Morgan Kaufmann.

2. B. E. Boser, I. M. Guyon, and V. N. Vapnik. A training algorithm for optimal margin classifiers. In *Proc. 5th Annu. Workshop on Comput. Learning Theory*, pages 144–152. ACM Press, New York, NY, 1992.

3. Leo Breiman. Bagging predictors. *Machine Learning*, 24(2):123–140, 1996.

4. Leo Breiman. Arcing the edge. Technical Report 486, Department of Statistics, University of California, Berkeley, 1997. Available at http://www.stat.berkeley.edu.

5. Leo Breiman. Bias, variance, and arcing classifiers. Technical Report 460, Department of Statistics, University of California, Berkeley, 1997. Available at http://www.stat.berkeley.edu.

6. Y. Freund. Boosting a weak learning algorithm by majority. *Information and Computation*, 121(2):256–285, September 1995. Also appeared in COLT90.

7. Yoav Freund and Robert E. Schapire. A decision-theoretic generalization of on-line learning and an application to boosting. *Journal of Computer and System Sciences*, 55(1):119–139, August 1997.

8. Jerome Friedman, Trevor Hastie, and Robert Tibshirani. Additive logistic regression: a statistical view of boosting. Unpublished manuscript available at http://www-stat.stanford.edu, 1998.

9. Ron Kohavi, Dan Sommerfield, and James Dougherty. Data mining using MLC++: A machine learning library in C++. In *Tools with Artificial Intelligence*. IEEE Computer Society Press, 1996. http://www.sgi.com/Technology/mlc.

10. D. G. Luenberger. *Linear and Nonlinear Programming*. Addison-Wesley, Reading, MA, 1984.

11. Llew Mason, Peter Bartlett, and Jonathan Baxter. Improved generalization through explicit optimization of margins. Technical report, Department of Systems Engineering, Research School of Information Sciences and Engineering, Australian National University, 1998.

12. J. R. Quinlan. Bagging, boosting and c4.5. In *Proceedings of the Thirteenth National Conference of Artificial Intelligence*, pages 725–730. AAAI Press and the MIT Press, 1996.

13. Gunnar Rätsch, Takashi Onoda, and Klaus-R. Müller. Soft margins for adaboost. Technical Report NC-TR-1998-021, NeuroCOLT2, 1998.

14. Robert E. Schapire, Yoav Freund, Peter Bartlett, and Wee Sun Lee. Boosting the margin: a new explanation for the effectiveness of voting methods. In *Proc. 14th International Conference on Machine Learning*, pages 322–330. Morgan Kaufmann, 1997.

15. Robert E. Schapire and Yoram Singer. Improved boosting algorithms using confidence-rated predictions. In *Proc. 11th Annu. Conf. on Comput. learning Theory*, 1998.

16. V. N. Vapnik. *Estimation of Dependences Based on Empirical Data*. Springer-Verlag, New York, 1982.

# Query by Committee, Linear Separation and Random Walks

Ran Bachrach, Shai Fine, and Eli Shamir*

Institute of Computer Science
The Hebrew University, Jerusalem, Israel
{ranb,fshai,shamir}@cs.huji.ac.il

**Abstract.** Recent works have shown the advantage of using *Active Learning* methods, such as the *Query by Committee* (QBC) algorithm, to various learning problems. This class of Algorithms requires an oracle with the ability to randomly select a consistent hypothesis according to some predefined distribution. When trying to implement such an oracle, for the linear separators family of hypotheses, various problems should be solved. The major problem is time-complexity, where the straight-forward *Monte Carlo* method takes exponential time.

In this paper we address some of those problems and show how to convert them to the problems of sampling from convex bodies or approximating the volume of such bodies. We show that recent algorithms for approximating the volume of convex bodies and approximately uniformly sampling from convex bodies using random walks, can be used to solve this problem, and yield an efficient implementation for the QBC algorithm. This solution suggests a connection between random walks and certain properties known in machine learning such as ε-net and support vector machines. Working out this connection is left for future work.

## 1 Introduction

In the *Active Learning* paradigm [3] the learner is given access to a stream of unlabeled samples, drawn at random from a fixed and unknown distribution and for every sample the learner decides whether to query the teacher for the label. Complexity in this context is measured by the number of requests directed to the teacher along the learning process. The reasoning comes from many real life problems where the teacher's activity is an expensive resource. For example, if one would like to design a program that classifies articles into two categories ("interesting" and "non-interesting") then the program may automatically scan as many articles as possible (e.g. through the Internet). However, articles which the program needs the teacher's comment (tag) - the teacher must actually read, and that is a costly task. The *Query By Committee* (QBC) algorithm [11] is an Active Learning algorithm acting in the *Bayesian* model of concept learning

---

* Partially supported by project I403-001.06/95 of the German-Israeli Foundation for Scientific Research [GIF].

[8] i.e. it assumes that the concept to be learned is chosen according to some fixed distribution known to the learning algorithm. The algorithm uses three oracles: The *Sample* oracle returns a random sample $x$, the *Label* oracle returns the label(tag) for a sample, and the *Gibbs* oracle returns a random hypothesis from the version space. The algorithm gets two parameters - accuracy ($\alpha$) and reliability ($\beta$) - and works as follows:

1. Call *Sample* to get a random sample $x$.
2. Call *Gibbs* twice to obtain two hypotheses and generate two predictions for the label of $x$.
3. If the predictions are not equal
   **Then** call *Label* to get the correct label for $x$.
4. If *Label* was not used for the last $t_k{}^1$ consecutive samples, where $k$ is the current number of labeled samples,
   **Then** call *Gibbs* once and output this last hypothesis
   **Else** return to the beginning of the loop (step 1).

A natural mean for tracing the progress of the learning process is the rate at which the size of the version space decreases. We adopt the notion of information gain as the measure of choice for the analysis of the learning process:

**Definition 1 (Haussler et. al. [8]).** *Let $\mathcal{V}_x = \{h \in \mathcal{V} | h(x) = c(x)\}$ be the version space after sample $x$ had been labeled*

- *The instantaneous information gain is $\mathcal{I}(x, c(x)) = -\log \Pr_{h \in \mathcal{V}}[h \in \mathcal{V}_x]$*
- *The expected information gain of a sample $x$ to is*

$$\mathcal{G}(x|\mathcal{V}) = \mathcal{H}(\Pr_{h \in \mathcal{V}}[h(x) = 1]) \tag{1}$$
$$= \Pr_{h \in \mathcal{V}}[h(x) = 1] \cdot \mathcal{I}(x, 1) + \Pr_{h \in \mathcal{V}}[h(x) = -1] \cdot \mathcal{I}(x, -1)$$

*where H is the binary entropy, i.e. $\mathcal{H}(p) = -p \log p - (1-p) \log(1-p)$.*

**Theorem 1 (Freund et. al. [6]).** *If a concept class $C$ has VC-dimension $0 < d < \infty$ and the expected information gain from the queries to Label Oracle made by QBC are uniformly lower bounded by $g > 0$ bits, then the following holds with probability larger than $1 - \beta$ over the choice of the target concept, the sequence of samples, and the choices made by QBC:*

1. *The number of calls to Sample is $m_0 = (\frac{d}{\alpha \beta g})^{O(1)}$.*
2. *The number of calls to Label is smaller then[2] $k_0 = \frac{10(d+1)}{g} \ln \frac{4m_0}{\beta}$.*
3. *The algorithm guarantees that*

$$\Pr_{c,h,QBC}[\Pr_x[h(x) \neq c(x)] \geq \alpha] \leq \beta \tag{2}$$

---

[1] $t_k = \frac{2\pi^2 (k+1)^2}{3\alpha\beta} \ln \frac{2\pi^2 (k+1)^2}{3\beta}$ is a correction of the expression given at ([6]).
[2] $k_0 = O(\log \frac{1}{\alpha\beta})$ results in an exponential gap between the number of queries made to *Label*, comparing to "regular" algorithms.

The main theme governing the proof of this theorem is the capability to bound the number of queries made by QBC in terms of $g$, the lower bound for the expected information gain: If the algorithm asks to tag all $m$ samples then $\Pr\left[\sum_i^m \mathcal{G}(x_i|\mathcal{V}) \geq (d+1)(\log \frac{\alpha m}{d})\right] < \frac{d}{em}$, meaning the accumulated information gain grows logarithmically with $m$. Obviously, when filtering out samples the accumulated information gain cannot be larger. On the other hand, $kg$ is a lower bound on the accumulated expected information gain from $k$ tagged samples. These two observations suggest that $kg \leq (d+1)(\log \frac{\alpha m}{d})$, which results in a bound on $k$ and implies that the gap between consecutive queried samples is expected to grow until the stop-condition will be satisfied. Theorem 1 can be augmented to handle general class of filtering algorithms: Let $L$ be an algorithm that filters out samples based on an internal probability assignment and previous query results. Using a stop-condition identical to the one used by the QBC algorithm and following the basic steps at the proof of theorem 1, one may conclude similar bounds on the number of calls $L$ makes to *Sample* and *Label* oracles.

By stating a lower bound on the expected information gain, Freund et. al. were able to identify several classes of concepts as learnable by the QBC algorithm. Among them are classes of perceptrons (linear separators) defined by a vector $w$ such that for any sample $x$:

$$c_w(x) = \begin{cases} +1, \text{ if } x \cdot w > 0 \\ -1, \text{ otherwise} \end{cases} \tag{3}$$

with the restriction that the version space distribution is known to the learner and both sample space and version space distributions are almost uniform. A question which was left open is how to efficiently implement the *Gibbs* oracle and thus reduce QBC to a standard learning model (using only *Sample* and *Label* oracles). It turns out that this question falls naturally into a class of approximating problems which got much attention in recent years: How to get an efficient approximation of volume or random sampling of rather complex defined and dynamically changing spaces. Moreover, unraveling the meaning of random walks employed by these approximate counting methods seems to have interesting implications in learning theory. Let us focus on the problem of randomly selecting hypotheses from the version space and limit our discussion to classes of linear separators: There are several known algorithms for finding a linear separator (e.g. the perceptron algorithm), but none of them suffice since we need to *randomly* select a separator in the version space. A possible straightforward solution is the use of the *Monte Carlo* mechanism: Assuming (as later we do) that the linear separators are uniformly distributed, we randomly select a point in the unit sphere[3], identifying this point as a linear separator, and check whether it is in the version space. If not, proceed with the sampling until a consistent separator will be selected. This process yields several problems, the most important of which is efficiency. Recall that the QBC algorithm assumes a lower bound $g > 0$

---

[3] pick $n$ normally distributed variables $\zeta_1 \ldots \zeta_n$ and normalize them by the square root of the sum of their squares

for the expected information gain from queried samples. Let $p \leq 1/2$ be such that $\mathcal{H}(p) = g$. Having $k$ tagged samples, the probability to select a consistent separator is smaller then $(1-p)^k$. This implies that the expected number of iterations the Monte Carlo algorithm makes until it finds a desired separator is greater then $(1-p)^{-k}$. If the total number of samples the algorithm uses is $m$, and $k$ is the number of tagged samples, then the computational complexity is at least $\Omega(m(1-p)^{-k})$. Plugging in the expected value for $k$ in the QBC algorithm, i.e. $\frac{10(d+1)}{g} \ln \frac{4m}{\beta}$, the Monte Carlo implementation results in a computational complexity exponential in $g$, $d$ (the VC-dimension, i.e. $n+1$ in our case) and also a depends on $m^2$. Furthermore, if the version space decreases faster then it's expected value, then finding a consistent linear separator will take even longer time. The algorithms we suggest in this paper work in time polynomial in $n, g$ and depend on $mk^{O(1)}$, i.e., they are exponentially better in terms of the VC-dimension and $g$ and also have better polynomial factors in terms of $m$. We also avoid the problem of rapid decrease in the size of the version space by employing a detecting condition.

## 1.1 Mathematical Notation

The sample space $\Omega$, is assumed to be a subset of $\Re^n$ and therefore a sample is a vector in $\Re^n$. A linear separator is a tuple $\{v, \text{offset}\}$ where $v$ is a vector in $\Re^n$ and offset $\in \Re$. To simplify notation we shall assume that each sample $x$ is taken from $\Re^{n+1}$ forcing $x_1 = 1$. Hence a linear separator is just a vector in $\Re^{n+1}$. The concept to be learned is assumed to be chosen according to a fixed distribution $\mathcal{D}$ over $\Re^{n+1}$. We denote by $x^i$ a queried sample and $t^i$ the corresponding tag, where $t^i \in \{-1, 1\}$. The version space $\mathcal{V}$ is defined to be $\mathcal{V} = \{v | \forall i (\langle x^i, v \rangle \cdot t^i) > 0\}$. Let $Y^i = t^i \cdot x^i$. Then a vector $v$ is a linear separator if $\forall i \langle Y^i, v \rangle > 0$. Using matrix notation we may further simplify notation by setting $Y^i$ to be the $i$'th row of matrix $A$ and writing $\mathcal{V} = \{v | Av > 0\}$.

## 1.2 Preliminary Observations

Upon receiving a new sample $x$, the algorithm needs to decide whether to query for a tag. The probability for labeling $x$ with $+1$ is: $P^+ = Pr_{\mathcal{D}}[v \in V^+]$ where $\mathcal{D}$ is the distribution induced on the version space $\mathcal{V}$ and $V^+ = \{v | Av > 0, \langle x, v \rangle \geq 0\}$. Similarly we define $V^-$ and $P^-$ which correspond to labeling $x$ with $-1$. The QBC algorithm decides to query for a tag only when the two hypotheses disagree on $x$'s label and this happens with probability $2P^+P^-$. Thus $P^+$ and $P^-$ are all we need in order to substitute *Gibbs* oracle and make this decision. Normalizing $||v|| = 1$, the version space of linear separators becomes subset of $n$ dimensional sphere $S^n$. Under the uniform distribution on $S^n$, the value of $P^+$ (and $P^-$) can be obtained by calculating $n+1$ dimensional volume: $P^+ = \frac{\text{Vol}(V^+)}{\text{Vol}(V)}$. Now $\mathcal{V}$, $V^+$ and $V^-$ are convex *simplexes* [4] in the $n+1$ dimensional unit ball. Having

---

[4] the term *simplex* is used to describe a conical convex set of the type $K = \{v \in \Re^n | Av > 0, ||v|| \leq 1\}$. Note that it is a nonstandrd use of this term.

$P^+$ and $P^-$, we can substitute the *Gibbs* oracle: Given a set of tagged samples and a new sample $x$, query the label of $x$ with probability $2P^+P^-$.

## 1.3 Few Results about Convex Bodies

In order to simulate the *Gibbs* oracle we seek efficient methods for calculating the volume of a convex body and uniformly sampling from it. Very similar questions relating convex bodies have been addressed by Dyer et. al. [4], Lovasz and Simonovits [9] and others.

**Theorem 2 (The Sampling Algorithm [9]).** *Let $K$ be a convex body such that $K$ contains at least 2/3 of the volume of the unit ball (B) and at least 2/3 of the volume of $K$ is contained in a ball of radius $m$ such that $1 \leq m \leq n^{3/2}$. For arbitrary $\epsilon > 0$ there exist a sampling algorithm that uses $O(n^4 m^2 \log^2(1/\epsilon)(n \log n + \log(1/\epsilon))$ operations on numbers of size $O(\log n)$ bits and returns a vector $v$ such that for every Lebesgue measurable set $L$ in $K$:*
$$|\Pr(v \in L) - \frac{Vol(L)}{Vol(K)}| < \epsilon$$

The algorithm uses random walks over the convex body $K$ as its method of traverse and it reaches every point of $K$ with almost equal probability. To complete this result, Grotchel et. al. [7] used the ellipsoid method to find an affine transformation $T_a$ such that given a convex body $K$, $B \subseteq T_a(K) \subseteq n^{3/2}B$. Assume that the original body $K$ is bounded in a ball of radius $R$ and contains a ball of radius $r$ then the algorithm finds $T_a$ in $O(n^4(|\log r| + |\log R|))$ operations on numbers of size $O(n^2(|\log r| + |\log R|))$ bits. Before we proceed, let us elaborate on the meaning of these results for our needs: When applying the sampling algorithm to the convex body $\mathcal{V}$, we will get $v \in \mathcal{V}$. Since $V^+$ and $V^-$ are both simplexes, then they are Lebesgue measurable, hence $|\Pr(v \in V^+) - P^+| < \epsilon$. Note that we are only interested in the proportions of $V^+$ and $V^-$ and the use of the affine transformation $T_a$ preserve these proportions. The sampling algorithm enables Lovasz and Simonovits to come out with an algorithm for approximating the volume of a convex body:

**Theorem 3 (Volume Approximation algorithm [9]).** *Let $K$ be a convex body[5] in $\Re^n$. There exists a volume approximating algorithm such that upon receiving error parameters $\epsilon, \delta \in (0, 1)$ and numbers $R$ and $r$ such that $K$ contains a ball of radius $r$ and is contained in a ball of radius $R$ centered at the origin, the algorithm outputs a number $\zeta$ such that with probability at least $1 - \delta$*

$$(1 - \epsilon) Vol(K) \leq \zeta \leq (1 + \epsilon) Vol(K) \tag{4}$$

*The algorithm works in time polynomial in $|\log R| + |\log r|, n, 1/\epsilon$ and $\log(1/\delta)$.*

For our purposes, this algorithm can estimate the expected information gained from the next sample. It also approximates the value of $P^+$ (and $P^-$) and thus

---

[5] $K$ is assumed to be given using a separation oracle.

we may simulate the *Gibbs* oracle by choosing to query for a tag with probability $2P^+(1 - P^+)$. Both the sampling algorithm and the volume approximation algorithm require the values of $R$ and $r$. Since in our case all convex bodies are contained in the unit ball $B$, then fixing $R = 1$ will suffice and we are left with the problem of finding $r$. However, it will suffice to find $r$ such that $\frac{r^*}{4} \leq r \leq r^*$ where $r^*$ is the maximal radius of a ball contained in $K$. Moreover, we will have to show that $r$ is not too small. The main part of this proof is to show that if the volume of $V^+$ is not too small, then $r$ is not too small (lemma 1). Since we learn by reducing the volume of the version space, this lemma states that the radius decreases in a rate proportional to the learning rate.

## 2 Modified Query By Committee Algorithms

In this section we present two variants of the QBC algorithm: the first uses approximation of the volume of convex bodies, while the second uses the technique for sampling from convex bodies. Both algorithms are efficient and maintain the exponential gap between labeled and unlabeled samples. QBC" is especially interesting from computational complexity perspective, while the mechanism in the basis of QBC' enables the approximation of the maximal a-posteriori (MAP) hypothesis in $Poly(\log m)$ time as well as direct access to the expected information gain from a query.

### 2.1 Using Volume Approximation in the QBC Algorithm (QBC')

Every Sample $x$ induces a partition of the version space $\mathcal{V}$ into two subsets $V^+$ and $V^-$. Since $\mathcal{V} = V^+ \cup V^-$ and they are disjoint, then $\mathrm{Vol}(\mathcal{V}) = \mathrm{Vol}(V^+) + \mathrm{Vol}(V^-)$ and $P^+ = \frac{\mathrm{Vol}(V^+)}{\mathrm{Vol}(V^+) + \mathrm{Vol}(V^-)}$. Hence, approximating these volumes results in approximation of $P^+$ that we can use instead of the original value. In order to use the volume approximation algorithm as a procedure, we need to bound the volumes of $V^+$ and $V^-$, i.e. find balls of radii $r^+$ and $r^-$ contained in $(V^+)$ and $(V^-)$ respectively. If both volumes are not too small then the corresponding radii are big enough and may be calculated efficiently using convex programming. If one of the volumes is too small then we are guaranteed that the other one is not too small since $\mathrm{Vol}(\mathcal{V})$ is not too small (lemma 7). It turns out that if one of the radii is very small then assuming that the corresponding part is empty (i.e. the complementary part is the full version space) is enough for simulating the *Gibbs* oracle (lemma 3). The QBC' algorithm follows:

Given $\alpha, \beta > 0$ and let $k$ be the current number of labeled samples,

define $t_k = \frac{1024\pi^4(k+1)^4 \log \frac{8\pi^2(k+1)^2}{3\beta}}{9\alpha^2\beta^2}$ , $\delta_k = \frac{3\beta}{4\pi^2(k+1)^2}$ , $\epsilon_k = \frac{\alpha\delta_k}{48}$ , $\mu_k = \frac{2\epsilon_k}{n}$

1. Call *Sample* to get a random sample $x$.
2. Use convex programming to simultaneously calculate the values of $r^+$ and $r^-$, the radii of balls contained in $V^+$ and $V^-$.

3. If $min(r^+, r^-) < \mu_k(max(r^+, r^-))^n$
   **Then** assume that the corresponding body is empty and **goto** 6.
4. Call the volume approximation algorithm with $r^+$ (and $r^-$) to get $\zeta^+$ (and $\zeta^-$) such that

$$(1 - \epsilon_k)\text{Vol}(V^+) \le \zeta^+ \le (1 + \epsilon_k)\text{Vol}(V^+)$$

   with probability greater then $1 - \delta_k$
5. Let $\widehat{P^+} = \frac{\zeta^+}{\zeta^+ + \zeta^-}$, with probability $2\widehat{P^+}(1 - \widehat{P^+})$ call *Label* to get the correct label of $x$.
6. **If** *Label* was not used for the last $t_k$ consecutive samples,
   **Then** call the sampling algorithm with $\epsilon = \frac{\beta}{2}$ to give an hypothesis and stop. **Else** return to the beginning of the loop (step 1).

With probability greater then $1 - \beta$ the time complexity of QBC' is $m$ times $Poly(n, k, \frac{1}{\alpha}, \frac{1}{\beta})$ (for each iteration). The number of samples that the algorithm uses is polynomial in the number of samples that the QBC algorithm uses. Furthermore, the exponential gap between the number of samples and number of labeled samples still holds.

## 2.2 Using Sampling in the QBC algorithm (QBC")

Another variant of QBC is the QBC" algorithm which simulate the *Gibbs* oracle by sampling, almost uniformly, two hypothesis from the version space:

Given $\alpha, \beta > 0$ and let $k$ be the current number of labeled samples, define $\beta_k = \frac{3\beta}{\pi^2(k+1)^2}$ , $t_k = \frac{8 \log 4/\beta_k}{\alpha\beta_k}$ , $\epsilon_k = \frac{\alpha\beta_k}{32}$ , $\mu_k = \frac{2}{n}\min(\epsilon_k, 1 - \epsilon_k)$

1. Call *Sample* to get a random sample $x$.
2. Call the sampling algorithm with $\epsilon_k$ and $r$ to get two hypotheses from the version space.
3. **If** the two hypotheses disagree on the label of $x$
   **Then** use convex programming to simultaneously calculate the values of $r^+$ and $r^-$, the radii of the balls contained in $V^+$ and $V^-$.
4. **If** $min(r^+, r^-) \ge \mu_k(max(r^+, r^-))^n$
   **Then** call *Label* to get the correct label and choose $r^+$ (or $r^-$), the radius of a ball contained in the new version space, to be used in step 2.
5. **If** *Label* was not used for the last $t_k$ consecutive samples,
   **Then** call the sampling algorithm with $\epsilon = \frac{\beta}{2}$ to give an hypothesis and stop.
   **Else** return to the beginning of the loop (step 1).

QBC" is very similar to QBC' but with one major difference: calculating new radius is conducted almost only when the version space changes and this happens only after querying for a tag. Hence each iteration takes $O(n^7 \log^2(1/\epsilon)(n \log n + \log(1/\epsilon))$ operations and an extra $Poly(n, 1/\epsilon, 1/\delta, k)$ is needed when a tag is asked. Due to the exponential gap between the number of samples and number of tagged samples, this algorithm may be attractive for practical use.

# 3 Deriving the Main Results

We start the analysis by presenting a useful lemma which bounds the radii of a ball contained in a simplex as a function of its volume. The algorithms for estimating the volume of a convex body, or sampling from it, work in time polynomial in $\log r$ ($R = 1$ in our case). The following lemma, gives a lower bound on the size of $r$, hence will be useful for analyzing the time-complexity of our algorithms.

**Lemma 1.** *Let $K$ be a convex body contained in the $n$-dimensional unit ball $B$ (assume $n > 1$). Let $v = Vol(K)$ then there is a ball of radius $r$ contained in $K$ such that*

$$r \geq \frac{1}{n} \frac{Vol(K)}{Vol(B)} = \frac{v\Gamma(\frac{n+2}{2})}{n\pi^{n/2}} \tag{5}$$

*Proof.* We shall assume that $K$ is given by a finite set of linear inequalities with the constraint that all the points in $K$ are within the unit ball. Let $r^*$ be the supremum of the radii of balls contained in $K$, and let $r \geq r^*$. We denote by $\partial K$ the boundary of $K$. Then $\partial K$ has a derivative at all points apart from a set of zero measure.

We construct a set $S$ by taking a segment of length $r$ for each point $y$ of $\partial K$ such that $\partial K$ has a derivative at $y$. We take the segment to be in direction which is orthogonal to the derivative at $y$ and pointing towards the inner part of $K$ (see figure 1).

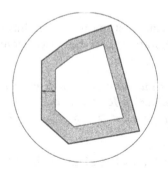

**Fig. 1.** An example of the process of generating the set $S$ (the gray area) by taking orthogonal segments to $\partial K$ (the bold line). In this case, the length $r$ (the arrow) is too small.

The assumption that $r \geq r^*$ implies $K \subset S$ up to a set of zero measure. To show this we look at the following: Let $x \in K$, then there is $\hat{r}$ which is the maximal radius of a ball contained in $K$ centered at $x$. If we look at the ball of radius $\hat{r}$ than it intersects $\partial K$ at least at one point. At this point, denote $y$, the derivative of $\partial K$ is the derivative of the boundary of the ball (the derivative exists). Hence the orthogonal segment to $y$ of length $\hat{r}$ reaches $x$. Since $\hat{r} \leq r^* \leq r$ then the orthogonal segment of length $r$ from $y$ reaches $x$. The only points that might not be in $S$ are the points in $\partial K$ where there is no derivative, but this is a set of measure zero. Therefore

$$\text{Vol}(S) \geq \text{Vol}(K) = v \tag{6}$$

But, by the definition of $S$ we can see that

$$\text{Vol}(S) \leq |\int_{\partial K} r| = r\text{Vol}(\partial K) \tag{7}$$

Note that $\text{Vol}(\partial K)$ is $n-1$ dimensional volume. Hence, we conclude that $v \leq r\text{Vol}(\partial K)$ or $r \geq \frac{v}{\text{Vol}(\partial K)}$. This is true for every $r \geq r^*$ therefore

$$r^* \geq \frac{v}{\text{Vol}(\partial K)} \tag{8}$$

It remains to bound the size of $\text{Vol}(\partial K)$. In [1] appendix C we show that the convex body with maximal surface is the unit ball itself (this result can be obtained from the isoperimetric inequalities as well). Since the volume of $n$-dimensional ball is $\frac{r^n \pi^{n/2}}{\Gamma(\frac{n+2}{2})}$ the $n-1$ dimension volume of its surface is $\frac{nr^{n-1}\pi^{n/2}}{\Gamma(\frac{n+2}{2})}$. Substituting $\text{Vol}(\partial K)$ with the volume of the surface of the unit ball in equation (8) we conclude that $r^* \geq \frac{v\Gamma(\frac{n+2}{2})}{n\pi^{n/2}}$. $\qquad\square$

*Remark 1.* Perhaps the lemma is known, but we could not find a reference. Eggleston [5] (also quoted at M. Berger's book *Géométrie*, 1990) gives a rather difficult proof of the lower bound $r \geq \frac{\min \text{width}(K)}{2\sqrt{n}}$ for $n$ odd (for even $n$ the bound is somewhat modified). The two lower bounds seem unrelated. Moreover, width$(K)$ seems hard to approximate by sampling.

Convex programming provides the tools for efficiently estimating the radius of the ball contained in a simplex as shown in the statement of the next lemma (proved in App. A):

**Lemma 2.** *Let $K$ be a simplex contained in the unit ball defined by $k$ inequalities. Let $r^*$ be the maximal radius of a ball contained in $K$. Using the ellipsoid algorithm, it is possible to calculate a value $r$, such that $r^* \geq r \geq r^*/4$, in time which is $Poly(n, |\log r^*|, k)$.*

We are now ready to present the main theorem for each variant of the QBC algorithm. However, since the difference in the analysis of the two algorithms provides no further insight we chose to describe here only the proof of QBC" which seems more adequate for practical use. The interested reader may find a detailed proofs for both algorithms in the comprehensive version [1].

**Theorem 4.** *Let $\alpha,\beta > 0$, let $n > 1$ and let $c$ be a linear separator chosen uniformly from the space of linear separators. Then algorithm QBC" (as described in section 2.2) returns an hypothesis $h$ such that*

$$Pr_{c,h}[Pr_x[c(x) \neq h(x)] > \alpha] < 1 - \beta \tag{9}$$

using $m_0 = (n, 1/\alpha, 1/\beta)^{O(1)}$ samples and $k_0 = O(n \log \frac{m_0}{\beta})$ labeled samples. With probability greater then $1 - \beta$, the time complexity is $m$ (the number of iterations) times $Poly(n, k, \frac{1}{\alpha}, \frac{1}{\beta})$ (the complexity of each iteration).

*Proof.* Our proof consists of three parts: the correctness of the algorithm, it's sample complexity and computational complexity. We base the proof on three lemmas which are specified at App. A.

In lemma 4 we show that if $q$ is the probability that QBC will ask to tag a sample $x$ and $\hat{q}$ is the probability that QBC" will ask to tag the same sample then $|q - \hat{q}| \leq 4\epsilon_k$. Using this result, we show in lemma 6 that if the algorithm didn't ask to tag more then $t_k$ consecutive samples and $\mathcal{V}$ is the version space then

$$\Pr_{c, h \in \mathcal{V}}[\Pr_x[c(x) \neq h(x)] > \alpha] \leq \beta/2 \tag{10}$$

therefore if we stop at this point and pick an hypothesis approximately uniformly from $\mathcal{V}$ with picking accuracy $\beta/2$, we get an algorithmic error of no more then $\beta$ and this completes the proof of the correctness of the algorithm.

We now turn to discuss the sample complexity of the algorithm. Following Freund et. al. [6] we need to show that at any stage in the learning process there is a uniform lower bound on the expected information gain from the next query. Freund et. al. showed that for the class of linear separators such a lower bound exists, when applying the original QBC algorithm under certain restriction on the distribution of the linear separators and the sample space. In corollary 2 we show that if $g$ is such a lower bound for the original QBC algorithm then there exists a lower bound $\hat{g}$ for the QBC" algorithm such that $\hat{g} \geq g - 4\epsilon_k$. Since $\epsilon_k \leq \alpha\beta$ we get a uniform lower bound $\hat{g}$ such that $\hat{g} \geq g - 4\alpha\beta$, so for $\alpha\beta$ sufficiently small $\hat{g} \geq g/2$. I.e. the expected information QBC" gain from each query it makes, is "almost" the same as the one gained by QBC.

Having this lower-bound on the expected information gain and using the augmented Theorem 1 , we conclude that the number of iterations QBC" will make is bounded by $Poly(n, \frac{1}{\alpha}, \frac{1}{\beta}, \frac{1}{g})$ while the number of queries it will make is less then $Poly(n, \log \frac{1}{\alpha}, \log \frac{1}{\beta}, \frac{1}{g})$.

Finally we would like to discuss the computational complexity of the algorithm. There are two main computational tasks in each iteration QBC" makes: First, the algorithm decides whether to query on the given sample. Second, it has to compute the radii of balls contained in $V^+$ and $V^-$.

The first task is done using twice the algorithm which approximate uniform sampling from convex bodies in order to obtain two hypotheses. The complexity of this algorithm is polynomial in $|\log \epsilon_k|, n, |\log r|$ where $\epsilon_k$ is the accuracy we need, $n$ is the dimension and $r$ is a radius of a ball contained in the body. In lemma 7 we bound the size of $r$ by showing that if the algorithm uses $m$ samples then with probability greater then $1 - \beta$, in every step $r \geq \frac{\beta \left(\frac{n}{\epsilon m}\right)^n}{n}$. Since we are interested in $\log r$ this bound suffice.

The other task is to calculate $r^+$ and $r^-$, which is done using convex programming as shown in lemma 2. It will suffice to show that at least one of them is "big enough" since we proceed in looking for the other value for no more then another $\log \mu_k$ iterations (a polynomial value): From lemma 7 we know that $\mathrm{Vol}\,(\mathcal{V}) \geq \frac{\beta\left(\frac{n}{em}\right)^n \pi^{n/2}}{\Gamma\left(\frac{n+2}{2}\right)}$ at every step. At least one of $V^+$ or $V^-$ has volume of at least $\frac{\mathrm{Vol}(\mathcal{V})}{2}$. Using the lower bound on the volume of $\mathcal{V}$ and lemma 1 we conclude that the maximal radius $r \geq \frac{\beta\left(\frac{n}{em}\right)^n}{2n}$.

We conclude that with probability greater then $1 - \beta$ the time-complexity of each iteration the QBC" algorithm is $\mathrm{Poly}(n, k, \log\frac{1}{\beta}, \log\frac{1}{\alpha})$. In the final iteration, the algorithm returns an hypothesis from the version space. Using the sampling algorithm this is done in polynomial time. Combined with the fact that there are at most $m_0$ iterations the statement of the theorem follows. □

## 4 Conclusions and Further Research

In this paper we presented a feasible way to simulate the *Gibbs* oracle picking almost uniformly distributed linear separators and thus reduce *Query by Committee* to a standard learning model. To this purpose, we used convex programming and formed a linkage to a class of approximation methods related to convex body sampling and volume approximation. These methods use random walks over convex bodies, on a grid which depends on the parameters $\epsilon$ and $\delta$, in a similar fashion to PAC algorithms. It seems that such random walks could be described using $\epsilon$-net terminology or alike. We thus suggest that this connection have further implication in Learning Theory.

Freund et. al. [6] assumed the existence of the *Gibbs* oracle and essentially used the information gain only for proving convergence of the QBC algorithm (Theorem 1). The use of the volume approximation technique (i.e. QBC') provides a direct access to the instantaneous information gain. This enable us to suggest another class of algorithms, namely *Information Gain Machines*, which make use of the extra information. Combining our results with the ones presented by Shawe-Taylor and Williamson [12] and McAllester [10] may allow to obtain generalization error estimates for such information gain machines and make use of QBC' ability to produce maximum a-posteriori estimate.

The two algorithms presented have to estimate a radius of a ball contained in a convex body, which in our case is the version space $\mathcal{V}$. Finding the center of a large ball contained in the version space is also an essential task in the theory of support vector machines (SVM) [2]. In this case the radius is the margin of the separator. It is also clear that QBC is a filtering algorithm which seeks samples that are going to be in the support set of the current version space. This similarity implies a connection between the two paradigms and is the subject of our current research.

# 5  Acknowledgment

We would like to thank also R. El-Yaniv, N. Linial and M. Kearns for their good advices.

# References

1. R. Bachrach, S. Fine, and E. Shamir. Query by committee, linear separation and random walks - full version. 1998. Available at http://www.cs.huji.ac.il/labs/learning/Papers/MLT_list.html.
2. C. Burges. A tutorial on support vector machines for pattern recognition. 1998. Available at http://svm.research.bell-labs.com/SVMdoc.html.
3. D. Cohn, L. Atlas, and R. Ladner. Training connectionist networks with queries and selective sampling. *Advanced in Neural Information Processing Systems 2*, 1990.
4. M. Dyer, A. Frieze, and R. Kannan. A random polynomial time algorithm for approximating the volume of convex bodies. *Journal of the Association for Computing Machinery*, 38, Number 1:1–17, 1991.
5. H. G. Eggleston. *Convexity*. Cambridge Univ. Press, 1958.
6. Y. Freund, H. Seung, E. Shamir, and N. Tishby. Selective sampling using the query by committee algorithm. *Macine Learning*, 28:133–168, 1997.
7. L. Grotchel, L. Lovasz, and A. Schrijver. *Geometric algorithms and Combinatorial Optimization*. Springer-Verlag, Berlin, 1988.
8. D. Haussler, M. Kearns, and R. E. Schapie. Bounds on the sample complexity of bayesian learning using information theory and the vc dimension. *Machine Learning*, 14:83–113, 1994.
9. L. Lovasz and M. Simonovits. Random walks in a convex body and an improved volume algorithm. *Random Structures and Algorithms*, 4, Number 4:359–412, 1993.
10. D. A. McAllester. Some pac-bayesian theorems. *Proc. of the Eleventh Annual Conference on Computational Learning Theory*, pages 230–234, 1998.
11. H. S. Seung, M. Opper, and H. Sompolinsky. Query by committe. *Proc. of the Fith Workshop on Computational Learning Theory*, pages 287–294, 1992.
12. J. Shawe-Taylor and R. C. Williamson. A pac analysis of a bayesian estimator. *Proc. of the Tenth Annual Conference on Computational Learning Theory.*, 1997.

# A  Lemmas for QBC"

**Corollary 1.** *Let $K$ be a simplex in the unit ball such that the maximal radius of the ball it contains is $r$. then*

$$\frac{r^n \pi^{n/2}}{\Gamma(\frac{n+2}{2})} \le Vol(K) \le \frac{rn\pi^{n/2}}{\Gamma(\frac{n+2}{2})} \tag{11}$$

*Proof.* The lower bound is obtained by taking the volume of the ball with radius $r$ contained in $K$, and the upper bound is a direct consequence of lemma 1.  □

*Proof (of lemma 2).* Let $A$ be the matrix representation of the $k$ inequalities defining $K$. Given a point $x \in K$, we would like to find $r^*$, the maximal radius of a ball centered at $x$ and contained in $K$. Any ball contained in $K$ and centered at $x$ is also contained in the unit ball (which is centered at the origin). Hence, its radius, $r$, must satisfy $||x|| + r \leq 1$. The ball with the maximal radius meets the boundary of $K$ and at these points the boundary of $K$ is tangent to that ball. If the boundary is defined by $A_i y = 0$, then the minimal distance between this boundary and the point $x$ is given by $|\langle A_i, x \rangle| = |A_i x|$ (assuming $A_i$ is normalized such that $||A_i||_2 = 1$). Since $x \in K$ then $|A_i x| = A_i x$, which implies that for any ball with a radius $r$ centered at $x$ and contained in $K$, $\forall i\ A_i x \geq r$. Else, the ball meets the spherical boundary thus $||x|| + r \geq 1$. This last discussion suggest that finding $r^*$ may be expressed as an optimization problem

$$r^* = \arg\max_r\{r | \exists x \text{ s.t. } ||x|| + r \leq 1, Ax \geq r\} \tag{12}$$

It is easy to see that this is a *convex programming* problem: Fix $r$ and assume that $x$ does not satisfies one of the conditions which defines the optimization problem. If there exists $i$ such that $\lambda = A_i x < r$ then the hyper-plane defined by $\{y | A_i y = \lambda\}$ is a separating hyper-plane. Otherwise, if $||x|| + r > 1$ then the hyper plane defined by $\{y | \langle y - x, x \rangle = 0\}$ is a separating hyper plane (this is the orthogonal hyper plane to the segment from the origin to $x$).

To conclude we need to show that the *ellipsoid algorithm* can do the job efficiently. First notice that $r^*$ is always bounded by 1. At lemma 7 we were able to show that $r^*$ is not worst then exponentially small. For our purposes, finding an $r$ such that $r \geq r^*/4$ will suffice. Note that if $r \geq r^*/4$ then the volume of a ball with the radius $r$ centered at $x$ and contained in $K$ is at least $(\frac{r^*}{4})^n \text{Vol}(B)$ where $\text{Vol}(B)$ is the volume of the $n$ dimensional unit ball. Hence, it is not worst than exponentially small in $\log(r^*)$ and $n$. Since $r^*$ is not too small, efficiently of the *ellipsoid algorithm* is guaranteed. □

**Lemma 3.** *Let $K_1$, $K_2$ be two convex simplexes and let $r_1$, $r_2$ be the maximal radii of corresponding contained balls. For $i = 1, 2$ let $v_i = \text{Vol}(K_i)$. Define $p = \frac{v_1}{v_1 + v_2}$, if $r_1 \leq \frac{\mu r_2^n}{n}$ then $p \leq \mu$.*

*Proof.* From corollary 1 it follows that $v_1 \leq \frac{r_1 n \pi^{n/2}}{\Gamma(n+2/2)}$ and $v_2 \geq \frac{r_2^n \pi^{n/2}}{\Gamma(n+2/2)}$. Therefore

$$\frac{v_1}{v_2} \leq \frac{n r_1}{r_2^n} \tag{13}$$

Let $\mu \leq 1$. Substituting $r_1 \leq \frac{\mu r_2^n}{n}$ we conclude that

$$p = \frac{v_1}{v_1 + v_2} \leq \frac{v_1}{v_2} \leq \mu \tag{14}$$

□

**Lemma 4.** *For any sample $x$, let $q$ be the probability that the QBC algorithm will query for a tag and let $\hat{q}$ be the similar probability for QBC". Then*

$$|q - \hat{q}| \leq 4\epsilon_k \tag{15}$$

*Proof.* We start by analyzing the case that the radii size condition of QBC" is satisfied, i.e. $min(r^+, r^-) \geq \mu_k(max(r^+, r^-))^n$. Let $p = \Pr_{u \in V}[u(x) = 1]$, then $q = 2p(1-p)$.

The QBC" algorithm samples two hypotheses, $h_1$ and $h_2$, from the version-space $V$. The sampling algorithm guarantees that

$$|\Pr_{h_1 \in V}[h_1 \in V^+] - \Pr[V^+]| \leq \epsilon_k \tag{16}$$

and the similarly for $V^-$ and $h_2$. Denote $a = \Pr_{h_1 \in V}[h_1 \in V^+]$ and $b = \Pr_{h_2 \in V}[h_2 \in V^-]$. Since $h_1$ and $h_2$ are independent random variables then $\hat{q} = 2ab$. Therefore, in order to bound $|q - \hat{q}|$ we need to maximize $|2p(1-p) - 2ab|$ subject to the restrictions $|p - a| \leq \epsilon_k$ and $|(1-p) - b| \leq \epsilon_k$. It is easy to check that the maximum is achieved when $|a - p| = \epsilon_k$ and $|b - (1-p)| = \epsilon_k$ and therefore

$$|2p(1-p) - 2ab| \leq 2\epsilon_k + 2\epsilon_k^2 \leq 4\epsilon_k \tag{17}$$

We now consider the case where the radii ratio condition fails. Without loss of generality, assume $r^+ < \mu_k(r^-)^n$. From lemma 3 it follows that $p < n\mu_k$ and by the definition of $\mu_k$ we get $p < 2min(\epsilon_k, 1 - \epsilon_k)$ which means that $q < 4min(\epsilon_k, 1 - \epsilon_k)(1 - 2min(\epsilon_k, 1 - \epsilon_k)) < 4\epsilon_k$. Therefore, by defining $\hat{q} = 0$ we maintain the difference $|q - \hat{q}| \leq 4\epsilon_k$. $\square$

**Lemma 5.** *Let $L$ be any samples filtering algorithm. For any sample $x$, let $q$ be the probability that the QBC algorithm will query for a tag and let $\hat{q}$ be the corresponding probability for $L$ and assume $|q - \hat{q}| \leq \gamma$. Let $g$ be a lower bound on the expected information gain for QBC. Then there exists a lower bound on the expected information gain for $L$, denoted by $\hat{g}$, such that*

$$\hat{g} \geq g - \gamma \tag{18}$$

*Proof.* Let $r(x)$ be the density function over the sample space $X$. Let $p(x)$ be the probability that $x$ is tagged 1, i.e. $p(x) = \Pr_{u \in V}[u(x) = 1]$, then $q(x) = 2p(x)(1 - p(x))$. Since $g$ is a lower bound on the expected information gain for the QBC algorithm then

$$g \leq \int_x r(x)q(x)\mathcal{H}(p(x))dx \tag{19}$$

since $|q - \hat{q}| \leq \gamma$, the expected information gain for $L$ is bounded by

$$\int_x r(x)\hat{q}(x)\mathcal{H}(p(x))dx \geq \int_x r(x)q(x)\mathcal{H}(p(x))dx - \gamma \geq g - \gamma \tag{20}$$

taking a close enough lower bound $\hat{g}$ for the leftmost term, the statement of the lemma follows. $\square$

**Corollary 2.** *Let $g$ be a lower bound on the expected information gain of the QBC algorithm. From lemmas 4 and 5 it follows that there exists $\hat{g} \geq g - 4\epsilon_k$ such that $\hat{g}$ is a lower bound on the expected information gain of QBC".*

**Lemma 6.** *Assume that after getting $k$ labeled samples, algorithm QBC" does not query for a tag in the next $t_k$ consecutive samples. If $c$ is a concept chosen uniformly from the version space and $h$ is the hypothesis returned by QBC", then*

$$Pr_{c,h}[Pr_x[c(x) \neq h(x)] > \alpha] \leq \beta/2 \tag{21}$$

*Proof.* We define *bad pair* to be a pair of hypotheses from the version space that differ on more then proportion $\alpha$ of the samples. We will want the algorithm to stop only when the queries it made form an $\left(\alpha, \frac{\beta_k}{4}\right)$-net, i.e. if two hypotheses are picked independently from the version space, the probability that they form a bad pair is less then $\frac{\beta_k}{4}$. We will show that if the algorithm did not make a query for $t_k$ consecutive samples, then the probability that the queries sampled do not form an $\left(\alpha - \frac{\beta_k}{4}\right)$-net, is bounded by $\beta_k/4$.

Let $W = \{(h_1, h_2) | Pr_x[h_1(x) \neq h_2(x)] \geq \alpha\}$. If $\Pr[W] \leq \beta_k/4$ then the probability that $(c, h)$ is a bad pair is bounded by $\beta_k/4$ (when picked uniformly).We would like to bound the probability that $\Pr[W] > \beta_k/4$ when QBC" didn't query for a tag for $t_k$ at the last consecutive samples:

If $\Pr[W] > \beta_k/4$, then the probability that the QBC algorithm will query for a tag is greater then $\alpha\beta_k/4$. From lemma 4 we conclude that the probability that the QBC" algorithm will query for a tag is greater then $\alpha\beta_k/4 - 4\epsilon_k$. Plugging in $\epsilon_k = \frac{\alpha\beta_k}{32}$ we conclude that the probability that QBC" will query for a tag is greater then $\alpha\beta_k/8$. Therefore, the probability that it won't query for a tag $t_k$ consecutive samples is bounded by $(1 - \alpha\beta_k/8)^{t_k}$. Using the well known relation $(1 - \varepsilon)^n \leq e^{-n\varepsilon}$ and plugging in $t_k = \frac{8 \log 4/\beta_k}{\alpha\beta_k}$ it follows that

$$\left(1 - \frac{\alpha\beta_k}{8}\right)^{t_k} \leq e^{-t_k \frac{\alpha\beta_k}{8}} = e^{-\frac{8\alpha\beta_k \log 4/\beta_k}{8\alpha\beta_k}} = e^{\log(\frac{\beta_k}{4})} = \frac{\beta_k}{4} \tag{22}$$

Hence, $\Pr_{x_1,x_2,\ldots}[\Pr[W] > \beta_k/4] \leq \beta_k/4$. Thus if the algorithm stops after $t_k$ consecutive unlabeled samples, the probability of choosing an hypothesis which forms a bad pair with the target concept is lower then $\beta_k/2$, since the probability of $W$ being bigger then $\beta_k/4$ is less then $\beta_k/4$, and if it is smaller than $\beta_k/4$ then the probability for mistake is bounded by $\beta_k/4$. Since $\beta_k = \frac{3\beta}{\pi^2(k+1)^2}$ it follows that $\sum_k \beta_k = \beta/2$ and we get the stated result. □

**Lemma 7.** *Let $a > 0$ and let $m$ be the number of calls to the Sample Oracle that QBC" (or QBC') makes (assume $m \geq n$) then the following holds with probability greater then $1 - 2^{-a}$:*

*Each intermediate version space the algorithm generates has a volume greater than $\frac{2^{-a}\left(\frac{d}{em}\right)^d \pi^{n/2}}{\Gamma\left(\frac{n+2}{2}\right)}$, and there is a ball of radius greater than $\frac{2^{-a}\left(\frac{d}{em}\right)^d}{n}$ contained in it.*

*Proof.* The final version space, the one that is being used when the algorithm stops, is the smallest of all intermediate version spaces. Moreover, if the algorithm was not filtering out samples, but querying labels for all samples, then the final version space would have been smaller. Since we are interested in the worst case, we will assume that the algorithm did not filter out any sample.

Fix $X$ a vector of samples, while $X^m$ is its first $m$ samples. Let $c$ be a concept chosen from $\Omega$. $X^m$ divides $\Omega$, the set of all concepts, to equivalence sets, two concepts are in the same set if they give the same label to all $m$ samples in $X^m$. If $\Omega$ has a VC-dimension $d$, we know from *Sauer's lemma* that the number of equivalence sets is bounded by $\left(\frac{em}{d}\right)^d$. Using the distribution $\Pr_c$ over $\Omega$ it follows that

$$\Pr_c \left[ -\log \Pr\left[C\right] \geq a + d\log \frac{em}{d} \right] \leq 2^{-a} \tag{23}$$

where $C$ is the equivalence set of $c$. We now turn to discuss the special case of linear separators and the uniform distribution over the unit ball, i.e. $\Omega$. Note that if $\mathcal{V}$ is the version space after getting the labels for $X^m$, then $\mathcal{V} = C$. Therefore $\Pr[C] = \frac{\mathrm{Vol}(\mathcal{V})}{\mathrm{Vol}(B)}$ where $\mathrm{Vol}(B)$ is the volume of the $n$-dimensional unit ball. Using (23) we get

$$\Pr_c \left[ -\log \mathrm{Vol}(\mathcal{V}) \geq a + d\log \frac{em}{d} - \log \mathrm{Vol}(B) \right] \leq 2^{-a} \tag{24}$$

Assume that $-\log \mathrm{Vol}(\mathcal{V}) \leq a + d\log \frac{em}{d} - \log \mathrm{Vol}(B)$ (this is true with probability greater then $1 - 2^{-a}$), from lemma 1 we know that there is a ball in $\mathcal{V}$ with radius $r$ such that $r \geq \frac{\mathrm{Vol}(\mathcal{V})\Gamma\left(\frac{n+2}{2}\right)}{n\pi^{n/2}}$. We conclude that there is a ball in $\mathcal{V}$ with radius $r$ such that

$$r \geq \frac{2^{-a} \left(\frac{d}{em}\right)^d \mathrm{Vol}(B)\Gamma\left(\frac{n+2}{2}\right)}{n\pi^{n/2}} \tag{25}$$

$\square$

# Hardness Results for Neural Network Approximation Problems

Peter Bartlett[1] and Shai Ben-David[2]

[1] Department of Systems Engineering
Australian National University
Canberra ACT 0200, Australia
`Peter.Bartlett@anu.edu.au`
[2] Department of Computer Science
Technion
Haifa 32000, Israel
`shai@cs.technion.ac.il`

**Abstract.** We consider the problem of efficiently learning in two-layer neural networks. We show that it is NP-hard to find a linear threshold network of a fixed size that approximately minimizes the proportion of misclassified examples in a training set, even if there is a network that correctly classifies all of the training examples. In particular, for a training set that is correctly classified by some two-layer linear threshold network with $k$ hidden units, it is NP-hard to find such a network that makes mistakes on a proportion smaller than $c/k^3$ of the examples, for some constant $c$. We prove a similar result for the problem of approximately minimizing the quadratic loss of a two-layer network with a sigmoid output unit.

## 1 Introduction

Previous negative results for learning two-layer neural network classifiers show that it is difficult to find a network that correctly classifies all examples in a training set. However, for learning to a particular accuracy it is only necessary to approximately solve this problem, that is, to find a network that correctly classifies *most* examples in a training set. In this paper, we show that this approximation problem is hard for several neural network classes.

The hardness of PAC style learning is a very natural question that has been addressed from a variety of viewpoints. The strongest non-learnability conclusions are those stating that no matter what type of algorithm a learner may use, as long as his computational resources are limited, he would not be able to predict a previously unseen label (with probability significantly better than that of a random guess). Such results have been derived by noticing that, in some precise sense, learning may be viewed as breaking a cryptographic scheme. These strong hardness results are based upon assuming the security of certain cryptographic constructions (and in this respect are weaker than hardness results that are based on computational complexity assumptions like $P \neq NP$ or even $RP \neq NP$). The weak side of these results is that they apply only to classes that are rich enough to encode a cryptographic mechanism. For example, under cryptographic assumptions, Goldreich, Goldwasser and Micali [6] show that it is difficult to learn boolean circuits over $n$ inputs with at most $p(n)$ gates, for some polynomial $p$. Kearns and Valiant [13] improve this result to circuits of polynomially many linear threshold gates and some constant (but unknown) depth. However, such classes are too rich to be considered useful for learning purposes.

Another line of research considers agnostic learning by natural hypothesis classes. In such a learning setting, no assumptions are made about the rule used to label the examples, and the learner is required to find a hypothesis in the class that minimizes the labeling errors over the training sample. If such a hypothesis class is relatively small (say, in terms of its VC-dimension), then it can be shown that such a hypothesis will have a good prediction ability.

There are quite a few hardness results in this framework. The first type are results showing hardness of finding a member of the hypothesis class that indeed minimizes the number of misclassification over a given labeled sample. Blum and Rivest [3] prove that it is NP-hard to decide if there is a two-layer linear threshold network with only two hidden units that correctly classifies *all* examples in a training sample. (Our main reduction uses an extension of the technique used by Blum and Rivest.) They also show that finding a conjunction of $k$ linear threshold functions that correctly classifies all positive examples and some constant proportion of negative examples is as hard as coloring an $n$-vertex $k$-colorable graph with $O(k \log n)$ colors (which has since been shown to be NP-hard [15]). DasGupta, Siegelmann and Sontag [4] extend Blum and Rivest's results to two-layer networks with piecewise linear hidden units. Megiddo [16] shows that it is NP-hard to decide if any boolean function of two linear threshold functions can correctly classify a training sample.

The weakness of such results is that, for the purpose of learning, one can settle for *approximating* the best hypothesis in the class, while the hardness results apply only to *exactly* meeting the best possible error rate.

Somewhat stronger are results showing the hardness of 'robust learning'. A robust learner should be able to find, for any given labeled sample, and for *every* $\epsilon > 0$, a hypothesis with training error rate within $\epsilon$ of the best possible within the class, in time polynomial in the sample size and in $1/\epsilon$. Höffgen and Simon [8] show that, assuming $RP \neq NP$, no such learner exists for some subclasses of the class of halfspaces. Judd [11] shows NP-hardness results for an approximate sample error minimization problem for certain linear threshold networks with many outputs.

One may argue, that, for all practical purposes, a learner may be considered successful once he finds a hypothesis that $\epsilon$ approximates the target (or the best hypothesis in a given class) for some *fixed* small $\epsilon$. Such learning is not ruled out by ruling out robust learning.

We are therefore led to the next level of hardness-of-learning results, showing hardness of approximating the best fitting hypothesis in the class to within some *fixed* error rate. Arora, Babai, Stern and Sweedyk [1] show that, for any constant, it is NP-hard to find a linear threshold function that has the ratio of the number of misclassifications to the optimum number below that constant. Höffgen and Simon [8] show a similar result. We extend this type of result to richer classes of neural networks.

The neural networks that we consider have two layers, with $k$ linear threshold units in the first layer and a variety of output units. For pattern classification, we consider output units that compute boolean functions, and for real prediction we consider sigmoidal output units. Both problems can be expressed in a probabilistic setting, in which the training data is generated by some probability distribution, and we attempt to find a function that has near-minimal expected loss with respect to this distribution (see, for example, [7]). For pattern classification, we use the discrete loss; for real estimation, we use the quadratic loss. In both cases, efficiently finding a network with expected loss nearly minimal is equivalent to efficiently finding a network that has the sample average of loss nearly minimal. In this paper, we give results that quantify the difficulty of these approximate sample error minimization problems. For the pattern classification problem, we show that it is NP-hard to find a network with $k$ linear threshold units in the first layer and an output unit that computes a conjunction that has proportion of data correctly classified within $c/k$ of optimal, for some constant $c$. We extend this result to two-layer linear threshold networks (that is, where the output unit is also a linear threshold unit). In this case, the problem is hard to approximate within $c/k^3$ for some constant $c$. This latter result applies even when there is a network that correctly classifies all of the data.

The case of quadratic loss has also been studied recently. Jones [10] considers the problem of approximately minimizing the sample average of the quadratic loss over a class of two-layer networks with sigmoid units in the first layer and a linear output unit with constraints on the size of the output weights. He shows that this approximation problem is NP-hard, for approximation accuracies of order $1/m$, where $m$ is the sample size. The weakness of these results is that the approximation accuracy is sufficiently small to ensure that every single training example has small quadratic loss, a requirement that exceeds the sufficiency conditions needed to ensure valid generalization. Vu [19] has used results on hardness of approximations to improve Jones' results. He shows that the problem of approximately minimizing the sample average of the quadratic loss of a two-layer network with $k$ linear threshold hidden units and a linear output unit remains hard when the approximation error is as large as $ck^{-3/2}d^{-3/2}$, where $c$ is a constant and $d$ is the input dimension. The hard samples in Vu's result have size that grows polynomially with $d$, so once again, the approximation threshold is a decreasing function of $m$.

In this paper, we also study the problem of approximately minimizing quadratic loss. We consider the class of two-layer networks with linear threshold units in the first layer and a sigmoid output unit (and no constraints on the output weights). We show that it is NP-hard to find such a network that has the sample average of the quadratic loss within $c/k^3$ of its optimal value, for some constant

c. This result is true even when the infimum over all networks of the error on the training data is zero. One should note that our results show hardness for an approximation value that is independent of input dimension and of the sample size.

All of the learning problems studied in this paper can be solved efficiently if we fix the input dimension and the number of hidden units $k$. In that case, the algorithm 'Splitting' described in [14] (see also [5]) efficiently enumerates all training set dichotomies computed by a linear threshold function.

# 2 Approximate Optimization Definitions

A maximization problem $A$ is defined as follows. Let $m_A$ be a non-negative objective function. Given an input $x$, the goal is to find a solution $y$ for which the objective function $m_A(x, y)$ is maximized. Define $\text{opt}_A(x)$ as the maximum value of the objective function. (We assume that, for all $x$, $m_A(x, \cdot)$ is not identically zero, so that the maximum is positive.) The *relative error* of a solution $y$ is defined as $(\text{opt}_A(x) - m_A(x, y))/\text{opt}_A(x)$.

Our proofs use *L-reductions* (see [17, 12]), which preserve approximability. An L-reduction from one optimization problem $A$ to another $B$ is a pair of functions $f$ and $g$ that are computable in polynomial time and satisfy the following conditions.

1. $f$ maps from instances of $A$ to instances of $B$
2. There is a positive constant $\alpha$ such that, for all instances $x$ of $A$, $\text{opt}_B(f(x)) \leq \alpha \text{opt}_A(x)$.
3. $g$ maps from instances of $A$ and solutions of $B$ to solutions of $A$.
4. There is a positive constant $\beta$ such that, for instances $x$ of $A$ and all solutions $y$ of $f(x)$, we have $\text{opt}_A(x) - m_A(x, g(x, y)) \leq \beta(\text{opt}_B(f(x)) - m_B(f(x), y))$.

The following lemma is immediate from the definitions.

**Lemma 1.** *Let $A$ and $B$ be maximization problems. Suppose that it is NP-hard to approximate $A$ with relative error less than $\delta$, and that $A$ L-reduces to $B$ with constants $\alpha$ and $\beta$. Then it is NP-hard to approximate $B$ with relative error less than $\delta/(\alpha\beta)$.*

Clearly, this lemma remains true if we relax condition (4) of the L-reduction, so that it applies only to solutions $y$ of an instance $f(x)$ that have relative error less than $\delta/(\alpha\beta)$.

For all of the problems studied in this paper, we define the objective function such that $\max_x \text{opt}_A(x) = 1$. With this normalization condition, we say that an L-reduction *preserves maximality* if $\text{opt}_A(x) = 1$ implies $\text{opt}_B(f(x)) = 1$. (This is a special case of Petrank's notion [18] of preserving the 'gap location' in reductions between optimization problems.) The following lemma is also trivial.

**Lemma 2.** *Let $A$ and $B$ be maximization problems. Suppose that it is NP-hard to approximate $A$ with relative error less than $\delta$, even for instances with*

$\text{opt}_A(x) = 1$. *If $A$ L-reduces to $B$ with constants $\alpha$ and $\beta$, and the L-reduction preserves maximality, then it is NP-hard to approximate $B$ with relative error less than $\delta/(\alpha\beta)$, even for instances with $\text{opt}_A(x) = 1$.*

## 3  Results

We first consider two-layer networks with $k$ linear threshold units in the first layer and an output unit that computes a conjunction. These networks compute functions of the form $f(x) = \bigwedge_{i=1}^{k} f_i(x)$, where each $f_i$ is a linear threshold function of the form $f_i(x) = \text{sgn}(w_i \cdot x - \theta_i)$ for some $w_i \in \mathbf{R}^n$, $\theta_i \in \mathbf{R}$. Here, $\text{sgn}(\alpha)$ is 1 if $\alpha \geq 0$ and 0 otherwise. Let $N_n^{\wedge,k}$ denote this class of functions.

MAX $k$-AND CONSISTENCY.
INPUT: A sequence $S$ of labelled examples, $(x_i, y_i) \in \{0,1\}^n \times \{0,1\}$.
GOAL: Find a function $f$ in $N_n^{\wedge,k}$ that maximizes the proportion of consistent examples, $(1/m)\,|\{i : f(x_i) = y_i\}|$.

The condition $\text{opt}_{\text{MAX } k\text{-AND CONSISTENCY}}(S) = 1$ in the following theorem corresponds to the case in which the training sample is consistent with some function in $N_n^{\wedge,k}$.

**Theorem 1.** *Suppose $k \geq 3$. It is NP-hard to approximate MAX $k$-AND CONSISTENCY with relative error less than $1/(238k)$. Furthermore, there is a constant $c$ such that even when $\text{opt}_{\text{MAX } k\text{-AND CONSISTENCY}}(S) = 1$ it is NP-hard to approximate MAX $k$-AND CONSISTENCY with relative error less than $c/k^2$.*

The class $N_n^{\wedge,k}$ is somewhat unnatural, since the output unit is constrained to compute a conjunction. Let $F$ be a set of boolean functions on $k$ inputs, and let $N_n^{F,k}$ denote the class of functions of the form $f(x) = g(f_1(x), \ldots, f_k(x))$, where $g \in F$ and $f_1, \ldots, f_k$ are linear threshold functions.
We do not know how to extend Theorem 1 to give a corresponding hardness result for the class $N_n^{F,k}$ defined on binary inputs. However, we can obtain results of this form if we allow rational inputs.

MAX $k$-$F$ CONSISTENCY.
INPUT: A sequence $S$ of labelled examples, $(x_i, y_i) \in \mathbf{Q}^n \times \{0,1\}$.
GOAL: Find a function $f$ in $N_n^{F,k}$ that maximizes the proportion of consistent examples, $(1/m)\,|\{i : f(x_i) = y_i\}|$.

**Theorem 2.** *For $k \geq 3$, there is a constant $c$ such that for any class $F$ of boolean functions containing the conjunction, it is NP-hard to approximate MAX $k$-$F$ CONSISTENCY with relative error less than $c/k^3$, even for instances with $\text{opt}_{\text{MAX } k\text{-}F \text{ CONSISTENCY}}(S) = 1$.*

Next we consider the class of two-layer networks with linear threshold units in the first layer and a sigmoid output unit. That is, we consider the class $N_n^{\sigma,k}$ of real-valued functions of the form

$$f(x) = \sigma\left(\sum_{i=1}^{k} v_i f_i(x) + v_0\right),$$

where $v_i \in \mathbf{R}$, $f_1, \ldots, f_k$ are linear threshold functions, and $\sigma : \mathbf{R} \to \mathbf{R}$ is a fixed function. We require that the fixed function $\sigma$ maps to the interval $[0, 1]$, is monotonically non-decreasing, and satisfies

$$\lim_{\alpha \to -\infty} \sigma(\alpha) = 0, \qquad \lim_{\alpha \to \infty} \sigma(\alpha) = 1.$$

(The limits 0 and 1 here can be replaced by any two distinct numbers.)

MAX $k$-$\sigma$ CONSISTENCY.
INPUT: A sequence $S$ of labelled examples, $(x_i, y_i) \in \mathbf{Q}^n \times ([0,1] \cap \mathbf{Q})$.
GOAL: Find a function $f$ in $N_n^{\sigma,k}$ that maximizes $1 - (1/m)\sum_{i=1}^{m}(y_i - f(x_i))^2$.

**Theorem 3.** *For $k \geq 3$, there is a constant $c$ such that it is NP-hard to approximate* MAX $k$-$\sigma$ CONSISTENCY *with relative error less than $c/k^3$, even for samples with* $\text{opt}_{\text{MAX } k\text{-}\sigma \text{ CONSISTENCY}}(S) = 1$.

## 4 Reductions

### 4.1 Learning with an AND output unit: MAX $k$-AND CONSISTENCY

We give an L-reduction to MAX $k$-CUT.

MAX $k$-CUT.
INPUT: A graph $G = (V, E)$.
GOAL: Find a colour assignment $c : V \to [k]$ that maximizes the proportion of multicoloured edges, $(1/|E|)\,|\{(v_1, v_2) \in E : c(v_1) \neq c(v_2)\}|$.

We use the following result, due to Kann, Khanna, Lagergren, and Panconesi [12], to prove the first part of Theorem 1.

**Theorem 4 ([12]).** *For $k \geq 2$, it is NP-hard to approximate* MAX $k$-CUT *with relative error less than $1/(34(k-1))$.*

For the second part of the theorem, we need a similar hardness result for $k$-colourable graphs. The following result is essentially due to Petrank [18]; Theorem 3.3 in [18] gives the hardness result without calculating the dependence of the gap on $k$. Using the reduction due to Papadimitriou and Yannakakis [17] that Petrank uses in the final step of his proof shows that this dependence is of the form $c/k^2$.

**Theorem 5 ([18]).** *For $k \geq 3$, there is a constant $c$ such that it is NP-hard to approximate* MAX $k$-CUT *with relative error less than $c/k^2$, even for $k$-colourable graphs.*

Given a graph $G = (V, E)$, we construct a sample $S$ for a MAX $k$-AND CONSISTENCY problem using a technique similar to that used by Blum and Rivest [3]. The key difference is that we use multiple copies of certain points in the training sample, in order to preserve approximability.

Suppose $|V| = n$, and relabel $V = \{v_1, \ldots, v_n\} \subset \{0, 1\}^n$, where $v_i$ is the unit vector with a 1 in the position $i$ and 0s elsewhere. Let $S$ consist of

- $a$ copies of $(0, 1)$ (where 0 is the all-0 vector in $\{0, 1\}^n$),
- $|\{v \in V : (v_i, v) \in E\}|$ copies of $(v_i, 0)$, for each $v_i \in V$, and
- one copy of $(v_i + v_j, 1)$, for each $(v_i, v_j) \in E$.

The number $a$ will be determined shortly. Clearly, $|S| = a + 3|E|$. The proof of Theorem 1 relies on the following two lemmas.

**Lemma 3.** For $k \geq 2$, $\mathrm{opt}_{\text{MAX }k\text{-AND CONSISTENCY}}(S) \leq (k/(k-1))\mathrm{opt}_{\text{MAX }k\text{-CUT}}(G)$. Furthermore, if $\mathrm{opt}_{\text{MAX }k\text{-CUT}}(G) = 1$ then $\mathrm{opt}_{\text{MAX }k\text{-AND CONSISTENCY}}(S) = 1$.

*Proof.* Let $c$ be the optimal colouring of $V$. Define hidden unit $i$ as $f_i(x) = \mathrm{sgn}(w_i \cdot x - \theta_i)$, where $\theta_i = -1/2$ and $w_i = (w_{i,1}, \ldots, w_{i,n}) \in \mathbf{R}^n$ satisfies $w_{i,j}$ takes value $-1$ if $c(v_j) = i$ and 1 otherwise. Clearly, the $a$ copies of $(0, 1)$ are correctly classified. It is easy to verify that each $(v_i, 0)$ is correctly classified. Finally, every labelled example $(v_i + v_j, 1)$ corresponding to an edge $(v_i, v_j) \in E$ has

$$h_l(v_i + v_j) = \begin{cases} 0 \text{ if } c(v_i) = c(v_j) = l \\ 1 \text{ otherwise,} \end{cases}$$

for $l = 1, \ldots, k$. Hence,

$$\mathrm{opt}_{\text{MAX }k\text{-AND CONSISTENCY}}(S) = \frac{a + 2|E| + |E|\mathrm{opt}_{\text{MAX }k\text{-CUT}}(G)}{a + 3|E|}. \tag{1}$$

But it is easy to show that every graph has $\mathrm{opt}_{\text{MAX }k\text{-CUT}}(G) \geq 1 - 1/k$. (A random colouring has this expected proportion of multicoloured edges.) Hence, we can approximate the linear relationship (1) by

$$\mathrm{opt}_{\text{MAX }k\text{-AND CONSISTENCY}}(S) \leq \frac{a + 2|E| + |E|(1 - 1/k)}{(a + 3|E|)(1 - 1/k)}\mathrm{opt}_{\text{MAX }k\text{-CUT}}(G)$$

$$= \left(\frac{k}{k-1} - \frac{|E|}{(k-1)(a + 3|E|)}\right)\mathrm{opt}_{\text{MAX }k\text{-CUT}}(G)$$

$$\leq \frac{k}{k-1}\mathrm{opt}_{\text{MAX }k\text{-CUT}}(G).$$

Finally, it is clear from (1) that $\mathrm{opt}_{\text{MAX }k\text{-CUT}}(G) = 1$ implies $\mathrm{opt}_{\text{MAX }k\text{-AND CONSISTENCY}}(S) = 1$.

**Lemma 4.** Set $a = 3|E| + 1$ and suppose that $k \geq 3$. For any MAX $k$-AND CONSISTENCY$(S)$ solution $f$ with relative error less than $1/(238k)$, we can find in polynomial time a MAX $k$-CUT$(G)$ solution $g$ with cost $c_g$, and $\mathrm{opt}_{\text{MAX }k\text{-CUT}}(G) - c_g \leq 7\left(\mathrm{opt}_{\text{MAX }k\text{-AND CONSISTENCY}}(S) - c_f\right)$.

*Proof.* Given a MAX $k$-AND CONSISTENCY(S) solution $f$, if

$$c_f > \frac{3|E|}{a + 3|E|},\tag{2}$$

then we know that $f(0) = 1$. To find a suitable choice for $a$, recall that $\text{opt}_{\text{MAX }k\text{-CUT}}(G) \geq 1 - 1/k$, so (1) implies $\text{opt}_{\text{MAX }k\text{-AND CONSISTENCY}}(S) \geq 1 - 1/k$. So if the relative error of $c_f$ is less than $1/(238k)$, we have

$$c_f > \left(1 - \frac{1}{k}\right)\left(1 - \frac{1}{238k}\right) > 1 - \left(\frac{1}{k} + \frac{1}{238k}\right) = 1 - \frac{239}{238k}.$$

Choosing $a = 3|E| + 1$ means that (2) will be true for $k \geq 3$.

Suppose that $f = \bigwedge_{i=1}^{k} f_i$. Define a colouring $g$ as follows: If $f(v_i) = 1$, set $g(v_i) = 1$, otherwise set $g(v_i) = \min\{j : f_j(v_i) = 0\}$, where the minimum is defined to be 1 if no $f_j(v_i) = 0$. For an edge $(v_i, v_j)$, if the edge is monochromatic (that is, $g(v_i) = g(v_j)$), then $f(v_i) = f(v_j) = 0$ implies $f(v_i + v_j) = 0$. To see this, suppose that $f(v_i) = 0$ and $f(v_j) = 0$. Then $g(v_i) = g(v_j)$ implies some $l$ has $f_l(v_i) = f_l(v_j) = 0$. But since we also have $f(0) = 1$, we must have $f(v_i + v_j) = 0$. For each example in $S$ that corresponds to a vertex $v \in V$, label the multiple copies with the pairs $(v, e)$ for all edges $e \in E$ of the form $e = (v, v')$. Then there is a 1-1 mapping between edges $e = (v_i, v_j)$ and triples $((v_1, e), (v_2, e), e)$. It follows that

$$|E|\left(\text{opt}_{\text{MAX }k\text{-CUT}}(G) - c_g\right) \leq |S|\left(\text{opt}_{\text{MAX }k\text{-AND CONSISTENCY}}(S) - c_f\right),$$

and with the choice of $a$ above, this is equivalent to

$$\text{opt}_{\text{MAX }k\text{-CUT}}(G) - c_g \leq \frac{6|E| + 1}{|E|}\left(\text{opt}_{\text{MAX }k\text{-AND CONSISTENCY}}(S) - c_f\right)$$
$$< 7\left(\text{opt}_{\text{MAX }k\text{-AND CONSISTENCY}}(S) - c_f\right).$$

Hence, we have an L-reduction from MAX $k$-CUT to MAX $k$-AND CONSISTENCY, with parameters $\alpha = k/(k-1)$ and $\beta = 7$, and this L-reduction preserves maximality. Together with Theorems 4 and 5, this implies Theorem 1.

## 4.2  Learning with an arbitrary output unit: MAX $k$-$F$ CONSISTENCY

We use the reduction from the proof of Theorem 1, and augment the input with two extra, rational, components, which we use to force the output unit to compute a conjunction. For $V = \{v_1, \ldots, v_n\} \subset \{0, 1\}^n$, we let $S$ consist of the following labelled points from $\{0, 1\}^n \cup \mathbf{Q}^2 \times \{0, 1\}$.

- $a$ copies of $((0, 0), 1)$,
- $|\{v \in V : (v_i, v) \in E\}|$ copies of $((0, v_i), 0)$, for each $v_i \in V$,
- one copy of $((0, v_i + v_j), 1)$, for each $(v_i, v_j) \in E$,
- $a$ copies of $((s, 0), 1)$ for $s \in S_{\text{in}} \subset \mathbf{Q}^2$, and

– $a$ copies of $((s, 0), 0)$ for $s \in S_{out} \subset \mathbf{Q}^2$,

where the sets $S_{in}$ and $S_{out}$ and the number $a$ will be defined shortly. Here, the first three types of labelled examples are those used in the reduction described in the proof of Theorem 1, augmented with two rational inputs set to zero. The sets $S_{in}$ and $S_{out}$ both have cardinality $3k$. Each point in $S_{in}$ is paired with a point in $S_{out}$, and this pair straddles some edge of a regular $k$-sided polygon in $\mathbf{R}^2$ that has vertices on the unit circle centred at the origin, as shown in Figure 1.

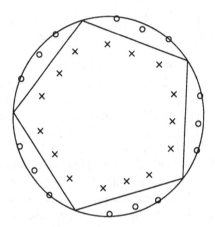

**Fig. 1.** The sets $S_{in}$ and $S_{out}$ used in the proof of Theorem 2, for the case $k = 5$. The points in $S_{in}$ are marked as crosses; those in $S_{out}$ are marked as circles.

(We call this pair of points a 'straddling pair'.) The midpoint of each pair lies on some edge of the polygon, and the line passing through the pair is perpendicular to that edge. The set of $3k$ midpoints (one for each pair) and the $k$ vertices of the polygon are equally spaced around the polygon. We use the weights and thresholds defined in the proof of Lemma 3, augmented with appropriate weights for the two additional inputs. We choose the output unit as a conjunction and arrange the new hidden unit weights so that the intersection of the hidden unit decision boundaries with the plane of the two additional inputs coincide with the $k$ sides of the polygon. It is now easy to verify the following lemma. The proof is essentially identical to that of Lemma 3.

**Lemma 5.** *For $k \geq 3$, $\mathrm{opt}_{\text{MAX } k\text{-F Consistency}}(S) \leq k/(k-1)\mathrm{opt}_{\text{MAX } k\text{-Cut}}(G)$. Furthermore, if $\mathrm{opt}_{\text{MAX } k\text{-Cut}}(G) = 1$ then $\mathrm{opt}_{\text{MAX } k\text{-F Consistency}}(S) = 1$.*

**Lemma 6.** *Set $a = 6|E|$ and suppose that $k \geq 2$. If $\mathrm{opt}_{\text{MAX } k\text{-F Consistency}}(S) = 1$, then for any MAX $k$-F CONSISTENCY$(S)$ solution $f$ with relative error less than $1/(13k)$, we can find in polynomial time a MAX $k$-CUT$(G)$ solution $g$ with cost $c_g$, and*

$$\mathrm{opt}_{\text{MAX } k\text{-Cut}}(G) - c_g \leq 9(4k+1)\left(\mathrm{opt}_{\text{MAX } k\text{-And Consistency}}(S) - c_f\right).$$

*Proof.* For a MAX $k$-$F$ CONSISTENCY(S) solution $f$, if

$$1 - c_f < \frac{a}{(6k+1)a + 3|E|}, \tag{3}$$

then we know that $f(0,0) = 0$ and $f(0,s)$ is 1 for $s \in S_{in}$ and 0 for $s \in S_{out}$. Condition (3) is equivalent to

$$a > \frac{(1-c_f)3|E|}{1 - (1-c_f)(6k+1)},$$

which follows from $a = 6|E|$ when the denominator is greater than 1/2. The latter is equivalent to $c_f > 1 - 1/(2(6k+1))$, and this is true when the relative error condition of the lemma is satisfied. So, under the conditions of the lemma, the MAX $k$-$F$ CONSISTENCY(S) solution $f$ correctly classifies the origin and the points straddling the polygon. Let $\alpha$ denote the distance between a point in $S_{in} \cup S_{out}$ and its associated edge. Clearly, since the points in $\{(s,0) : s \in S_{in}\}$ are labelled 1 and those in $\{(s,0) : s \in S_{out}\}$ are labelled 0, for every straddling pair described above, any function in $N_n^{F,k}$ that is consistent with these points has some hidden unit whose decision boundary separates the pair. It is easy to show using elementary trigonometry that there is a constant $c$ such that, if $\alpha < c/k$, no line in $\mathbf{R}^2$ can pass between more than three of these pairs, and no line can pass between three unless they all straddle the same edge of the polygon. Since $k$ lines must separate $3k$ straddling pairs, and the origin must be classified as 1, any function in $N_n^{F,k}$ that is consistent with the points from $S_{in} \cup S_{out}$ is a conjunction of $k$ linear threshold functions. We continue in the same way as the proof of Lemma 4, obtaining

$$\text{opt}_{\text{MAX } k\text{-CUT}}(G) - c_g \leq \frac{|S|}{|E|} \left( \text{opt}_{\text{MAX } k\text{-}F \text{ CONSISTENCY}}(S) - c_f \right).$$

Substituting $|S| = a(6k+1) + 3|E| = 9|E|(4k+1)$ gives the result. It is easy to show that the result is also true if the components of vectors in $S_{in}$ and $S_{out}$ must be ratios of integers, provided the integers are allowed to be as large as $ck^2$, for some constant $c$. Hence, for each $k$, the number of bits needed to represent $S$ is linear in the size of the graph $G$.

These lemmas show that we have an L-reduction from MAX $k$-CUT for $k$-colourable graphs to MAX $k$-$F$ CONSISTENCY, with parameters $\alpha = k/(k-1)$ and $\beta = 9(4k+1)$, and this L-reduction preserves maximality. Combining this with Theorem 5 gives Theorem 2.

## 4.3 Learning with a sigmoid output unit: MAX $k$-$\sigma$ CONSISTENCY

We give an L-reduction from MAX $k$-$F$ CONSISTENCY to MAX $k$-$\sigma$ CONSISTENCY, where $F$ is the class of linear threshold functions. Given a sample $S$ for a MAX $k$-$F$ CONSISTENCY problem, we use the same sample for the

MAX $k$-$\sigma$ CONSISTENCY problem. Trivially[1], if $\text{opt}_{\text{MAX } k\text{-}F \text{ Consistency}}(S) = 1$ then $\text{opt}_{\text{MAX } k\text{-}\sigma \text{ Consistency}}(S) = 1$. Furthermore, we have the following lemma.

**Lemma 7.** *For a solution $f$ to MAX $k$-$\sigma$ CONSISTENCY with cost $c_f$, we can find a solution $h$ for MAX $k$-$F$ CONSISTENCY with cost $c_h$, and*

$$\text{opt}_{\text{MAX } k\text{-}F \text{ Consistency}}(S) - c_h \leq \frac{1}{4}\left(\text{opt}_{\text{MAX } k\text{-}\sigma \text{ Consistency}}(S) - c_f\right).$$

*Proof.* Suppose that

$$f(x) = \sigma\left(\sum_{i=1}^{k} v_i f_i(x) + v_0\right).$$

Without loss of generality, assume that $\sigma(0) = 1/2$. (In any case, adjusting $v_0$ gives a function $\tilde{\sigma}$ that satisfies $\inf\{\alpha : \tilde{\sigma}(\alpha) > 1/2\} = 0$, which suffices for the proof.) Now, if we replace $\sigma(\cdot)$ by $\text{sgn}(\cdot)$, we obtain a function $h$ for which $h(x_i) \neq y_i$ implies $(f(x_i) - y_i)^2 \geq 1/4$. It follows that $1 - c_h \leq (1 - c_f)/4$, as required.

Thus, for the case $\text{opt}_{\text{MAX } k\text{-}F \text{ Consistency}}(S) = 1$, we have an L-reduction from MAX $k$-$F$ CONSISTENCY to MAX $k$-$\sigma$ CONSISTENCY, with parameters $\alpha = 1$ and $\beta = 1/4$, and this L-reduction preserves maximality. Theorem 3 follows from Theorem 2.

## 5  Future Work

It seems likely that the relative error bounds in Theorems 2 and 3 can be improved to $c/k^2$. This would be immediate if Theorem 4 were also true for $k$-colourable graphs.

It would be interesting to extend the hardness result for networks with real outputs to the case of a linear output unit with a constraint on the size of the output weights. We conjecture that a similar result can be obtained, with a relative error bound that—unlike Vu's result for this case [19]—does not decrease as the input dimension increases.

It would also be worthwhile to extend the results to show that it is difficult to find a hypothesis that has expected loss nearly minimal over some neural network class, whatever hypothesis class is used. There is some related work in this direction. Theorem 7 in [3] shows that finding a conjunction of $k'$ linear threshold functions that correctly classifies a set that can be correctly classified by a conjunction of $k$ linear threshold functions is as hard as colouring a $k$-colourable graph with $n$ vertices using $k'$ colours, which has since been shown to be hard for $k' = O(kn^\alpha)$ for some $\alpha > 0$ [15]. The cryptographic results

---

[1] In this problem, the maximum might not exist since the restriction of the function class to the set of training examples is infinite, so we consider the problem of approximating the supremum.

mentioned in Section 1 do not have such strong restrictions on the hypothesis class, but only apply to classes that are apparently considerably richer than the neural network classes studied in this paper.

**Acknowledgments** This research was supported in part by the Australian Research Council.

# References

1. Sanjeev Arora, Laszlo Babai, Jacques Stern, and Z. Sweedyk. Hardness of approximate optima in lattices, codes, and linear systems. *Journal of Computer and System Sciences*, 54(2):317–331, 1997.
2. Eric B. Baum. On learning a union of half-spaces. *Journal of Complexity*, 6:67–101, 1990.
3. A.L. Blum and R.L. Rivest. Training a 3-node neural network is NP-complete. *Neural Networks*, 5(1):117–127, 1992.
4. Bhaskar DasGupta, Hava T. Siegelmann, and Eduardo D. Sontag. On the complexity of training neural networks with continuous activation functions. *IEEE Transactions on Neural Networks*, 6(6):1490–1504, 1995.
5. András Faragó and Gábor Lugosi. Strong universal consistency of neural network classifiers. *IEEE Transactions on Information Theory*, 39(4):1146–1151, 1993.
6. O. Goldreich, S. Goldwasser, and S. Micali. How to construct random functions. *Journal of the ACM*, 33:792–807, 1986.
7. D. Haussler. Decision theoretic generalizations of the PAC model for neural net and other learning applications. *Inform. Comput.*, 100(1):78–150, September 1992.
8. Klaus-U. Höffgen, Hans-U. Simon, and Kevin S. Van Horn. Robust trainability of single neurons. *J. of Comput. Syst. Sci.*, 50(1):114–125, 1995.
9. David S. Johnson and F. P. Preparata. The densest hemisphere problem. *Theoretical Computer Science*, 6:93–107, 1978.
10. Lee K. Jones. The computational intractability of training sigmoidal neural networks. *IEEE Transactions on Information Theory*, 43(1):167–713, 1997.
11. J. S. Judd. *Neural Network Design and the Complexity of Learning*. MIT Press, 1990.
12. Viggo Kann, Sanjeev Khanna, Jens Lagergren, and Alessandro Panconesi. On the hardness of approximating max-$k$-cut and its dual. Technical Report CJTCS-1997-2, Chicago Journal of Theoretical Computer Science, 1997.
13. Michael Kearns and Leslie G. Valiant. Cryptographic limitations on learning Boolean formulae and finite automata. In *Proceedings of the Twenty First Annual ACM Symposium on Theory of Computing*, pages 433–444, 1989.
14. Wee Sun Lee, Peter L. Bartlett, and Robert C. Williamson. Efficient agnostic learning of neural networks with bounded fan-in. *IEEE Transactions on Information Theory*, 42(6):2118–2132, 1996.
15. Carsten Lund and Mihalis Yannakakis. On the hardness of approximating minimization problems. *Journal of the ACM*, 41(5):960–981, 1994.
16. Nimrod Megiddo. On the complexity of polyhedral separability. *Discrete Computational Geometry*, 3:325–337, 1988.
17. C. H. Papadimitriou and M. Yannakakis. Optimization, approximation, and complexity classes. *Journal of Computer and System Science*, 43:425–440, 1991.

18. Erez Petrank. The hardness of approximation: Gap location. *Computational Complexity*, 4(2):133–157, 1994.

19. Van H. Vu. On the infeasibility of training neural networks with small squared errors. In Michael I. Jordan, Michael J. Kearns, and Sara A. Solla, editors, *Advances in Neural Information Processing Systems*, volume 10, pages 371–377. The MIT Press, 1998.

# Learnability of Quantified Formulas

Víctor Dalmau[1] and Peter Jeavons[2]

[1] Departament LSI, Universitat Politécnica de Catalunya
dalmau@lsi.upc.es
[2] Department of Computer Science, Royal Holloway, University of London, UK
p.jeavons@dcs.rhbnc.ac.uk

**Abstract.** We consider the following classes of quantified formulas. Fix a set of basic relations called a basis. Take conjunctions of these basic relations applied to variables and constants in arbitrary ways. Finally, quantify existentially or universally some of the variables. We introduce some conditions on the basis that guarantee efficient learnability. Furthermore, we show that with certain restrictions on the basis the classification is complete. We introduce, as an intermediate tool, a link between this class of quantified formulas and some well-studied structures in Universal Algebra called clones. More precisely, we prove that the computational complexity of the learnability of these formulas is completely determined by a simple algebraic property of the basis of relations, their clone of polymorphisms. Finally, we use this technique to give a simpler proof of the already known dichotomy theorem over boolean domains and we present an extension of this theorem to bases with infinite size.

## 1 Introduction

The problem of learning an unknown formula under some determined protocol has been widely studied. The inevitable trade-off between the expressive power of a family of formulas and the resources needed to learn them has forced researchers to study restricted classes of formulas. Among them, propositional formulas have received particular attention. It is known that learning general propositional formulas is hard [3, 17] in the usual learning models and some efficiently learnable subclasses of boolean formulas, especially inside CNF and DNF, have been identified (see [1, 2, 5, 12] for example).

First-order logic is a formalism with superior expressive power, but it is not so well studied from the computational point of view (see [18] and futher references in that paper). An active line of research in predicate logics is, for instance, *Inductive Logic Programming (ILP)* [20, 21].

In a recent paper, Dalmau [7], inspired by a well known dichotomy on the satisfiability of boolean formulas proved by Schaefer [25], introduced a framework to study the learnability of quantified boolean formulas and proved a complete classification for finite bases. The main goal of this paper is to further continue that line of research by extending those results to domains of arbitrary size, since quantification makes more sense when it can be applied to arbitrary variables and not neccesarily to boolean ones.

As a main intermediate tool for our study we introduce a link with some well known algebraic structures, called *clones* in Universal Algebra. This approach has been introduced in a different context by Jeavons et al. [15] and it has been succesful in the study of the Constraint Satisfaction Problem (CSP) [13–16]. We prove that the learning complexity of a family of quantified formulas over a finite domain is completely determined by its clone of polymorphisms.

As a first application of this new technique we introduce two families of efficiently learnable classes, namely, coset generating (CG) and near-unanimity (NU) bases containing, as a particular case, the learnable classes for the boolean domain. Furthermore, we provide some evidence that these families of learnable formulas are complete. More precisely, we show that if we restrict the formulas in certain ways we obtain a dichotomy. Despite the fact that there exists a dichotomic classification for the boolean domain, a full dichotomy for arbitrary domains is not known and seems likely to be hard to be found, since the clone lattice that characterizes the learnability of quantified formulas is rather involved; actually it is uncountable. For the boolean domain, the clone lattice is simpler and has been completely characterized by Post [24]. This description allows us to give an alternative proof of the dichotomy theorem in [7] and to extend it to infinite bases.

The positive learnability results are obtained using an apparently simple algorithm, called the *Generating Set (GS) Algorithm*. This algorithm exploits the intersection closure property of some representation classes. Learnable classes are efficiently learnable with equivalence queries in the model of exact learning with queries, as defined by Angluin [1]. This fact is rather striking since in all the dichotomic classifications the rest of the classes are shown not to be learnable even in the more powerful model of PAC-prediction with membership queries as defined by Angluin and Kharitonov [3]. Another characteristic feature of the learnable classes is that every concept in them can be described as the minimum concept containing a set of examples with size polynomial in the number of attributes (variables). This fact has some interesting consequences. First, the computational complexity of learning these classes only depends on the number of attributes but not on the length of the particular representation, strengthening the dichotomy. Second, the total number of concepts with a determined number of atributes is a number singly exponential in the number of attributes.

For space limitation some of the proofs are not included. We refer the reader to the full-version paper [8] for proofs missing in this paper and for further technical details.

## 2   Formulas and Relations

Let $V = \{x_1, x_2, \ldots\}$ be an infinite set of variables. Let $D$ be a fixed finite set called the *domain*. An assignment is a vector in $D^*$. If $x$ is a string, $|x|$ denotes its length. For any assignment $t \in D^*$ and for any integer $j \leq |t|$, $t[j] \in D$

denotes the $j$th component of $t$. A relation of rank $k$ (or $k$-ary relation) over $D$ is a subset of $D^k$.

We use the term *formula* in a wide sense, to mean any well-formed formula, formed from variables, constants, logical connectives, parentheses, relation symbols, and existential and universal quantifiers.

Let $S = \{R_1, R_2, \ldots\}$ be any set where each $R_i$ is a relation of rank $k_i$. $R_i$ denotes both the relation and its symbol. The set of *quantified formulas with constants over the basis* $S$, denoted by $\exists\forall\text{-Form}_C(S)$, is the smallest set of formulas such that:

a.- For all $R \in S$ of rank $k$, $R(y_1, \ldots, y_k) \in \exists\forall\text{-Form}_C(S)$ where $y_i \in V \cup D$ for $1 \leq i \leq k$.

b.- For all $F, G \in \exists\forall\text{-Form}_C(S)$, $F \wedge G \in \exists\forall\text{-Form}_C(S)$.

c.- For all $F \in \exists\forall\text{-Form}_C(S)$ and for all $x \in V$, $\exists x F \in \exists\forall\text{-Form}_C(S)$.

d.- For all $F \in \exists\forall\text{-Form}_C(S)$ and for all $x \in V$, $\forall x F \in \exists\forall\text{-Form}_C(S)$.

If we remove condition **(d)** in the previous definition we obtain a reduced class of formulas called *existentially quantified formulas with constants over the basis* $S$, denoted by $\exists\text{-Form}_C(S)$. Furthermore, if we also remove condition **(c)** we obtain a more reduced class called *formulas with constants over the basis* $S$ and denoted by $\text{Form}_C(S)$.

If in the previous definitions we replace $y_i \in V \cup D$ by $y_i \in V$ in **(a)**, we obtain the constant-free counterpart of the previous sets of formulas denoted by $\exists\forall\text{-Form}(S)$, $\exists\text{-Form}(S)$, $\text{Form}(S)$ respectively.

Each formula $F$ defines a relation $[F]$ if we apply the usual semantics of first-order logic and the variables are taken in lexicographical order. This operator can be extended to sets of formulas: For every set of relations $S$ we define $\text{Rel}(S) = \{[F] : F \in \text{Form}(S)\}$. Similarly, we also define $\exists\forall\text{-Rel}(S)$, $\exists\text{-Rel}(S)$, $\text{Rel}_C(S)$, $\exists\forall\text{-Rel}_C(S)$, and $\exists\text{-Rel}_C(S)$.

## 3  Generating Set Algorithm

In this paper we consider two models of learning, both of which are fairly standard: Angluin's model of exact learning from queries [1] and the model of PAC-prediction with membership queries as defined by Angluin and Kharitonov [3]. We also assume some familiarity with the prediction with membership reduction (see [3] for details).

Most of the terminology about learning comes from [3]. Strings over $X = D^*$ will represent both examples and concept names. A *representation of concepts* $\mathcal{C}$ is any subset of $X \times X$. We interpret an element $\langle u, x \rangle$ of $X \times X$ as consisting of a *concept name* $u$ and an *example* $x$. The example $x$ is a member of the concept $u$ if and only if $\langle u, x \rangle \in \mathcal{C}$. Define the *concept represented by* $u$ as $K_{\mathcal{C}}(u) = \{x : \langle u, x \rangle \in \mathcal{C}\}$. The *set of concepts represented by* $\mathcal{C}$ is $K_{\mathcal{C}} = \{K_{\mathcal{C}}(u) : u \in X\}$.

We will focus on representation classes for formulas. These representation classes have a stratified structure, that is, every concept contains examples of the same size. For any stratified representation class $\mathcal{C}$ we define $K_{\mathcal{C},n}$ as the set of concepts in $\mathcal{C}$ with examples of length $n$. We say that a stratified representation class $\mathcal{C}$ is intersection-closed if:

$$\forall c_1, c_2 \in K_{\mathcal{C},n} \Rightarrow \exists c_3 \in K_{\mathcal{C},n} \quad K_{\mathcal{C}}(c_3) = K_{\mathcal{C}}(c_1) \cap K_{\mathcal{C}}(c_2)$$

When $\mathcal{C}$ is intersection-closed, then, for any set of examples $H$ of the same length, we can consider the intersection of all the concepts in $\mathcal{C}$ containing $H$, denoted by $\langle H \rangle_{\mathcal{C}}$. We will say that $H$ is a *generating set* of the concept $\langle H \rangle_{\mathcal{C}}$.

Notice that closure under intersection depends only on the set of concepts $K_{\mathcal{C}}$ and does not depend at all on the particular representation class $\mathcal{C}$. In fact, we can consider generating sets as an alternative representation class for the same collection of concepts. More formally, given a set of examples $H$, we say that an example $x$ belongs to the class represented by $H$ iff $x \in \langle H \rangle_{\mathcal{C}}$.

A representation class has to be *polynomial-time evaluable*, that is, it has to be decidable in polynomial time if a vector belongs to the class. We will focus on representation classes fulfilling this condition. For the remainder of this section we will assume that we are dealing with polynomial-time evaluable representation classes but we will have to take into consideration this property later when we present concrete examples.

This representation class suggests an immediate learning algorithm using equivalence queries: Start with an empty set of generators and keep asking equivalence queries and adding vectors until the set is complete. We call this algorithm the *Generating Set (GS) Algorithm* and we state it for future reference.

Algorithm **GS**
$H = \emptyset$,
while $EQ(\langle H \rangle_{\mathcal{C}})=$ 'no' do
    Let $c$ be the conterexample,
    $H = H \cup \{c\}$,
endwhile,
return $\langle H \rangle_{\mathcal{C}}$.

Algorithm **GS** can be applied to any intersection-closed representation class $\mathcal{C}$. There is a canonical algorithm for learning intersection-closed classes in the PAC model [27] called the *Closure Algorithm*: The output of this algorithm is always $\langle H \rangle_{\mathcal{C}}$ where $H$ contains all the positive samples [22]. Algorithm **GS** is a direct adaptation of the Closure algorithm. Consequently, it is possible to extend the results in this paper to nested differences of intersection-closed classes using an approach similar to [10].

It is possible to convert this algorithm to a proper algorithm finding for every set of generators $H$, a concept $c$ equivalent to $\langle H \rangle_{\mathcal{C}}$, but this step can be computationally expensive.

Clearly, algorithm **GS** always finds the target concept, the only drawback is its time complexity, since it can require an exponential number of equivalence queries. In consequence, we are interested in characterizing the cases in which algorithm **GS** learns a representation class with a polynomial number of queries. First, we need the following definition:

**Definition 1.** *Let $\mathcal{C}$ be an intersection-closed representation class of concepts, and let $u = (x_0, x_1, \ldots, x_m)$ be a list of vectors in $D^n$. If for every $1 \leq i \leq m$, $x_i \notin \langle \{x_0, \ldots, x_{i-1}\} \rangle_{\mathcal{C}}$ then we call $u$ an* additive sequence *over $\mathcal{C}^n$.*

Clearly, an additive sequence is just a different reformulation of a possible sequence of counterexamples provided by algorithm **GS**. A representation class is learnable using algorithm **GS** if the size of every possible sequence of counterexamples can be bounded by a polynomial in the size of the examples and the size of the representation class. We do not consider the size of the representation class. This choice make analysis simpler, since we obtain indepence from the particular representation class. Furthermore, as we will see later (Section 5), there is some evidence that this restriction does not make any difference when we are dealing with quantified formulas. Formally, we say that a representation class $\mathcal{C}$ is *polynomially bounded* if it is intersection-closed and every additive sequence over $\mathcal{C}^n$ has size polynomial in $n$.

**Theorem 1.** *Let $\mathcal{C}$ be a polynomially bounded representation class. Then $\mathcal{C}$ is polynomially learnable with improper equivalence queries using algorithm **GS**. Furthermore, $\mathcal{C}$ is also learnable with a polynomial number of proper equivalence queries (not necessarily in polynomial time).*

Finally, notice that every intersection-closed representation class contained in a polynomially bounded representation class is also polynomially bounded.

# 4 Learning Subuniverses

The following definitions are fairly standard (see [19] for example). An *algebra* is an ordered pair $(D, \Phi)$ such that $D$ is a nonempty set, called the *universe*, and $\Phi$ is a set of finite operations[1] over $D$. There are some standard ways to assemble new algebras from those already at hand. The chief tools we will use are the formation of subuniverses and the formation of direct powers.

Let $\varphi$ be an $m$-ary operation over $D$, and let $E$ be a subset of $D$. We say that $E$ is closed under $\varphi$ (or $\varphi$ preserves $E$) if and only if $\forall d_1, \ldots, d_m \in E$, $\varphi(d_1, \ldots, d_m) \in E$.

Let $(D, \Phi)$ be an algebra. A subset $E$ of $D$ closed under every operation in $\Phi$ is called a subuniverse of $(D, \Phi)$. Let $(D, \Phi)$ be an algebra and $n$ any positive

---

[1] Technically, $\Phi$ is an indexed system of operations rather than a mere set of operations. However, we consider that presenting it as a set of operations is simpler for the purposes of this paper.

integer. The *direct power* of $(D, \Phi)$, denoted $(D, \Phi)^n$ is the algebra $(D^n, \{\varphi^n | \varphi \in \Phi\})$, where for every $m$-ary operation $\varphi$, $\varphi^n$ is the function given by

$$\varphi^n(x_1, \ldots, x_m) = \langle \varphi(x_1[1], \ldots, x_m[1]), \ldots, \varphi(x_1[n], \ldots, x_m[n]) \rangle$$

Direct power is the natural way to extend the algebra to tuples of elements. From now on, due to the correspondence between an algebra and its direct powers we will do some notation abuse and for instance we will say that an $n$-ary relation $R$ over $D$ is closed under an operation $\varphi : D \to D$, meaning that $R$ is closed under $\varphi^n$. Furthermore, we will say that a formula $F$ over $D$ is closed under $\varphi$ if and only if $[F]$ is closed under $\varphi$. Moreover, we will say that a set of relations (formulas) is closed under a operation $\varphi$ if every relation (formula) in the set is closed under $\varphi$. Let $\varphi$ be an operation over $D$. Operation $\varphi$ is said to be exhaustive if its image is $D$. Operation $\varphi$ is said to be idempotent if it satisfies $\varphi(x, x, \ldots, x) = x$. Idempotent operations are exhaustive. For any set $\Phi$ of operations, we define $Idem(\Phi)$ as the subset containing exactly the idempotent operations in $\Phi$.

It is straighforward to see from the definition that the property of being closed under some operation is preserved by some of the classes of relations described in Section 2.

**Lemma 1.** *Let $S$ be a set of logical relations closed under some operation $\varphi$ over $D$. Then, $\exists\text{-Rel}(S)$ is also closed under $\varphi$. Furthermore, if $\varphi$ is exhaustive then $\exists\forall\text{-Rel}(S)$ is closed under $\varphi$. Furthermore, if $\varphi$ is idempotent then $\exists\forall\text{-Rel}_C(S)$ is closed under $\varphi$.*

The intersection of any collection of subuniverses of an algebra $(D, \Phi)$ is again a subuniverse. In consequence, we can define generating sets for subuniverses in an analogous way to the previous section. This applies as well to direct powers. More precisely, let $H$ be a subset of $D^n$, the intersection $\langle H \rangle_{(D, \Phi)}$ of all subuniverses of the direct power $(D, \Phi)^n$ containing $H$ will be called the *subuniverse generated by $H$*.

Consequently, a reasonable way to represent subuniverses is using generating sets. We call $\mathcal{C}_{(D, \Phi)}$ the class of subuniverses of some direct power $(D, \Phi)^n$ represented by sets of generators. Since algebras define representation classes, concepts introduced in the previous section are applicable to algebras. So, we will say that an algebra $(D, \Phi)$ is polynomially evaluable or polynomially bounded if so is $\mathcal{C}_{(D, \Phi)}$.

We can turn these results in algebras into results about quantified formulas by considering closure operations. The next theorem summarizes the results.

**Theorem 2.** *Let $\mathcal{F}$ be a class of formulas closed under a polynomially bounded algebra $(D, \Phi)$. Then the following conditions hold:*

(a) *$\mathcal{F}$, $Form([\mathcal{F}])$, and $\exists\text{-Form}([\mathcal{F}])$ are polynomially learnable with improper equivalence queries,*

*(b) Form([ℱ]) and ∃-Form([ℱ]) are learnable with a polynomial number of proper equivalence queries (not necessarily in polynomial time),*

*(c) If every operation in Φ is exhaustive, then conditions (a) and (b) are also satisfied by ∃∀-Form([ℱ]).*

*(d) If every operation in Φ is idempotent, then conditions (a) and (b) are also satisfied by Form$_C$([ℱ]), ∃-Form$_C$([ℱ]), and ∃∀-Form$_C$([ℱ]).*

**Proof.** Condition **(a)** is a direct consequence of the definition of polynomially bounded algebra, Lemma 1, and the first part of Theorem 1. To show condition **(b)** just consider that both classes of concepts are intersection-closed and apply the second part of Theorem 1. Condition **(c)** follows from the fact that closure under an exhaustive operation is preserved by universal quantification. Finally, condition **(d)** is due to the fact that closure under an idempotent operation is preserved by constantification, and that idempotentence implies exhaustivity. ∎

In the remainder of this section we will introduce two families of operations, namely, coset generating operations and near-unanimity operations, such that the class of subuniverses of algebras containing one of these operations is polynomially bounded. In consequence, every class of quantified formulas with a basis preserved by some function in one of these families is polynomially learnable using algorithm **GS**. We just define these families and present the positive learnability results.

### 4.1 Coset Generating Operations

**Definition 2.** *An operation $\varphi : D^3 \to D$, is called a 'coset generating (CG) operation' if for all $x, y, z, u \in D$,*

*1. $\varphi(x, x, y) = \varphi(y, x, x) = y$*
*2. $\varphi(\varphi(x, y, z), z, u) = \varphi(x, y, u)$*
*3. $\varphi(u, z, \varphi(z, y, x)) = \varphi(u, y, x)$*

It is easy to adapt the proof of Proposition 2.2 in [26] to show that the previous definition is equivalent to the existence of some group $(D, \cdot)$ such that $\varphi(x, y, z) = x \cdot y^{-1} \cdot z$.

If $(D, \cdot)$ is abelian, we have a particular kind of CG operation called an affine operation. Affine operations have been intensively studied in universal algebra (see [26] for example). It is well known (see [14] for example) that for every affine operation over a finite set $D$ of prime size, the subuniverses of its direct power are exactly the subsets of $D^n$ that can be expressed as a system of counting functions modulo $|D|$. The learnability of these formulas has already been shown in [6] using a similar strategy. The next result generalizes this result to arbitrary CG operations.

**Theorem 3.** *Let $\varphi$ be a coset generating operation, and let $\mathcal{F}$ be a set of formulas closed under $\varphi$, then $\mathcal{C}_{(D,\varphi)}$ is polynomial-time evaluable and polynomially learnable with proper equivalence queries. Furthermore, the class $∃∀$-Form$_C$([ℱ]) is polynomially learnable with equivalence queries in $\mathcal{C}_{(D,\varphi)}$.*

**Proof.** The proof contains mainly two results. We have to show that algebras containing CG operations are polynomially bounded and polynomially evaluable. First we prove that $(D, \varphi)$ is polynomially bounded:

Let $u = \{x_0, \ldots, x_m\}$ be any additive sequence over $(D, \varphi)^n$. By Lemma 3 in Section 5.7 in [19], $\langle \{x_0, \ldots, x_m\} \rangle_{(D,\varphi)}$ is a right coset of a subgroup $J$ of the product group $(D, \cdot)^n$, so we can take $x_0$ as a representative of the coset and consider the set $H = \{x_0 \cdot x_0^{-1}, x_1 \cdot x_0^{-1}, \ldots, x_m \cdot x_0^{-1}\}$ as a generating set for the subgroup $J$. From the fact that $\{x_0, \ldots, x_m\}$ is an additive sequence we have that $H$ is independent in the sense that no element in $H$ can be generated from the remainder. Therefore, the cardinality of the subgroup is at least $2^m \leq |D|^n$, which gives a polynomial bound for the size of the basis $m$.

The proof of the polynomial-time evaluability mimics the proof of Theorem 32 in [9] but it is not entirely straightforward.

Let $H = \{x_0, \ldots, x_m\}$ be any set of vectors over $D^n$. Let $(D, \cdot)$ be the group associated with $\varphi$. As has been pointed out in the previous proof, $\langle H \rangle_{(D,\varphi)}$ is a right coset of a subgroup $J$ of the product group $(D, \cdot)^n$. We can take $x_0$ as a representative of the coset and it is not hard to prove that $\{x_0 \cdot x_0^{-1}, x_1 \cdot x_0^{-1}, \ldots, x_m \cdot x_0^{-1}\}$ is a generating set of the subgroup $J$. So, the problem is reduced to the problem of deciding whether a vector $y_0$ belongs to a group represented by a set of generators.

Consider the tower of subgroups $G_i$, $0 \leq i \leq n$ where $G_i$ is the subgroup of $J$ obtained fixing the first $i$ components to 0. A right coset representation of this tower can be efficiently constructed using algorithm 7 in [11][2].

Now we will present a polynomial-time algorithm that, given a right coset representation for the tower of subgroups, decides whether $y_0 \in G_0$, proving the polynomial-time evaluability of CG operations.

Let $a_1, \ldots, a_r$ be the right coset representatives of $G_0$ in $G_1$. Let $T = \{a_i : 1 \leq i \leq r, a_i[1] = y_0[1]\}$ be the subset of the representatives coinciding with $y_0$ in the first component. It is clear that if $|T| = 0$ then $y_0 \notin G_0$. On the other hand, we have $|T| \leq 1$, otherwise, let $a_i, a_j$ be two different elements in $T$, then $(a_j \cdot a_i^{-1})$ has a 0 as first component and, in consequence, belongs to $G_1$ (incidentally, this fact proves that the size of the coset representation is not too large).

Therefore, let $a_i$ be the unique representative in $T$. Since, $y_0 \in G_0$ iff $y_0 \cdot a_i^{-1} \in G_1$, now we proceed with $y_1 = y_0 \cdot a_i^{-1}$ and $G_1$ as we did before for $y_0$ and $G_0$ and so on. If during some step $j$ of this process we find that there does not exist any coset representative of $G_j$ in $G_{j+1}$ coinciding with $y_j$ in the $j+1$ component

---

[2] It is convenient to notice that algorithm 7 requires a polynomial procedure for testing membership in $G_i$, a condition that in our case is not satisfied, since we are precisely interested in this procedure for $G_0$. However, this condition can be relaxed noticing that all the elements generated by algorithm 7 already belong to $G_0$. In this case, membership in $G_i$ is straightforward: just check that the first $i$ components are equal to 0.

then we know that the answer is *no*. Otherwise, after $n$ repetitions the answer is *yes*. ∎

## 4.2 Near-unanimity Operations

**Definition 3.** *An operation $\varphi : D^k \to D$, is called a 'near-unanimity (NU) operation' if for all $x, y \in D$, $\varphi(x, y, y, \ldots, y) = \varphi(y, x, y, \ldots, y) = \cdots = \varphi(y, y, \ldots, y, x) = y$.*

A near-unanimity operation of rank 3 is also called *majority* operation. For near-unanimity operations it is even possible to prove proper learnability.

**Theorem 4.** *Let $\varphi$ be a near-unanimity operation, and let $\mathcal{F}$ be a set of formulas closed under $\varphi$, then $\mathcal{C}_{(D,\varphi)}$ is polynomial-time evaluable and polynomially learnable with proper equivalence queries. Furthermore, the class $\exists\forall\text{-Form}_C([\mathcal{F}])$ is polynomially learnable with proper equivalence queries.*

To prove this result we have to introduce some notation. Let $R$ be an $n$-ary relation over $D$ and let $I = (i_1, \ldots, i_k)$ be a list of indices chosen from $\{1, \ldots, n\}$. The projection $\pi_I(R)$ is defined to be the $k$-ary relation

$$\pi_I(R) = \{\langle t[i_1], \ldots, t[i_k]\rangle | t \in R\}$$

The projection of a tuple $t$, $\pi_I(t)$ is defined similarly.

**Definition 4.** *An $n$-ary relation $R$ over $D$ is said to be $r$-decomposable if it contains all $n$-tuples $t$ such that $\pi_I(t) \in \pi_I(R)$ for all lists of indices $I$, from the set $\{1, 2, \ldots, n\}$ with $|I| \leq r$.*

From [4] we have this useful property.

**Theorem 5.** *Every relation $R$ over $D$, closed under a near-unanimity operation of arity $r$ is $(r-1)$-decomposable.*

Using this property, it is an easy task to prove that near-unanimity functions are polynomially bounded.

**Lemma 2.** *Let $\varphi$ be a NU operation over a finite domain $D$. Then $(D, \varphi)$ is polynomially bounded.*

**Proof.** Let $r$ be the arity of $\varphi$ and let $u = \{x_0, \ldots, x_m\}$ be any additive sequence over $(D, \varphi)^n$. For every $1 \leq i \leq m-1$, the set $H_i = \langle\{x_0, \ldots, x_i\}\rangle_{(D,\varphi)}$ is $(r-1)$-decomposable. We know that $x_{i+1} \notin H_i$, so there exists some set of indices $I$, with $|I| \leq r-1$ such that $\pi_I(x_{i+1}) \notin \pi_I(H_i)$. This implies that $\pi_I(x_{i+1}) \neq \pi_I(x_j)$ for every $0 \leq j \leq i$. The result follows from the fact that there are only a polynomial number of choices for $\pi_I(x)$. ∎

The intuition underlying this result is the following: every relation closed under a near-unanimity operation of arity $r$ is decomposable as a conjunction of relations of fixed arity $r - 1$, therefore the problem of learning this class of relations is reduced to the problem of learning conjunctions of clauses of a fixed arity that can be solved using a similar approach to the one that is known for learning $(r - 1)$-CNF [1]. An empty basis can be regarded as a conjunction containing a full $(r - 1)$-ary relation for every possible set with at most $r - 1$ indices. Every time we add a tuple to the basis, we remove in every relation the tuples falsified by the new tuple. We have a polynomial number of such tuples and with every addition to the basis we remove at least one.

Finally, we prove the polynomial-time evaluability of near-unanimity operations.

**Lemma 3.** *Let $\varphi$ be a NU operation over a finite domain $D$. Then $(D, \varphi)$ is polynomially evaluable.*

**Proof.** Let $r$ be the arity of $\varphi$, let $H$ be a set of tuples over $D^n$ and let $x$ be a tuple over $D^n$. It is easy to see that $x \in \langle H \rangle_{(D,\varphi)}$ iff for every list of indices $I$ over $\{1, 2, \ldots, n\}$ with $|I| \leq r - 1$, there exists some tuple $u$ in $H$, such that $\pi_I(u) = \pi_I(x)$. Clearly, this condition can be checked in polynomial time. ∎

Finally we have to prove that it is possible to get proper learnability for quantified formulas. In fact, we establish a general conditions that guarantees proper learnability in some more cases.

**Lemma 4.** *Let $\mathcal{F}$ be a class of formulas closed under a near-unanimity operation $\varphi$ of arity $r$ and closed under existential quantification, conjunction and renaming of variables. Then $\mathcal{F}$ is polynomial learnable with proper equivalence queries.*

**Proof.** We only need to prove that for every set $H$ of models over $D^n$, it is possible to find a formula equivalent to $R = \langle H \rangle_{e_{\mathcal{F}}}$ in polynomial time. Consider for every set $I = \{i_1, \ldots, i_{r-1}\}$ of $r - 1$ indices, the relation $\pi_I(R)$. Clearly, this relation is obtained by some formula $F_{\pi_I(R)}$ in $\mathcal{F}$ (the set of relations of rank $r - 1$ in $\mathcal{F}$ is finite and fixed, and therefore a list of formulas generating all of them can be precalculated). By the $r - 1$ decomposability of $R$ the following formula is equivalent to $R$.

$$\bigwedge_{I=\{i_1,\ldots,i_r\},1\leq i_1\leq\ldots\leq i_r\leq n} F_{\pi_I(R)}(x_{i_1}, \ldots, x_{i_r})$$

∎

Summarizing,

**Corollary 1.** *Let $\mathcal{F}$ be a class of formula closed under a near-unanimity operation $\varphi$. Then the following classes of formulas are polynomial-time learnable with proper equivalence queries: $\exists\text{-Form}([\mathcal{F}])$, $\exists\forall\text{-Form}([\mathcal{F}])$, $\exists\text{-Form}_C([\mathcal{F}])$, and $\exists\forall\text{-Form}_C([\mathcal{F}])$.*

# 5 Non-learnability results

In previous sections we have used algebraic properties of relations to prove learn-ability results. More precisely, we used closure operations to show that algorithm **GS** can learn efficiently some sets of formulas. In fact, the link between the complexity of learning some classes of quantified formulas and closure operations is even tighter: closure operations of quantified formulas determine the learnability complexity.

**Definition 5.** *Let $S$ be a set of relations over $D$. Define $Pol(S)$ (polymorphisms of $S$) to be the set of all operations, $\varphi$, on $D$ such that every relation in $S$ is closed under $\varphi$.*

The polymorphisms of a set have a known structure, **(a)** they contain all the projections, i.e., functions that return one of their arguments, and **(b)** they are closed under composition. Any set of operations satisfying these conditions is called a *Clone* [26]. The set of all clones over some finite set $D$ forms a lattice. The set of polynomrphisms of a class of formulas determines its learning complexity.

**Theorem 6.** *Let $S$ and $S_0$ be sets of relations over a finite set $D$,*

1. *If $Pol(S) \subseteq Pol(S_0)$, and $\exists$-Form$(S)$ is polynomially predictable with membership queries so is $\exists$-Form$(S_0)$.*
2. *If $Idem(Pol(S)) \subseteq Idem(Pol(S_0))$, and $\exists$-Form$_C(S)$ is polynomially predictable with membership queries, so is $\exists$-Form$_C(S_0)$.*

Therefore from now on, it is justified to talk about the complexity of learning an algebra $(D, \Phi)$ meaning by that, the set of quantified formulas closed under all the operations in the algebra. That allows us to use the body of knowledge from universal algebra about clones. Theorem 6 also holds for some other learning models as for example: exact learning with equivalence queries, PAC-learning and PAC-prediction and the models obtained by adding membership queries to them. Since in this section we are interested in non-learnability results, we only state the theorem for the strongest model: PAC-prediction with membership queries .

The original aim of this paper was to extend the dichotomic classification for the learnability of boolean formulas [7] to larger domains. Unfortunately, the 2-element domain is rather particular and whereas the clone lattice for the boolean domain is countable and was fully identified by Post [24], the clone lattice for larger domains is more involved. In fact, it is known [28] that the clone lattice for $|D| \geq 3$, contains uncountably many clones. This fact seems to indicate that it will be hard to find a complete classification for larger domains.

However, in this section we will show that restricting the lattice of clones in some ways, i.e., considering only minimal clones and only plain clones we obtain a dichotomy. This fact provides some evidence that the known learnable families, i.e., CG and NU operations, are complete. We will consider clones containing only idempotent operations. This assumption is justified by the fact that clones containing only idempotent operations correspond to the closure operations of classes of formulas containing constants (Theorem 6).

Atoms in the clone lattice are called *minimal clones*. Learnability of minimal clones is completely classified.

**Theorem 7.** *(Dichotomy Theorem for minimal clones) Let $S$ be a set of relations, such that $Pol(S) = (D, \varphi)$ is minimal. Then, if $\varphi$ is a majority operation or an affine operation then $\exists\forall$-$Form_C(S)$ is polynomially learnable with improper equivalence queries, otherwise $\exists$-$Form_C(S)$ is not polynomially predictable even with membership queries under cryptographic assumptions.*

An algebra is called *plain* iff it is simple and has no nonsingleton proper subalgebras. Plain algebras also have a complete classification.

**Theorem 8.** *(Dichotomy Theorem for plain clones) Let $S$ be a finite set of relations, such that $Pol(S)$ is plain. Then, if $Pol(S)$ contains a near-unanimity operation or an affine operation then $\exists\forall$-$Form_C(S)$ is polynomially learnable with improper equivalence queries, otherwise $\exists$-$Form_C(S)$ is not polynomially predictable even with membership queries under cryptographic assumptions.*

# 6 Boolean Case revisited

In this section we review the already known results about the learnability of quantified boolean formulas [7] under the perspective provided by its connection with clone theory, in order to simplify the proof and strengthen the results.

We start by introducing the dichotomy theorem for the learnability of quantified boolean formulas with constants. The following definitions are from [7] but the notation has been slightly adapted for convenience:

A boolean relation is *bijunctive* if it can be expressed as a CNF where every clause has at most 2 literals. A boolean relation is said to be *k-weakly monotone* (resp. *k-weakly antimonotone*) $(k \geq 3)$ if can be expressed as a CNF where every clause is either (i) the disjunction of at most $k$ unnegated variables (resp. negated variables) or (ii) the disjunction of at most two literals with at most one negated (resp. unnegated) variable. A boolean relation is *weakly monotone* (WM) (resp. *weakly antimonotone* (WA)) if it is $k$-ary weakly monotone (resp. $k$-ary weakly antimonotone) for some $k \geq 3$. Finally, a boolean relation $R$ is *linear* if it is logically equivalent to some system of equations over $GF(2)$.

These definitions are extended in a natural way to sets of relations. We say, for example, that a set of relations $S$ is bijunctive iff every relation in $S$ is bijunctive. In [7] it is shown that under certain assumptions, quantified formulas are learnable iff the basis is bijunctive, weakly monotone, weakly antimonotone or linear.

Diagram 1 represents the idempotent Post lattice, that is, the lattice of clones on a 2-element set [24] restricted to idempotent operations. Nodes in figure 1

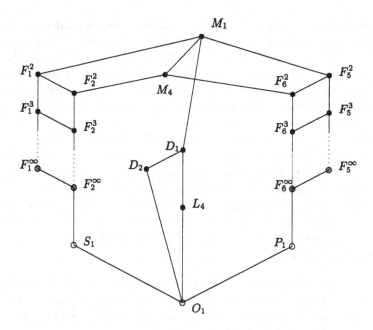

**Fig. 1.** Post Lattice restricted to idempotent operations

are labeled according to Post's notation (see [23] for a simple description of the lattice). Grey nodes denote clones generated by an infinite set of relations. Black nodes denote clones containing a near-unanimity or an affine function. The following table establishes the correspondence between these clones and the learnable classes in the boolean case.

| bijunctive | $\varphi_{D_2}(x,y,z) = xy \vee yz \vee zx$ |
|---|---|
| $k$-ary WM | $\varphi_{F_2^k}(x_1,\ldots,x_{k+1}) = \bigwedge_{j=1}^{k+1}(x_1 \vee .. \vee x_{j-1} \vee x_{j+1} \vee .. \vee x_{k+1})$ |
| $k$-ary WA | $\varphi_{F_6^k}(x_1,\ldots,x_{k+1}) = \bigvee_{j=1}^{k+1}(x_1 \wedge .. \wedge x_{j-1} \wedge x_{j+1} \wedge .. \wedge x_{k+1})$ |
| linear | $\varphi_{L_4}(x,y,z) = x \oplus y \oplus z$ |

Every entry in the table, constituted by a class of basis $C$ and an operation $\varphi$, has to be interpreted in the following way: a basis $S$ belongs to the class $C$ iff $\varphi \in \mathrm{Pol}(S)$. On the other hand, operation $\varphi_X$ generates clone $X$.

Clearly, $\varphi_{L_4}$ is an affine operation, and $\varphi_{D_2}$, $\varphi_{F_2^k}$, and $\varphi_{F_6^k}$ are near-unanimity operations. So, the learnability of these classes follows directly from Theorems 3 and 4. As the lattice is ordered from bottom to top according to inclusion, the remainder of the black nodes contain also a near-unanimity or an affine operation inherited from some ancestor.

The remainder of the clones are depicted as white nodes in figure 1. Let us now analyze them. Consider clone $P_1$, which is generated by the conjunction operation. It is known that every Horn formula is closed under conjunction and in particular so is $[\overline{x} \vee \overline{y} \vee z]$. On the other hand, clone $S_1$ is generated by the disjunction operation, so it preserves all anti-Horn formulas, in particular $[x \lor y \lor \bar{z}]$. Therefore, every clone generated by a finite set of relations and not containing any near-unanimity or any affine operation preserves either $[\bar{x} \lor \bar{y} \lor z]$ or $[x \lor y \lor \bar{z}]$ and, as it is shown in [7], the associated set of quantified formulas is not polynomially predictable with membership queries under cryptographic assumptions. This simple reasoning gives us an alternative proof of the involved case analysis in [7].

A direct way to extend the boolean case in [7] is to classify the grey nodes in figure 1 in order to deal with bases containing an infinite number of relations. Obviously, we have to define some uniformity to deal with this case. We choose the size of the minimum CNF expression, since CNF formulas have conjuntive form (and therefore, are convenient to our framework that includes closure under conjunction) and have the maximum expressive power, since if we choose any other natural representation class strictly containing CNF we only obtain trivial non-learnability results.

**Definition 6.** *Let $F$ be any formula in $\exists \forall\text{-}Form_C(S)$ where $S$ can contain an infinite number of boolean relations. We define the size of $F$, $|F|$ as the length of the formula obtained by replacing in $F$ every occurrence of a relation $R(x_1, \ldots, x_m)$ by the minimum equivalent CNF.*

**Theorem 9.** *(Generalized Dichotomy Theorem for quantified boolean formulas) For every set of boolean relations $S$,*

1. *If $S$ is bijunctive, linear, or k-weakly monotone or k-weakly antimonotone for some $k \geq 3$, then $\exists \forall\text{-}Form_C(S)$ is polynomially learnable with (proper) equivalence queries.*
2. *Else if $S$ is linear, then $\exists \forall\text{-}Form_C(S)$ is polynomially learnable with (improper) equivalence queries.*
3. *Else if $S$ is monotone or antimonotone, then $\exists \forall\text{-}Form_C(S)$ is polynomially learnable with (improper) equivalence queries and membership queries.*
4. *Else if $S$ is weakly monotone or weakly antimonotone then DNF is prediction with membership-reducible to $\exists \forall\text{-}Form_C(S)$.*
5. *Else $\exists \forall\text{-}Rel_C(S)$ is not polynomially predictable with membership queries under the assumption that public key encryption systems secure against chosen ciphertext attack exist.*

It is interesting to point out is that whereas for the finite basis case membership queries are no help, i.e., for every finite basis the corresponding set of quantified formulas is either polynomially learnable with equivalence queries alone or not predictable even with membership queries, they turn out to be necessary to study the infinite case, since the class of monotone formulas is not known to be learnable with equivalence queries alone.

# References

1. D. Angluin. Queries and Concept Learning. *Machine Learning*, 2:319–342, 1988.
2. D. Angluin, M. Frazier, and L. Pitt. Learning Conjunctions of Horn Clauses. *Machine Learning*, 9:147–164, 1992.
3. D. Angluin and M. Kharitonov. When won't Membership Queries help. *Journal of Computer and System Sciences*, 50:336–355, 1995.
4. K.A. Baker and A.F. Pixley. Polynomial Interpolation and the Chinese Remainder Theorem for Algebraic Systems. *Math. Z.*, 1975.
5. N.H. Bshouty. Exact learning boolean functions via the monotone theory. *Information and Computation*, pages 146–153, November 1995.
6. Zhixiang Chen and Steven Homer. Learning counting functions with queries. *Theoretical Computer Science*, 180(1–2):155–168, 10 June 1997.
7. V. Dalmau. A Dichotomy Theorem for Learning Quantified Boolean Formulas. In *10th Annual ACM Conference on Computational Learning Theory COLT'97*, pages 193–200, 1997.
8. V. Dalmau and P. Jeavons. Learnability of Quantified Formulas. Technical Report CSD-TR-98-10, Royal Holloway, University of London, UK, 1998.
9. T. Feder and M.Y. Vardi. The Computational Structure of Monotone Monadic SNP and Contraint Satisfaction: A Study through Datalog and Group Theory. *SIAM J. Computing*, 28(1):57–104, 1998.
10. D. Helmbold, R. Sloan, and M. Warmuth. Learning Nested Differences of Intersection-Closed Concept Classes. *Machine Learning*, 5(2):165–196, 1990.
11. M.C. Hoffmann. *Group-Theoretic Algorithms and Graph Isomorphism*, volume 136 of *Lecture Notes in Computer Science*. Springer-Verlag, 1982.
12. Jeffrey C. Jackson. An Efficient Membership-query Algorithm for Learning DNF with respect to the Uniform Distribution. *Journal of Computer and System Sciences*, 55(3):414–440, December 1997.
13. P. Jeavons, D. Cohen, and M.C. Cooper. Constraints, Consistency and Closure. *Artificial Intelligence*, 101:251–265, 1988.
14. P. Jeavons, D. Cohen, and M. Gyssens. A Unifying Framework for Tractable Constraints. In *1st International Conference on Principles and Practice of Constraint Programming, CP'95, Cassis (France), September 1995*, volume 976 of *Lecture Notes in Computer Science*, pages 276–291. Springer-Verlag, 1995.
15. P. Jeavons, D. Cohen, and M. Gyssens. Closure Properties of Constraints. *Journal of the ACM*, 44(4):527–548, July 1997.
16. P. Jeavons and M. Cooper. Tractable Constraints on Ordered Domains. *Artificial Intelligence*, 79:327–339, 1996.
17. Michael Kearns and Leslie Valiant. Cryptographic limitations on learning Boolean formulae and finite automata. *Journal of the ACM*, 41(1):67–95, January 1994.
18. W. Maass and G. Turán. On Learnability and Predicate Logic. In *Bar-Ilan Symposium onf the Foundations of Artificial Intelligence, BISFAI'95*, pages 75–85, 1995.
19. R.N. McKenzie, G.F. McNulty, and W.F. Taylor. *Algebras, Lattices and Varieties*, volume 1. Wadsworth and Brooks, 1987.
20. S. Muggleton, editor. *Inductive Logic Programming*. Academic Press, 1992.
21. S. Muggleton and L. De Raedt. Inductive Logic Programming: Theory and Methods. *Journal of Logic Programming*, 19/20:7:629–679, 1994.
22. B.K. Natarajan. On Learning Boolean Functions. In *9thAnnual ACM Symposium on Theory of Computing, STOC'87*, pages 296–304, 1987.

23. N. Pippenger. *Theories of Computability*. Cambridge University Press, 1997.
24. E.L. Post. *The Two-Valued Iterative Systems of Mathematical Logic*, volume 5 of *Annals of Mathematics Studies*. Princeton, N.J, 1941.
25. T.J. Schaefer. The Complexity of Satisfiability Problems. In *10th Annual ACM Symposium on Theory of Computing*, pages 216–226, 1978.
26. A. Szendrei. *Clones in Universal Algebra*, volume 99 of *Seminaires de Mathématiques Supéreiores*. University of Montreal, 1986.
27. L. Valiant. A Theory of the Learnable. *Comm. ACM*, 27(11):1134–1142, 1984.
28. Yu.I. Yanov and A.A. Muchnik. On the existence of $k$-valued closed classes without a finite basis. *Dokl. Akad. Nauk SSSR*, 127:44–46, 1959. In russian.

# Learning Multiplicity Automata from Smallest Counterexamples

Jürgen Forster

Universität Bochum, Germany
forster@lmi.ruhr-uni-bochum.de

**Abstract.** We show that multiplicity automata (MAs) with size $n$ and input alphabet $\Sigma$ can efficiently be learned from $n(n+1)|\Sigma| + 2$ smallest counterexamples. This improves on an earlier result of Bergadano and Varricchio. A unique representation for MAs is introduced. Our algorithm learns this representation. We also show that any learning algorithm for MAs needs at least $\frac{1}{64}n^2|\Sigma|$ smallest counterexamples. Thus our upper bound on the number of counterexamples cannot be improved substantially.

## 1 Introduction

We study the problem of *learning* an unknown *target concept* $f$ that is an element of a known set $\mathcal{F}$. A *learning algorithm* gets information about $f$ only by posing *queries* to a teacher. If $\mathcal{F}$ is a set of functions from a set $X$ to a set $Y$, typical queries are *equivalence queries* (*EQs*) and *membership queries* (*MQs*). For a function $g : X \to Y$ (the *hypothesis*), the teacher answers to an EQ($g$) query with "YES" if $g$ is equal to the target concept $f$, and returns a *counterexample* $x \in X$, i.e., an element $x \in X$ with $f(x) \neq g(x)$, otherwise. For $x \in X$ the teacher answers a MQ($x$) query with the value $f(x)$.

If there is an ordering on $X$, we can also investigate equivalence queries that return *smallest counterexamples* (*EQSC queries*). When the learning algorithm poses an EQSC query for $g : X \to Y$ and $g$ is not equal to the target concept $f$, the teacher answers with the smallest $x \in X$ for which $f(x) \neq g(x)$, and with the value $f(x) \in Y$.

The running time of an efficient learning algorithm must be polynomial in parameters describing the complexity of the target concept and in the length of the longest counterexample ever returned by the teacher.

Two interesting classes of functions for $\mathcal{F}$ are the functions accepted by DFAs and by MAs. Learnability of DFAs has been studied intensively. DFAs cannot be learned efficiently from MQs alone, or from EQs alone (see [2]). But Angluin has shown in [1] that DFAs can efficiently be learned with MQs and EQs. This algorithm was improved by Rivest and Shapire in [9]. Ibarra and Jiang have shown in [8] that, given the canonical ordering on $\Sigma^*$, DFAs of size $n$ can be learned efficiently with at most $|\Sigma|n^3$ EQSC queries. Birkendorf, Böker and Simon proved in [5] that even $|\Sigma|n^2$ counterexamples are sufficient. In [4], Bergadano and Varricchio have shown that MAs of size $n$ can be learned with $O(n^5|\Sigma|)$ EQSC queries. Our main result in Sect. 4 is that $n(n+1)|\Sigma| + 2$ EQSC queries suffice. In addition, we show in Sect. 5 that this result cannot be improved substantially. Our learning algorithm has similarities to the algorithm for learning DFAs from smallest counterexamples of Birkendorf, Böker and Simon. E.g., the set of minimum representants of a DFA used in [5] corresponds to the set $R(f)$ that we define in Sect. 3 for a recognizable function $f$. We also use elements of the algorithm of Bergadano and Varricchio, namely prefixtree representations and the solving of systems of linear equations. Their algorithm is competitive to our algorithm (with respect to the number of queries and running time) in the special case where the target MA maps only words of a fixed length to non-zero. However, they perform a reduction of the general case to this special case which makes their algorithm less efficient.

## 2   Definitions and Notations

The set of natural numbers $1, 2, 3, \ldots$ is denoted by $\mathbb{N}$. Let $\mathbb{N}_0 := \mathbb{N} \cup \{0\}$. An *input alphabet* is a finite set. In this article $\Sigma$ is always an ordered input alphabet. $\Sigma^*$ is the set of all words $x = x_1 \cdots x_n$ of a finite length $|x| = n$ with $x_1, \ldots, x_n \in \Sigma$. $\varepsilon$ is the word of length zero. The words $x_1 \cdots x_n$, $x_1 \cdots x_{n-1}$, $\ldots$, $x_1$, $\varepsilon$ are the *prefixes* of $x$, the words $x_1 \cdots x_n$, $x_2 \cdots x_n$, $\ldots$, $x_n$, $\varepsilon$ are the *suffixes* of $x$. A set $M \subseteq \Sigma^*$ is called *prefix-closed* if all prefixes of every element of $M$ also belong to $M$. For a non-empty, prefix-closed set $R \subseteq \Sigma^*$ and $c \in \Sigma^* \setminus R$ there are unique $r \in R$, $a \in \Sigma$, $z \in \Sigma^*$ so that $c = raz$ and $ra \notin R$. $r$ ist the longest prefix of $c$ that is an element of $R$. We call $(r, a, z)$ the *R-decomposition* of $c$. For two words $x = x_1 \cdots x_n, y = y_1 \cdots y_m \in \Sigma^*$, we say that $x$ is *canonically smaller* than $y$, denoted by $x < y$, if $n < m$ or if $n = m$ and there is a number $i \in \{1, \ldots, n\}$ such that $x_1 \cdots x_{i-1} = y_1 \cdots y_{i-1}$ and $x_i < y_i$.

Throughout the article $K$ is a field. For $n \in \mathbb{N}$, $K^n$ denotes the vector space of $n$-dimensional column vectors $x$. $x^\top$, the transposed vector of $x$, is a row vector. For a set $M \subseteq K^n$, $\mathrm{span}(M)$ is the linear hull of $M$. $e_1, \ldots, e_n$ are the unit vectors, in particular $e_1 = (1, 0, \ldots, 0)^\top$. For $m, n \in \mathbb{N}$, $K^{m \times n}$ is the set of $m \times n$ matrices with entries from $K$. We also look at infinite matrices. For sets $V, W$, $K^{V \times W}$ is the set of matrices with rows labeled by the elements of $V$ and columns labeled by the elements of $W$. The rank $rk(A)$ of a matrix $A \in K^{V \times W}$ is the supremum of the ranks of all finite submatrices.

For functions $f, g : \Sigma^* \to K$, $f \neq g$ we define $\mathrm{mincex}(f, g) \in \Sigma^*$ to be the (canonically) smallest word $x \in \Sigma^*$ such that $f(x) \neq g(x)$. For an expression $A$, we write

$$[A] = \begin{cases} 1, & \text{if } A \text{ is true,} \\ 0, & \text{otherwise.} \end{cases}$$

The function $\chi_L : \Sigma^* \to K$ with $\chi_L(x) = [x \in L]$, $x \in \Sigma^*$, is the *characteristic function* of the set $L \subseteq \Sigma^*$.

For $n \in \mathbb{N}$, $\mu : \Sigma^* \to K^{n \times n}$ is a *morphism of monoids* if $\mu(x_1 \cdots x_m) = \mu(x_1) \cdots \mu(x_m)$ for all $m \in \mathbb{N}_0$, $x_1, \ldots, x_m \in \Sigma$. If $\mu : \Sigma^* \to K^{n \times n}$ is a morphism of monoids and $\gamma \in K^n$ is a vector, $(\mu, \gamma)$ is the *multiplicity automaton (MA)* of size $n$ for the function $f : \Sigma^* \to K$ with $f(x) = e_1^\top \mu(x) \gamma$, $x \in \Sigma^*$. A function $f : \Sigma^* \to K$ is called *recognizable* if there is a MA for $f$.

For a function $f : \Sigma^* \to K$, $H^f = (f(xy))_{x,y \in \Sigma^*}$ is the *Hankel matrix* of $f$. $Z_x^f = (f(xy))_{y \in \Sigma^*}$ is the the row of $H^f$ for prefix $x \in \Sigma^*$. It is well known that a set $L \subseteq \Sigma^*$ can be represented by a DFA if and only if the number of distinct rows of the Hankel matrix of $\chi_L$ is finite. In [3] (see also [6,7]) it is shown that a function $f : \Sigma^* \to K$ is recognizable if and only if the Hankel matrix $H^f$ has finite rank. Then $\mathrm{rk}(H^f)$ is the size of a minimal MA for $f$.

## 3 Prefixtree Representations

In this section, we look at another representation for recognizable functions, namely prefixtree representations. They were introduced in [4]. In addition, we investigate prefixtree representations that respect the canonical ordering on $\Sigma^*$. They will by very useful when we present the algorithm of Sect. 4 which learns from canonically smallest counterexamples.

**Definition 1.** *Let $R \subseteq \Sigma^*$ be a finite, non-empty, prefix-closed set, let $\alpha : R \to K$ be a function, and let $\lambda^{ra,s} \in K$, $r, s \in R$, $a \in \Sigma$, be numbers, such that $\lambda^{ra,s} = [ra = s]$ if $ra \in R$. $(R, \alpha, \lambda)$ is called a* prefixtree representation *(of size $|R|$) of the function $f : \Sigma^* \to K$ with*

$$f(x_1 \cdots x_m) = \sum_{s_1, \ldots, s_m \in R} \lambda^{x_1, s_1} \lambda^{s_1 x_2, s_2} \cdots \lambda^{s_{m-1} x_m, s_m} \alpha(s_m)$$

*for $m \in \mathbb{N}_0$, $x_1, \ldots, x_m \in \Sigma$.*

If we think of the elements of $R$ as states of the prefixtree representation, we can consider the numbers $\lambda^{ra,s}$ as weights for the transition from state $r$ to state $s$ when the next input letter is $a$. If $ra$ is an element of $R$, the weight is one if $ra = s$ and zero otherwise.

Prefixtree representations are special MAs: Let $(R, \alpha, \lambda)$ be a prefixtree representation of $f$ and let $n = |R|$. We can write $R = \{r_1, \ldots, r_n\}$ with $r_1 = \varepsilon$. Let $\mu : \Sigma^* \to K^{n \times n}$ be the morphism of monoids with $\mu(a) = (\lambda^{r_i a, r_j})_{1 \le i, j \le n}$, $a \in \Sigma$, and let $\gamma := (\alpha(r_1), \ldots, \alpha(r_n))^\top \in K^n$. Then $(\mu, \gamma)$ is a MA for $f$. Because of the requirement $\lambda^{ra,s} = [ra = s]$ if $ra \in R$, we have $f|_R = \alpha$ and

$$Z_{ra}^f = \sum_{s \in R} \lambda^{ra,s} Z_s^f \tag{1}$$

for $r \in R$, $a \in \Sigma$. We say that $(R, \alpha, \lambda)$ is a *canonical prefixtree representation* if $\lambda^{ra,s} = 0$ for all $s > ra$. Then

$$Z_{ra}^f = \sum_{s \in R, s \le ra} \lambda^{ra,s} Z_s^f . \tag{2}$$

We now show that for any recognizable function $f : \Sigma^* \to K$ there is a unique canonical prefixtree representation of size $\mathrm{rk}(H^f)$. This representation is learned by the algorithm in Sect. 4. Let

$$R(f) = \{r \in \Sigma^* \mid Z_r^f \notin \mathrm{span}\{Z_s^f \mid s \in \Sigma^*, s < r\}\} \ .$$

$R(f)$ is the set of prefixes $r \in \Sigma^*$ for which the row for $r$ of the Hankel matrix $H^f$ is not a linear combination of the rows for prefixes that are smaller than $r$ in the canonical ordering. $R(f)$ is prefix-closed. For all $r \in \Sigma^*$,

$$Z_r^f \in \mathrm{span}\{Z_s^f \mid s \in R(f), s \leq r\} \ . \tag{3}$$

$(Z_s^f)_{s \in R(f)}$ is a basis of $\mathrm{span}\{Z_r^f \mid r \in \Sigma^*\}$, thus $\mathrm{rk}(H^f) = |R(f)|$. Using (2) we can prove that $R(f) \subseteq R$ for any canonical prefixtree representation $(R, \alpha, \lambda)$ of $f$.

**Proposition 1.** *Every non-zero recognizable function $f : \Sigma^* \to K$ has a unique canonical prefixtree representation $(R, \alpha, \lambda)$ of size $\mathrm{rk}(H^f)$.*

**Proof.** Existence: Let $R = R(f)$, $\alpha = f|_R$. Since $(Z_s^f)_{s \in R}$ is a basis of $\mathrm{span}\{Z_s^f \mid s \in \Sigma^*\}$, there are numbers $\lambda^{ra,s} \in K$, $r, s \in R$, $a \in \Sigma$, such that

$$Z_{ra}^f = \sum_{s \in R} \lambda^{ra,s} Z_s^f \tag{4}$$

for $r \in R$, $a \in \Sigma$. Since these numbers are unique and because of (3), $(R, \alpha, \lambda)$ is a canonical prefixtree representation. Because of (4) and $\alpha = f|_R$, $(R, \alpha, \lambda)$ is a prefixtree representation of $f$. There holds $|R| = |R(f)| = \mathrm{rk}(H^f)$.

Uniqueness: If $(R, \alpha, \lambda)$ is a prefixtree representation of $f$ with size $\mathrm{rk}(H^f)$, we have $R = R(f)$ (this follows from $R(f) \subseteq R$ and $|R(f)| = \mathrm{rk}(H^f) = |R|$). The function $\alpha$ must be equal to $f|_R$. Since $(Z_s^f)_{s \in R(f)}$ is linearly independent and because of (1), the numbers $\lambda^{ra,s}$ are unique. ∎

## 4 The MA Learning Algorithm

In this section we prove the following theorem.

**Theorem 1.** *There is a learning algorithm that learns the unique canonical prefixtree representation of size $n = \mathrm{rk}(H^f)$ of any recognizable function $f : \Sigma^* \to K$ with at most $n(n+1)|\Sigma| + 2$ EQSC queries in time $O(n^5|\Sigma|)$.*

Before we look at the algorithm, we describe the variables we are going to use. $k$ is an integer variable that counts the iterations of the main loop. For all $k$, $(R_k, \alpha_k, \lambda_k)$ is a prefixtree representation of the $k$'th hypothesis $f_k : \Sigma^* \to K$. $c_k = \mathrm{EQSC}(f_k) = \mathrm{mincex}(f_k, f)$ denotes the smallest counterexample for $f_k$; $(r_k, a_k, z_k)$ is the $R_k$-decomposition of $c_k$. For some words $r \in \Sigma^*$ and some $a \in \Sigma$, we store suffixes $z \in \Sigma^*$ of counterexamples $raz$ in lists $L_{ra}$.

In each iteration of the main loop, the algorithm tries to solve a system of linear equations. If the system has a solution, it is not necessary to enlarge the current hypothesis and only the numbers $\lambda^{r_k a_k, s}$, $s \in R_k$, are changed for the new hypothesis. Otherwise, the word $r_k a_k$ is added to the set $R_k$ in the procedure EXTEND.

**Algorithm 1.**
```
1: INIT;
2: k := 1;
3: Repeat:
4:      Let (r_k, a_k, z_k) be the R_k-decomposition of c_k;
5:      Append z_k to the list L_{r_k a_k};
6:      While there exists a tuple of numbers (ξ_s)_{s∈R_k, s<ra} that solves all
```
equations $f(r_k a_k z) = \sum_{s \in R_k, s < r_k a_k} f(sz)\xi_s$ with $z$ element of $L_{r_k a_k}$:

$$
7: \quad \text{For } r, s \in R_k, a \in \Sigma \text{ let } \lambda^{ra,s} := \begin{cases} \lambda_k^{ra,s}, & ra \neq r_k a_k, \\ \xi_s, & ra = r_k a_k, s < r_k a_k, \\ 0, & ra = r_k a_k, s > r_k a_k; \end{cases}
$$

```
8:          c := EQSC(R_k, α_k, λ);
9:          If c > c_k:
10:             (R_{k+1}, α_{k+1}, λ_{k+1}) := (R_k, α_k, λ); c_{k+1} := c;
11:             Go to Line 14;
12:         Append the z ∈ Σ* for which c = r_k a_k z to the list L_{r_k a_k};
13:     EXTEND;
14:     k := k + 1;
```

INIT:
```
I1: c_0 := EQSC(0);
I2: R_1 := {ε};
I3: α_1(ε) := f(ε);
I4: λ_1^{a,ε} := 0 for a ∈ Σ;
I5: For a ∈ Σ initialize L_a as the empty list;
I6: c_1 := EQSC(R_1, α_1, λ_1);
```

EXTEND:

E1: $R_{k+1} := R_k \cup \{r_k a_k\}$;

$$
\text{E2: } \alpha_{k+1}(r) := \begin{cases} \alpha_k(r), & r \in R_k, \\ f(r_k a_k), & r = r_k a_k, \end{cases} \quad \text{for } r \in R_{k+1};
$$

$$
\text{E3: } \lambda_{k+1}^{ra,s} := \begin{cases} \lambda_k^{ra,s}, & r, s \in R_k, ra \neq r_k a_k, \\ [ra = s], & ra = r_k a_k, \\ \sum_{t \in R_k} \lambda_k^{r_k a_k, t} \lambda_k^{ta,s}, & r = r_k a_k, s \in R_k, \\ 0, & \text{otherwise,} \end{cases} \quad \text{for } r, s \in R_{k+1}, a \in \Sigma;
$$

E4: For $a \in \Sigma$ initialize $L_{r_k a_k a}$ as the empty list;

E5: $c_{k+1} := EQSC(R_{k+1}, \alpha_{k+1}, \lambda_{k+1})$;

If an EQSC query returns "YES", the algorithm stops immediately and outputs the correct prefixtree representation (or a MA computed from this prefixtree representation).

By induction on $k$, we see that all $(R_k, \alpha_k, \lambda_k)$ and all $(R_k, \alpha_k, \lambda)$ are canonical prefixtree representations and that $\alpha_k = f|_{R_k}$ for all $k$. (Note that if $\lambda_{k+1}^{ra,s} \neq 0$ for $r = r_k a_k$, $s \in R_k$ in Line E3, then there is a $t \in R_k$ such that $\lambda_k^{r_k a_k, t} \lambda_k^{ta,s} \neq 0$. Because of the induction hypothesis $t \leq r_k a_k = r$ and $s \leq ta \leq ra$ follow.)

It is not evident how some of the lines of the algorithm can be executed. We make some remarks about those lines. In Line 4, $c_k$ has a $R_k$-decomposition since $f_k(c_k) \neq f(c_k)$ (thus $c_k \notin R_k$). In Line 6, the numbers $f(r_k a_k z)$, $f(sz)$ are known: For every $z$ from the list $L_{r_k a_k}$, $r_k a_k z$ is a counterexample returned by an EQSC query for some prefixtree representation $(R, \alpha, \lambda)$. The teacher has made $f(r_k a_k z)$ known and the values $f(sz)$ can be computed with $(R, \alpha, \lambda)$, since $sz$ is smaller than $r_k a_k z$. In Proposition 2, we prove that $r_k a_k$ is a prefix of $c$ in Line 12. In Line I3, we know the value $f(\varepsilon)$ because the teacher has made $f(c_0) = f(\varepsilon)$ known if $c_0 = \varepsilon$, and we know that $f(\varepsilon) = 0$ if $c_0 \neq \varepsilon$. In Line E2, either $f(r_k a_k)$ has been made known by the teacher (if $z_k = \varepsilon$) or $r_k a_k < r_k a_k z_k = c_k$, and $f(r_k a_k)$ can be computed with the prefixtree representation $(R_k, \alpha_k, \lambda_k)$.

**Proposition 2.** $r_k a_k$ is a prefix of $c$ whenever Line 12 is executed.

**Proof.** We know $c \leq c_k$. If $c = c_k$, the assertion is evident. (However, the proof of Proposition 5 will show that this case never occurs.) Otherwise, let $h$ be the function with prefixtree representation $(R_k, \alpha_k, \lambda)$. Since mincex$(h, f) = c < c_k = $ mincex$(f_k, f)$, we have $c = $ mincex$(f_k, h)$. Since $c \notin R_k$, $c$ has a $R_k$-decomposition $(r, a, z)$. Assume that $ra \neq r_k a_k$. Then $\lambda^{ra,s} = \lambda_k^{ra,s}$ for $s \in R_k$, and (2) yields

$$\sum_{s \in R_k, s < ra} \lambda_k^{ra,s} f_k(sz) = f_k(raz) \neq h(raz)$$

$$= \sum_{s \in R_k, s < ra} \lambda^{ra,s} h(sz) = \sum_{s \in R_k, s < ra} \lambda_k^{ra,s} h(sz) \ .$$

Thus there is a $s \in R_k$, $s < ra$, such that $f_k(sz) \neq h(sz)$. Since $sz < raz = c = $ mincex$(f_k, h)$, this is a contradiction. ∎

The next proposition is a crucial observation. It explains the choice of the $\lambda_k^{ra,s}$ in Line E3.

**Proposition 3.** The sequence $c_k$, $k \geq 1$, is non-decreasing.

**Proof.** Let $k \geq 1$. If $c_{k+1}$ is computed in Line 10, we have $c_{k+1} > c_k$. If $c_{k+1}$ is computed in Line E5, we have $R_{k+1} = R_k \cup \{r_k a_k\}$ and we look at the two cases $z_k = \varepsilon$ and $z_k \neq \varepsilon$.

Case 1: $z_k = \varepsilon$. Since $r_k a_k = c_k = $ mincex$(f_k, f)$ and $c_{k+1} = $ mincex$(f_{k+1}, f)$, we have to show that $f_k(x) = f_{k+1}(x)$ for all $x \in \Sigma^*$, $x < r_k a_k$. We show this by induction on $x$, looking at the elements of $\Sigma^*$ in the canonical order. If $x \in R_k$, then $f_k(x) = f(x) = f_{k+1}(x)$. If $x \notin R_k$, let $(r, a, z)$ be the $R_k$-decomposition of $x$. Since $ra \leq raz = x < r_k a_k$, we know that $ra \neq r_k a_k$. Thus $(r, a, z)$ is also the $R_{k+1}$-decomposition of $x$ and we have

$$f_k(x) = f_k(raz) = \sum_{s \in R_k, s < ra} \lambda_k^{ra,s} f_k(sz)$$

$$= \sum_{s \in R_{k+1}, s < ra} \lambda_{k+1}^{ra,s} f_{k+1}(sz) = f_{k+1}(raz) = f_{k+1}(x) \ .$$

Case 2: $z_k \neq \varepsilon$. We show $f_{k+1} = f_k$. This would follow from

$$\forall i \in \mathbb{N}_0, x \in R_{k+1}, y \in \Sigma^i : \quad f_{k+1}(xy) = f_k(xy) \ .$$

We show the latter assertion by induction on $i$. For $i = 0$, the assertion follows from $f_{k+1}(x) = f(x) = f_k(x)$ for $x \in R_{k+1}$. (Note that $f_k(r_k a_k) = f(r_k a_k)$ since $r_k a_k < r_k a_k z_k = c_k = \text{mincex}(f_k, f)$.) Let $i > 0$ and assume that the assertion is true for $0, \ldots, i-1$. Let $x \in R_{k+1}$, $y \in \Sigma^i$. The induction base implies that $f_{k+1}(xy) = f_k(xy)$ if $xy \in R_{k+1}$. Otherwise, let $(r, a, z)$ be the $R_{k+1}$-decomposition of $xy$. Using $|z| < |y|$ and the induction hypothesis, we get $f_{k+1}(sz) = f_k(sz)$ for $s \in R_{k+1}$. Since $ra \notin R_{k+1}$, we know $ra \neq r_k a_k$. Thus if $r \in R_k$, then

$$f_{k+1}(xy) = f_{k+1}(raz) = \sum_{s \in R_{k+1}} \lambda_{k+1}^{ra,s} f_{k+1}(sz)$$

$$= \sum_{s \in R_k} \lambda_k^{ra,s} f_k(sz) = f_k(raz) = f_k(xy) \ .$$

If $r \notin R_k$, i.e., $r = r_k a_k$, then

$$f_{k+1}(xy) = f_{k+1}(raz) = \sum_{s \in R_{k+1}} \lambda_{k+1}^{ra,s} f_{k+1}(sz)$$

$$= \sum_{s \in R_k} \left( \sum_{t \in R_k} \lambda_k^{r_k a_k, t} \lambda_k^{ta,s} \right) f_{k+1}(sz) = \sum_{t \in R_k} \lambda_k^{r_k a_k, t} \left( \sum_{s \in R_k} \lambda_k^{ta,s} f_k(sz) \right)$$

$$= \sum_{t \in R_k} \lambda_k^{r_k a_k, t} f_k(taz) = f_k(r_k a_k az) = f_k(raz) = f_k(xy) \ .$$

■

Since all prefixtree representations $(R_k, \alpha_k, \lambda_k)$ and $(R_k, \alpha_k, \lambda)$ are canonical prefixtree representations, we know that $R(f) \subseteq R_k$ if an $\text{EQSC}(R_k, \alpha_k, \lambda_k)$ query or an $\text{EQSC}(R_k, \alpha_k, \lambda)$ query respectively returns "YES". The following proposition shows that $R_k = R(f)$ in this case, i.e., $(R_k, \alpha_k, \lambda_k)$ or $(R_k, \alpha_k, \lambda)$ respectively is the unique prefixtree representation of $f$ from Proposition 1.

**Proposition 4.** $R_k \subseteq R(f)$ for all $k$.

**Proof.** In Line I2 we know $\varepsilon \in R(f)$ since $f \neq 0$. We have to show that $r_k a_k \in R(f)$ whenever the procedure EXTEND is invoked. Suppose that there is a $k$ such that $r_k a_k \notin R(f)$ and EXTEND is invoked. Then there is a finite set $S \subseteq \Sigma^*$ with $s < r_k a_k$ for $s \in S$ and there are numbers $\lambda_s \in K$ for $s \in S$ such that

$$Z^f_{r_k a_k} = \sum_{s \in S} \lambda_s Z^f_s \ .$$

Since $(R_k, \alpha_k, \lambda_k)$ is a canonical prefixtree representation for $f_k$, there are numbers $\mu_{s,t} \in K$ for $s \in S$, $t \in R_k$, $t \leq s$, such that

$$Z^{f_k}_s = \sum_{t \in R_k, t \leq s} \mu_{s,t} Z^{f_k}_t \ , \quad s \in S \ .$$

The system in Line 6 had no solution. Thus there is an element $z$ in the list $L_{r_k a_k}$, such that

$$f(r_k a_k z) \neq \sum_{t \in R_k, t < r_k a_k} f(tz) \left( \sum_{s \in S, t \leq s} \lambda_s \mu_{s,t} \right) \ . \tag{5}$$

$z$ was added to $L_{r_k a_k}$ because of the counterexample $r_k a_k z$. From Proposition 3, we know $r_k a_k z \leq c_k$. For $s \in S$, $t \in R_k$, $t \leq s$, we have $tz \leq sz < r_k a_k z \leq c_k = \mathrm{mincex}(f_k, f)$, i.e., $f_k(tz) = f(tz)$, $f_k(sz) = f(sz)$. Hence,

$$f(r_k a_k z) = \sum_{s \in S} \lambda_s f(sz) = \sum_{s \in S} \lambda_s f_k(sz) = \sum_{s \in S, t \in R_k, t \leq s} \lambda_s \mu_{s,t} f_k(tz)$$

$$= \sum_{s \in S, t \in R_k, t \leq s} \lambda_s \mu_{s,t} f(tz) = \sum_{t \in R_k, t < r_k a_k} f(tz) \left( \sum_{s \in S, t \leq s} \lambda_s \mu_{s,t} \right) \ ,$$

which contradicts (5). ∎

By now we know that suffixes are added to at most $n|\Sigma|$ lists $L_{ra}$ with $r \in R(f)$, $a \in \Sigma$. The next proposition gives an upper bound on the number of elements in any of the lists.

**Proposition 5.** *For every $r \in \Sigma^*$, $a \in \Sigma$, the list $L_{ra}$ contains at most $n + 1$ elements.*

**Proof.** We can show inductively that

$$f(raz) = \sum_{s \in R_k, s < ra} f(sz) \lambda^{ra,s}$$

for $r \in R_k$, $a \in \Sigma$, $ra \notin R_k$ and $z$ from the list $L_{ra}$ whenever an EQSC query for some prefixtree representation $(R_k, \alpha_k, \lambda)$ is posed. The easy proof is omitted here.

Let $r \in \Sigma^*$, $a \in \Sigma$. Assume that the elements $z_1, \ldots, z_l$ were added to $L_{ra}$ in this order. For $1 \leq i \leq l$, the word $raz_i$ was returned by an $\mathrm{EQSC}(R, \alpha, \lambda)$ query. $(R, \alpha, \lambda)$ is a canonical prefixtree representation, $R \subseteq R(f)$, $(r, a, z_i)$ is the $R$-decomposition of $raz_i$, and we have

$$f(raz) = \sum_{s \in R, s < ra} f(sz)\lambda^{ra,s} \ , \quad z \in \{z_1, \ldots, z_{i-1}\} \ .$$

Let $g : \Sigma^* \to K$ be the function with prefixtree representation $(R, \alpha, \lambda)$. Since

$$f(raz_i) \neq g(raz_i) = \sum_{s \in R, s < ra} \lambda^{ra,s} g(sz_i) = \sum_{s \in R, s < ra} f(sz_i)\lambda^{ra,s} \ ,$$

in the system

$$f(raz) = \sum_{s \in R(f), s < ra} f(sz)\xi_s \ , \quad z \in \{z_1, \ldots, z_l\} \ ,$$

the equation for $z_i$ is independent of the equations for $z_1, \ldots, z_{i-1}$. Since there are at most $|R(f)| = n$ variables, there cannot be more than $n + 1$ independent equations. Thus $l \leq n + 1$. ∎

**Proposition 6.** *The learning algorithm poses at most $n(n + 1)|\Sigma| + 2$ EQSC queries.*

**Proof.** For every EQSC query, except the first and the last one, an element is added to some list $L_{ra}$ with $r \in R(f)$, $a \in \Sigma$. Together with Proposition 5, this yields the assertion. ∎

Using the last two propositions and the following lemma, we can show that the running time of Algorithm 1 is $O(n^5|\Sigma|)$.

**Lemma 1.** *For recognizable functions $f, g : \Sigma^* \to K$, $f \neq g$, there is a word $c \in \Sigma^*$ such that $f(c) \neq g(c)$ and $|c| \leq \mathrm{rk}(H^f) + \mathrm{rk}(H^g) - 1$.*

**Proof.** Let $c = c_1 \cdots c_m \in \Sigma^*$ be a shortest word such that $f(c) \neq g(c)$. Let $x_i = c_1 \cdots c_i$, $y_i = c_{i+1} \cdots c_m$ for $0 \leq i \leq m$, $d = f(c) - g(c) \neq 0$.

$$((f - g)(x_i y_j))_{0 \leq i,j \leq m} = \begin{pmatrix} d & 0 & \cdots & 0 \\ * & \ddots & \ddots & \vdots \\ \vdots & \ddots & \ddots & 0 \\ * & \cdots & * & d \end{pmatrix}$$

is a regular submatrix of $H^{f-g}$. Thus $m + 1 \leq \mathrm{rk}(H^{f-g}) \leq \mathrm{rk}(H^f) + \mathrm{rk}(H^g)$. ∎

# 5 A Lower Bound on the Number of EQSC Queries

Using a method from [5], we show that the upper bound on the number of EQSC queries from Sect. 4 cannot be improved substantially. Let

$$\mathcal{H} := \{f : \Sigma^* \to K \mid f \text{ is recognizable}\} \ .$$

For $\mathcal{F} \subseteq \mathcal{H}$ let $\mathrm{SC}(\mathcal{F})$ be the smallest number $m \in \mathbb{N}_0 \cup \{\infty\}$ such that $m$ EQSC queries are needed in the worst case to learn any function in $\mathcal{F}$. If $1 \leq \mathrm{SC}(\mathcal{F}) < \infty$, we have

$$\mathrm{SC}(\mathcal{F}) = 1 + \min_{h \in \mathcal{H}} \max_{f \in \mathcal{F}} \mathrm{SC}(\{g \in \mathcal{F} \mid \mathrm{mincex}(g, f) > \mathrm{mincex}(h, f)\}) \ . \qquad (6)$$

Because of $\mathrm{SC}(\mathcal{F}) \geq 1$, the target concept is unknown. So the learner has to pose an EQSC($h$) query (this leads to the summand 1) for some $h \in \mathcal{H}$ (so we have to take the minimum). Every $f \in \mathcal{F}$ can be the target concept (so we take the maximum). If $h \in \mathcal{H}$ is the hypothesis and $f \in \mathcal{F}$ is the target concept, the learning algorithm cannot know which of the concepts that are still conceivable after receiving the counterexample $\mathrm{mincex}(h, f)$ is the target concept. The "version space" of still conceivable concepts consists of all functions $g$ satisfying $\mathrm{mincex}(g, f) > \mathrm{mincex}(h, f)$.

With this equation and the SC-dimension, that we introduce now, we will prove the lower bound. The SC-dimension is comparable to the VC-dimension, see [10]. We call a finite set $S \subseteq \Sigma^*$ *SC-shattered* for $\mathcal{F}$ if there is a subset $\mathcal{G} \subseteq \mathcal{F}$ such that

$$\{g|_S \mid g \in \mathcal{G}\} = \{g : S \to \{0, 1\}\}$$

and such that the elements of $\mathcal{G}$ all yield the same value on all $x \in \Sigma^* \setminus S$, $x < \max(S)$. The *SC-dimension* of $\mathcal{F}$ is

$$\mathrm{SCdim}(\mathcal{F}) := \sup\{|S| \mid S \subseteq \Sigma^* \text{ is SC-shattered for } \mathcal{F}\} \ .$$

**Proposition 7.** *For every set $\mathcal{F} \subseteq \mathcal{H}$, $\mathrm{SC}(\mathcal{F}) \geq \mathrm{SCdim}(\mathcal{F})$.*

**Proof.** We show inductively:

$$\forall d \in \mathbb{N}_0, \mathcal{F} \subseteq \mathcal{H} : \quad \mathrm{SCdim}(\mathcal{F}) \geq d \ \Rightarrow \ \mathrm{SC}(\mathcal{F}) \geq d \ . \qquad (7)$$

This is evident for $d = 0$. Let $d > 0$ and assume that (7) is true for $d - 1$. There is a SC-shattered set $S = \{s_1, \ldots, s_d\}$ for $\mathcal{F}$ with $s_1 < s_2 < \cdots < s_d$. Let $\mathcal{G}$ be a subset of $\mathcal{F}$ such that

$$\{g|_S \mid g \in \mathcal{G}\} = \{g : S \to \{0, 1\}\}$$

and such that the elements of $\mathcal{G}$ all yield the same value on all words $x \in \Sigma^* \setminus S$, $x < s_d$. For every $h \in \mathcal{H}$, there is a function $f \in \mathcal{G}$ such that $f(s_1) \neq h(s_1)$. $\tilde{S} = \{s_2, \ldots, s_d\}$ is SC-shattered for

$$\tilde{\mathcal{F}} = \{g \in \mathcal{F} \mid \mathrm{mincex}(h, f) < \mathrm{mincex}(g, f)\} \ .$$

(This can be shown using the set $\tilde{\mathcal{G}} = \{g \in \mathcal{G} \mid g(s_1) = f(s_1)\}$; because of $\mathrm{mincex}(h, f) \leq s_1 < s_2 \leq \mathrm{mincex}(g, f)$ for $g \in \tilde{\mathcal{G}} \subseteq \mathcal{G}$, we have $\tilde{\mathcal{G}} \subseteq \tilde{\mathcal{F}}$.) Thus $\mathrm{SCdim}(\tilde{\mathcal{F}}) \geq d - 1$. Because of (7), $\mathrm{SC}(\tilde{\mathcal{F}}) \geq d - 1$. Because of (6), $\mathrm{SC}(\mathcal{F}) \geq 1 + (d - 1) = d$. ∎

**Proposition 8.** *Let* $\mathcal{F} = \{f : \Sigma^* \to K \mid \mathrm{rk}(H^f) \leq n\}$. *If* $n \geq 4$ *and* $|\Sigma| \geq 2$ *then* $\mathrm{SC}(\mathcal{F}) \geq \mathrm{SCdim}(\mathcal{F}) > \frac{1}{64}n^2|\Sigma|$.

**Proof.** There are $a, b \in \Sigma$ such that $a \neq b$. We show that

$$S = \{a, b\}^{\lfloor \log_2 n \rfloor - 2} \cdot \Sigma \cdot \{a, b\}^{\lfloor \log_2 n \rfloor - 2}$$

is SC-shattered for $\mathcal{F}$. Since

$$|S| = 2^{\lfloor \log_2 n \rfloor - 2} \cdot |\Sigma| \cdot 2^{\lfloor \log_2 n \rfloor - 2} > (2^{\log_2 n - 3})^2 |\Sigma| = \frac{1}{64}n^2|\Sigma| \ ,$$

this proves the assertion. Let $\mathcal{G} = \{f : \Sigma^* \to \{0, 1\} \mid f(x) = 0 \text{ for } x \in \Sigma^* \setminus S\}$. We show $\mathcal{G} \subseteq \mathcal{F}$. A function $f \in \mathcal{G}$ is non-zero only for words of length $2\lfloor \log_2 n \rfloor - 3$. Thus

$$\mathrm{rk}(H^f) = \sum_{k=0}^{\lfloor \log_2 n \rfloor - 2} \left( \mathrm{rk}(f(xy))_{x \in \{a,b\}^k, y \in \Sigma^*} + \mathrm{rk}(f(xy))_{x \in \Sigma^*, y \in \{a,b\}^k} \right)$$

$$\leq \sum_{k=0}^{\lfloor \log_2 n \rfloor - 2} 2 \cdot 2^k < 2 \cdot 2^{\lfloor \log_2 n \rfloor - 1} \leq n \ ,$$

where $\{a, b\}^k = \{x_1 \cdots x_k \mid x_1, \ldots, x_k \in \{a, b\}\}$. ∎

This shows that in order to learn the class of recognizable functions whose Hankel matrices have rank at most $n$, more than $\frac{1}{64}n^2|\Sigma|$ EQSC queries are needed.

# 6 Acknowledgements

The author is grateful to Hans Ulrich Simon, Andreas Birkendorf and Ricki Wegner for calling his attention to this problem and for a lot of helpful suggestions.

# References

1. Angluin, D.: Learning Regular Sets from Queries and Counterexamples. Information and Computation **75** (1987) 87–106
2. Angluin, D.: Negative Results for Equivalence Queries. Machine Learning **5** (1990) 121–150
3. Beimel, A., Bergadano, F., Bshouty, N., Kushilevitz, E., Varricchio, S.: On the Applications of Multiplicity Automata in Learning. Proceedings of the 37th Annual Symposium on Foundations of Computer Science (1996) 349–358

4. Bergadano, F., Varricchio, S.: Learning Behaviors of Automata from Shortest Counterexamples. Proceedings of the 2nd European Conference on Computational Learning Theory (EUROCOLT 1995) 380–391

5. Birkendorf, A., Böker, A., Simon, H. U.: Learning Deterministic Finite Automata from Smallest Counterexamples. Proceedings of the 9th Annual ACM/SIAM Symposium on Discrete Algorithms (SODA 1998) 599–608

6. Carlyle, J. W., Paz, A.: Realization by Stochastic Finite Automata. Journal of Computer and System Sciences **5** (1971) 26–40

7. Fliess., M.: Matrices de Hankel. J. Math. Pures Appl. **53** (1974) 197–222. Erratum in vol. 54

8. Ibarra, O. H., Jiang, T.: Learning Regular Languages from Counterexamples. Journal of Computer and System Sciences **43** (1991) 299–316

9. Rivest, R. L., Shapire, R. E.: Inference on Finite Automata Using Homing Sequences. Information and Computation **103** (1993) 299–347

10. Vapnik, V. N., Chervonenkis, A. Y.: On the Uniform Convergence of Relative Frequencies of Events to their Probabilities. Theor. Probability and Appl. **16** (1971) 264–280

# Exact Learning when Irrelevant Variables Abound

David Guijarro[1]*, Víctor Lavín[1]**, and Vijay Raghavan[2]***

[1] Department LSI, Universitat Politècnica de Catalunya, Jordi Girona Salgado, 1-3, Barcelona 08034, Spain, {david,vlavin}@lsi.upc.es
[2] Box 1679-B, Computer Science Department, Vanderbilt University, Nashville, TN 37235, raghavan@vuse.vanderbilt.edu

**Abstract.** We prove the following results. Any Boolean function of $O(\log n)$ relevant variables can be exactly learned with a set of non-adaptive membership queries alone and a *minimum* sized decision tree representation of the function constructed, in polynomial time. In contrast, such a function cannot be exactly learned with equivalence queries alone using general decision trees and other representation classes as hypotheses.

Our results imply others which may be of independent interest. We show that truth-table minimization of decision trees can be done in polynomial time, complementing the well-known result of Masek that truth-table minimization of DNF formulas is NP-hard. The proofs of our negative results show that general decision trees and related representations are not learnable in polynomial time using equivalence queries alone, confirming a folklore theorem.

## 1  Introduction

Exact learning using queries is a well-studied model in computational learning. Of the many kinds of queries considered by Angluin [1], membership and equivalence queries have established themselves as the standard combination to be used for exact learning.

Some results that characterize learnability with a polynomial number of polynomially sized queries are known. For example, Angluin [2] showed that the presence of the *approximate fingerprint* property for a concept class is a sufficient condition for non-learnability with equivalence queries alone. Using this characterization, Angluin showed that equivalence queries do not suffice for learning deterministic or nondeterministic finite automata, context-free grammars, or general CNF or DNF formulas. Later on, Gavaldà [11] proved this property to be

* Supported by the Esprit EU BRA program under project 20244 (ALCOM-IT) and the EC Working Group NeuroCOLT2 - EP27150.
** Supported by the Esprit EU BRA program under project 20244 (ALCOM-IT) and the EC Working Group NeuroCOLT2 - EP27150.
*** This work was supported by NSF grant CCR-9510392.

not only sufficient but also a necessary condition. On the other hand, Goldman and Kearns [13] showed that if a concept class is learnable with a polynomial number of membership queries alone, then it has *polynomial teaching dimension*. Moreover, the converse holds provided the concept class is projection closed, as shown by Hellerstein et al. [15]. Finally, it is known [15] that a concept class is learnable with a polynomial number of equivalence and membership queries if and only if that class has *polynomial certificates*.

Decision trees are a popular representation of Boolean functions, which form the basic inference engine used in many machine learning programs. The learnability of decision trees has been well-studied in the learning theory community. For example, it is known [14] that $\mu$-decision trees are exactly learnable with equivalence and membership queries, but neither type of query alone suffices for polynomial learning. Bshouty [5] has shown that general decision trees are learnable with extended equivalence queries (the hypotheses used are depth-three formulas) and membership queries. It is not known whether general decision trees are learnable with proper equivalence queries and membership queries, nor is it known whether decision trees are properly PAC-learnable with or without membership queries.

In this paper, we focus on concepts that depend on very few variables. Since Littlestone's seminal work [17] on this topic, such concept classes have been well studied in learning theory [4, 7, 10]. Recently, Damaschke [8, 9] studied exact learning of Boolean functions when irrelevant attributes abound, primarily in the model of learning with membership queries alone. He was able to show that a set $X$ of *non-adaptive* membership queries can be constructed in time polynomial in $n$, the number of variables, so that $X$ suffices to exactly learn every Boolean function of $O(\log n)$ variables in polynomial time. Moreover, a truthtable representing the learned Boolean function can be constructed in polynomial time as well. Here, we offer a simple alternative proof of this result and show in addition that a decision tree of *minimum* size to represent the learned function can also be constructed in polynomial time. In contrast, we show that such functions cannot be learned with equivalence queries alone using as hypotheses decision trees or other popular representation classes. Our result implies a folk theorem that general decision trees cannot be properly learned with equivalence queries alone.

Our positive result shows that truth-table minimization of decision trees can be done in polynomial time. This may be contrasted with the well-known result of Masek cited in Garey and Johnson's book [12] that truth-table minimization of DNF formulas is NP-hard.

The rest of the paper is organized as follows. Section 2 has definitions used in the rest of the paper. Section 3 has our positive results on exact learning with non-adaptive membership queries when irrelevant variables abound and Section 4 has the negative results for exact learning such concepts with equivalence queries.

## 2 Preliminaries

We use standard terminology in learning theory. See [2] for more detailed descriptions of the learning model and a formalization of *concept classes, representation classes, examples*, etc.

We consider learning algorithms that make equivalence queries or membership queries to a teacher. The teacher answers the equivalence queries according to a target concept $c \in \mathcal{C}$. More precisely, an *equivalence query* is a representation $r \in \mathcal{R}$ of some concept in $\mathcal{C}$, and the answer is either YES, if the concept represented by $r$ is equivalent to $c$, or a counterexample in the symmetric difference of $c$ and the concept represented by $r$, otherwise. A *membership query* is an example and the answer is either YES or NO, depending how the target concept classifies that example.

We are interested in Boolean concepts or, in other words, Boolean functions defined over a finite set of Boolean variables $\{x_1, \ldots, x_n\}$. The classes of representations we consider here are the following:

1. *DT (Decision Trees).* A decision tree $d$ is a binary tree where the leaves are labeled either 0 or 1, and each internal node is labeled with a variable. Given an *assignment* $\alpha \in \{0,1\}^n$, $d(\alpha)$ is evaluated by starting at the root and iteratively applying the following rule, until a leaf is reached: let the variable at the current node be $x_i$; if the value of $\alpha$ at position $i$ is 1 then branch right; otherwise branch left. If the leaf reached is labeled 0 (resp. 1) then $d(\alpha) = FALSE$ (resp. $TRUE$). The size of a decision tree is its number of nodes. The decision-tree size ($DT$-size) of a Boolean function $f$ is the size of the smallest decision tree that can represent $f$.

2. *CDNF.* A CDNF formula is a pair $(f, g)$, where $f$ is a DNF formula and $g$ is a CNF formula and $f \equiv g$. It is convenient to define the size of such a formula as $\max\{n, m, p\}$, where $n$ is the number of variables over which the formulas $f$ and $g$ are defined, $m$ is the number of terms in $f$, and $q$ is the number of clauses in $g$. The CDNF-size of a Boolean function is the size of the smallest CDNF formula that can represent it.

   Equivalent but slightly different definitions of CDNF formulas and their sizes can be found in [5] and [15]. In [5], it is shown that CDNF formulas can be exactly learned in polynomial time with extended equivalence queries (of depth-3 formulas) and membership queries. In [15], it is shown that CDNF formulas are polynomial-query learnable with proper equivalence queries and membership queries. Here, we show that this latter result is tight: we show that proper equivalence queries alone do not suffice for polynomial-query learnability.

3. *Self-Dual DNF (Self-Dual CNF).* A DNF (CNF) formula $f$ is self-dual if $f(\alpha) \neq f(\bar{\alpha})$ for all $\alpha \in \{0,1\}^n$, where $\bar{\alpha}$ is the bitwise complement of $\alpha$. We direct the reader to [3] for work on the self-dual formulas.

4. $\log n$-*DNF* $\cap$ $\log n$-*CNF.* This class contains the functions representable both as DNF formulas whose terms have at most $\log n$ literals, and CNF formulas whose clauses have at most $\log n$ literals. For our purposes, we

consider a representation in this class to be a pair $(f, g)$, where $f$ is a $\log n$-DNF formula and $g$ is a $\log n$-CNF formula. The size of such a pair is the same as its CDNF size.

There are several results in learning theory about this interesting class. Notice that this class contains the class of $\log n$-depth decision trees, shown to be exactly learnable in polynomial time [16] with membership queries. (The output of the learning algorithm is not a $\log n$-depth decision tree but a representation based on Fourier coefficients.) In [6], it was shown that $\log n$-DNF $\cap$ $\log n$-CNF is learnable with membership queries and an NP-oracle, in a representation of depth-3 Boolean formulas. Finally, in [15] it was shown that this class is properly learnable with membership queries and an oracle for NP $\cap$ co-NP. It is open whether this class is properly learnable with membership queries alone in polynomial time. Here we show that the class is not polynomial-query learnable with equivalence queries alone.

5. *BP (Branching programs).* A branching program is a directed, acyclic graph, with a unique node of in-degree 0 (called the *root*), and two nodes of out-degree 0 (called *leaves*) , one labeled 0, and the other labeled 1; each non-leaf node of the graph contains a variable, and has outdegree exactly two. Assignments are evaluated following the same rule as for decision trees.

A branching program is in the class $\log n$-*depth BP* if its longest pat h has length at most $\log n$. The size of a branching program is the number of nodes in it.

General branching programs are known to be not learnable with equivalence and membership queries. (See [19] for a detailed study of subclasses of branching programs according to learnability.) In [15], it is shown that the subclass of $\log n$-depth branching programs is properly learnable with membership queries and an oracle for NP $\cap$ co-NP—it is open whether the oracle can be dispensed with. Here we show that the class is not polynomial-query learnable with equivalence queries alone.

## 3 Learning with Non-Adaptive Membership Queries

Let $\mathcal{F}_{n,r}$ denote the set of Boolean functions over $n$ variables which depend on at most $r$ variables. The following is a restatement of a result of Damaschke [8, 9].

**Theorem 1.** *There exists a set of assignments, $X$, of size at most a polynomial in $2^r$ and $\log n$ such that a truth-table for any function $f \in \mathcal{F}_{n,r}$ can be learned solely by making membership queries on the set $X$. Moreover, the set $X$ and the truth-table can be constructed in time polynomial in $2^r$ and $n$.*

We independently arrived at a proof of the above theorem; however, Damaschke's result has sharper bounds for the construction of $X$ and the time to do the inference of the truth-table than our proof provides. For the sake of completeness, we outline our simple proof of the above theorem.

Use the deterministic construction in [18] to obtain a $(n, r)$-universal set $B$ of size $2^{O(r)} \log n$ in time polynomial in $2^r$ and $n$. Let $B'$ be the set of all assignments at Hamming distance 1 from an assignment in $B$; thus $|B'| \leq n \cdot |B|$. Let $X = B \cup B'$. Now, to learn any function $f \in \mathcal{F}_{n,r}$, make membership queries on all the assignments in $X$. Clearly, if we get a different answer for two assignments which differ only in variable $v$, then $v$ must be in the set $R$ of relevant variables of $f$. Conversely, the facts that $B$ is a $(n, r)$-universal set and that $|R| \leq r$ guarantee us that if a variable $v$ is in $R$ then there are two assignments in $X$ which differ only in variable $v$ for which we will get different answers to membership queries. Thus we can find the set $R$ in the claimed time. Once $R$ is found, we can construct a truth table of $2^{|R|}$ entries by searching in $X$ for every projection over the variables in $R$ and logging the answer to the membership query.

Next, we prove the following theorem to conclude that a decision tree of minimum size can be output for the learned function $f \in \mathcal{F}_{n,r}$ in time polynomial in $2^r$.

**Theorem 2.** *A decision tree of minimum size representing a function $f$ can be constructed in polynomial time given a complete truth-table of $f$.*

**Proof:** Let $V$ be the set of $r$ variables over which $f$ is defined and let $\Gamma$ be a truth-table of $f$ of $2^r$ entries.

We construct a table $P$ of size $3^r$, indexed by partial assignments on the $r$ variables. In position $\alpha$ of this array we shall place a decision tree of minimum size which computes the function $f_\alpha$ obtained by projecting $f$ to the partial assignment $\alpha$. That is,

$$P[\alpha] = \text{ a minimum size DT for } f_\alpha$$

Note that once $P$ is computed then a minimum size decision tree for $f$ is obtained by reading off the entry $P[\lambda]$, where $\lambda$ is the empty partial assignment.

For any tree $T$, let $|T|$ denote the size of $T$ and for any Boolean function $g$, let $|g|$ denote the decision tree size of $g$. For any partial assignment $\alpha$ and for any variable $v$ not assigned a value in $\alpha$, let $\alpha \cup \{v \leftarrow b\}$ denote the partial assignment by extending $\alpha$ by assigning the value $b \in \{0, 1\}$ to $v$. Now, $P$ may be constructed by using a dynamic programming approach after observing these facts:

1. For each (complete) assignment $\alpha$ over all $r$ variables, the minimum size decision tree for $f_\alpha$ is just a constant 0 or 1 node obtained by looking up the value of $f(\alpha)$ in the truth-table $\Gamma$.
2. For every partial assignment $\alpha$ over some set $X \subset V$ of fewer than $r$ variables, if there exists a variable $v \in V - X$ such that $f_{\alpha \cup \{v \leftarrow 0\}} \equiv f_{\alpha \cup \{v \leftarrow 1\}}$, then $f_\alpha \equiv f_{\alpha \cup \{v \leftarrow 0\}}$. Consequently, the entry $P[\alpha]$ may be filled by copying the entry for $P[\alpha \cup \{v \leftarrow 0\}]$.
3. For every partial assignment $\alpha$ over some set $X \subset V$ of fewer than $r$ variables, if there exists no variable $v \in V - X$ such that $f_{\alpha \cup \{v \leftarrow 0\}} \equiv f_{\alpha \cup \{v \leftarrow 1\}}$, then

$$|f_\alpha| = \min_{v \in V - X} \{1 + |f_{\alpha \cup \{v \leftarrow 0\}}| + |f_{\alpha \cup \{v \leftarrow 1\}}|\}.$$

Consequently, the entry $P[\alpha]$ may be found by first finding a variable $v$ for which the minimum of the above equation is achieved and then constructing a tree with $v$ as the root node and $P[\alpha \cup \{v \leftarrow 0\}]$ $P[\alpha \cup \{v \leftarrow 1\}]$ as the left and right children respectively of $v$.

Clearly, the dynamic programming approach to filling the entries of $P$ can be accomplished in time polynomial in $2^r$. ∎

An immediate corollary of the above theorems is that Boolean functions of $O(\log n)$ relevant variables can be exactly learned using non-adaptive membership queries and a decision tree of minimum size for the learned function output in time polynomial in $n$.

f $D$

# 4   Learning with Equivalence Queries

## 4.1   Approximate Fingerprints

We recall the following definitions from [2, 11]. Let $\mathcal{C}$ denote a class of concepts defined over an instance space of $\Sigma^*$ (where $\Sigma$ is a finite alphabet), $\mathcal{R}$ a representation class for $\mathcal{C}$, $w$ a string from $\Sigma^*$, $b$ an element of $\{0, 1\}$, and $\alpha > 0$ a real number. We say that the pair $\langle w, b \rangle$ is an $\alpha$-approximate fingerprint with respect to $C$ if

$$|\{c \in \mathcal{C} : \chi_c(w) = b\}| < \alpha|\mathcal{C}|.$$

That is, the number of concepts in $\mathcal{C}$ that agree with the classification $b$ of $w$ is strictly less than the fraction $\alpha$ of the total number of concepts in $\mathcal{C}$.

A sequence of concept classes is a sequence $C_1, C_2, C_3, \ldots$ such that each $C_i$ is a class of concepts. Such a sequence is polynomially bounded (with respect to a given representation $\mathcal{R}$) if there exists a polynomial $p(n)$ such that for all $c \in C_n$, there is a representation $r \in \mathcal{R}$ such that $c(r) = c$ and $|r| \leq p(n)$.

A representation of concepts $\mathcal{R}$ is said to have the approximate fingerprint property if there exists a polynomially bounded sequence of concept classes $T_1, T_2, T_3, \ldots$, and a polynomial $p(n)$ such that for any polynomial $q(n)$, for infinitely many $n$, $T_n$ contains at least two concepts and if $r \in \mathcal{R}$ and $|r| \leq q(n)$ then there exists a string $w \in \Sigma^*$ of length at most $p(n)$ such that $\langle w, \chi_{c(r)}(w) \rangle$ is a $1/q(n)$-approximate fingerprint with respect to $T_n$. That is,

$$|\{c \in T_n : \chi_c(w) = \chi_{c(r)}(w)\}| < |T_n|/q(n),$$

where $c(r)$ is the concept associated to $r$.

Since we are dealing with Boolean concepts defined over $n$ variables, the polynomial $p(n)$ that bounds the length of the words, can be set to $n$. The notion of approximate fingerprints was introduced as a means of proving non-learnability of certain classes in the equivalence query model using the following theorem.

**Theorem 3.** [2]
*Let $\mathcal{R}$ be a representation class of concepts with the approximate fingerprint property. Then there is no algorithm for exact identification of $\mathcal{R}$ using polynomially many equivalence queries of polynomial size.*

## 4.2 The Negative Results

We now show that none of the classes considered here can be exactly learned with equivalence queries alone, even when the number of relevant variables is $O(\log n)$. Since we do not restrict the hypothesis space of equivalence queries to only hypotheses of $O(\log n)$ relevant variables, our results imply that the general classes (with potentially more relevant variables) are also not learnable with equivalence queries alone. Indeed, this is how the results are stated and proved below.

Our results for all the classes considered here use the same central idea. We first illustrate the technique for the class DT of decision trees.

In order to prove approximate fingerprints for DT, we need the following lemma.

**Lemma 1.** *Let $k > 0$ be some fixed constant. If $d$ is a decision tree of size at most $n^k$, over $n$ variables, then there exists an assignment $\alpha$ such that either*

*(a) $\alpha$ contains at most $k \log n$ 1's and $d(\alpha) = 1$, or*
*(b) $\alpha$ contains at most $k \log n$ 0's and $d(\alpha) = 0$.*

**Proof**: Since each of the $2^n$ assignments reaches some leaf of $d$ after being evaluated, and $d$ has at most $n^k$ leaves, $d$ must have a path $p$ of length at most $\log(n^k) = k \log n$. The assignment $\alpha$ can be constructed by satisfying $p$ first and then filling the rest of the positions with 1's or 0's as necessary.

**Theorem 4.** *The class DT has approximate fingerprints.*

**Proof**: Let $T_n$ be the target class of functions that represent the majority of $\log n$ variables chosen out of $n$ variables. Clearly, $|T_n| = \binom{n}{\log n}$.
Clearly, the $DT$-size of each function in $T_n$ is at most $n$. Therefore, it suffices to show that for any fixed constant $k$, and for infinitely many $n$, and any $DT$ $d$ of size at most $n^k$, the assignment $\alpha$ whose existence is guaranteed by Lemma 1 satisfies the property that fewer than $|T_n| n^{-k}$ of the functions in $T_n$ classify $\alpha$ the same way as $d$.

Without loss of generality, assume that $\log n$ is an even integer. (This avoids floors and ceilings.) The number of functions in $T_n$ that accept (reject) an assignment with $k \log n$ 1's (respectively, 0's) is

$$\sum_{p=\frac{\log n}{2}}^{\log n} \binom{k \log n}{p} \binom{n - k \log n}{\log n - p}.$$

Using $n^k$ as an upper bound for $\binom{k\log n}{p}$ this sum turns out to be less than

$$n^k \sum_{p=0}^{\frac{\log n}{2}} \binom{n - k\log n}{p},$$

which is less than

$$n^k(1 + \frac{\log n}{2})\binom{n - k\log n}{\frac{\log n}{2}} = r(n).$$

Now $\frac{r(n)}{|T_n|}$ can be shown to be less than

$$\frac{n^k(1 + \frac{\log n}{2})(\log n)^{\frac{\log n}{2}}}{(n - \log n + 1)^{\frac{\log n}{2}}},$$

which is less than $n^{-k}$ for $n > 2^{ck}$, where $c$ is some constant.  ∎

We now show that the remaining classes considered here have approximate fingerprints.

**Corollary 1.** *The following classes have approximate fingerprints:*

1. *CDNF Formulas*
2. *Self-Dual DNF Formulas and Self-Dual CNF Formulas*
3. *$\log n$–DNF $\cap$ $\log n$–CNF*
4. *$\log n$–depth BP*

**Proof:** The proof follows easily if we first use the following propositions for each of the above classes instead of Lemma 1.

Let $k > 0$ be some fixed constant.

- *For every CDNF formula $h = (f, g)$ over $n$ variables, of size at most $n^k$, there exists an assignment $\alpha$ that either (a) contains at most $k\log(2n)$ 1's and $h(\alpha) = 1$, or (b) contains at most $k\log(2n)$ 0's and $h(\alpha) = 0$.*
  To see this, note that the DNF formula $f + \bar{g}$ has at most $2 \cdot n^k$ terms and is identically true, i.e., it accepts all $2^n$ assignments. Consequently, such a formula must have a term $t$ that accepts at least $\frac{2^n}{2 \cdot n^k}$ assignments, whence the length of $t$ is at most $k\log(2n)$. The assignment $\alpha$ can now be constructed by satisfying the literals in $t$ and then padding the remaining variables with 0's or 1's according to whether $t$ is a term in $f$ or corresponds to a clause in $g$ respectively.
- *For every self-dual DNF formula $f$ of at most $n^k$ terms over $n$ variables, there exists an assignment $\alpha$ that either (a) contains at most $k\log(2n)$ 1's and $f(\alpha) = 1$, or (b) contains at most $k\log(2n)$ 0's and $f(\alpha) = 0$.*
  Let $\sim f$ denote the DNF formula obtained from $f$ by complementing every literal in every term of $f$. Then, by the definition of self-dual formulas, it follows that $\sim f \equiv \bar{f}$. Therefore, $f + \sim f$ is identically true and the existence of $\alpha$ is proved in an identical manner to that of CDNF formula $h$ above. Note that an analogous statement holds for self-dual CNF formulas.

- *For every $\log n$–DNF $\cap$ $\log n$–CNF formula $f$ of size at most $n^k$, there exists an assignment $\alpha$ that either (a) contains at most $\log(n)$ 1's and $f(\alpha) = 1$, or (b) contains at most $\log(n)$ 0's and $f(\alpha) = 0$.*
  This is obvious.
- *For every $\log n$-depth BP $h$ of size at most $n^k$ over $n$ variables, there exists an assignment $\alpha$ that either (a) contains at most $k \log(n)$ 1's and $h(\alpha) = 1$, or (b) contains at most $k \log(n)$ 0's and $h(\alpha) = 0$.*
  This follows along the same lines as the proof of Lemma 1.

With this change, the proof of Theorem 4 can be used with very slight modifications to show that all of these classes have approximate fingerprints. In particular, the target class $T_n$ remains the same for all the classes, and each function in $T_n$ has a representation of size at most $n$ in each of these classes. ∎
A final note. Since the target class defined in Theorem 4 is monotone, the monotone versions of all the classes mentioned above (including DT) also have approximate fingerprints, and are therefore not learnable with equivalence queries alone.

## 5 Acknowledgments

We thank O. Watanabe, T. Tsukiji and C. Domingo for communicating the problem of exact learning Boolean functions of few relevant variables with membership queries. We also thank L. Hellerstein for pointing us to the work of Peter Damaschke.

## References

1. D. Angluin. Queries and Concept Learning. *Machine Learning*, 2, (1988), 319-342.
2. D. Angluin. Negative Results for Equivalence Queries. *Machine Learning*, 5, (1990), 121-150.
3. J. C. Bioch and T. Ibaraki. Complexity of Identification and Dualization of Positive Boolean Functions. *Information and Computation*, 123:50–63, 1995.
4. A. Blum, L. Hellerstein, N. Littlestone. Learning in the Presence of Finitely or Infinitely Many Attributes. *Journal of Computer and System Science*, pages 50:32–40, 1995.
5. N. Bshouty. Exact Learning Boolean Functions via the Monotone Theory. *Information and Computation*, 123(1):146–153, Nov 1995.
6. N. Bshouty, R. Cleve, S. Kannan, and C. Tamon. Oracles and Queries that are Sufficient for Exact Learning. *Proceedings of the Seventh Annual ACM Conference on Computational Learning Theory*, pages 130–139, 1994.
7. N.H. Bshouty, L. Hellerstein. Attribute-efficient Learning in Query and Mistake Bound Models. *Proceedings of the Ninth Conference on Computational Learning Theory*, pages 235–243, 1996.
8. P. Damaschke. Adaptive versus Non-Adaptive Attribute-Efficient Learning. *Proceedings of the 35th ACM Symposium on Theory of Computing*, pages 590–596, 1998.

9. P. Damaschke. Computational Aspects of Parallel Attribute-Efficient Learning. *To appear in: Proceedings of the 9th International Workshop on Al gorithmic Learning Theory*, 1998.

10. A. Dhagat, L. Hellerstein. PAC Learning with Irrelevant Attributes. *Proceedings of the 35th IEEE Foundations of Computer Science*, pages 64–75, 1994.

11. R. Gavaldà. On the Power of Equivalence Queries. *Proceedings of the 2nd European Conference on Computa tional Learning Theory*, (1993), 193-203.

12. M.R. Garey and D.S. Johnson. Computers and Intractability: A Guide to the Theory of NP-Completeness . W.H. Freeman and Company, New York, 1979.

13. S. Goldman, M. Kearns. On the Complexity of Teaching. *Proceedings of the 4rd Workshop on Computational Learn ing Theory*, (1991), 303-314.

14. T. Hancock. Identifying $\mu$-Formula Decision Trees with Queries. *Proceedings of the Third Annual Workshop on Computational Learning Theory*, pages 23–37, 1990.

15. L. Hellerstein, K. Pillaipakkamnatt, V. Raghavan, D. Wilkins. How Many Queries are Needed to Learn? *Proceedings of the 27th ACM Symposium on the Theory of Computing*, (1995), 190-199.

16. E. Kushilevitz and Y. Mansour. Learning Decision Trees Using the Fourier Spectrum. *SIAM Journal of Computing*, 22(6):1331–1348, 1993.

17. N. Littlestone. Learning Quickly When Irrelevant Variables Abound. *Machine Learning*, 2:285–318, 1988.

18. J. Naor and M. Naor. Small-bias probability spaces: Efficient constructions and applications. *Proceedings of the 22nd ACM Symposium on the Theory of Computing*, (1990), 312-323.

19. D. Wilkins. Learning Restricted-Read Branching Programs with Queries. *Ph.D. Thesis*, Vanderbilt University, 1995.

# An Application of Codes to Attribute–Efficient Learning

Thomas Hofmeister

Informatik 2, Universität Dortmund, D–44221 Dortmund, Germany
`hofmeist@Ls2.cs.uni--dortmund.de`

**Abstract.** We design asymptotically optimal query strategies for the class of parity functions which contain at most $k$ essential variables. The number of questions asked is at most twice the number asked by an optimal strategy. The strategy presented is even non–adaptive. For fixed $k$, the number of questions is optimal up to additive constants. Our results improve upon results by Uehara, Tsuchida and Wegener [6].

## 1 Introduction

One part of algorithmic learning theory is concerned with the problem of identifying an object from a set of objects by querying a teacher. Usually, the main aim is to keep the number of questions as small as possible. Two other possible cost measures are given by the time that it takes the learner to decide which questions to ask and the time needed to deduce from the answers the object, but this aspect is sometimes neglected.

In this paper, we consider a problem which is known in learning theory under the name "attribute–efficient learning with $k$ essential attributes". A more precise definition will be given shortly. We will show that parity–check matrices can be used to obtain so–called non–adaptive and adaptive strategies for learning parity functions.

The previously best known results for the class considered are by Uehara, Tsuchida and Wegener [6]. We give a different approach to designing query strategies and extend the positive results from adaptive to non–adaptive learning strategies.

A recent paper by Damaschke [2] is concerned with the learning of arbitrary function classes and it gives a good survey of the known results. In that paper, well–known combinatorial structures are exploited, like "$r$–universal sets", and a new structure is designed which is given the name "$r$–wise bipartite connected families". Since those structures are designed to cope with arbitrary classes, it should not be a surprise that for special classes, other combinatorial objects will be more efficient.

Let us now give a formal introduction to the considered problem. Let $\mathcal{B}_n$ be the class of all Boolean functions on $n$ variables.

A subset $\mathcal{F}$ of $\mathcal{B}_n$ is considered to be a concept class. During the learning process, we want to find out which function $f \in \mathcal{F}$ has been chosen by a teacher (or an adversary). Our task is to identify the function chosen by the teacher by asking questions, more precisely, our query consists in presenting an input $a \in \{0,1\}^n$. The teacher answers with the value $f(a)$. There are two possible models which can be considered, namely, the adaptive and the non–adaptive model. In the non–adaptive model, the learner has to make all queries at once, i.e., the queries are not allowed to depend on previous answers of the teacher. In the adaptive model, the teacher gives his answer after each query, and the learner is allowed to let his queries depend on all previously given answers.

Given a concept class $\mathcal{F}$, the cost of a (deterministic) query strategy is the maximum number of questions asked, given any function $f \in \mathcal{F}$, before the learner has identified $f$. Since the answers of the teacher are $\{0,1\}$–valued, a standard information theoretic argument shows that $\lceil \log |\mathcal{F}| \rceil$ is a lower bound for the number of questions asked. It is also clear that we can identify any chosen function by asking at most $2^n$ questions. Our goal is to determine the number of questions which is necessary and sufficient.

## 2  Basic Definitions

Here, we review some of the basic notions and properties known in coding theory which we will apply later on. The interested reader may consult the books by Lidl and Niederreiter [4], by Hoffman et al. [3] and by Peterson and Weldon [5] for further details.

In general, codes are defined over finite fields $\mathbb{F}$, but since we are dealing with the field $\mathbb{Z}_2 = \{0,1\}$ only, we adapt the definitions to this special case.

For two 0–1–vectors $v = (v_1, \ldots, v_n)$ and $w = (w_1, \ldots, w_n)$, let $d(v, w)$ denote the Hamming distance between the two, i.e., $d(v, w) = |\{ i \mid v_i \neq w_i \}|$.

**Definition 1.** *Given a subset $C \subseteq \{0,1\}^n$ with $|C| \geq 2$, we define the minimum Hamming distance $d(C)$ as follows:*

$$d(C) = \min\{ d(c_1, c_2) \mid c_1 \neq c_2 \in C \}.$$

In our considerations, linear codes will prove to be useful.

**Definition 2.** *Let $H$ be an $(n-k) \times n$–matrix of rank $n-k$ and with entries from $\{0,1\}$. The set*
$$C := \{ \underline{c} \in \{0,1\}^n \mid H \cdot \underline{c} = \underline{0} \}$$
*is called a linear $(n,k)$–code. The matrix $H$ is referred to as the parity–check matrix of the code $C$.*

(Note that here and in the sequel, we do the matrix–vector multiplications over the field $\mathbb{Z}_2$.)

If the code $C$ which corresponds to a parity–check matrix $H$ has Hamming distance $d$, then we will say that $H$ has code distance $d$.

The following equivalence is well–known (see e.g. Lemma 8.14 in the book by Lidl and Niederreiter [4]):

**Proposition 1.** *A parity–check matrix $H$ has code distance $s+1$ if and only if any $s$ columns of $H$ are linearly independent over the field $\mathbb{Z}_2$.*

There exists a large amount of constructions of linear codes with certain distances. One of the few which makes a general statement is the so–called Gilbert–Varshamov bound. It states the following (see e.g. [4], Theorem 8.27):

**Theorem 1. Gilbert–Varshamov bound:** *There exists a linear $(n, k)$–code with minimum distance at least $d$ whenever*

$$2^{n-k} > \sum_{i=0}^{d-2} \binom{n-1}{i}.$$

## 3 Learning Parity Functions with $k$ Essential Variables

We consider the following two concept classes.

**Definition 3.** $PAR(k, n) \subseteq \mathcal{B}_n$ *is the set of all parity functions which depend on exactly $k$ variables. $PAR_{\leq}(k, n)$ is the set of all parity functions which depend on at most $k$ variables. I.e.,*

$$PAR(k, n) = \{f_S \mid f_S = \bigoplus_{i \in S} x_i, S \subseteq \{1, \ldots, n\}, |S| = k\},$$

$$PAR_{\leq}(k, n) = \{f_S \mid f_S = \bigoplus_{i \in S} x_i, S \subseteq \{1, \ldots, n\}, |S| \leq k\}.$$

The variables that a function depends on are often called "essential" variables. It should be clear that any query strategy for learning $PAR_{\leq}(k, n)$ can be used as a query strategy for $PAR(k, n)$, since the latter class is a subset of the former. The class $PAR(k, n)$ contains exactly $\binom{n}{k}$ Boolean functions, and thus a lower bound of $\lceil \log \binom{n}{k} \rceil$ queries holds. Both classes can be learned with at most $n$ queries, since the learner may ask the $n$ queries $e_1, \ldots, e_n$, where $e_i$ is the input having a 1 in the $i$–th component and a 0 everywhere else. Due to symmetry, the complexity of learning $PAR(k, n)$ is the same as the complexity of learning $PAR(n-k, n)$. For $k > n/2$, the class $PAR_{\leq}(k, n)$ contains more than $2^{n-1}$ functions, and thus $n$ queries are sufficient and necessary. We can restrict to $k \leq \lfloor n/2 \rfloor$ in the following.

By using binary search, the class $PAR(1, n)$ can obviously be learned with $\lceil \log n \rceil$ queries, which is optimal. We are interested in the query complexity for larger $k$.

Assume that the teacher is keeping secret a parity function $f_S$ which the learner wants to determine. It will be more convenient to view a query $a \in \{0, 1\}^n$ as the set $A = \{i \mid 1 \leq i \leq n, a_i = 1\}$. A basic strategy applied in [6] is to determine the elements $s \in S$ one by one. Let us make this more precise:

If the learner chooses some $a$ (resp. some set $A$) and asks for the value of $f_S(a)$, then the answer determines whether $S \cap A$ contains an even or an odd number of ones. This suggests the following "binary search procedure":

Given a subset $A$ such that $|S \cap A|$ is odd, i.e., $f_S(a) = 1$, we can identify one $s \in S$ with at most $\lceil \log |A| \rceil \leq \lceil \log n \rceil$ queries. Namely, we partition $A = A_1 \cup A_2$ such that $0 \leq |A_1| - |A_2| \leq 1$. One of those two sets must contain an odd number of elements from $S$, hence by asking one query we obtain a smaller set which contains an odd number of elements from $S$. By repeating this procedure, we obtain a set $A^*$ of cardinality 1, i.e., $A^* = \{s\}$ such that $|S \cap A^*|$ is odd, i.e., $s \in S$. This takes at most $\lceil \log n \rceil$ queries.

If $k$ is odd and if we are to learn $PAR(k, n)$ then we can start the binary search procedure with $A = \{1, \ldots, n\}$. But how do we start the procedure if $k$ is even? So far, we have described the same approach as in [6]. There, different solutions are proposed in order to obtain an $a$ such that $f_S(a) = 1$. We first show that coding theory offers alternative solutions to this problem. Because of the binary search phase, the approach from [6] only yields adaptive learning strategies. We show how to obtain non–adaptive learning strategies which even use the optimal number of queries.

## 4  Finding an Input on Which the Teacher Says "Yes"

We have seen that it may be crucial to find a "1–input", one, on which the secret parity function evaluates to 1. We show how this can be accomplished with the help of parity check matrices.

We can interpret the rows of a matrix $H \in \{0, 1\}^{m \times n}$ in a canonical fashion as describing $m$ subsets $A_1, \ldots, A_m$, each from the set $\{1, \ldots, n\}$.

A parity function $f_S$ can be seen as a column vector $v$ of length $n$ which has $v_i = 1$ if $i \in S$ and $v_i = 0$ otherwise. (Thus, the Hamming distance between parity functions can also be defined.)

If $v$ is the vector corresponding to the secret parity function, then the teacher's answers on the inputs $A_1, \ldots, A_m$ are described by the product $H \cdot v$, more precisely, $(H \cdot v)_i$ is the answer of the teacher on query $A_i$.

In order to find a 1–input for parities with $k$ essential variables, it is enough to find a matrix $H$ with $n$ columns such that no sum of $k$ columns of $H$ is equal to the zero vector. (Let us denote this property as the "$k$–sum–property".) The reason is that for such a matrix $H$, any answer $H \cdot v$ of the teacher will not be zero, and thus reveal a 1–input $A_i$.

A parity–check matrix $H$ with code distance $k + 1$ (see Definition 2) fulfills the $j$–sum–property for all $j = 1, \ldots, k$:

Assume that $H$ has $m$ rows and $n$ columns. By Proposition 1, any set of $j \leq k$ columns is linearly independent over $\mathbb{Z}_2$, in particular, no sum of $1 \leq j \leq k$ columns is equal to zero.

We can convince ourselves easily that, because of this property, parity–check matrices can be used in the same fashion in order to find a 1–input when the secret function is from $PAR_{\leq}(k,n)$. If none of the inputs is a 1–input, then the secret parity function is the empty parity function.

# 5  Designing Learning Strategies

Let us start by showing a bound for matrices which have the $k$–sum–property. The proof is completely analogous to the proof of the Gilbert–Varshamov bound. Note that the lemma only makes sense if $k$ is even, because otherwise we could take the matrix which has a single row of ones only.

**Lemma 1.** *Let $k \geq 2$. There is a matrix $H$ with at most $m \geq 1$ rows and $n$ columns which has the $k$–sum–property whenever the following holds:*

$$2^m > \binom{n-1}{k-1}.$$

**Proof.** Choose any vector from $\{0,1\}^m$ as the first column of $H$. Now assume that $j \leq n-1$ columns have already been chosen such that no $k$ columns of them add up to zero. There are $\binom{j}{k-1}$ ways to choose $k-1$ of those columns, hence at most $\binom{j}{k-1}$ columns are forbidden as column $j+1$. Since $\binom{j}{k-1} \leq \binom{n-1}{k-1} < 2^m$, there is at least one vector left which we can choose as the $j+1$-th column. ∎

As a consequence, for a secret parity function $f \in PAR(k,n)$, ($k$ even), we can find an $a$ with $f(a) = 1$ with $m$ queries, whenever $m > \log\binom{n-1}{k-1}$. Unfortunately, this helps us only in finding one variable. After that, the task remains to identify a parity function on a smaller number of variables.

It turns out that matrices which have the $j$–sum–property for all $j = 1,\ldots,k$ simultaneously are the solution to the problem. Parity–check matrices are such matrices.

We first describe a procedure which also contains binary search phases:

**Theorem 2.** *Let $A_1,\ldots,A_m$ be the subsets of $\{1,\ldots,n\}$ corresponding to the rows of a parity–check matrix with code distance $k+1$. Then the class $PAR_{\leq}(k,n)$ can be learned adaptively with at most $m + k \cdot \lceil \log n \rceil$ queries.*

**Proof.** Note that no $1 \leq j \leq k$ columns in the parity–check matrix add to the zero column. First, we ask the teacher for the values of $f_S(A_1),\ldots,f_S(A_m)$. If $S \neq \emptyset$, then for at least one $i$, we have that $|A_i \cap S|$ is odd and with $\lceil \log n \rceil$ more questions we can identify one variable $s \in S$ by binary search. It remains to identify the parity function $f_{S\setminus\{s\}}$. The teacher still gives the answers for the function $f_S$, but we can think of "replacing" him by a teacher for the function $f_{S\setminus\{s\}}$. This can be achieved by replacing any answer $f_S(A)$ of him by $f_S(A) \oplus f_{\{s\}}(A)$.

Now, the procedure can be iterated. In a more algorithmic notation, the query strategy looks as follows and it is easy to see that the number of queries is at most $m + k\lceil \log n \rceil$.

```
Identified := ∅;  stop := false;
for i = 1,...,m do answerᵢ = f_S(Aᵢ);
while not stop do
begin
   find an i such that answerᵢ = 1;
   if no such i exists, then stop := true;
   Otherwise:
      identify an s ∈ S \ Identified by binary search on Aᵢ \ Identified.
      Identified := Identified ∪ {s};
      "replace the current teacher" by a teacher for f_{S\Identified}.
      for i = 1,...,m do answerᵢ := answerᵢ ⊕ f_{s}(Aᵢ);
end;
return Identified;
```

∎

In order to keep the number of queries small, we should use parity–check matrices with few rows only. We will consider concrete constructions in Section 6.

Surprisingly, it will turn out that the above adaptive learning strategy is not competitive enough and that we can design nearly optimal learning strategies that are even non–adaptive. Let us turn to the construction of such non–adaptive learning strategies.

We need the following lemma, in which we again identify parity functions $f_S$ with binary vectors of length $n$. It is implicitly equivalent to Proposition 1.

**Lemma 2.** *Let $f$ be an arbitrary parity function. If $H$ is a $\{0,1\}$–matrix in which each set of $t$ columns is linearly independent, then the set $C = \{g \mid H \cdot g = H \cdot f\}$ has Hamming distance at least $t + 1$.*

Note that if $f$ is the secret parity function, then the set $C$ can be seen as the set of parity functions consistent with the answers of the teacher.

**Proof.** Let $c_1 \neq c_2 \in C$. Then, $H \cdot (c_1 \oplus c_2) = (H \cdot c_1) \oplus (H \cdot c_2)$ is equal to the zero vector. If $c_1$ and $c_2$ have Hamming distance less than $t + 1$, then $c_1 \oplus c_2$ contains at most $t$ ones. Thus, a set of at most $t$ column vectors of $H$ would be linearly dependent. ∎

We obtain the following application:

**Theorem 3.** *Let $H$ be a matrix in which each set of $2k$ columns is linearly independent. Let $A_1,\ldots,A_m$ be the sets corresponding to the rows of $H$. $PAR_{\leq}(k,n)$ can be learned non–adaptively by asking the $m$ queries $A_1,\ldots,A_m$.*

**Proof.** Assume that there are two parity functions $f_S$ and $f_{S'}$ consistent with the answer of the teacher. By Lemma 2, they must have Hamming distance at least $2k+1$. This is not possible for parity functions on at most $k$ essential variables. ∎

The correspondence between non–adaptive learning strategies and parity–check matrices also holds in the other direction.

**Lemma 3.** *A set $\{a_1, \ldots, a_m\}$ of vectors $a_i \in \{0,1\}^n$ which is a non–adaptive learning strategy for $PAR_\leq(k,n)$ can be turned into a parity–check matrix with code distance $2k+1$ and at most $m$ rows.*

**Proof.** We can assume w.l.o.g. that no subset of $\{a_1, \ldots, a_m\}$ is a non–adaptive learning strategy for $PAR_\leq(k,n)$ as well. As a consequence, the $a_i$ are linearly independent over $\mathbb{Z}_2$. Now consider the matrix where the $a_i$ are arranged as rows.

It is enough to prove that the sum of any $j$ columns, $1 \leq j \leq 2k$, is not equal to the zero vector. Assume the contrary, i.e., assume that (w.l.o.g.) the columns $1, \ldots, j$ add up to the zero vector. If $j \leq k$, then the parity function $f_\emptyset = 0$ and the parity function $x_1 \oplus \cdots \oplus x_j$ both yield the same answers by the teacher, hence they cannot be distinguished by the learning strategy. If $j > k$, then one can consider the parity function $f_{\{1,\ldots,k\}}$ and the parity function $f_{\{k+1,\ldots,j\}}$ and argue as before. ∎

Lemma 3 allows us to transfer lower bounds known in coding theory to lower bounds on the number of queries necessary in non–adaptive learning strategies.

# 6 Nearly–Optimal Non–Adaptive Strategies

In this section, we show how known constructions from coding theory can be applied to obtain non–adaptive learning strategies which are nearly optimal in the class of all (adaptive or non–adaptive) learning strategies.

We could use the Gilbert–Varshamov bound (Theorem 1) to obtain a parity–check matrix $H$ with $m$ rows which has code distance $k+1$ if $2^m > \sum_{i=0}^{k-1} \binom{n-1}{i}$. If $k \leq n/3$, the right hand side is smaller than $\binom{n}{k}$ and by Theorem 2, we would obtain an adaptive learning strategy with at most $\lceil \log \binom{n}{k} \rceil + k \lceil \log n \rceil$ queries, but the strategy used in the following theorem leads to a better bound:

**Theorem 4.** *If $k \leq n/2$, then $PAR_\leq(k,n)$ can be learned non–adaptively with at most $2 \cdot \log \binom{n}{k} + 1$ queries.*

The lower bound of $\lceil \log \binom{n}{k} \rceil$ already holds for the function class $PAR(k,n)$ and all (adaptive or non–adaptive) strategies. Thus, the query number in Theorem 4 is asymptotically optimal.

**Proof.** We use the Gilbert–Varshamov construction to obtain a parity–check matrix with $m$ rows and code distance $2k+1$ which exists if

$$2^m > \sum_{i=0}^{2k-1} \binom{n-1}{i} =: S_1 ,$$

i.e., $m = 1 + \lfloor \log S_1 \rfloor$ is enough. Observe that (for $k \le n/2$) $S_1 \le \binom{n}{k}\binom{n}{k-1} \le$ $\binom{n}{k}^2$: We have $S_1 = \binom{n}{2k-1} + \binom{n}{2k-3} + \cdots + \binom{n}{1}$ and thus $S_1$ can be interpreted as the number of choices to pick a subset of odd cardinality at most $2k-1$ from an $n$–element set. Every such subset can also be obtained by first choosing a $k$–element subset $A$ of $\{1,\ldots,n\}$, then choosing a $k-1$–element subset $B$ of $\{1,\ldots,n\}$ and taking the symmetric difference of both. Thus $S_1 \le \binom{n}{k}\binom{n}{k-1}$ and $m \le 1 + \lfloor \log S_1 \rfloor \le 1 + \lfloor 2\log\binom{n}{k}\rfloor$ and by Theorem 3 this number of queries is enough. ∎

The strategy from Theorem 4 improves the results from [6] and it also has the advantage of being non–adaptive, in contrast to the strategies given in [6].

The maybe more important aspect here is that by using parity–check matrices, we have made applicable other constructions from coding theory as well.

Until now, we have neglected the efficiency with which these parity–check matrices can be constructed. Codes that can efficiently be constructed are the so–called BCH–codes. The following theorem shows how they can be applied to obtain very efficient non–adaptive strategies.

**Theorem 5.** *Let $n = 2^w - 1$ for some $w \ge 2$. There is a non–adaptive learning strategy for learning $PAR_\le(k,n)$ with at most $k\log(n+1)$ queries. The set of queries can be constructed in polynomial time.*

**Proof.** Choose some $2t + 1 \le n$. Then it is known (see e.g. the paper by Alon, Babai and Itai [1], Proposition 6.5) that we can construct a matrix $H$ which is the parity–check matrix of a BCH code with minimum distance $2t+2$ as follows:[1] Let $x_1,\ldots,x_n$ be $n$ column vectors of length $w$ over $\mathbb{Z}_2$ which binary represent the $n$ nonzero elements of the Galois field with $2^w$ elements. Then the matrix $H$ has $wt$ rows and $n$ columns and is constructed as follows:

$$H = \begin{pmatrix} x_1 & x_2 & x_3 & \cdots & x_n \\ x_1^3 & x_2^3 & x_3^3 & \cdots & x_n^3 \\ \cdots & \cdots & \cdots & \cdots \\ x_1^{2t-1} & x_2^{2t-1} & x_3^{2t-1} & \cdots & x_n^{2t-1} \end{pmatrix}.$$

Since $w = \log(n+1)$, and since we are looking for codes with Hamming distance at least $2k+1$, we choose $t=k$ and obtain a matrix with $k\log(n+1)$ rows. Thus, the corresponding non–adaptive learning strategy uses $k\log(n+1)$ queries. ∎

If $n$ is not of the form that fits Theorem 5, we can consider the smallest $N > n$ which is of the appropriate form, i.e., some $N \le 2n-1$. Since $PAR_\le(k,n)$ can be seen as a subset of $PAR_\le(k,N)$, we obtain the following corollary:

**Corollary 1.** *For every $n \ge 3$, there is a non–adaptive learning strategy for learning $PAR_\le(k,n)$ with at most $k\log n + k$ queries. The set of queries can be constructed in polynomial time.*

---

[1] If $2t + 2 = n + 1$, then the code contains only one codeword.

Since the lower bound $\log \binom{n}{k}$ is at least $k \log \frac{n}{k} = k \log n - k \log k$, the strategy used in the corollary is, for fixed $k$, optimal up to a constant additive term.

The query strategies described in [6] are not constructive since they do not compute the query set in polynomial time. In that paper, a constructive query strategy based on "splitters" – as suggested by the present author – is mentioned which has a query number of $O(k^4 \log n)$. Hence the above bound improves on this query number and, in addition, our strategy has the advantage of being non–adaptive.

## 7    Fine–Tuning

We give a sketch of how the number of queries could be reduced further in special cases.

Assume that we are given a matrix $H$ with $n$ columns in which each $2k-2$ columns are linearly independent. Ask the teacher for the values of the secret parity function on the rows $H_i$. By Lemma 2, the set of parity functions consistent with the answers has Hamming distance at least $2k-1$. As a consequence, if $f_{S_1}$ and $f_{S_2}$, both from $PAR(k,n)$, are consistent with the answers, then $S_1 \cap S_2 = \emptyset$. We are thus left with at most $\lfloor n/k \rfloor$ candidate functions from $PAR(k,n)$ and they have disjoint variable sets. We can determine which of those parity functions the teacher has in mind by at most $\lceil \log \lfloor n/k \rfloor \rceil$ queries. The reason for this is that, as in the case of $PAR(1,n)$, we can use binary search.

As an application, we show that the above leads to a query strategy which for the class $PAR(2,n)$ needs at most one query more than the trivial lower bound $\lceil \log \binom{n}{2} \rceil$:

**Theorem 6.** $PAR(2,n)$ can be learned adaptively with at most

$$\lceil \log n \rceil + \lceil \log(\lfloor n/2 \rfloor) \rceil \leq \left\lceil \log \binom{n}{2} \right\rceil + 1 \quad queries.$$

**Proof.** We represent the numbers $0, \ldots, n-1$ as binary vectors of length $\lceil \log n \rceil$. Then we choose $H$ to be the $\lceil \log n \rceil \times n$ matrix which contains these bit vectors as columns. Matrix $H$ has the 2–sum–property. Our strategy queries the teacher for his answers on the rows of $H$.

Since two parities from $PAR(2,n)$ have Hamming distance either 2 or 4, the set of parity functions from $PAR(2,n)$ consistent with the answers of the teacher has Hamming distance 4, i.e., they are all on disjoint variable sets. By the remarks before the theorem, we can determine by $\lceil \log \lfloor n/2 \rfloor \rceil$ additional queries which of the remaining candidate parity functions is the secret one. The inequality stated in the theorem follows from standard calculations.

Another way to see the bound is to observe that in the matrix $H$, every row contains at most $\lfloor n/2 \rfloor$ many ones. Hence, a binary search on the corresponding row reveals one variable and the second is also determined by the first one. ∎

# 8 Remarks

We have neglected the question how efficiently the learner can determine the secret parity function $f_S$ from the answers of the teacher. It should be clear that due to the close connection to coding theory, this problem can be solved with the usual techniques of error–correction, but we refrain from making these connections more explicit since it was our main aim to demonstrate the usefulness of parity–check matrices for optimizing the query number.

# References

1. N. Alon, L. Babai and A. Itai, *A Fast and Simple Randomized Parallel Algorithm for the Maximal Independent Set Problem*, Journal of Algorithms 7, 1986, 567–583.
2. P. Damaschke, *Adaptive Versus Nonadaptive Attribute-Efficient Learning*, Proc. of the 30th Annual ACM Symposium on the Theory of Computing (STOC), 1998, 590–596.
3. D. Hoffman, D. Leonard, C. Lindner, K. Phelps, C. Rodger and J. Wall, *Coding Theory, the Essentials*, Marcel Dekker, 1991.
4. R. Lidl and H. Niederreiter, *Introduction to Finite Fields and Their Applications*, Cambridge University Press, 1994.
5. W. Peterson and E. Weldon, *Error–Correcting Codes*, MIT Press, 2nd edition, 1972.
6. R. Uehara, K. Tsuchida and I. Wegener, *Identification of Partial Disjunction, Parity, and Threshold Functions*, Proc. of the European Conference on Computational Learning Theory (Eurocolt), 1997, 171–184. To appear in Theoretical Computer Science.

# Learning Range Restricted Horn Expressions[*]

Roni Khardon

Division of Informatics
University of Edinburgh
The King's Buildings
Edinburgh EH9 3JZ
Scotland
roni@dcs.ed.ac.uk

**Abstract.** We study the learnability of first order Horn expressions from equivalence and membership queries. We show that the class of range restricted Horn expressions, where every term in the consequent of every clause appears also in the antecedent of the clause, is learnable. The result holds both for the model where interpretations are examples (learning from interpretations) and the model where clauses are examples (learning from entailment).

The paper utilises a previous result on learning function free Horn expressions. This is done by using techniques for flattening and unflattening of examples and clauses, and a procedure for model finding for range restricted expressions. This procedure can also be used to solve the implication problem for this class.

## 1 Introduction

We study the problem of exactly identifying universally quantified first order Horn expressions using Angluin's [Ang88] model of exact learning. Much of the work in learning theory has dealt with learning of Boolean expressions in propositional logic. Early treatments of relational expressions were given by [Val85,Hau89], but only recently more attention was given to the subject in framework of Inductive Logic Programming [MDR94,Coh95a,Coh95b]. It is clear that the relational learning problem is harder than the propositional one and indeed except for very restricted cases it is computationally hard [Coh95b]. To tackle this issue in the propositional domain various queries and oracles that allow for efficient learning have been studied [Val84,Ang88]. In particular, propositional Horn expressions are known to be learnable in polynomial time from equivalence and membership queries [AFP92,FP93]. In the relational domain, queries have been used in several systems [Sha83,SB86,DRB92,MB92] and results on learnability in the limit were derived [Sha91,DRB92]. More recently progress has been made on the problem of learning first order Horn expressions

---
[*] This work was partly supported by EPSRC Grant GR/M21409.

from equivalence and membership queries using additional constraints or other additional queries [Ari97,RT97,Kha98,RT98,RS98].

In particular [Kha98] shows that universally quantified function free Horn expressions are exactly learnable in several models of learning from equivalence and membership queries. This paper extends these results to a class of expressions allowing the use of function symbols. In particular, we present algorithms for learning *range restricted* Horn expressions where every term in the consequent of a clause appears also (possibly as a subterm) in the antecedent of the clause. In fact, our results hold for a more expressive class, *weakly range restricted* Horn expressions, that allows for some use of equalities in the antecedent of a clause.

Several kinds of examples have been considered in the context of learning first order expressions. The natural generalisation of the setup studied in propositional logic suggests that examples are interpretations of the underlying language. That is, a positive example is a model of the expression being learned. Another view suggests that a positive example is a sentence that is logically implied by the expression, and in particular Horn clauses have been used as examples. These two views have been called *learning from interpretations* and *learning from entailment* respectively [DR97] and were both studied before. We present algorithms for learning weakly range restricted Horn expressions in both settings. We also show that the implication problem for such expressions is decidable, and provide an upper bound for its complexity. This motivates the use of this class since learned expressions can be used as a knowledge base in a system in a useful way.

The result for learning from interpretations is derived by exhibiting a reduction to the function free case, essentially using flattening - replacing function symbols with predicate symbols of arity larger by one [Rou92]. The reduction uses flattening and unflattening of examples and clauses, and an axiomatisation of the functionality of the new predicates. Learning from entailment is then shown possible by reducing it to learning from interpretations under the given restrictions. This relies on a procedure for model finding for this class, which also proves the decidability of inference for it. We also derive learnability results for range restricted expressions as corollaries. Interestingly, despite the use of reduction, for learning from entailment we can use range restricted expressions as the hypothesis language, but for learning from interpretations hypotheses are weakly range restricted.

The rest of the paper is organised as follows. The next section provides preliminary definitions. Section 3 presents range restricted expressions and some of their basic properties. Sections 4 and 5 develop the results on learning from interpretations and learning from entailment respectively, and Section 6 discusses the implication problem. The concluding section discusses related work and directions for future work.

## 2 Preliminaries

### 2.1 First Order Horn Expressions

We follow standard definitions of first order expressions; for these see [CK90,Llo87]. The learning problems under consideration assume a pre-fixed known and finite signature $S$ of the language. That is, $S = (P, F)$ where $P$ is a finite set of predicates, and $F$ is a finite set of function symbols, each with its associated fixed arity. Constants are simply 0-ary function symbols and are treated as such. In addition a set of variables $x_1, x_2, x_3, \ldots$ is used to construct expressions.

We next define *terms* and their depth. A variable is a term of depth 0. A constant is a term of depth 0. If $t_1, \ldots, t_n$ are terms, each of depth at most $i$ (and one with depth precisely $i$) and $f \in F$ is a function symbol of arity $n$, then $f(t_1, \ldots, t_n)$ is a term of depth $i + 1$.

An *atom* is an expression $p(t_1, \ldots, t_n)$ where $p \in P$ is a predicate symbol of arity $n$ and $t_1, \ldots, t_n$ are terms. An atom is called a *positive literal*; a *negative literal* is an expression $\neg l$ where $l$ is a positive literal. A clause is a disjunction of literals where all variables are taken to be universally quantified. A Horn clause has at most one positive literal and an arbitrary number of negative literals. A Horn clause $\neg p_1 \vee \ldots \vee \neg p_n \vee p_{n+1}$ is equivalent to its "implicational form" $p_1 \wedge \ldots \wedge p_n \to p_{n+1}$. When presenting a clause in this way we call $p_1 \wedge \ldots \wedge p_n$ the *antecedent* of the clause and $p_{n+1}$ the *consequent* of the clause. A Horn expression is a conjunction of Horn clauses.

The truth value of first order expressions is defined relative to an interpretation $I$ of the predicates and function symbols in $S$ [Llo87]. Interpretations are also called *structures* in model theory [CK90] and we use these terms interchangeably. An interpretation $I$ includes a domain $D$ which is a (finite) set of elements. For each function symbol $f \in F$ of arity $n$, $I$ associates a mapping from $D^n$ to $D$; if $f(a_1, \ldots, a_n)$ is associated with $a$ we say that $f(a_1, \ldots, a_n)$ *corresponds to* $a$ in $I$. For each predicate symbol $p \in P$ of arity $n$, $I$ specifies the truth value of $p$ on $n$-tuples over $D$. The *extension* of a predicate in $I$ is the set of positive instantiations of it that are true in $I$. In structural domains [Hau89,Kha96,RTR96], domain elements are objects in the world and an instantiation describes properties and relations of objects. We therefore refer to domain elements as *objects*. Let $str(S)$ be the set of structures (interpretations) for the signature $S$.

The truth value of an expression in an interpretation $I$ is defined in a standard way [CK90,Llo87]. Note that a Horn clause is not true (falsified) in $I$ iff there is a variable assignment (a substitution) that simultaneously satisfies the antecedent and falsifies the consequent. The terms (1) $T$ is true in $I$, (3) $I$ satisfies $T$, (4) $I$ is a model of $T$, and (5) $I \models T$, have the same meaning. Let $T_1, T_2 \in \mathcal{H}(S, =)$ then $T_1$ implies $T_2$, denoted $T_1 \models T_2$, if every model of $T_1$ is also a model of $T_2$.

### 2.2 The Learning Model

We define here the scheme of learning from interpretations [DRD94]. Learning from entailment [FP93], where examples are clauses in the language is defined in

Section 5. An example is an interpretation; an example $I$ is positive for a target expression $T$ if $I \models T$ and negative otherwise. Examples of this form have been used before by various authors including [Hau89,DRD94,RT97,Kha98].

We use Angluin's model of learning from Equivalence Queries (EQ) and Membership Queries (MQ) [Ang88]. Let $\mathcal{H}$ be a class under consideration, $\mathcal{H}'$ a (possibly different) class used to represent hypotheses, and let $T \in \mathcal{H}$ be the target expression. For membership queries, the learner presents an interpretation $I$ and the oracle MQ returns "yes" iff $I \models T$. For equivalence queries, the learner presents a hypothesis $H \in \mathcal{H}'$ and the oracle EQ returns "yes" if for all $I$, $I \models T$ iff $I \models H$; otherwise it returns a counter example $I$ such that $I \models T$ and $I \not\models H$ (a positive counter example) or $I \not\models T$ and $I \models H$ (a negative counter example).

In the learning model, $T \in \mathcal{H}$ is fixed by an adversary and hidden from the learner. The learner has access to EQ and MQ and must find an expression $H$ equivalent to $T$ (under the definition above). If there is an algorithm that performs this task we say that $\mathcal{H}$ *is learnable with hypothesis in* $\mathcal{H}'$, or, when $\mathcal{H}' = H$, just $\mathcal{H}$ *is learnable*. For complexity we measure the running time of the algorithm and the number of times it makes queries to EQ and MQ. It is known [Lit88,Ang88] that learnability in this model implies pac-learnability [Val84].

## 3 Range Restricted Horn Expressions

**Definition 1. (definite clauses)** *A clause is definite if it includes precisely one positive literal. For a signature $S$, let $\mathcal{H}(S)$ be the set of Horn expressions over $S$ in which all clauses are definite.*

**Definition 2. (range restricted clauses)** *A definite Horn clause is called range restricted[1] if every term that appears in its consequent also appears in its antecedent, possibly as a subterm of another term. For a signature $S$, let $\mathcal{H}_R(S)$ be the set of Horn expressions over $S$ in which all clauses are definite and range restricted.*

For example, the clause $(p_1(f_1(f_2(x)), f_3()) \rightarrow p_2(f_2(x), x))$ is range restricted, but the clause $(p_1(f_1(f_2(x)), f_3()) \rightarrow p_2(f_1(x), x))$ is not. We also consider clauses with a limited use of equality in their antecedent.

**Definition 3. (equational form)** *A definite clause $C$ with equalities in its antecedent and where every non-equational literal includes only variables as terms, and every equational literal is of the form $(x_{i_{n+1}} = f(x_{i_1}, \ldots, x_{i_n}))$ where $f \in F$ and $x_{i_j}$ are variables is in equational form. For a signature $S$, let $\mathcal{H}(S, =)$ be the set of Horn expressions over $S$ in which all clauses are definite and in equational form.*

---

[1] A similar restriction has been used before by several authors. Unfortunately, in a previous version of [Kha98] it was called "non-generative" while in other work it was called "generative" [MF92]. The term "range-restricted" was used in database literature for the function free case [Min88]. Here we use a natural generalisation for the case with function symbols.

Every range restricted clause can be transformed into an equational form by unfolding terms bottom-up and replacing them with variables. Formally, for $T \in \mathcal{H}_R(\mathcal{S})$, transform each clause $C$ in $T$ as follows. Find a term $f(x_1, \ldots, x_n)$ in $C$ all of whose sub-terms are variables (this includes constants) and rewrite the clause by replacing all occurrences of this term with a new variable $z$, and adding a new literal $(z = f(x_1, \ldots, x_n))$ to the antecedent of $C$. For example the clause

$$p_1(x_1, f_1(x_2)) \wedge p_2(f_2()) \to p_1(x_1, f_2())$$

is first transformed (using $f_1(x_2)$) into

$$(z_1 = f_1(x_2)) \wedge p_1(x_1, z_1) \wedge p_2(f_2()) \to p_1(x_1, f_2())$$

and then (using the constant $f_2()$) into

$$((z_1 = f_1(x_2)) \wedge (z_2 = f_2())) \wedge p_1(x_1, z_1) \wedge p_2(z_2) \to p_1(x_1, z_2)).$$

In the equational form of range restricted clauses each new variable $z_i$ has one defining equation, and we may think of the variables involved in the equation as its ancestors. For example, $x_2$ is an ancestor of $z_1$ in the example above. Constructed in this way all variables that appear in equational literals are ancestors of some variable in the original literals. Since the clause is range restricted this holds for variables in the consequent as well. We will consider the case where $z_i$ may have more than one such equation as in

$$((z_1 = f_3(x_1)) \wedge (z_1 = f_1(x_2)) \wedge (z_2 = f_2())) \wedge p_1(x_1, z_1) \wedge p_2(z_2) \to p_1(x_1, z_2))$$

but where the variables in equations are still ancestors in this sense.

**Definition 4. (root variables, legal ancestor)** *Let $C$ be a definite Horn clause in equational form. (1) The variables appearing in non-equational literals in the antecedent are called* root *variables. (2) Root variables are legal ancestors. (3) If an equational literal $(z = f(x_1, \ldots, x_n))$ appears in the antecedent and $z$ is a legal ancestor then $x_1, \ldots, x_n$ are also legal ancestors.*

**Definition 5. (weakly range restricted clauses)** *A definite Horn clause in equational form is called* weakly range restricted *if every variable that appears in its consequent or in equational literals is a legal ancestor. For a signature $\mathcal{S}$, let $\mathcal{H}_R(\mathcal{S}, =)$ be the set of Horn expressions over $\mathcal{S}$ in which all clauses are definite and weakly range restricted.*

The following proposition (proof omitted) shows that we can replace range restricted expressions with their equational form.

**Proposition 1.** *Let $T \in \mathcal{H}_R(\mathcal{S})$ and let $T'$ be the equational form of $T$ computed as above then for all $I \in str(\mathcal{S})$, $I \models T$ if and only if $I \models T'$.*

We next define legal objects in interpretations to play a role similar to legal ancestors in clauses.

**Definition 6. (legal objects)** *Let $I \in str(S)$, and let $D$ be the domain of $I$.*
*(1) If $p(a_1, \ldots, a_n)$ is true in $I$ for $p \in P$ then $a_1, \ldots, a_n$ are legal objects.*
*(2) If $f(a_1, \ldots, a_n)$ is mapped to $a_{n+1}$ in $I$ where $f \in F$ and $a_{n+1}$ is a legal object then $a_1, \ldots, a_n$ are legal objects.*

The main property of weakly range restricted expressions used in our constructions is the fact that their truth value of is not effected by non-legal objects.

**Lemma 1.** *Let $I \in str(S)$, let $C$ be a weakly range restricted clause, and let $\theta$ be a mapping of the variables of $C$ into objects of $I$. If $I \not\models C\theta$ then all objects mapped by $\theta$ are legal objects.*

**Proof.** Assume that $\theta$ maps a variable of $C$ to a non-legal object. If the equational literals in the antecedent of $C$ are not satisfied in $I$ by $\theta$, then $I \models C\theta$.
Notice that if a variable $x$ is mapped to a non-legal object in $I$ and $(z = f(\ldots, x, \ldots))$ is true in $I$ then $z$ is also mapped to a non-legal object. Now, since every variable is an ancestor of some root variable in $C$, if the equational literals of $C$ are satisfied in $I$ by $\theta$, then some root variable is mapped to a non-legal object by $\theta$. By definition this implies that an atom $p(\ldots)$ in the antecedent of $C$ is made false by $\theta$. Therefore $I \models C\theta$. ∎

## 4 Learning from Interpretations

We first define a modified signature of the language above. Similar transformations have been previously used under the name of flattening [Rou92] (see also [NCDW97]). For each function symbol $f$ of arity $n$, define a new predicate symbol $f_p$ of arity $n + 1$. Let $F_p$ be the new set of predicates so defined, $S' = (P \cup F_p, \emptyset)$ be the modified signature, $\mathcal{H}_R(S')$ the set of range restricted (and function free) Horn expressions over the predicates in $P \cup F_p$, and $str(S')$ be the set of interpretations for $S'$.

Reductions appropriate for learning with membership queries were defined in [AK95] where they are called pwm-reductions. Three transformations are required. The *representation transformation* maps $T \in \mathcal{H}_R(S)$ to $T' \in \mathcal{H}_R(S')$, the *example transformation* maps $I \in str(S)$ to $I' \in str(S')$, and the *membership queries transformation* maps $I' \in str(S')$ to $\{Yes, No\} \cup str(S)$. Intuitively, the learner for $T \in \mathcal{H}_R(S)$ will be constructed out of a learner for $T' \in \mathcal{H}_R(S')$ (the image of the representation transformation) by using the transformations. The obvious properties required of these transformations guarantee correctness. The example and representation transformations guarantee that the learner receives correct examples for $T'$ and the membership query transformation guarantees that queries can be either answered immediately or transferred to the membership oracle for $T$.

*The Representation Transformation:* Let $T \in \mathcal{H}(S, =)$ be a Horn expression, then the expression $flat(T) \in \mathcal{H}_R(S')$ is formed by replacing each equational literal $(z = f(x_1, \ldots, x_n))$ with the corresponding atom $f_p(x_1, \ldots, x_n, z)$. Thus, the equational clause given above is transformed to:

$$f_{3p}(x_1, z_1) \wedge f_{1p}(x_2, z_1) \wedge f_{2p}(z_2) \wedge p_1(x_1, z_1) \wedge p_2(z_2) \rightarrow p_1(x_1, z_2).$$

The definitions of root variables and legal ancestors hold for the flat versions as well. We also axiomatise the fact that the new predicates are functional. Our treatment diverges from previous uses of flattening [Rou92] in that the function symbols are taken out of the language. For every $f \in F$ of arity $n$ let

$$exist_f = (\forall x_1, \forall x_2 \ldots, \forall x_n, \exists z, f_p(x_1, \ldots, x_n, z))$$
$$unique_f = (\forall x_1, \forall x_2 \ldots, \forall x_n, \forall z_1, \forall z_2,$$
$$f_p(x_1, \ldots, x_n, z_1) \wedge f_p(x_1, \ldots, x_n, z_2) \rightarrow (z_1 = z_2))$$

Let $\phi_f = exist_f \wedge unique_f$, $\phi_F = \wedge_{f \in F} \phi_f$, and $\mathcal{A}_{unique} = \wedge_{f \in F} unique_f$. We call $exist_f$ the existence clause of $f$ and $unique_f$ the uniqueness clause.

*The Example Transformation:* Let $I$ be an interpretation for $S$, then $flat(I)$ is an interpretation for $S'$ defined as follows. The domain of $flat(I)$ is equal to the domain of $I$ and the extension of predicates in $P$ is the same as in $I$. The extension of a predicate $f_p \in F_p$ of arity $n + 1$ is defined in a natural way to include all tuples $(a_1, \ldots, a_n, a_{n+1})$ where $a_i$ are domain elements and $f(a_1, \ldots, a_n)$ corresponds to $a_{n+1}$ in $I$.

**Lemma 2.** *For all $T \in \mathcal{H}(S, =)$ and for all $I \in str(S)$:*
*(1) $flat(I) \models \phi_F$.*
*(2) $I \models T$ if and only if $flat(I) \models flat(T)$.*

**Proof.** Since each constant and each term are mapped to precisely one domain element in $I$, part (1) is true by the construction of $flat(I)$. For (2) note that $flat(T)$ and the equational form of $T$ have the same variables, and $I$ and $flat(I)$ have the same domain. Let $\theta$ be a mapping of these variables to the domain. By construction, $(z = f(x_1, \ldots, x_n))\theta$ is true in $I$ if and only if $f_p(x_1, \ldots, x_n, z)\theta$ is true in $flat(I)$. Moreover, predicates in $P$ have the same extension in $I$ and $flat(I)$. Therefore, a falsifying substitution for one can be used as a falsifying substitution for the other. ∎

*The Membership Queries Transformation:* A mapping converting structures from $str(S')$ to $str(S)$ is a bit more involved. Let $J \in str(S')$; if $J \models \phi_F$ then the previous mapping can simply be reversed, and we denote it by $unflat(J)$. Otherwise there are two cases. If $J$ falsifies the uniqueness clause, it is in some sense inconsistent with the intension for usage of the functional predicates. Such interpretations are not output by the algorithm of [Kha98] when learning $\mathcal{H}_R(S')$ and hence we do not need to deal with them. If $J$ satisfies the uniqueness clause (of all function symbols) but falsifies the existence axiom then some information on the interpretation of the function symbols is missing. In this case we complete it by introducing a new domain element $*$ and defining $complete(J) \in str(S')$ to be the interpretation in which every ground instance of the existence clauses which is false in $J$ is made true by adding a positive atom whose last term is $*$. For example, if there is no $b$ such that $f_p(1, b)$ is true in $J$ then we add $f_p(1, *)$ to $complete(J)$. For any $J \in str(S')$ such that $J \models A_{unique}$, the interpretation $J$ is transformed in this way into $unflat(complete(J))$. Note that the object $*$ is non-legal (cf. Definition 6) in $unflat(complete(J))$.

**Lemma 3.** *For all $T \in \mathcal{H}_R(S, =)$ and for all $J \in str(S')$ such that $J \models A_{unique}$ the following conditions are equivalent.*
*(1) $J \models flat(T)$.*
*(2) $complete(J) \models flat(T)$.*
*(3) $unflat(complete(J)) \models T$.*

**Proof.** Since $unflat(complete(J))$ is in $str(S)$ and $flat(unflat(complete(J))) = complete(J)$, Lemma 2 implies that (2) and (3) are equivalent. Now, if $J \not\models flat(T)\theta$ for some $\theta$ then since the $complete()$ construction does not change the truth value for atoms whose objects are in $J$ we also have $complete(J) \not\models flat(T)\theta$. Thus (2) implies (1).

Finally, if $unflat(complete(J)) \not\models T\theta$ then by Lemma 1, $\theta$ does not use non-legal objects, and in particular the object $*$. Hence we can use $\theta$ in $J$ and the argument in Lemma 2 shows that $J \not\models flat(T)\theta$. Therefore (1) implies (3). ∎

For $S = (P, F)$ let $|S| = |P| + |F|$ be the number of symbols in the signature.

**Theorem 1.** *The class $\mathcal{H}_R(S, =)$ is learnable from equivalence and membership queries with hypothesis in $\mathcal{H}_R(S')$.*
*For $T \in \mathcal{H}_R(S, =)$ with $m$ clauses and at most $t$ variables, the algorithm makes $O(mt^{t+2r}|S|^2)$ equivalence queries, $O((nm + m^2 t^t)|S|t^r)$ membership queries, and its running time is polynomial in $n^t + t^t + m + |S| + t^r$, where $n$ is the number of objects in the largest counter example presented to the algorithm, and $r$ is the maximal arity of predicates and function symbols in $S$.*

**Proof.** The theorem follows from properties of pwm-reductions [AK95] and the result in [Kha98] showing that $\mathcal{H}_R(S')$ is learnable. The idea is that when learning $T \in \mathcal{H}_R(S, =)$ we will run the algorithm A2 from [Kha98] to learn the expression $flat(T) \in \mathcal{H}_R(S')$. When A2 presents $H \in \mathcal{H}_R(S')$ to an equivalence query we interpret this by saying that $I \in str(S)$ is a model of $H$ if and only if $flat(I) \models H$. Hence given a counter example $I$ we simply compute $flat(I)$ and present it as a counter example to A2. Lemma 2 and the above interpretation guarantee that the examples it receives are correct. When A2 presents $J$ for a membership query, we compute $unflat(complete(J))$, present it to MQ and return its answer to A2. Lemma 3 guarantees that the answer is correct. By Corollary 11 of [Kha98] we get that A2 will find an expression equivalent to $flat(T)$. The complexity bound follows from [Kha98]. ∎

## 4.1 Modifying the Hypothesis Language

The previous theorem produces a hypothesis in $\mathcal{H}_R(\mathcal{S}')$ while the target expression is in $\mathcal{H}_R(\mathcal{S}, =)$. We next show how to use a hypothesis in $\mathcal{H}_R(\mathcal{S}, =)$.

We first need to describe the hypothesis of the learning algorithm $A2$ from [Kha98]. The algorithm maintains a set of interpretations $S \subseteq str(\mathcal{S}')$ such that for each $J \in S$, $J \not\models flat(T)$. The hypothesis is $H = \wedge_{J \in S} rel\text{-}cands(J)$ where $rel\text{-}cands(J)$ is a set of clauses produced as follows. First take the conjunction of positive atoms true in $J$ as an antecedent and an atom false in $J$ as a consequent. Each such choice of consequent generates a ground clause. Considering each ground clause separately, substitute a unique variable to each object in the clause to get a clause in $rel\text{-}cands(J)$.

We generate clauses over $\mathcal{S}$ by reversing the $flat()$ operation; namely, replacing every literal $f_p(x_1, \ldots, x_n, x_{n+1})$ (where $f_p \in F_p$) by the corresponding literal $(x_{n+1} = f(x_1, \ldots, x_n))$. For $C \in rel\text{-}cands(J)$ let $unflat(C)$ be the resulting clause. Notice that $unflat(C)$ is in $\mathcal{H}(S, =)$ but it may not be in $\mathcal{H}_R(\mathcal{S}, =)$ since some of the variables in its equality literals may not be legal ancestors (cf. Definition 4). Since the clauses in question are in $\mathcal{H}(S, =)$, and since $flat(unflat(C)) = C$, the following is a special case of Lemma 2.

**Lemma 4.** *For all $I \in str(\mathcal{S})$, for all $J \in str(\mathcal{S}')$, and for all $C \in rel\text{-}cands(J)$, $I \models unflat(C)$ if and only if $flat(I) \models C$.*

When applied in this way we can see that a hypothesis modified by $unflat()$ attracts precisely the same counter examples and we get learnability with expressions over the signature $\mathcal{S}$. A further improvement is needed to generate a hypothesis in $\mathcal{H}_R(\mathcal{S}, =)$. Define legal objects of interpretation over $\mathcal{S}'$ in accordance with the definition for $\mathcal{S}$ (so that the same thing results when flattening). Let $J \in str(\mathcal{S}')$ be an interpretation with domain $D$. For $D' \subset D$ let $J_{|D'}$ be the projection of $J$ over $D'$. Namely, the interpretation where the domain is $D'$ and an atom $q(a_1, \ldots, a_n)$, where $a_1, \ldots, a_n \in D'$, is true in $J_{|D'}$ if and only if it is true in $J$.

**Lemma 5.** *Let $T \in \mathcal{H}_R(\mathcal{S}, =)$ and $J \in str(\mathcal{S}')$, such that $J \models A_{unique}$. Let $D$ be the domain of $J$ and let $a \in D$ be a non-legal object in $J$. Then $unflat(complete(J)) \models T$ if and only if $unflat(complete(J_{|\{D \setminus a\}})) \models T$.*

**Proof.** Since $a$ is non-legal in $J$ if and only if it is non-legal in $unflat(complete(J))$, Lemma 1 implies that if $unflat(complete(J)) \not\models T\theta$ then $\theta$ does not use $a$. Similarly, $\theta$ does not use the object $*$. Since the extension of predicates and mapping of functions over the other objects is not changed it follows that $unflat(complete(J_{|\{D \setminus a\}})) \not\models T\theta$.

For the other direction, if $unflat(complete(J_{|\{D \setminus a\}})) \not\models T\theta$ then by the same argument $\theta$ does not use the object $*$. Again, since the extension of predicates and mapping of functions over the other objects is not changed, $\theta$ can be used in $unflat(complete(J))$ without changing the truth value of $T$. ∎

Since a membership query of the algorithm (i.e. whether $J \models \text{flat}(T)$) is translated to a membership query for $T$ (i.e. whether $\text{unflat}(\text{complete}(J)) \models T$) the lemma indicates that *all* non-legal objects can be dropped from $J$ before making the membership query. This fact is utilised in the next section.

For our current purpose it suffices to observe that in *A2* dropping of objects happens by default. In particular, whenever the algorithm *A2* (with its optional step taken) puts an interpretation $J$ into the set $S$ (that generates its hypothesis as discussed above), it makes sure that $J \not\models \text{flat}(T)$ and for every object $a$ in the domain $D$ of $J$, it holds that $J_{|\{D\backslash a\}} \models \text{flat}(T)$. If this does not hold then it uses $J_{|\{D\backslash a\}}$ instead of $J$. Therefore, by Lemma 5 we get that all objects in all interpretations in $S$ are legal objects. This in turn implies that the hypothesis is in $\mathcal{H}_R(S, =)$.

**Theorem 2.** *The class $\mathcal{H}_R(S, =)$ is learnable from equivalence and membership queries.*

For a clause $C \in \mathcal{H}_R(S)$, by *the number of distinct terms in $C$* we mean the number of distinct elements in the set of all terms in $C$ and all their subterms. For example, $(p(x, f_1(x), f_2(f_1(x)), f_3()) \rightarrow q(f_1(x)))$ has 4 distinct terms $x, f_3(), f_1(x), f_2(f_1(x))$.

**Corollary 1.** *The class $\mathcal{H}_R(S)$ is learnable from equivalence and membership queries with hypothesis in $\mathcal{H}_R(S, =)$. The complexity is as in the previous theorem where $t$ is the maximal number of distinct terms in a clause in the target expression.*

**Proof.** Learnability follows since by Proposition 1 every $T \in \mathcal{H}_R(S)$ has an equivalent expression in $\mathcal{H}_R(S, =)$. It remains to observe that each distinct term in a clause $C \in \mathcal{H}_R(S)$ is mapped to a variable in the equational form. ∎

## 5   Learning from Entailment

In this model examples are clauses in the underlying language $\mathcal{H}$ [FP93]. An example $C \in \mathcal{H}$ is positive for $T \in \mathcal{H}$ if $T \models C$. The equivalence and membership oracles are defined accordingly. For membership queries, the learner presents a clause $C$ and the oracle EntMQ returns "yes" iff $T \models C$. For equivalence queries, the learner presents a hypothesis $H \in \mathcal{H}'$ and the oracle EntEQ returns "yes" if for all $I$, $I \models T$ iff $I \models H$; otherwise it returns a counter example $C$ such that $T \models C$ and $H \not\models C$ (a positive counter example) or $T \not\models C$ and $H \models C$ (a negative counter example).

Since one can identify non-legal objects and (by Lemma 5) drop them before making a membership query, the following lemma indicates that we can replace MQ by EntMQ for clauses in $\mathcal{H}_R(S, =)$.

**Lemma 6.** *Let $T \in \mathcal{H}_R(S, =)$ and let $J \in \text{str}(S')$ be such that $J \models \mathcal{A}_{unique}$ and all objects in $J$ are legal objects. Then $\text{unflat}(\text{complete}(J)) \not\models T$ if and only if $T \models \text{unflat}(C)$ for some $C \in \text{rel-cands}(J)$.*

**Proof.** Let $I = unflat(complete(J))$. First note that by construction $I \not\models unflat(C)$ for all $C \in rel\text{-}cands(J)$. Hence if $T \models unflat(C)$ for some such $C$ then $I \not\models T$.

For the other direction, let $\gamma$ be the (reverse) substitution that is used when generating $rel\text{-}cands(J)$. Let $R$ be a clause in $T$ and $\theta$ a substitution such that $I \not\models R\theta$. The antecedent of $R$ is satisfied by $\theta$ in $I$ and, by Lemma 1, $\theta$ does not use the object $*$. Therefore $ant(R)\theta\gamma \subseteq ant(unflat(C))$ for all $C \in rel\text{-}cands(J)$, where $ant()$ refers to the antecedent part of the clause considered as a set of literals. (The resulting substitution $\theta\gamma$ is a variable renaming that may unify several variables into one.) Since in $rel\text{-}cands(R)$ all range restricted consequents are considered, we get that for some $C' \in rel\text{-}cands(J)$, $R\theta\gamma \subseteq unflat(C')$, where here we consider a clause as a set of literals. (In other words $R$, $\theta$-subsumes $unflat(C')$ [Plo70].) We therefore get that $T \models R \models R\theta\gamma \models unflat(C')$. ∎

The following lemma provides a model finding algorithm for $\mathcal{H}_R(\mathcal{S}, =)$.

**Lemma 7.** *Given $H \in \mathcal{H}_R(\mathcal{S}, =)$ and a clause $C \in \mathcal{H}_R(\mathcal{S}, =)$ such that $H \not\models C$, one can find an interpretation $I \in str(\mathcal{S})$ such that $I \models H$ and $I \not\models C$ in time $O(|H| \cdot |\mathcal{S}| \cdot n^{t+r})$ where $|H|$ is the number of clauses in $H$, $n$ is the number of terms in $C$, $t$ is the maximal number of variables in a clause of $H$, and $r$ is the maximal arity.*

**Proof.** The idea is to generate an interpretation from $C$ and then make sure (by forward chaining) that it is a model of $H$ but not of $C$.

Generate a structure $I_0 \in str(\mathcal{S})$ as follows. First, introduce a unique domain element for each term in $C$ and then join elements if their terms are equated in the antecedent of $C$; let this domain be $D$.[2] The extension of predicates in $I_0$ includes precisely the atoms corresponding to the antecedent of $C$ and the mapping of domain elements produced. Let $p$ be the (ground atom which is the) consequent of $C$ under this mapping. The mapping of function symbols includes the initial mapping used when constructing $D$. It is then extended (as in the *complete()* construction) by adding another domain element $*$ and mapping each term $f(a_1, \ldots, a_n)$ that has not yet been assigned to $*$. Note that $*$ is a non-legal object.

Next, let $I = I_0$ and run forward chaining on $H$ adding positive atoms to $I$. That is, repeat the following procedure: find a clause $C$ in $H$ and a substitution $\theta$ such that $I \not\models C\theta$ and add the atom corresponding to the consequent of $C\theta$ to $I$. This results in an interpretation $I$ whose domain size is at most the number of distinct terms in $C$ plus 1, and which is a model of $H$. This is true since $H$ is definite and the domain of $I_0$ is finite and hence by adding atoms to $I_0$ we eventually get to a state where all clauses are satisfied (there is a finite number of atoms that can be added). We claim that $p$ is not in $I$ and hence $I \not\models C$.

---

[2] Note that there is no need to perform equational reasoning here and a syntactic matching suffices. This is true since in $\mathcal{H}_R(\mathcal{S}, =)$ all terms are of depth 0 or 1.

Since $H \in \mathcal{H}_R(\mathcal{S}, =)$, by Lemma 1 if $I \not\models H\theta$ then $\theta$ does not use the object $*$. Hence forward chaining does not produce any positive atoms containing the object $*$. Inductively, this shows that no such atom is true in $I$.

Let $J$ be some interpretation such that $J \models H$ and $J \not\models C$ (which exists by the condition of the lemma). Let $\theta$ be such that $J \not\models C\theta$ and let $q$ be the consequent of $C\theta$. Clearly, $q$ is not true in $J$. Moreover, there is a mapping from objects in $I_0$ (apart from $*$) to the objects in $J$ that are used in $C\theta$, so that all positive atoms true in $I_0$ are true in $J$ under this mapping, and all equalities true in $I_0$ (apart from ones referring to $*$) are true in $J$ under this mapping. Namely, a homomorphic embedding [CK90] of $flat(I_0)_{|D}$ into $flat(J)$.

Finally, assume that $p$ is in $I$. Since its forward chaining does not use the object $*$, we can use the same chaining under the homomorphism to generate $q$ in $J$, and therefore since $J \models H$, $q$ is in $J$, a contradiction.

The complexity bound follows since in each iteration we can check whether forward chaining adds a new atom in time $|H|n^t$ and there are at most $|\mathcal{S}|n^r$ iterations. ∎

The above process is similar of the use of the chase procedure to decide on uniform containment of database queries [Sag88]. Since we have access to EntMQ we can make sure that all clauses in the hypothesis of the algorithm are implied by the target function. (This essentially replaces the positive counter examples in the interpretations setting with EntMQ in the entailment setting.) Thus, the following lemma indicates that in the presence of EntMQ we can replace EQ by EntEQ.

**Lemma 8.** *Let $T \in \mathcal{H}_R(\mathcal{S}, =)$, $H \in \mathcal{H}_R(\mathcal{S}, =)$ and $T \models H$. Given a positive (clause) counter example $C \in \mathcal{H}_R(\mathcal{S}, =)$ such that $T \models C$ and $H \not\models C$ one can find a negative (interpretation) counter example $I$ such that $I \not\models T$ and $I \models H$.*

**Proof.** This easily follows from the previous lemma since $I \not\models C$ and $T \models C$ implies $I \not\models T$. ∎

We therefore get that the class is learnable. The complexity of the algorithm is as in the interpretation setting (though a slightly more careful argument is needed).

**Theorem 3.** *The class $\mathcal{H}_R(\mathcal{S}, =)$ is learnable from entailment equivalence queries and entailment membership queries.*

As before we can get a learnability result for $\mathcal{H}_R(\mathcal{S})$; this time, however, we can use a hypothesis in $\mathcal{H}_R(\mathcal{S})$. Note that when learning $T \in \mathcal{H}_R(\mathcal{S})$, interpretation counter examples constructed by the model finding algorithm have a special structure. In particular, since $C \in \mathcal{H}_R(\mathcal{S})$ (in Lemma 8) every object in $I$ (of Lemma 7) has a unique term associated with it (as generated from $C$). It follows that in the clauses generated in *rel-cands*() each variable has at most one defining equation. Therefore, the clauses can be "folded back" from the equational form into a range restricted form.

**Theorem 4.** *The class $\mathcal{H}_R(\mathcal{S})$ is learnable from entailment equivalence queries and entailment membership queries.*

# 6 The Implication Problem

Once expressions are learned as above one would want to use them as a knowledge base in a system, for example to infer properties implied by this knowledge. It is therefore useful if the implication problem is decidable and its complexity is bounded. It is easy to see that the model finding algorithm from Lemma 7 can be used to decide the implication problem.

**Corollary 2.** *The implication problem for $\mathcal{H}_R(\mathcal{S}, =)$ is decidable in time $O(|H| \cdot |S| \cdot n^{t+r})$.*

We note that similar problems have been studied in database theory; checking whether $I \models H$ corresponds to query evaluation, and checking whether $H \models C$ corresponds to uniform containment [Sag88]. Completeness results for these problems parametrised by the number of variables in a clause follow from [PY97].

# 7 Discussion

We have shown that weakly range restricted Horn expressions are learnable from equivalence and membership queries, both for learning from interpretations and for learning from entailment. In the special case where the target expression is range restricted, we can use range restricted expressions as the hypothesis language for learning from entailment. For learning from interpretations hypotheses are weakly range restricted. Our results use flattening and unflattening of examples and clauses and a model finding procedure for this class.

The learning algorithm is similar to the algorithm for learning from entailment in the propositional case [FP93] as well as several previous ILP algorithms. In fact, the construction in Lemma 7 corresponds to elaboration in [SB86] and saturation in [Rou92], and flattening has been used before in [Rou92]. The pairing procedure from [Kha98] is similar to LGG computation [Plo70] used in many systems. In addition the dropping of non-legal literals is similar to what is done in [Rou92]. As we have shown a combination of these steps is formally justified in that it leads to convergence for range restricted Horn expressions.

Previous work in [Ari97,RT98,RS98] pursued similar problems in the context of learning from entailment. These works use oracles that are stronger than the ones used here in that they provide information on the syntax of the learned expression (using the order on atoms for acyclic expressions or otherwise information on subsumption rather than implication). On the other hand they derive complexity bounds that are lower than the ones here, in particular avoiding the exponential dependence on the number of terms in a clause. This is partly due to use of strong oracles and partly due to the the fact that different subclasses of Horn expressions are studied.

A natural question from the discussion above is whether the exponential dependence on the number of terms can be avoided without using the additional oracles. On the other hand, relaxing the requirement that clauses are range restricted is also of interest since many standard logic programs use recursive patterns that do not conform to it. Finally, in the model inference problem [Sha91] the learner is trying to acquire information about a model rather than a formula. In contrast with the scenario here the domain and mapping of function symbols are fixed and hence the nature of the problem is different. More work is needed to clarify these issues.

# References

[AFP92]    D. Angluin, M. Frazier, and L. Pitt. Learning conjunctions of Horn clauses. *Machine Learning*, 9:147–164, 1992.

[AK95]     D. Angluin and M. Kharitonov. When won't membership queries help? *Journal of Computer and System Sciences*, 50:336–355, 1995.

[Ang88]    D. Angluin. Queries and concept learning. *Machine Learning*, 2(4):319–342, 1988.

[Ari97]    H. Arimura. Learning acyclic first-order Horn sentences from entailment. In *Proceedings of the International Conference on Algorithmic Learning Theory*. Springer-verlag, 1997. LNAI 1316.

[CK90]     C. Chang and J. Keisler. *Model Theory*. Elsevier, Amsterdam, Holland, 1990.

[Coh95a]   W. Cohen. PAC-learning recursive logic programs: Efficient algorithms. *Journal of Artificial Intelligence Research*, 2:501–539, 1995.

[Coh95b]   W. Cohen. PAC-learning recursive logic programs: Negative result. *Journal of Artificial Intelligence Research*, 2:541–573, 1995.

[DR97]     L. De Raedt. Logical settings for concept learning. *Artificial Intelligence*, 95(1):187–201, 1997. See also relevant Errata.

[DRB92]    L. De Raedt and M. Bruynooghe. An overview of the interactive concept learner and theory revisor CLINT. In S. Muggleton, editor, *Inductive Logic Programming*. Academic Press, 1992.

[DRD94]    L. De Raedt and S. Dzeroski. First order *jk*-clausal theories are PAC-learnable. *Artificial Intelligence*, 70:375–392, 1994.

[FP93]     M. Frazier and L. Pitt. Learning from entailment: An application to propositional Horn sentences. In *Proceedings of the International Conference on Machine Learning*, pages 120–127, Amherst, MA, 1993. Morgan Kaufmann.

[Hau89]    D. Haussler. Learning conjunctive concepts in structural domains. *Machine Learning*, 4(1):7–40, 1989.

[Kha96]    R. Khardon. Learning to take actions. In *Proceedings of the National Conference on Artificial Intelligence*, pages 787–792, Portland, Oregon, 1996. AAAI Press.

[Kha98]    R. Khardon. Learning function free Horn expressions. Technical Report ECS-LFCS-98-394, Laboratory for Foundations of Computer Science, Edinburgh University, 1998. A preliminary version of this paper appeared in COLT 1998.

[Lit88]    N. Littlestone. Learning quickly when irrelevant attributes abound: A new linear-threshold algorithm. *Machine Learning*, 2:285–318, 1988.

[Llo87]    J.W. Lloyd. *Foundations of Logic Programming*. Springer Verlag, 1987. Second Edition.

[MB92]    S. Muggleton and W. Buntine. Machine invention of first order predicates by inverting resolution. In S. Muggleton, editor, *Inductive Logic Programming*. Academic Press, 1992.

[MDR94]    S. Muggleton and L. De Raedt. Inductive logic programming: Theory and methods. *Journal of Logic Programming*, 20:629–679, 1994.

[MF92]    S. Muggleton and C. Feng. Efficient induction of logic programs. In S. Muggleton, editor, *Inductive Logic Programming*. Academic Press, 1992.

[Min88]    J. Minker, editor. *Foundations of Deductive Databases and Logic Programming*. Morgan Kaufmann, 1988.

[NCDW97]    S. Nienhuys-Cheng and R. De Wolf. *Foundations of Inductive Logic Programming*. Springer-verlag, 1997. LNAI 1228.

[Plo70]    G. D. Plotkin. A note on inductive generalization. In B. Meltzer and D. Michie, editors, *Machine Intelligence 5*, pages 153–163. American Elsevier, 1970.

[PY97]    C. H. Papadimitriou and M. Yannakakis. On the complexity of database queries. In *Proceedings of the symposium on Principles of Database Systems*, pages 12–19, Tucson, Arizona, 1997. ACM Press.

[Rou92]    C. Rouveirol. Extensions of inversion of resolution applied to theory completion. In S. Muggleton, editor, *Inductive Logic Programming*. Academic Press, 1992.

[RS98]    K. Rao and A. Sattar. Learning from entailment of logic programs with local variables. In *Proceedings of the International Conference on Algorithmic Learning Theory*. Springer-verlag, 1998. LNAI 1501.

[RT97]    C. Reddy and P. Tadepalli. Learning Horn definitions with equivalence and membership queries. In *International Workshop on Inductive Logic Programming*, pages 243–255, Prague, Czech Republic, 1997. Springer. LNAI 1297.

[RT98]    C. Reddy and P. Tadepalli. Learning first order acyclic Horn programs from entailment. In *International Conference on Inductive Logic Programming*, pages 23–37, Madison, WI, 1998. Springer. LNAI 1446.

[RTR96]    C. Reddy, P. Tadepalli, and S. Roncagliolo. Theory guided empirical speedup learning of goal decomposition rules. In *International Conference on Machine Learning*, pages 409–416, Bari, Italy, 1996. Morgan Kaufmann.

[Sag88]    Y. Sagiv. Optimizing datalog programs. In J. Minker, editor, *Foundations of Deductive Databases and Logic Programming*. Morgan Kaufmann, 1988.

[SB86]    C. Sammut and R. Banerji. Learning concepts by asking questions. In R. Michalski, J. Carbonell, and T. Mitchell, editors, *Machine Learning : An AI Approach, Volume II*. Morgan Kaufman, 1986..

[Sha83]    E. Y. Shapiro. *Algorithmic Program Debugging*. MIT Press, Cambridge, MA, 1983.

[Sha91]    E. Shapiro. Inductive inference of theories from facts. In J. Lassez and G. Plotkin, editors, *Computational Logic*, pages 199–254. MIT Press, 1991.

[Val84]    L. G. Valiant. A theory of the learnable. *Communications of the ACM*, 27(11):1134–1142, 1984.

[Val85]    L. G. Valiant. Learning disjunctions of conjunctions. In *Proceedings of the International Joint Conference of Artificial Intelligence*, pages 560–566, Los Angeles, CA, 1985. Morgan Kaufmann.

# On the Asymptotic Behavior of a Constant Stepsize Temporal-Difference Learning Algorithm

Vladislav Tadić

Mihajlo Pupin Institute, Volgina 15, 11000 Belgrade, Serbia, Yugoslavia
etadicv@ubbg.etf.bg.ac.yu

**Abstract.** The mean-square asymptotic behavior of constant stepsize temporal-difference algorithms is analyzed in this paper. The analysis is carried out for the case of a linear (cost-to-go) function approximation and for the case of Markov chains with an uncountable state space. An asymptotic upper bound for the mean-square deviation of the algorithm iterations from the optimal value of the parameter of the (cost-to-go) function approximator achievable by temporal-difference learning is determined as a function of stepsize.

**Keywords.** Temporal-difference learning, reinforcement learning, dynamic programming, cost-to-go function approximation, Markov chains.

## 1   Introduction

Predicting the expected long-term future cost of a stochastic system modelled as an uncontrolled Markov chain is a problem of great importance in the fields such as time-series analysis and automatic control (see e.g., [3]) These predictions have typically the form of a cost-to-go function, which itself is of a central role in the area of dynamic programming (see e.g., [2]). Several methods have been developed for predicting the values of a cost-to-go function associated to an uncontrolled Markov chain: Monte Carlo and maximum likelihood methods in the fields of statistics and automatic control (see e.g., [7]) and temporal-difference learning in the area of machine learning (see e.g., [3], [10]). Among them, temporal-difference is probably the most efficient and undoubtedly the most general and simplest to be implemented. Basically, temporal-difference learning algorithms are a parametric recursive method for approximating the cost-to-go function (associated to an uncontrolled Markov chain) as a function of the (chain) current state. Aiming at improving the approximations of the cost-to-go function on the basis of collected observations, these algorithms update the parameter of the function approximator whenever the observation of the chain transition and associated cost becomes available.

Due to good performances and a wide range of applications, various properties of temporal-difference learning algorithms have extensively been considered in a great number of papers (see e.g., [3], [10] and references cited therein; see the same references for details on the application of temporal-difference learning). Their convergence properties (almost sure convergence, convergence in mean, convergence of mean and rate of convergence) have been studied in [3] – [6] and [9] – [16]. However, the analysis presented in these papers corresponds exclusively to decreasing stepsize temporal-difference algorithms. Since the decreasing stepsize algorithms typically exhibit a poor convergence rate, the analysis of the corresponding constant stepsize algorithms is much more interesting (at least from the application point of view).

In this paper, the mean-square asymptotic behavior of constant stepsize temporal-difference algorithms is analyzed. The analysis is carried out for the case of a linear (cost-to-go) function approximation and for the case of Markov chains with an uncountable state space. An asymptotic upper bound for the mean-square deviation of the algorithm iterations from the optimal value of the parameter of the (cost-to-go) function approximator achievable by temporal-difference learning is determined as a function of stepsize. The results presented in this paper are an extension of the results of [15] to the constant stepsize algorithms and to the case of Markov chains with an uncountable state space. Other problems related to temporal-difference learning algorithms (almost sure convergence, rate of convergence, non-linear function approximation and stabilization) are considered in [11] – [14]

## 2  Algorithm and Assumptions

Temporal-difference learning algorithms with function approximation are defined by the following difference equations:

$$\theta_{n+1} = \theta_n + \gamma \varepsilon_{n+1} \delta_{n+1}, \quad n \geq 0, \tag{1}$$

$$\delta_{n+1} = g(X_{n+1}, X_{n+2}) + \alpha f(\theta_n, X_{n+2}) - f(\theta_n, X_{n+1}), \quad n \geq 0, \tag{2}$$

$$\varepsilon_{n+1} = \sum_{i=0}^{n} (\alpha \lambda)^{n-i} \nabla_\theta f(\theta_n, X_{i+1}), \quad n \geq 0. \tag{3}$$

$f : R^d \times R^{d'} \to R$ and $g : R^{d'} \times R^{d'} \to R$ are Borel-measurable functions and $f(\cdot, x)$, $x \in R^{d'}$, is differentiable. $\alpha \in (0, 1)$, $\lambda \in [0, 1]$ and $\gamma \in (0, \infty)$ are constants, while the algorithm initial value $\theta_0$ is an arbitrary vector from $R^d$. $\{X_n\}_{n \geq 0}$ is an $R^{d'}$-valued random process defined on a probability space $(\Omega, \mathcal{F}, \mathcal{P})$.

Let $f_*(x) = E(\sum_{n=0}^{\infty} \alpha^n g(X_n, X_{n+1}) | X_0 = x)$, $x \in R^{d'}$, be a discounted cost-to-go function associated to $\{X_n\}_{n \geq 0}$. The algorithm (1) – (3) aims at determining the parameter $\theta \in R^d$ such that $f(\theta, \cdot)$ approximates $f_*(\cdot)$. If $\lambda = 1$, this reduces to determining $\theta \in R^d$ such that $f(\theta, \cdot)$ approximates $f_*(\cdot)$ optimally in the $L^2(\mu)$ sense, i.e., to the minimization of the criterion function $J_*(\theta) = \int (f(\theta, x) - f_*(\theta))^2 \mu(dx)$, $\theta \in R^d$ (for details see [15]).

In this paper, the algorithm (1) – (3) is analyzed for the following case:

(i) $\{X_n\}_{n\geq 0}$ is a homogenous Markov chain,

(ii) $f(\theta, x) = \theta^T \phi(x)$, $\forall \theta \in R^d$, $\forall x \in R^{d'}$, where $\phi : R^{d'} \to R^d$ is a Borel-measurable function.

Let $R^+$ and $R_0^+$ be the sets of positive and non-negative reals (respectively), while $\|\cdot\|$ denotes the Euclidean vector norm, the Frobenius matrix norm and the total variation of signed measures. Let $P(x, \cdot)$, $x \in R^{d'}$, be the transition probability of $\{X_n\}_{n\geq 0}$ (i.e., $\mathcal{P}(X_{n+1} \in B | X_n) = P(X_n, B)$ w.p.1, $\forall B \in \mathcal{B}^{d'}$, $n \geq 0$), while $\tilde{g}(x) = \int g(x, x')P(x, dx')$, $x \in R^{d'}$. For $x \in R^{d'}$ and $B \in \mathcal{B}^{d'}$, let $P_0(x, B) = I_B(x)$ and $P_{n+1}(x, B) = \int P_n(x', B)P(x, dx')$, $n \geq 0$. For $x \in R^{d'}$, let $(P_n \phi)(x) = \int \phi(x')P_n(x, dx')$, $(P_n \tilde{g})(x) = \int \tilde{g}(x')P_n(x, dx')$ and $\phi_n(x) = \alpha(P_{n+1}\phi)(x) - (P_n\phi)(x)$, $n \geq 0$. The assumptions under which the algorithm (1) – (3) is analyzed are as follows:

**A1.** $g(\cdot, \cdot)$ and $\phi(\cdot)$ are locally bounded.

**A2.** $\{X_n\}_{n\geq 0}$ has a unique invariant measure $\mu(\cdot)$.

**A3.** There exists a constant $r \in R^+$ such that $\mu(x : \|x\| > r) = 0$ and $P(x, x' : \|x'\| > r) = 0$, $\forall x \in R^{d'}$.

**A4.** There exists a locally bounded Borel-measurable function $\psi : R^{d'} \to R_0^+$ such that

$$\sum_{i=0}^{\infty} \left\| \int \phi(x')(P_n\phi^T)(x')(P_i - \mu)(x, dx') \right\| \leq \psi(x); \quad \forall x \in R^{d'}, \ n \geq 0,$$

$$\sum_{i=0}^{\infty} \left\| \int \phi(x')(P_n\tilde{g})(x')(P_i - \mu)(x, dx') \right\| \leq \psi(x); \quad \forall x \in R^{d'}, \ n \geq 0.$$

**A5.** $\int \phi(x)\phi^T(x)\mu(dx)$ is negative definite.

*Remark 1.* A1 and A3 imply

$$P_n(x, x' : \|x'\| > r) = 0; \quad \forall x \in R^{d'}, \ n \geq 1, \tag{4}$$

$$\sup_{\|x\|\leq t} \int |g(x, x')|P(x, dx') \leq \sup_{\|x\|\leq t, \|x'\|\leq r} |g(x, x')| < \infty, \quad \forall t \in R^+. \tag{5}$$

$$\sup_{x \in R^{d'}} \int \int |g(x', x'')|P(x', dx'')P_n(x, dx')$$
$$\leq \sup_{\|x\|, \|x'\|\leq r} |g(x, x')| < \infty, \quad n \geq 1, \tag{6}$$

$$\sup_{x \in R^{d'}} \int \|\phi(x)\|P_n(x, dx') \leq \sup_{\|x\|\leq r} \|\phi(x)\| < \infty, \quad n \geq 1, \tag{7}$$

wherefrom it can easily be deduced that $\tilde{g}(\cdot)$ and the terms of the sums appearing in A4 are well-defined and finite.

A1 corresponds to the properties of $g(\cdot,\cdot)$ and $\phi(\cdot)$, while A2 – A5 refer to those of $\{X_n\}_{n\geq 0}$. A1 represents probably the mildest assumption on $g(\cdot,\cdot)$ and $\phi(\cdot)$ under which the algorithm (1) – (3) can still be analyzed. On the other hand, A2 requires $\{X_n\}_{n\geq 0}$ to exhibit a certain asymptotic stationarity, while A4 virtually demands this "asymptotic steady-state" to be reached sufficiently fast. The assumptions of this kind are natural for learning in the Markovian environments and standardly appear in the analysis of the corresponding (learning) algorithms (for details see [3] and references cited therein). A3 requires $\{X_n\}_{n\geq 0}$ to be essentially bounded. Since any implementation of the algorithm (1) – (3) involves a uniform truncation of the input data (due to the finite precision of implementing machines), this requirement is not restrictive (at least not from the application point of view). A5 can be thought of as a form of "persistency of excitation" condition (for details see e.g., [7], [8]). If $\{X_n\}_{n\geq 0}$ has a finite state-space $\{x_1,\ldots,x_m\}$, it reduces to the requirement that $\mu(x = x_i) > 0$, $1 \leq i \leq m$, and that $[\phi(x_1)\ldots\phi(x_m)]$ is a full row-rank matrix (i.e., that its rows are linearly independent).

Using A3 and (4), it can easily be deduced that

$$\left\| \int \phi(x')(P_n\phi^T)(x')(P_i - \mu)(x,dx') \right\|$$
$$\leq C^2 \|(P_i - \mu)(x,\cdot)\|; \quad \forall x \in R^{d'},\ n \geq 0,\ i \geq 1,$$

$$\left\| \int \phi(x')(P_n\tilde{g})(x')(P_i - \mu)(x,dx') \right\|$$
$$\leq C^2 \|(P_i - \mu)(x,\cdot)\|; \quad \forall x \in R^{d'},\ n \geq 0,\ i \geq 1,$$

where $C = \sup_{\|x\|\leq r} \max\{|\tilde{g}(x)|, \|\phi(x)\|\}$. Then, it is obvious that A4 holds if A2 and A3 are satisfied and if $\sum_{n=0}^{\infty} \|(P_i - \mu)(x,\cdot)\| < \infty,\ \forall x \in R^{d'}$. Consequently, A2 – A4 are satisfied if $\{X_n\}_{n\geq 0}$ is a geometrically ergodic Markov chain with bounded state-space, which itself includes the case of irreducible aperiodic Markov chain with finite state-space (see e.g. [8]). Moreover, A1 – A5, with the exception of only A3, cover the assumptions adopted in [15].

## 3  Analysis

For $x$, $x' \in R^{d'}$, $y \in R^d$ and $z = (x,x',y)$, let $U(z) = y(\alpha\phi(x') - \phi(x))^T$ and $u(z) = yg(x,x')$, while

$$\Pi(z,B) = \int I_B(x',x'',\alpha\lambda y + \phi(x'))P(x',dx''), \quad \forall B \in R^{d+2d'}.$$

Let $Z_n = (X_n, X_{n+1}, \varepsilon_n)$, $n \geq 0$, while $\theta_* = -U_*^{-1}u_*$ and

$$U_* = -\int \phi(x)\phi^T(x)\mu(dx) + (1-\lambda)\alpha\sum_{n=0}^{\infty}(\alpha\lambda)^n \int \phi(x)(P_{n+1}\phi^T)(x)\mu(dx),$$

$$u_* = \sum_{n=0}^{\infty} (\alpha\lambda)^n \int \int \phi(x)(P_n\tilde{g})(x)\mu(dx).$$

Then, it can easily be deduced that $\{Z_n\}_{n\geq 0}$ is a homogenous Markov process satisfying $\mathcal{P}(Z_{n+1} \in B|Z_n) = \Pi(Z_n, B)$ w.p.1, $\forall B \in \mathcal{B}^{d+2d'}$, $n \geq 0$. For an interpretation of $\theta_*$ and an upper bound for the error in approximating $f_*(\cdot)$ by $\theta_*^T\phi(\cdot)$ see [15].

**Lemma 1.** *Let A1 – A3 and A5 hold. Then, $f_*(\cdot), U_*, u_*$ and $\theta_*$ are well-defined and finite.*

**Proof.** Using (4) – (7), it can easily be deduced that there exists a locally bounded Borel-measurable function $\varphi : R^{d'} \to R_0^+$ such that

$$\max\{|(P_n\tilde{g})(x)|, \|(P_n\phi)(x)\|\} \leq \varphi(x); \quad \forall x \in R^{d'}, n \geq 0. \tag{8}$$

Let $K = \sup_{\|x\|\leq r} \varphi(x)$. As

$$E\left(\sum_{n=0}^{\infty} \alpha^n |g(X_n, X_{n+1})| \Big| X_0 = x\right)$$

$$= \sum_{n=0}^{\infty} \alpha^n \int \int |g(x', x'')| P(x', dx'') P_n(x, dx'); \quad \forall x \in R^{d'}, n \geq 0,$$

$$\int \|\phi(x)\phi^T(x)\|\mu(dx) \leq K^2,$$

$$\sum_{n=0}^{\infty} (\alpha\lambda)^n \int \|\phi(x)(P_{n+1}\phi^T)(x)\|\mu(dx) \leq (1 - \alpha\lambda)^{-1}K^2,$$

$$\sum_{n=0}^{\infty} (\alpha\lambda)^n \int \|\phi(x)(P_n\tilde{g})(x)\|\mu(dx) \leq (1 - \alpha\lambda)^{-1}K^2$$

(due to A3 and (8)), it is obvious that $U_*$ and $u_*$ are also well-defined and finite. On the other hand, owing to the Lyapunov inequality, it is obtained

$$\int (\theta^T(P_n\phi)(x))^2 \mu(dx) \leq \int \int (\theta^T\phi(x'))^2 P_n(x, dx')\mu(dx)$$

$$= \int (\theta^T\phi(x))^2 \mu(dx); \quad \forall \theta \in R^d, n \geq 0.$$

Consequently,

$$\left|\int \theta^T\phi(x)(P_n\phi^T)(x)\theta\mu(dx)\right|$$

$$\leq \left(\int (\theta^T\phi(x))^2\mu(dx)\right)^{1/2} \left(\int (\theta^T(P_n\phi)(x))^2\mu(dx)\right)^{1/2}$$

$$\leq \int (\theta^T\phi(x))^2\mu(dx); \quad \forall \theta \in R^d, n \geq 0.$$

Then, it can easily be deduced that

$$\theta^T U_* \theta = (1 - \lambda)\alpha \sum_{n=0}^{\infty} (\alpha\lambda)^n \int \theta^T \phi(x)(P_{n+1}\phi)(x)\theta\mu(dx)$$

$$- \int (\theta^T \phi(x))^2 \mu(dx)$$

$$\leq -(1 - \alpha)(1 - \alpha\lambda)^{-1} \int (\theta^T \phi(x))^2 \mu(dx)$$

$$= -(1 - \alpha)(1 - \alpha\lambda)^{-1}\theta^T \left( \int \phi(x)\phi^T(x)\mu(dx) \right) \theta, \quad \forall \theta \in R^d,$$

wherefrom it immediately follows that $U_*$ is negative definite and that $\theta_*$ is well-defined and finite. ∎

**Lemma 2.** *Let A1 – A3 hold. Then, $(\Pi^n U)(\cdot)$ and $(\Pi^n u)(\cdot)$ are well-defined, finite and satisfy the following relations for all $x$, $x' \in R^{d'}$, $y \in R^d$ and $z = (x, x', y)$:*

$$(\Pi^{n+1}U)(z) = \sum_{i=0}^{n} (\alpha\lambda)^i \int \phi(x'')\phi_i^T(x'')P_{n-i}(x', dx'')$$

$$+ (\alpha\lambda)^{n+1}y\phi_n^T(x), \quad n \geq 0, \tag{9}$$

$$(\Pi^{n+1}u)(z) = \sum_{i=0}^{n} (\alpha\lambda)^i \int \phi(x'')(P_i\tilde{g})(x'')P_{n-i}(x', dx'')$$

$$+ (\alpha\lambda)^{n+1}y(P_n\tilde{g})(x'), \quad n \geq 0. \tag{10}$$

**Proof.** Due to A1, A3 and (4) – (7), it is obvious that $(\Pi^n U)(z)$, $(\Pi^n u)(z)$ and the right-hand sides of (9) and (10) are well-defined and finite for all $x$, $x' \in R^{d'}$, $y \in R^d$, $z = (x, x', y)$ and $n \geq 0$ (notice that A1 and A3 imply that $U(\cdot)$ and $u(\cdot)$ are locally bounded and that $\Pi^n(z, \cdot)$ is compactly supported for all $z \in R^{d+2d'}$, $n \geq 0$). The relations (9) and (10) themselves will be proved by mathematical induction.

It can easily be deduced from the definition of $P_i(\cdot, \cdot)$ that the following relations are satisfied for all $x$, $x' \in R^{d'}$, $y \in R^d$ and $z = (x, x', y)$:

$$(\Pi^1 U)(z) = \int (\alpha\lambda y + \phi(x'))(\alpha\phi(x'') - \phi(x'))^T P(x', dx'')$$

$$= (\alpha\lambda y + \phi(x'))(\alpha(P_1\phi)(x') - \phi(x'))^T$$

$$= \int \phi(x'')\phi_0^T(x'')P_0(x', dx'') + \alpha\lambda y\phi_0^T(x),$$

$$(\Pi^1 u)(z) = \int (\alpha\lambda y + \phi(x'))g(x', x'')P(x', dx'')$$

$$= (\alpha\lambda y + \phi(x'))\tilde{g}(x')$$

$$= \alpha\lambda y\tilde{g}(x') + \int \phi(x'')\tilde{g}(x'')P_0(x',dx'').$$

Now, let us suppose that (9) and (10) hold for some $n \geq 0$ and for all $x$, $x' \in R^{d'}$, $y \in R^d$ and $z = (x, x', y)$. Then, it can easily be deduced from the definition of $\Pi(\cdot, \cdot)$ that the following relations are satisfied for all $x$, $x' \in R^{d'}$, $y \in R^d$ and $z = (x, x', y)$:

$$(\Pi^{n+1}U)(z) = \sum_{i=0}^{n}(\alpha\lambda)^i \int\int \phi(x''')\phi_i^T(x''')P_{n-i}(x'',dx''')P(x',dx'')$$

$$+ (\alpha\lambda)^{n+1}\int (\alpha\lambda y + \phi(x'))\phi_n^T(x'')P(x',dx'')$$

$$= \sum_{i=0}^{n}(\alpha\lambda)^i \int \phi(x'')\phi_i^T(x'')P_{n-i+1}(x',dx'')$$

$$+ (\alpha\lambda)^{n+1}(\alpha\lambda y + \phi(x'))\phi_{n+1}^T(x')$$

$$= \sum_{i=0}^{n+1}(\alpha\lambda)^i \int \phi(x'')\phi_i^T(x'')P_{n-i+1}(x',dx'')$$

$$+ (\alpha\lambda)^{n+1}y\phi_{n+1}^T(x'),$$

$$(\Pi^{n+1}u)(z) = \sum_{i=0}^{n}(\alpha\lambda)^i \int\int \phi(x''')(P_i\tilde{g})(x''')P_{n-i}(x'',dx''')P(x',dx'')$$

$$+ (\alpha\lambda)^{n+1}\int (\alpha\lambda y + \phi(x'))(P_n\tilde{g})(x'')P(x',dx'')$$

$$= \sum_{i=0}^{n}(\alpha\lambda)^i \int \phi(x'')(P_i\tilde{g})(x'')P_{n-i+1}(x',dx'')$$

$$+ (\alpha\lambda)^{n+1}(\alpha\lambda y + \phi(x'))(P_{n+1}\tilde{g})(x')$$

$$= \sum_{i=0}^{n+1}(\alpha\lambda)^i \int \phi(x'')(P_i\tilde{g})(x'')P_{n-i+1}(x',dx'')$$

$$+ (\alpha\lambda)^{n+2}y(P_{n+1}\tilde{g})(x').$$

This completes the proof. ∎

**Lemma 3.** *Let A1 – A4 hold. Then, there exist locally bounded Borel-measurable functions $V : R^{d+2d'} \to R^{d\times d}$ and $v : R^{d+2d'} \to R^d$ such that $(\Pi V)(\cdot)$ and $(\Pi v)(\cdot)$ are also locally bounded and such that*

$$U(z) - U_* = V(z) - (\Pi V)(z), \quad \forall z \in R^{d+2d'}, \tag{11}$$

$$u(z) - u_* = v(z) - (\Pi v)(z), \quad \forall z \in R^{d+2d'}. \tag{12}$$

**Proof.** It can easily be deduced from (5) – (7) that there exists a locally bounded Borel-measurable function $\varphi : R^{d'} \to R_0^+$ such that

$$\max\{\|(P_n\phi)(x)\|, |(P_n\tilde{g})(x)|\} \leq \varphi(x); \quad \forall x \in R^{d'}, \ n \geq 0. \tag{13}$$

Let $K = \sup_{\|x\| \leq r} \varphi(x)$. Then, it follows from A3 and (13) that

$$\sum_{i=n+1}^{\infty} (\alpha\lambda)^i \int \|\phi(x)(P_{i+j}\phi)(x)\|\mu(dx) \leq (1-\alpha\lambda)^{-1}(\alpha\lambda)^{n+1}K^2; \quad n, j \geq 0, \tag{14}$$

$$\sum_{i=n+1}^{\infty} (\alpha\lambda)^i \int \|\phi(x)(P_i\tilde{g})(x)\|\mu(dx) \leq (1-\alpha\lambda)^{-1}(\alpha\lambda)^{n+1}K^2, \quad n \geq 0, \tag{15}$$

while A4 implies

$$\sum_{n=0}^{\infty} \sum_{i=0}^{n} (\alpha\lambda)^i \left\| \int \phi(x')(P_{i+j}\phi^T)(x')(P_{n-i} - \mu)(x, dx') \right\|$$

$$= \sum_{i=0}^{\infty} (\alpha\lambda)^i \sum_{n=0}^{\infty} \left\| \int \phi(x')(P_{i+j}\phi^T)(x')(P_n - \mu)(x, dx') \right\|$$

$$\leq (1-\alpha\lambda)^{-1}\psi(x); \quad \forall x \in R^{d'}, \ j \geq 0, \tag{16}$$

$$\sum_{n=0}^{\infty} \sum_{i=0}^{n} (\alpha\lambda)^i \left\| \int \phi(x')(P_i\tilde{g})(x')(P_{n-i} - \mu)(x, dx') \right\|$$

$$= \sum_{i=0}^{\infty} (\alpha\lambda)^i \sum_{n=0}^{\infty} \left\| \int \phi(x')(P_i\tilde{g})(x')(P_n - \mu)(x, dx') \right\|$$

$$\leq (1-\alpha\lambda)^{-1}\psi(x), \quad \forall x \in R^{d'}. \tag{17}$$

On the other hand, using Lemma 2, it is obtained

$$(\Pi^{n+1}U)(z) - U_* = \sum_{i=0}^{n} (\alpha\lambda)^i \int \phi(x'')\phi_i^T(x'')(P_{n-i} - \mu)(x', dx'')$$

$$- \sum_{i=n+1}^{\infty} (\alpha\lambda)^i \int \phi(x'')\phi_i^T(x'')\mu(dx'')$$

$$+ (\alpha\lambda)^{n+1}y\phi_n^T(x'), \quad n \geq 0,$$

$$(\Pi^{n+1}u)(z) - u_* = \sum_{i=0}^{n} (\alpha\lambda)^i \int \phi(x'')(P_i\tilde{g})(x'')(P_{n-i} - \mu)(x', dx'')$$

$$- \sum_{i=n+1}^{\infty} (\alpha\lambda)^i \int \phi(x'')(P_i\tilde{g})(x'')\mu(dx'')$$

$$+ (\alpha\lambda)^{n+1}y(P_n\tilde{g})(x'), \quad n \geq 0,$$

for all $x$, $x' \in R^{d'}$, $y \in R^d$ and $z = (x, x', y)$. Then, owing to (13) – (15), it can easily be deduced that the following relations also hold for all $x$, $x' \in R^{d'}$, $y \in R^d$ and $z = (x, x', y)$:

$$\|(\Pi^{n+1}U)(z) - U_*\| \leq \sum_{i=0}^{n}(\alpha\lambda)^i \left\| \int \phi(x'')(P_{i+1}\phi^T)(x'')(P_{n-i} - \mu)(x', dx'') \right\|$$
$$+ \sum_{i=0}^{n}(\alpha\lambda)^i \left\| \int \phi(x'')(P_i\phi^T)(x'')(P_{n-i} - \mu)(x', dx'') \right\|$$
$$+ 2(\alpha\lambda)^{n+1}\varphi(x')\|y\| + 2(\alpha\lambda)^{n+1}(1 - \alpha\lambda)^{-1}K^2, \quad n \geq 0,$$

$$\|(\Pi^{n+1}u)(z) - u_*\| \leq \sum_{i=0}^{n}(\alpha\lambda)^i \left\| \int \phi(x'')(P_i\tilde{g})(x'')(P_{n-i} - \mu)(x', dx'') \right\|$$
$$+ (\alpha\lambda)^{n+1}\varphi(x')\|y\| + (\alpha\lambda)^{n+1}(1 - \alpha\lambda)^{-1}K^2, \quad n \geq 0.$$

Therefore and owing to (16) and (17), it is obtained that

$$\sum_{n=1}^{\infty} \|(\Pi^n U)(z) - U_*\| \leq 2(1 - \alpha\lambda)^{-1}(\alpha\lambda(1 - \alpha\lambda)^{-1}K^2 + \alpha\lambda\varphi(x')\|y\| + \psi(x')),$$

$$\sum_{n=1}^{\infty} \|(\Pi^n u)(z) - u_*\| \leq (1 - \alpha\lambda)^{-1}(\alpha\lambda(1 - \alpha\lambda)^{-1}K^2 + \alpha\lambda\varphi(x')\|y\| + \psi(x'))$$

for all $x$, $x' \in R^{d'}$, $y \in R^d$ and $z = (x, x', y)$. Let $V(z) = \sum_{n=0}^{\infty}((\Pi^n U)(z) - U_*)$ and $v(z) = \sum_{n=0}^{\infty}((\Pi^n u)(z) - u_*)$, $z \in R^{d+2d'}$. Then, it can easily be deduced that $V(\cdot)$, $(\Pi V)(\cdot)$, $v(\cdot)$ and $(\Pi v)(\cdot)$ are well-defined, locally bounded and satisfy (11) and (12) (notice that $(\Pi V)(z) = \sum_{n=1}^{\infty}((\Pi^n U)(z) - U_*)$ and $(\Pi v)(z) = \sum_{n=1}^{\infty}((\Pi^n u)(z) - u_*)$, $\forall z \in R^{d+2d'}$). ∎

**Theorem 1.** *Let A1 – A5 hold and let $\theta_0$ be an arbitrary deterministic vector from $R^d$. Then, there exist constants $\gamma_*$, $C_* \in R^+$ (depending on $\alpha$, $\lambda$, $r$, $\mu(\cdot)$, $g(\cdot, \cdot)$ and $\phi(\cdot)$, and not depending on $\gamma$ and $\theta_0$) such that*

$$\varlimsup_{n \to \infty} E\|\theta_n - \theta_*\|^2 \leq C_*\gamma, \quad \forall\gamma \in (0, \gamma_*).$$

**Proof.** Let $-\lambda_m$ denote the largest eigenvalue of $U_*$, while $K = \sup_{\|x\| \leq r}\|\phi(x)\|$. Let

$$L = \sup\{\|U(z)\|, \|u(z)\|, \|V(z)\|, \|v(z)\|, \|(\Pi V)(z)\|, \|(\Pi v)(z)\|$$
$$: \|z\| \leq 2r + (1 - \alpha\lambda)^{-1}K\}$$

and $M = (1 + L)(1 + \|\theta_*\|)$. Let $\gamma_* = \min\{2\lambda_m^{-1}, 2^{-4}M^{-3}\}$ and suppose that $\gamma \in (0, \gamma_*)$. Let $\mathcal{F}_n = \sigma\{Z_0, \ldots, Z_n\}$, $A_n = U(Z_n)$, $B_n = V(Z_n)$ and $\tilde{B}_n = (\Pi V)(Z_n)$, $n \geq 0$, while $a_n = U(Z_n)\theta_* + u(Z_n)$, $b_n = V(Z_n)\theta_* + v(Z_n)$ and

$\tilde{b}_n = (\Pi V)(Z_n)\theta_* + (\Pi v)(Z_n)$, $n \geq 0$. Since $\|X_n\| \leq r$ w.p.1, $n \geq 1$ (due to (4)), it is obtained

$$\|\varepsilon_{n+1}\| \leq \sum_{i=0}^{n}(\alpha\lambda)^{n-i}\|\phi(X_{i+1})\| \leq (1-\alpha\lambda)^{-1}K \ w.p.1, \quad n \geq 0.$$

Consequently, $\|Z_n\| \leq 2r + (1-\alpha\lambda)^{-1}K$ w.p.1, $n \geq 1$, wherefrom

$$\max\{\|A_n\|, \|a_n\|, \|B_n\|, \|b_n\|, \|\tilde{B}_n\|, \|\tilde{b}_n\|\} \leq M \ w.p.1, \quad n \geq 1, \qquad (18)$$

immediately follows. Let $x_n = \theta_n - \theta_*$ and $T_n = \|x_n\|^2 + 2\gamma x_n^T \tilde{B}_n x_n + 2\gamma x_n^T \tilde{b}_n$, $n \geq 0$. Then, it is straightforward to verify that

$$x_{n+1} = x_n + \gamma(A_{n+1}x_n + a_{n+1}), \quad n \geq 0, \qquad (19)$$

$$\begin{aligned}
T_{n+1} = {} & T_n + 2\gamma x_n^T U_* x_n + 2\gamma x_n^T((B_{n+1} - \tilde{B}_n)x_n + b_{n+1} - \tilde{b}_n) \\
& + \gamma^2\|A_{n+1}x_n + a_{n+1}\|^2 \\
& + 2\gamma^2((\tilde{B}_{n+1} + \tilde{B}_{n+1}^T)x_n + \tilde{b}_{n+1})^T(A_{n+1}x_n + a_{n+1}) \\
& + 2\gamma^3(A_{n+1}x_n + a_{n+1})^T \tilde{B}_{n+1}(A_{n+1}x_n + a_{n+1}), \quad n \geq 0. \qquad (20)
\end{aligned}$$

Using (18), (19) and the fact that $\theta_0$ is deterministic, it can easily be deduced that $\sigma\{\theta_n\} \subseteq \mathcal{F}_n$, $n \geq 0$, and

$$\|x_n\| \leq (1+\gamma K)^n(\|\theta_0\| + \|\theta_*\|) + \gamma K \sum_{i=1}^{n-1}(1+\gamma K)^i, \quad n \geq 0. \qquad (21)$$

Therefore and owing to the fact that $E(B_{n+1}|\mathcal{F}_n) = \tilde{B}_n$ and $E(b_{n+1}|\mathcal{F}_n) = \tilde{b}_n$ w.p.1, $n \geq 0$ (notice that $E(V(Z_{n+1})|\mathcal{F}_n) = (\Pi V)(Z_n)$ and $E(v(Z_{n+1})|\mathcal{F}_n) = (\Pi v)(Z_n)$ w.p.1, $n \geq 0$), it is obvious that

$$E(x_n^T(B_{n+1} - \tilde{B}_n)x_n|\mathcal{F}_n) = 0 \ w.p.1, \quad n \geq 0,$$

$$E(x_n^T(b_{n+1} - \tilde{b}_n)|\mathcal{F}_n) = 0 \ w.p.1, \quad n \geq 0.$$

Consequently,

$$E(x_n^T((B_{n+1} - \tilde{B}_n)x_n + b_{n+1} - \tilde{b}_n)) = 0, \quad n \geq 0. \qquad (22)$$

On the other hand, (18) implies

$$\|A_{n+1}x_n + a_{n+1}\|^2 \leq 2M^2(1 + \|x_n\|^2), \quad n \geq 0, \qquad (23)$$

$$|(A_{n+1}x_n + a_{n+1})^T \tilde{B}_{n+1}(A_{n+1}x_n + a_{n+1})| \leq 2M^3(1 + \|x_n\|^2), \quad n \geq 0, \qquad (24)$$

$$\begin{aligned}
& |((\tilde{B}_{n+1} + \tilde{B}_{n+1}^T)x_n + \tilde{b}_{n+1})^T(A_{n+1}x_n + a_{n+1})| \\
& \leq M^2(1 + 2\|x_n\|)(1 + \|x_n\|) \leq 4M^2(1 + \|x_n\|^2), \quad n \geq 0, \qquad (25)
\end{aligned}$$

$$|T_n - \|x_n\|^2| \leq 2M\gamma\|x_n\|^2 + 2M\gamma\|x_n\|$$
$$\leq 4M\gamma\|x_n\|^2 + 2M\gamma \leq 2^{-1}\|x_n\|^2 + 2M\gamma, \quad n \geq 1 \qquad (26)$$

(notice that $4M\gamma \leq 2^{-1}$). Since $x_n^T U_* x_n \leq -\lambda_m\|x_n\|^2$, $n \geq 0$, it directly follows from (20) and (22) – (26) that

$$E(T_{n+1}) \leq E(T_n) - 2\lambda_m\gamma E\|x_n\|^2 + 16M^3\gamma^2(1 + E\|x_n\|^2)$$
$$\leq E(T_n) - \lambda_m\gamma E\|x_n\|^2 + 16M^3\gamma^2, \quad n \geq 1 \qquad (27)$$

(notice that $\gamma \leq 1$, $\lambda_m \geq 16M^3\gamma$ and that (21) and (26) imply $E|T_n| < \infty$, $n \geq 1$), while (26) yields

$$E\|x_n\|^2 \geq 2^{-1}E(T_n) - M\gamma, \quad n \geq 1, \qquad (28)$$

$$E\|x_n\|^2 \leq 2E(T_n) + 4M\gamma, \quad n \geq 1. \qquad (29)$$

Due to (27) and (28), it is obtained

$$E(T_{n+1}) \leq (1 - 2^{-1}\lambda_m\gamma)E(T_n) + M(\lambda_m + 16M^2)\gamma^2, \quad n \geq 1,$$

wherefrom

$$E(T_n) \leq (1 - 2^{-1}\lambda_m\gamma)^{n-1}E(T_1) + M(\lambda_m + 16M^2)\sum_{i=0}^{n-2}(1 - 2^{-1}\lambda_m\gamma)^i, \quad n \geq 1,$$

immediately follows. Therefore,

$$\varlimsup_{n\to\infty} E(T_n) \leq 2M(1 + 16M^2\lambda_m^{-1})\gamma$$

(notice that $2^{-1}\lambda_m\gamma < 1$), which, together with (29), implies

$$\varlimsup_{n\to\infty} E\|\theta_n - \theta_*\|^2 = \varlimsup_{n\to\infty} E\|x_n\|^2 \leq 8M(1 + 8M^2\lambda_m^{-1})\gamma.$$

This completes the proof. ∎

## 4 Conclusion

The mean-square asymptotic behavior of constant stepsize temporal-difference algorithms has been analyzed in this paper. The analysis has been carried out for the case of a linear (cost-to-go) function approximation and for the case of Markov chains with an uncountable state space. An asymptotic upper bound for the mean-square error deviation of the algorithm iterations from the optimal value of the parameter of the (cost-to-go) function approximator achievable by temporal-difference learning has been determined as a function of stepsize. The results presented in this paper are an extension of the results of [15] to the constant stepsize algorithms and to the case of Markov chains with an uncountable state space.

# References

1. A. Benveniste, M. Metivier, P. Priouret, Adaptive Algorithms and Stochastic Approximation, Springer Verlag, 1990.
2. D. P. Bertsekas, Dynamic Programming and Optimal Control, Athena Scientific, 1995.
3. D. P. Bertsekas, J. N. Tsitsiklis, Neuro-Dynamic Programming, Athena Scientific, 1996.
4. P. D. Dayan, The convergence of $TD(\lambda)$ for general $\lambda$, Machine Learning 8 (1992), pp. 341–362.
5. P. D. Dayan, T. J. Sejnowski, $TD(\lambda)$ converges with probability 1, Machine Learning 14 (1994), pp. 295–301.
6. T. Jaakola, M. I. Jordan, S. P. Singh, On the convergence of stochastic iterative dynamic programming algorithms, Neural Computation 6 (1994), pp. 1185–1201.
7. P. R. Kumar, P. Varaiya, Stochastic Systems: Estimation, Identification and Adaptive Control, Prentice Hall, 1986.
8. S. P. Meyn, R. L. Tweedie, Markov Chains and Stochastic Stability, Springer Verlag, 1993.
9. R. S. Sutton, Learning to predict by the methods of temporal-differences, Machine Learning 3 (1988), pp. 9–44.
10. R. S. Sutton, A. G. Barto, Reinforcement Learning: An Introduction, MIT Press, 1998.
11. V. Tadić, On the convergence of stochastic iterative algorithms and their applications to machine learning, in preparation.
12. V. Tadić, On the robustness of stochastic iterative algorithms and their applications to machine learning, in preparation.
13. V. Tadić, A stabilization of a class of stochastic iterative algorithms and its application to machine learning, in preparation.
14. V. Tadić, Almost sure exponential convergence of constant stepsize temporal-difference learning algorithms, in preparation.
15. J. N. Tsitsiklis, B. Van Roy, An analysis of temporal-difference learning with function approximation, IEEE Transactions on Automatic Control 42 (1997), pp. 674–690.
16. J. N. Tsitsiklis, B. Van Roy, Feature-based methods for large scale dynamic programming, Machine Learning 22 (1996), pp. 59–94.

# Direct and Indirect Algorithms for On-line Learning of Disjunctions*

D. P. Helmbold, S. Panizza and M. K. Warmuth

Department of Computer Science
University of California at Santa Cruz
dph/panizza/manfred@cse.ucsc.edu

**Abstract.** It is easy to design on-line learning algorithms for learning $k$ out of $n$ variable monotone disjunctions by simply keeping one weight per disjunction. Such algorithms use roughly $O(n^k)$ weights which can be prohibitively expensive. Surprisingly, algorithms like Winnow require only $n$ weights (one per variable) and the mistake bound of these algorithms is not too much worse than the mistake bound of the more costly algorithms. The purpose of this paper is to investigate how the exponentially many weights can be collapsed into only $O(n)$ weights. In particular, we consider probabilistic assumptions that enable the Bayes optimal algorithm's posterior over the disjunctions to be encoded with only $O(n)$ weights. This results in a new $O(n)$ algorithm for learning disjunctions which is related to the Bylander's BEG algorithm originally introduced for linear regression. Beside providing a Bayesian interpretation for this new algorithm, we are also able to obtain mistake bounds for the noise free case resembling those that have been derived for the Winnow algorithm. The same techniques used to derive this new algorithm also provide a Bayesian interpretation for a normalized version of Winnow.

## 1 Introduction

We consider the problem of learning $k$ out of $n$ variable monotone disjunctions, where $k$ is typically much smaller than $n$, in an on-line setting. In this setting learning proceeds in a sequence of trials; on each trial the learning algorithm observes a boolean instance, predicts the instance's classification, and then is told the correct classification for the instance.

Most on-line learning algorithms use a set of weights or parameters to represent their current hypothesis. In this paper on-line learning algorithms always have three parts: a *prediction rule* which maps the instance and weights to a prediction, an *update function* which specifies how the algorithm's weights are modified, and an *update policy* indicating when the update function should be

---

* The first and third authors are supported by NSF grant CCR 9700201. The second author is supported by a research fellowship from the University of Milan and by a Eurocolt grant.

applied. The update policies considered in this paper are: 1) update after each trial, and 2) only update after trials where the algorithm makes an incorrect prediction. Algorithms with the latter policy are called *mistake-driven* (or conservative) [Lit89,Lit95].

When learning monotone disjunctions, some algorithms keep one weight per disjunction (i.e. a total of $\binom{n}{k}$ weights). We call such algorithms *direct algorithms* since the weights directly encode the confidence in or likelihood of each individual disjunction.

There are other algorithms that learn disjunctions while maintaining only $O(n)$ weights. We call such algorithms *indirect algorithms* since they indirectly encode their confidences in the disjunctions using $O(1)$ weights per variable. Surprisingly these more efficient algorithms learn disjunctions almost as well as the direct algorithms. The first such indirect algorithm was Littlestone's Winnow algorithm [Lit88,Lit89].

In this paper we are primarily interested in a performance criteria that makes no probabilistic assumptions about how the data is generated. On the contrary the examples can be chosen by an adversary and the goal is to make *relatively* few mistakes compared to the number of mistakes made by the best monotone disjunction on the sequence of examples being observed [Lit88,Lit89].

The Bayesian approach is a popular way to design and analyze on-line algorithms. Bayes learning algorithms use probabilistic assumptions about the world and data observed in past trials to construct a posterior distribution over the class of disjunctions. These algorithms then predict the most likely classification with respect to the current posterior. It is well known that when the instances are generated and labeled according to the probabilistic assumptions, then Bayes algorithm minimizes the expected total number of mistakes.

By comparing the world model assumed by a Bayes algorithm to the actual situation, one can get important intuition about how well (or poorly) the algorithm will perform. Relative mistake bounds give a much different kind of intuition, and their worst-case nature may be overly pessimistic. Relating these two styles of algorithms will give important insight into existing algorithms and lead to new approaches for designing learning algorithms.

For many direct algorithms with good relative mistake bounds it is easy to work out a nice Bayesian interpretation for the algorithms' prediction rule and update function by making appropriate probabilistic assumptions on how the data is generated. For instance, the direct Weighted Majority (WM) [LW94] algorithm's weights are posterior probabilities over the set of disjunctions of up to $k$ variables under the assumption of i.i.d. label noise with a known rate. The algorithm predicts with the label having the highest posterior probability. Although the direct WM algorithm has a clean Bayesian interpretation, until now, it has been unclear if there also exists a Bayesian interpretation for the more efficient indirect algorithms which have good relative mistake bounds.

In this paper we present a general technique for deriving indirect algorithms from Bayes optimal algorithms that make certain probabilistic assumptions about how the instances and labels are generated. In particular, we show that with some independence assumptions, the posterior distribution over monotone disjunctions kept by the direct Bayes algorithm can be encoded with only $O(n)$ weights. These assumptions lead to indirect algorithms whose updates and prediction functions have a clear Bayesian interpretation. Our technique has been applied to derive two indirect algorithms whose updates and prediction functions coincide with those used by Normalized Winnow[1] (first analyzed in [Lit95a]) and a new classification variant of Bylander's BEG algorithm[2] [Byl97] (two indirect algorithms with good relative loss bounds). This suggests that there may be more indirect algorithms that combine the strengths of the Bayesian and relative mistake bound settings.

It is important to observe that the similarity between these algorithms does not extend to the update policy. All known indirect algorithms with good relative mistake bounds must use the mistake-driven update policy, and all Bayes algorithms update their posteriors after each trial.

The classical method for using independence assumptions to simplify the direct Bayes algorithm gives the indirect Naive Bayes algorithm. However, no relative loss bounds have been proven for Naive Bayes or its mistake-driven variant. The mistake-driven variant has performed better in experiments, but both versions are very sensitive to redundant attributes and neither performs as well as Winnow [Lit95].

The precursor of this research is a paper by Nick Littlestone [Lit96] (see also [LM97]) in which he uses a Bayesian approach to derive an indirect prediction algorithm, the Singly Variant Bayes algorithm (SVB), for learning linearly separable functions (which include disjunctions). Rather than using a prior over the set of all monotone disjunctions, the SVB algorithm uses a uniform prior over the set of disjunctions of size one. This leads to a different style of indirect update than the ones considered in this paper. A good mistake bound for learning disjunctions with SVB has been proven only for the noise-free case, and Winnow's bound is much better when learning disjunctions.

The next two sections review the on-line learning of disjunctions and the direct Bayes algorithm. Our general technique for deriving indirect algorithms from direct Bayes algorithms is presented in Section 4. To keep the presentation as simple as possible, we specialize the presentation to derive the linear threshold classification algorithm related to Bylander's BEG algorithm [Byl97]. In Section 5 we briefly describe how the same technique can be applied to obtain a Bayesian interpretation of the normalized variant of Winnow.

---

[1] Normalized Winnow is identical to Winnow except that for computing its linear threshold predictions it uses the normalized instead of the un-normalized weights.

[2] Throughout this paper we call the algorithm using the update function of Figure 1 BEG because it is related to the update used by Bylander's Binary Exponentiated Gradient algorithm [Byl97] for linear regression. When the gradient w.r.t. the square loss used in the derivation of Bylander's algorithm is replaced by the gradient w.r.t. the "linear hinge loss", we get the update function of Figure 1. This "linear hinge loss" can be used to motivate other linear threshold classification algorithms such as the Perceptron algorithm and Winnow [GW98].

## 2 An Overview of On-line Learning of Disjunctions

In the Mistake Bound model introduced by Littlestone [Lit88,Lit89], the goal of the learner is to make a number of mistakes not much greater than the best classifier in some comparison class. In this paper we use monotone disjunctions over $n$ variables as the comparison class. Such disjunctions are boolean formulas of the form $x_{i_1} \vee x_{i_2} \vee \ldots \vee x_{i_k}$ where the indices $i_j$ belong to $\{1, \ldots, n\}$ and the size $k$ is at most $n$. It is natural to represent a monotone disjunction $d$ by the $n$-dimensional binary vector indicating which variables are in the disjunction. For example, when $n = 5$ we will specify the disjunction $x_1 \vee x_3$ by the binary vector $(1, 0, 1, 0, 0)$. Given a monotone disjunction $d \in \{0, 1\}^n$ and an instance $x \in \{0, 1\}^n$, the prediction of $d$ on $x$ is defined to be the boolean value $d(x) = 1$ if $d \cdot x \geq 1$ and 0 otherwise.

Good learning algorithms in the mistake bound model make a number of mistakes not much larger than twice[3] the number of mistakes made by the best disjunction on an *arbitrary* sequence of examples. This can be easily achieved for direct algorithms, such as direct WM. No known indirect algorithms achieve this goal. In fact, for indirect algorithms it is only possible to prove relative mistake bounds that are not much larger than twice[4] the number of attribute errors of the best disjunction. A disjunction's *attribute errors* are those bits in the instances that must be changed so that the disjunction correctly labels the modified instances. For disjunctions of size $k$, the number of attribute errors can be up to a factor of $k$ larger than the number of classification errors. These additional mistakes appear to be a necessary consequence of the indirect algorithm's improved computational efficiency. This penalty occurs only in the presence of noise; in the noise-free case both direct and indirect algorithms have similar $O(k \log n)$ mistake bounds (see [Lit89]).

## 3 The Direct Bayes Algorithm for Disjunctions

It is straightforward to apply Bayes methods (see, e.g. [DH73]) to the on-line learning of disjunctions in the presence of noise. For instance, we might assume that the unknown sequence is generated as follows. First, a "target" disjunction $d$ is chosen at random from some prior distribution $P(\cdot \mid \lambda)$ on the space of all monotone disjunctions over $n$ variables, where $\lambda$ denotes the empty sequence. Second, each instance-label pair $(x_t, y_t)$ of the sequence $S^\ell = (x_1, y_1), \ldots, (x_\ell, y_\ell)$ is drawn at random according to some probability distribution $P(\cdot|d)$ such that $P((x_t, y_t) \mid S^{t-1}, d) = P(y_t \mid x_t, d) P(x_t \mid d)$ where

---

[3] The factor of two disappears when a probabilistic prediction is allowed, so that the direct algorithm's expected (w.r.t. its internal randomization) number of mistakes should not be much larger than the number of mistakes made by the best disjunction [LW94].

[4] Again, the factor of two multiplying the number of attribute errors disappears when a probabilistic prediction is allowed [AW98].

$P(x_t \mid d) = P(x_t)$ and $P(y_t \mid x_t, d) = \nu^{|y_t - d(x_t)|} (1 - \nu)^{(1 - |y_t - d(x_t)|)}$. In other words, each label $y_1, \ldots y_\ell$ of the sequence of examples $S^\ell$ differs from that predicted by the selected disjunction with a probability that depends on an arbitrary but fixed "noise rate" $\nu \in (0, 1/2)$.

In this probabilistic setting, it is not too difficult to see that the Bayes prediction rule simply outputs the label $\hat{y}_t$ such that

$$\hat{y}_t = \arg \max_{y \in \{0,1\}} \left\{ \sum_{d \in \{0,1\}^n} \nu^{|y - d(x_t)|} (1 - \nu)^{(1 - |y - d(x_t)|)} P(d \mid S^{t-1}) \right\}. \quad (1)$$

At the end of every trial the current posterior distribution over the class of monotone disjunctions is then updated according to Bayes rule.

Different choices of the noise rate $\nu$ produce different versions of the Bayes optimal predictor (1). For instance, if $\beta < 1$ and $\nu = \beta/(\beta + 1)$, then the Bayes prediction algorithm is identical (up to a trivial rescaling of the weights) to the direct WM algorithm that always updates with factor $\beta$.

## 4 A Technique for Deriving Indirect Algorithms

In this section we present a general technique for deriving indirect prediction algorithms for learning disjunctions. In particular we show that when some independence assumptions are made regarding the generation of the instances and labels, then the posterior distribution over disjunctions kept by the direct Bayes algorithm can be encoded with only $O(n)$ weights. By appropriately fixing the unknown parameters of the model we obtain simple update rules for the $O(n)$ weights encoding the posterior. To simplify the presentation, we specialize our technique for the case where the update function is like the one used by Bylander's BEG algorithm [Byl97]. We also show that when this update function is combined with the Bayes prediction rule, then the resulting mistake-driven indirect algorithms do provably well in the adversarial noise free setting when learning disjunctions.

It is not easy to encode the Bayes posterior over disjunctions with only $n$ weights. Our approach uses an expanded label space where each variable has its own label bit. This vector-label prediction problem enables us to sidestep the normalization constant that would otherwise appear when the successive posterior distributions are computed, allowing an easy factorization of the posteriors. Combining this expansion with a natural loss function yields Bayes algorithms that predict the bit 1 whenever the posterior probability of the all-1 label vector $1^n$ is greater than the posterior probability of the all-0 vector $0^n$. Thus these Bayes algorithms for the vector-label problem can be used to solve the original disjunction problem by simply converting the binary labels into the $1^n$ or $0^n$ vector-labels.

So far we have been unable to obtain interesting algorithms without going through this vector-label problem. Neither considering the label as a stochastic function of the attributes, nor considering the attributes as corrupted versions of the label seemed to work. In the first case we were unable to decompose the problem because of a normalizing factor depending on all of the components. Although the posteriors factored in the second case, the resulting algorithms were not Winnow-like, and we were unable to prove relative loss bounds for them.

## 4.1 The Bayesian Framework

In this section we consider a *vector-label* prediction problem where the sequence of examples $S^\ell = (x_1, y_1), \ldots, (x_\ell, y_\ell)$ consists of instances $x_t = (x_{t,1}, \ldots x_{t,n}) \in \{0,1\}^n$ and vector-labels $y_t = (y_{t,1}, \ldots y_{t,n}) \in \{0,1\}^n$. We will use a natural loss function between Booleans and vector-labels so that the predictions made by the algorithm are the Boolean predictions required for the disjunction problem.

In Section 3 we assumed that the unknown sequence $S^\ell = (x_1, y_1), \ldots, (x_\ell, y_\ell)$ is generated by first selecting a "target" disjunction $d$ according to some prior distribution $P(\cdot \mid \lambda)$ over the class of all monotone disjunctions and then by drawing each instance-label pair $(x_t, y_t)$ of the sequence $S^\ell$ at random according to some probability distribution $P(\cdot|d)$ on $\{0,1\}^n \times \{0,1\}^n$. However, here we assume that the probability distributions of the model satisfy the following assumptions.

**Model $\mathcal{M}$**

**AS1** $P(d \mid \lambda) = \prod_{i=1}^n P(d_i \mid \lambda)$.
**AS2** $P((x_t, y_t) \mid S^{t-1}, d) = P(y_t \mid x_t, d) \, P(x_t \mid d)$
**AS3** $P(x_t \mid d) = P(x_t)$
**AS4** $P(y_t \mid x_t, d) = \prod_{i=1}^n P(y_{t,i} \mid x_t, d) = \prod_{i=1}^n P(y_{t,i} \mid x_{t,i}, d_i)$

The assumptions of "model $\mathcal{M}$" are designed so that the posterior probabilities over disjunctions have the following product form.

**Lemma 1.** *Under model $\mathcal{M}$, for any sequence $S^t$ we have that*

$$P(d \mid S^t) = \prod_{i=1}^n P(d_i \mid S_i^t), \tag{2}$$

*where $S_i^t = (x_{1,i}, y_{1,i}), \ldots (x_{t,i}, y_{t,i})$.*

**Proof.** The proof is by induction on $t$. If $t = 0$ then $S^t = \lambda$ and the thesis holds by **AS1**. Assume that $P(d \mid S^{t-1}) = \prod_{i=1}^n P(d_i \mid S_i^{t-1})$. We now show that the decomposition also holds for $S^t$. Using Bayes Rule and assumptions **AS1** through **AS4** it is not difficult to see that

$$
\begin{aligned}
P(d \mid S^{t-1}, (x_t, y_t)) &= \frac{P(d \mid S^{t-1}) \, P((x_t, y_t) \mid S^{t-1}, d)}{\sum_{d' \in \{0,1\}^n} P((x_t, y_t) \mid S^{t-1}, d') \, P(d' \mid S^{t-1})} \\
&= \frac{P(d \mid S^{t-1}) \, P(y_t \mid x_t, d) \, P(x_t \mid d)}{\sum_{d' \in \{0,1\}^n} P(y_t \mid x_t, d') \, P(x_t \mid d') \, P(d' \mid S^{t-1})} \\
&= \frac{\prod_{i=1}^n P(d_i \mid S_i^{t-1}) \, P(y_{t,i} \mid x_{t,i}, d_i)}{\sum_{d' \in \{0,1\}^n} \prod_{i=1}^n P(y_{t,i} \mid x_{t,i}, d_i') \, P(d_i' \mid S_i^{t-1})},
\end{aligned} \tag{3}
$$

where the first equality follows from Bayes Rule, the second equality from assumptions **AS2** and the third equality follows from assumptions **AS3**, **AS4** and the inductive hypothesis. Now, since in the denominator of (3) we are summing over all $d' \in \{0,1\}^n$, sum and product can be switched and thus (3) can equivalently be written as

$$
\begin{aligned}
P(d \mid S^{t-1}, (x_t, y_t)) &= \prod_{i=1}^{n} \left( \frac{P(d_i \mid S_i^{t-1}) \, P(y_{t,i} \mid x_{t,i}, d_i) \, P(x_{t,i} \mid d_i)}{\sum_{d_i' \in \{0,1\}} P(y_{t,i} \mid x_{t,i}, d_i') \, P(x_{t,i} \mid d_i') \, P(d_i' \mid S_i^{t-1})} \right) \\
&= \prod_{i=1}^{n} \frac{P(S_i^{t-1} \mid d_i) \, P((x_{t,i}, y_{t,i}) \mid d_i) \, P(d_i \mid \lambda)}{\sum_{d_i' \in \{0,1\}} P(S_i^{t-1} \mid d_i') \, P((x_{t,i}, y_{t,i}) \mid d_i') \, P(d_i' \mid \lambda)},
\end{aligned}
$$

where in the first equality we have used assumption **AS3** and in the second equality we have applied Bayes Rule to $P(d_i \mid S_i^{t-1})$. Finally, observing that $P((x_{t,i}, y_{t,i}) \mid d_i) = P((x_{t,i}, y_{t,i}) \mid S_i^{t-1}, d_i)$ and that $P(S_i^{t-1} \mid d_i) \, P((x_{t,i}, y_{t,i}) \mid S_i^{t-1}, d_i) = P(S_i^{t-1}(x_{t,i}, y_{t,i}) \mid d_i)$ we obtain by simple manipulations

$$
\begin{aligned}
P(d \mid S^{t-1}, (x_t, y_t)) &= \prod_{i=1}^{n} \frac{P(S_i^{t-1}(x_{t,i}, y_{t,i}) \mid d_i) \, P(d_i \mid \lambda)}{\sum_{d_i' \in \{0,1\}} P(S_i^{t-1}(x_{t,i}, y_{t,i}) \mid d_i') \, P(d_i' \mid \lambda)} \\
&= \prod_{i=1}^{n} \frac{P(S_i^{t-1}(x_{t,i}, y_{t,i}), d_i)}{P(S_i^{t-1}(x_{t,i}, y_{t,i}))} = \prod_{i=1}^{n} P(d_i \mid S_i^{t-1}(x_{t,i}, y_{t,i})).
\end{aligned}
$$

This concludes the proof. ∎

Thus maintaining the posterior $P(d \mid S^t)$ reduces to maintaining the $n$ independent posteriors $P(d_i \mid S_i^t)$, each of which can be encoded with a single weight.

Before further proceeding in the analysis of our Bayesian framework it is important to point out an important difference between our set of assumptions and the ones used by the popular Naive Bayes algorithm.

Both methodologies make some simplifying assumptions regarding the generation of the instances and labels that allow them to use only $O(n)$ time per trial when learning disjunctions. Naive Bayes simply assumes that the attribute values are conditionally independent given the label, i.e. for any instance $x_t$ and label $y_t$,

$$
P(x_t \mid y_t) = \prod_{i=1}^{n} p(x_{t,i} \mid y_t). \tag{4}
$$

However, Naive Bayes makes no use of the fact that the examples are generated by some target disjunctions. Our model allows the algorithm to track the posterior probabilities of the various disjunctions. Despite the simple assumption (4), Domingos and Pazzani [DP96] show that if the instances are drawn uniformly at random, then Naive Bayes is optimal for learning disjunctions in the average case setting. However, experimental results reported by Littlestone [Lit95] show that Naive Bayes is not optimal in the relative mistake bound setting even when it is run in a conservative way.

**An Update Rule for the Posterior Probabilities** We now consider a particular family of distributions, $\{P_{\beta_0,\beta_1,\gamma}(y \mid x,d)\}_{x,y,d\in\{0,1\}}$, for which the weights encoding the Bayes posteriors are easily updated. This family has the noise parameters $0 < \gamma < 1$, $0 < \beta_0 < 1$, and $\beta_1 > 1$, and is defined as follows:

$$P_{\beta_0,\beta_1,\gamma}(y \mid x,d) =$$

$$\begin{cases} \left(\left(\frac{\beta_1-1}{\beta_1-\beta_0}\right)^{1-d}\left(\beta_0\frac{\beta_1-1}{\beta_1-\beta_0}\right)^d\right)^{1-y}\left(\left(\frac{1-\beta_0}{\beta_1-\beta_0}\right)^{1-d}\left(\beta_1\frac{1-\beta_0}{\beta_1-\beta_0}\right)^d\right)^y, & \text{if } x = 1 \\ \gamma^{1-y}(1-\gamma)^y, & \text{otherwise} \end{cases}$$

Parameter $\gamma$ is the probability that the label is flipped to 1 when $x = 0$, and the $\beta$ parameters jointly encode different noise probabilities for the case when $x = 1$, $d = 1$, and the case when $x = 1$, $d = 0$.

After seeing a new example, the weights encoding the posterior are updated as in Bylander's BEG algorithm.

**Theorem 1.** *Let $S$ be the sequence of examples through trial $t$ and let $(x, y)$ be the example received at trial $t + 1$. If for each $i = 1,\ldots,n$, the probability $P(y_i \mid x_i,d_i)$ is equal to $P_{\beta_0,\beta_1,\gamma}(y_i \mid x_i,d_i)$ and $P(d_i \mid S_i) = w_i^{d_i}(1 - w_i)^{1-d_i}$, then in model $\mathcal{M}$*

$$P(d \mid S) = \prod_{i=1}^{n} w_i^{d_i}(1 - w_i)^{1-d_i}, \quad P(d \mid S, (x,y)) = \prod_{i=1}^{n} \tilde{w}_i^{d_i}(1 - \tilde{w}_i)^{1-d_i} \quad (5)$$

$$\text{where} \quad \tilde{w}_i = w_i \frac{(\beta_{y_i})^{x_i}}{1 - w_i + w_i(\beta_{y_i})^{x_i}}. \quad (6)$$

**Proof Sketch.** By using assumption **AS3**, a case analysis shows that for the distribution $P(y_i \mid x_i,d_i)$ assumed in the theorem, the Bayes rule for computing successive posterior probabilities for the components $\{d_i\}_{i=1}^n$ reduces to equation (6). In fact, a more tedious analysis can be used to show that the distribution $P_{\beta_0,\beta_1,\gamma}(y_i \mid x_i,d_i)$ is the *only* distribution (under our four assumptions) for which identity (6) holds. The theorem then follows by combining this Bayesian single component update rule with the product decomposition (2). ∎

Notice that update rule (6) is independent of the parameter $\gamma$ that specifies the distribution $P_{\beta_0,\beta_1,\gamma}$. This is because when $x = 0$, the disjunction cannot evaluate to 1, and the probability that $y = 1$ is the (unknown) noise rate. This value can be set to any value $0 < \gamma < 1$ without affecting the update rule.

**A Bayes Predictor for Bit-labels** The next step is to map the posterior distribution (5) and the current instance into a prediction. Since the disjunction problem requires single bit predictions (rather than vector-labels), we define a natural loss function between vector-labels and bit-labels that is 1 if and only if some component of the vector-label differs from the bit-label, i.e. for $y_t \in$

$\{0,1\}^n$ and $y \in \{0,1\}$, the function $L^n(\boldsymbol{y}_t, y) = 1$ if $\exists j$ such that $y_{t,j} \neq y$, and $L^n(\boldsymbol{y}_t, y) = 0$ otherwise.

The Bayes optimal algorithm for this loss and probabilistic model $\mathcal{M}$ predicts the binary label $\hat{y}$ that minimizes the expected loss, i.e.

$$\hat{y}_t = \arg \min_{y \in \{0,1\}} \sum_{\boldsymbol{y}_t \in \{0,1\}^n} L^n(\boldsymbol{y}_t, y) P(\boldsymbol{y}_t \mid \boldsymbol{x}_t, S^{t-1}). \tag{7}$$

It is not difficult to see that this simplifies to

$$\hat{y}_t = \arg \max_{y \in \{0,1\}} P(y^n \mid \boldsymbol{x}_t, S^{t-1}), \tag{8}$$

where $y^n$ is the $n$-dimensional vector with each component set to $y$. Thus the Bayes optimal prediction is the bit $y$ for which the corresponding vector $y^n$ is more likely.

Prediction (8) can be expressed in a dot product form over a transformed weight space as shown by the following result.

**Theorem 2.** *Let $S = (\boldsymbol{x}_1, y_1), \ldots, (\boldsymbol{x}_{t-1}, y_{t-1})$ be the sequence of examples observed before trial $t$ and let $\boldsymbol{x}_t$ be the instance received at the beginning of trial $t$. If $P(y \mid x_{t,i}, d_i)$ is some $P_{\beta_0, \beta_1, \gamma}(y \mid x_{t,i}, d_i)$, then under model $\mathcal{M}$ decision rule (8) can be expressed in the following form:*

$$\hat{y}_t = \begin{cases} 1 & \text{if } \boldsymbol{x}_t \cdot \boldsymbol{z}_t > \theta \\ 0 & \text{otherwise} \end{cases}$$

*where $\theta = n \ln(\gamma/(1-\gamma))$ and $z_{t,i} = \ln \left( \dfrac{\gamma(1-\beta_0)}{(1-\gamma)(\beta_1-1)} \dfrac{1 + w_{t,i}(\beta_1-1)}{1 + w_{t,i}(\beta_0-1)} \right)$.*

**Proof Sketch.** Under model $\mathcal{M}$ it is not difficult to see that

$$P(\boldsymbol{y}_t \mid \boldsymbol{x}_t, S) = \frac{P(\boldsymbol{x}_t)}{P(\boldsymbol{x}_t \mid S)} \prod_{i=1}^n \left( \sum_{d_i \in \{0,1\}} P(y_{t,i} \mid x_{t,i}, d_i) P(d_i \mid S_i) \right). \tag{9}$$

Substituting the expression for $P(\boldsymbol{y}_t \mid \boldsymbol{x}_t, S)$ given in (9) in the Bayes Decision rule (8) we obtain

$$\hat{y}_t = \arg \max_{y \in \{0,1\}} \prod_{i=1}^n \left( \sum_{d_i \in \{0,1\}} P(y \mid x_{t,i}, d_i) P(d_i \mid S_i) \right). \tag{10}$$

The thesis then follows, by simple manipulations, from (10) and the facts

$$\sum_{d_i \in \{0,1\}} P(y=1 \mid x_{t,i}, d_i) P(d_i \mid S_i) = \left[ \frac{1-\beta_0}{\beta_1 - \beta_0} (1 + w_{t,i}(\beta_1-1)) \right]^{x_{t,i}} (1-\gamma)^{1-x_{t,i}}$$

$$\sum_{d_i \in \{0,1\}} P(y=0 \mid x_{t,i}, d_i) P(d_i \mid S_i) = \left[ \frac{\beta_1 - 1}{\beta_1 - \beta_0} (1 + w_{t,i}(\beta_0-1)) \right]^{x_{t,i}} \gamma^{1-x_{t,i}}.$$

---

*Bayes*-BEG

**Input:** $0 \leq \beta_0 < 1$, $\beta_1 > 1$, $0 < \gamma < 1$, and $n \geq 1$

**Initialization:** Let $(w_{1,1}, \ldots w_{1,n})$ be a weight vector in $[0,1]^n$

For $t = 1, 2 \ldots$

**Prediction Rule:** Upon receiving the instance $\boldsymbol{x}_t$, if $\boldsymbol{x}_t \cdot \boldsymbol{z}_t > \theta$ then predict 1, otherwise predict 0, where

$$z_{t,i} = \ln \left( \frac{\gamma(1-\beta_0)}{(1-\gamma)(\beta_1-1)} \frac{(1+w_{t,i}(\beta_1-1))}{(1+w_{t,i}(\beta_0-1))} \right) \text{ and } \theta = n \ln(\gamma/(1-\gamma)).$$

**Update Function:** Observe vector-label $\boldsymbol{y}_t$ and for each $i = 1, \ldots, n$ set

$$w_{t+1,i} = w_{t,i} \frac{\beta_{y_{t,i}}^{x_{t,i}}}{1 - w_{t,i} + w_{t,i}\beta_{y_{t,i}}^{x_{t,i}}}. \tag{11}$$

**Update Policy:** Update in all trials.

---

**Fig. 1.** The *Bayes*-BEG algorithm.

■

We call the indirect algorithm using the prediction rule of Theorem 2 and the update function (6) described in Theorem 1 the *Bayes*-BEG algorithm. The algorithm is summarized in Figure 1. Its always-update version minimizes the probability of a mistake with respect to the discrete loss $L^n$ when the vector-labels are generated by $P_{\beta_0,\beta_1,\gamma}(y \mid x, d)$ as per model $\mathcal{M}$. However, when learning disjunctions it will only see the vector-labels $1^n$ and $0^n$.

## 4.2 The Mistake-driven *Bayes*-BEG Algorithm

We now turn from the probabilistic setting to the adversarial setting where we analyze MD-*Bayes*-BEG, the mistake-driven version of *Bayes*-BEG, assuming the algorithm only sees the vector-labels $1^n$ and $0^n$ that correspond to the labels for the disjunction problem. We use $M_{\mathbf{alg}}(S)$ to denote the number of mistakes made by algorithm "alg" on sequence $S$.

We start by proving a mistake bound for the MD-*Bayes*-BEG algorithm when $\beta_0 = 0$.

**Theorem 3.** *Let* $n \geq 2$, $c = ((e+1)/(e-1))^{1/n}$ *and set* $\gamma = c/(1+c)$, $\beta_1 = 1+c$ *and* $\beta_0 = 0$. *Furthermore, let* $w_{1,i} = 1/n$ *for* $i = 1, \ldots n$. *Then for all sequences* $S = (\boldsymbol{x}_1, y_1), \ldots, (\boldsymbol{x}_\ell, y_\ell)$ *such that there exists a monotone disjunction consistent with* $S$ *we have*

$$M_{\textit{MD-Bayes-BEG}}(S) \leq 6.48 + 2.48k \left( 1 + \left| \ln_2 \left( \frac{2(n-1)}{(1+c)(e-1)} \right) \right| \right), \tag{12}$$

*where* $k$ *is the number of relevant variables in the target disjunction.*

**Proof.** The bound is proven by following the same approach used in Section 5 of Littlestone [Lit88]. As in [Lit88], we call every trial where the algorithm predicts $\hat{y}_t = 0$ and $y_t = 1$ a *promotion* step and every trial where $\hat{y}_t = 1$ but $y_t = 0$ an *elimination* step. Since the MD-*Bayes*-BEG prediction algorithm is mistake-driven, its number of mistakes is equal to the number of promotion steps, $p$, plus the number of elimination steps, $d$, made by the algorithm. The theorem is then proved by bounding the number of promotion and elimination steps.

To avoid confusion, in the rest of the proof we will call the weights $z$ used in the dot product prediction the "z-weights", and the weights $w$ associated with the attributes the "w-weights".

Let $Z_t = \sum_{i=1}^{n} z_{t,i}$ be the total z-weight at the beginning of trial $t$. Since for any $i \in \{1, \ldots n\}$ and $t = 1, \ldots, \ell$, $z_{t,i} \geq 0$ and $z_{t,i}$ only increases/decreases during promotion/elimination steps it follows that $Z_1 + p Z_{gain} - d Z_{lost} \geq 0$, where $Z_{gain}$ is an upper bound on the total z-weight gained during a promotion step and $Z_{lost}$ is a lower bound on the total z-weight lost during an elimination step. By solving it with respect to $d$ we obtain that $d \leq (Z_1/Z_{lost}) + p(Z_{gain}/Z_{lost})$. Hence, the number of mistakes made by MD-*Bayes*-BEG can be upper bounded by

$$M_{\text{MD-}Bayes\text{-BEG}}(S) \leq \frac{Z_1}{Z_{lost}} + p\left(1 + \frac{Z_{gain}}{Z_{lost}}\right). \tag{13}$$

We now estimate the quantities in the right hand side of (13). For the total initial z-weight, $Z_1 = \sum_{i=1}^{n} z_{1,i}$, it is easy to see that when $c = (e+1)/(e-1)$ and $w_{1,i} = 1/n$ $(i = 1, \ldots, n)$, we have $Z_1 = n \ln\left(1 + \frac{\beta_1}{n-1}\right) \leq 2\beta_1$, where the inequality follows from the fact that for $r > 0$ we have $\ln(1+r) \leq r$ and $n/(n-1) \leq 2$ for $n \geq 2$. Similarly, $Z_{lost} > \theta$ since during each elimination step we have $\sum_{i=1}^{n} x_{t,i} z_{t,i} > \theta$ and $z_{t+1,i} = 0$ for any attribute $x_{t,i}$ such that $x_{t,i} = 1$. For $Z_{gain}$ the analysis is more involved. First note that if $x_{t,i} = 1$ the corresponding weight $w_{t,i}$ is updated to $w_{t+1,i} = w_{t,i}\beta_1/(1 - w_{t,i} + w_{t,i}\beta_1)$. Substituting $w_{t+1,i}$ into $z_{t+1,i}$ and observing that for $w_{t,i} \in [0,1]$ the ratio $z_{t+1,i}/z_{t,i}$ is decreasing with respect to $w_{t,i}$ and $\lim_{w_{t,i} \to 0} z_{t+1,i}/z_{t,i} = (1+c)$, we obtain $z_{t+1,i}/z_{t,i} \leq (1+c)$. Now, $Z_{gain} = \sum_{i=1}^{n} x_{t,i}(z_{t+1,i} - z_{t,i}) \leq c \sum_{i=1}^{n} x_{t,i} z_{t,i} \leq c\theta$, where the last inequality follows from the fact that during a promotion step we have $\sum_{i=1}^{n} x_{t,i} z_{t,i} \leq \theta$.

We now bound the number of promotion steps incurred by the algorithm. We first observe that if the w-weight assigned to each relevant attribute is $> 1/g(c)$ where $g(c) = 1 + ((1+c)(e-1)/2)$, then $z_{t,i} > n \ln(\gamma/(1-\gamma))$ and positive examples are correctly classified by MD-*Bayes*-BEG. By simple manipulation it is not difficult to see that if $x_{t,i} = 1$ and $w_{t,i} = 1-1/(1+(1+c)^{-k})$ then at the end of a promotion step the updated weight $w_{t+1,i}$ is $w_{t+1,i} = 1-1/(1+(1+c)^{-k+1})$. By expressing the initial and final weights of a relevant attribute in this form, we have that the number of promotion steps per relevant attribute can be upper bounded by $\lceil |\ln_{c+1}((2(n-1))/((1+c)(e-1)))| \rceil$ and thus,

$$p \leq k \left\lceil \left| \ln_{c+1}\left(\frac{2(n-1)}{(1+c)(e-1)}\right) \right| \right\rceil \leq k \left(1 + \left| \ln_2\left(\frac{2(n-1)}{(1+c)(e-1)}\right) \right| \right) \tag{14}$$

Bound (12) then immediately follows by plugging the above estimates for $Z_1$, $Z_{lost}$, $Z_{gain}$ and $p$ into (13) and by observing that $1 < c < \sqrt{(1+e)/(e-1)}$. ∎

The *Bayes*-BEG update function with $\beta_0 = 0$ sets $w_{t+1,i}$ to 0 whenever $x_{t,i} = 1$ and $y_t = 0$, and the multiplicative nature of the update ensures that $w_i$ remains 0 thereafter. Therefore, if an example has the label 0 but all the variables are 1, then all of the weights get set to zero and the algorithm is no longer able to predict 1. This indicates that the $\beta = 0$ version of *Bayes*-BEG is unable to tolerate noise.

On the other hand, if $\beta_0 > 0$ then the weights will always be positive. Even if the weight of a variable in the best disjunction gets driven down by noisy examples, the multiplicative update will allow it to recover before the algorithm makes too many additional mistakes. Although the exact analysis with noise is difficult, the next result shows that noise tolerant versions of the algorithm (with $\beta_0 > 0$) also have similar noise-free mistake bounds.

**Theorem 4.** *Let $n \geq 2$, $q = 16/10$, $\epsilon = 9/10$ and set $\gamma/(1-\gamma) = q^{1/(n-1)}$, $\beta_0 = 1 - (q^{3/2} - 1 + \epsilon)/((1+q)(q^{1/(2(n-1))}))$ and $\beta_1 = 1 + (q^{3/2} - 1 + \epsilon)/(1+q)$. Then for all sequences $S = (x_1, y_1), \ldots, (x_\ell, y_\ell)$ such that there exists a monotone disjunction consistent with $S$ we have*

$$M_{MD\text{-}Bayes\text{-}BEG}(S) \leq 24.79 + 8.44k \ln(n-1) + 5.76k, \qquad (15)$$

*where $k$ is the number of relevant variables in the target disjunction.*

**Proof Sketch.** It is similar to the proof of Theorem 3, but now, rather than analyzing the change in the total weight $Z_t = \sum_{i=1}^{n} z_{t,i}$, where the $z_{t,i}$ are the weights used in the dot product prediction, we analyze the change in the total weight $Y_t = \sum_{i=1}^{n} y_{t,i}$ where $y_{t,i} = \ln((1 + w_{t,i}(\beta_1 - 1))/(1 - w_{t,i}(1 - \beta_0)))$. Details of the proof are omitted. ∎

## 4.3 The Thresholded-BEG Algorithm

An indirect algorithm related to *Bayes*-BEG results when the update function of Figure 1 is combined with the simple thresholded dot product prediction rule used by Winnow. That is, the algorithm rather than predicting with the prediction rule of Figure 1, predicts 1 if $x_t \cdot w_t > \theta$, and 0 otherwise. We call the resulting algorithm Thresholded-BEG.

This algorithm is much easier to analyze with the existing relative mistake bound techniques [Lit89,AW98], and it is not difficult to get relative mistake bounds for it even in the noisy case. For instance, if no information besides the number $n$ of attributes is given, then the following bound on the number of mistakes made by the algorithm on any sequence of examples where the best disjunctions incurs at most $A$ attribute errors can be proven. Recall that the attribute errors of a disjunction $d$ are those bits in the Boolean instances that have to be changed so that $d$ correctly labels the modified instances.

**Theorem 5.** *Let $\alpha > 1$ and set $\beta_1 = \alpha, \beta_0 = 1/\alpha$ and $\theta = (\alpha \ln \alpha)/(\alpha^2 - 1)$. Let $w_1 > 0$. Then for all sequences $S$ such that there exists a monotone disjunction with at most $A$ attribute errors on $S$, we have*

$$M_{Thresholded-BEG}(S) \leq (\alpha + 1)\frac{\text{dist}_{bre}(u, w_1) + A \ln \alpha}{\ln \alpha}, \qquad (16)$$

*where $\text{dist}_{bre}(u, w_{1,i}) = \sum_{i=1}^{n} u_i \ln(u_i/w_{1,i}) + (1 - u_i) \ln((1 - u_i)/(1 - w_{1,i}))$ is the binary relative entropy between the target disjunction $u$ and the initial weight vector $w_1$ used by the algorithm.*

**Proof Sketch.** The technique used to derive the mistake bound is similar to Auer and Warmuth's [AW98]. The analysis proceeds by showing that the distance between the weight vector $w_t$ used by the algorithm and a target weight vector $u$ decreases whenever the algorithm makes a mistakes. However, our analysis uses the binary relative entropy as a potential function. Details of the proof are omitted. ∎

It is interesting to observe that bound (16) of Theorem 5 has the same form as the bound derived for Winnow in [AW98], except that in the latter the binary relative entropy of (16) is replaced by the un-normalized relative entropy $\text{dist}_{ure}(u, w_{1,i}) = \sum_{i=1}^{n} u_i \ln(u_i/w_{1,i}) + w_{1,i} - u_i$.

Better results can be obtained if the algorithm has some additional information regarding the sequence to be predicted. For instance, if the number $A$ of attribute errors of the best disjunction is known in advance, then the parameters of the algorithm can be optimally tuned to obtain bounds similar to those derived in [AW98] (although with slightly worse constants). For example, in the noise-free case, i.e. when the algorithm knows ahead of time that there exists a monotone disjunction consistent with $S$ ($A = 0$), we get a bound that is incomparable to Theorem 3.

**Corollary 1.** *Let $n \geq 2$ and set $\beta_0 = 0, \beta_1 = e$ and $\theta = 1/e$. Furthermore, let $w_{1,i} = 1/n$ for $i = 1, \ldots, n$. Then for all sequences $S = (x_1, y_1), \ldots, (x_\ell, y_\ell)$ such that there exists a monotone disjunction consistent with $S$ we have*

$$M_{Thresholded-BEG}(S) \leq 3.76 + 2.72k \ln(n), \qquad (17)$$

*where $k$ is the number of relevant variables in the target disjunction.*

## 5   The Normalized Winnow Algorithm

The Normalized Winnow algorithm [Lit95a] is another mistake-driven linear threshold algorithm for on-line learning disjunctions with a good relative mistake bound. This algorithm is identical to Winnow except that it normalizes its weights before computing the linear threshold prediction. Techniques like those employed in Subsection 4.1 show that Normalized Winnow is also closely related to Bayesian methods.

Whereas the prior on disjunctions used in Subsection 4.1 was a product of $n$ Bernoulli distributions, the prior we found useful for Normalized Winnow is the $n$-fold product of a distribution over $\{1, 2, \ldots, n\}$. Since sampling this prior gives a vector in $\{1, 2, \ldots, n\}^n$, most of the $2^n$ disjunctions will be represented by several possible outcomes. For example, the disjunction $x_1 \vee x_3 \vee x_7$ is represented by all vectors containing only 1's, 3's, and 7's, and at least one of each.

Under model $\mathcal{M}$ (with a slight modification to assumption **AS4** for the new prior) the posterior probabilities over the space $\{1, 2, \ldots, n\}^n$ can also be represented as an $n$-fold product distribution. As before, the vector-label problem is used to decouple the attributes and obtain this result. It turns out that the posterior probabilities/weights of the integers in $\{1, 2, \ldots, n\}$ are updated in the same way as the weights of the Normalized Winnow algorithm. With the loss function defined in Section 4.1, the Bayes-optimal predictions are the same thresholded dot products between the instances and weights used by the Normalized Winnow algorithm. This establishes a close correspondence between Normalized Winnow and Bayes methods.

Although the relationship between Normalized Winnow and its corresponding Bayes algorithm is analogous to the relationship between indirect *Bayes*-BEG and BEG, there are two subtle differences. Indirect *Bayes*-BEG uses a logarithmic function of the weights in its dot-product prediction rule, while Normalized Winnow and its corresponding Bayes algorithm both predict with the simple thresholded dot-product between the weights (or probabilities) and the instance. However, the predictions of the Bayes algorithm remain a simple thresholded dot-product only as long as the vector-labels are either $1^n$ or $0^n$. Vector-labels containing both 1s and 0s break the symmetry and the Bayes optimal prediction is no longer a dot product.

The technical details for relating Normalized Winnow to Bayesian methods are more complex than for the new classification variant of BEG, but the basic approach is the same. It is now natural to ask if the original (un-normalized) Winnow algorithm also has a corresponding Bayesian interpretation. Our attempts in this direction have been unsuccessful. Using Poisson distributions to encode the prior and posteriors over disjunctions appears promising since it corresponds to the un-normalized relative entropy used to analyze Winnow [Lit89,AW98]. However, Winnow's weights do not seem to encode the proper Poisson posteriors.

## 6 Conclusions

The Winnow family of algorithms is surprisingly good at learning disjunctions in the relative mistake bound model. These algorithms are very efficient, using only $O(n)$ weights. The goal of this research is to gain a better understanding of this family by exploring its relationship to Bayesian methods. Although we have not yet answered this question for Winnow itself, we do have a Bayesian interpretation for the prediction and update rules used by Normalized Winnow and a new classification variant of BEG.

We started by investigating the assumptions necessary to encode the posteriors over monotone disjunctions kept by Bayes algorithms with only $O(n)$ weights. Our methods lead to computationally efficient algorithms which are motivated by a Bayesian analysis. For one of these algorithms, indirect *Bayes*-BEG, we have examined how its mistake-driven variant performs in the relative mistake bound model when learning disjunctions. In the noise free case we have shown that this variant has mistake bounds with the same form as the best known indirect algorithms for learning disjunctions. Further results imply that this algorithm can tolerate noise, but the complexity of its predictions makes the analysis difficult.

# References

[AW98] Auer, P., Warmuth, M. K.: Tracking the best disjunction. Journal of Machine Learning, Special issue on concept drift. **32** (2) (1998)

[Byl97] Bylander, T.: The binary exponentiated gradient algorithm for learning linear functions. Unpublished manuscript, private communication, (1997)

[DP96] Domingo, P., Pazzani, M.: Beyond independence: conditions for the optimality of the simple Bayesian classifier. Proc. 13th International Conference on Machine Learning, (1996) 105–112

[DH73] Duda, R. O., Hart, P. E.: Pattern Classification and Scene Analysis. Publisher Wiley (1973)

[GW98] Gentile, C., Warmuth, M. K.: Hinge Loss and Average Margin. Advances in Neural Information Processing Systems. Morgan Kaufmann, (1998)

[Lit88] Littlestone, N.: Learning when Irrelevant Attributes Abound: A New Linear-threshold Algorithm. Machine Learning. **2** (1988) 285–318 (Earlier version in FOCS87)

[Lit89] Littlestone, N.: Mistake Bounds and Logarithmic Linear-threshold Learning Algorithms. PhD thesis, Technical Report UCSC-CRL-89-11, University of California Santa Cruz (1989)

[Lit95] Littlestone, N.: Comparing several linear-threshold learning algorithms on tasks involving superfluous attributes. In Proc. 12th International Conference on Machine Learning. Morgan Kaufmann, (1995) 353–361

[Lit95a] Littlestone, N.: "Private Communication"

[Lit96] Littlestone, N.: Mistake-driven Bayes sports: bounds for symmetric apobayesian learning algorithms. Technical report, NEC Research Institute, Princeton, NJ. (1996)

[LM97] Littlestone, N., Mesterharm, C.: An Apobayesian Relative of Winnow. Advances in Neural Information Processing Systems. Morgan Kaufmann, (1997)

[LW94] Littlestone, N., Warmuth, M. K.: The weighted majority algorithm. Information and Computation. **108** (1994) 212–261. (Earlier version in FOCS89)

# Averaging Expert Predictions

Jyrki Kivinen[1] and Manfred K. Warmuth[*2]

[1] Department of Computer Science, P.O. Box 26 (Teollisuuskatu 23), FIN-00014
University of Helsinki, Finland; e-mail Jyrki.Kivinen@cs.Helsinki.FI
[2] Department of Computer Science, University of California, Santa Cruz, CA 95064,
USA; e-mail manfred@cse.ucsc.edu

**Abstract.** We consider algorithms for combining advice from a set of
experts. In each trial, the algorithm receives the predictions of the experts and produces its own prediction. A loss function is applied to measure the discrepancy between the predictions and actual observations.
The algorithm keeps a weight for each expert. At each trial the weights
are first used to help produce the prediction and then updated according to the observed outcome. Our starting point is Vovk's Aggregating
Algorithm, in which the weights have a simple form: the weight of an
expert decreases exponentially as a function of the loss incurred by the
expert. The prediction of the Aggregating Algorithm is typically a nonlinear function of the weights and the experts' predictions. We analyze
here a simplified algorithm in which the weights are as in the original
Aggregating Algorithm, but the prediction is simply the weighted average of the experts' predictions. We show that for a large class of loss
functions, even with the simplified prediction rule the additional loss of
the algorithm over the loss of the best expert is at most $c \ln n$, where
$n$ is the number of experts and $c$ a constant that depends on the loss
function. Thus, the bound is of the same form as the known bounds for
the Aggregating Algorithm, although the constants here are not quite as
good. We use relative entropy to rewrite the bounds in a stronger form
and to motivate the update.

## 1 Introduction

The focus of this paper is a certain class of on-line learning algorithms. In on-line
learning the algorithm receives one by one a sequence of inputs $x_t$ and makes
after each $x_t$ a *prediction* $\hat{y}_t$. For each input $x_t$ there is also a corresponding
*outcome* (or desired output) $y_t$ which is revealed to the learner after it has made
its prediction $\hat{y}_t$.

To define our on-line learning problem more closely, we need to specify which
sequences $((x_1, y_1), \ldots, (x_\ell, y_\ell))$ are allowed as inputs, and what is the criterion
for judging the quality of the predictions $\hat{y}_t$. Regarding the input sequences, we
take a worst-case view that given some domain $X$ for the inputs and $Y$ for the
outcomes, for each $t$ the pair $(x_t, y_t)$ can be any element of $X \times Y$. In particular,

* Supported by NSF grant CCR 9700201

the pairs need not come from any probability distribution, and we make no assumptions about possible dependence between $y_t$ and $x_t$. In this paper we consider mainly the case $X = [0,1]^n$ for some $n$ and $Y = [0,1]$. Many of the results have obvious extensions to larger ranges of real inputs and outputs. We sometimes also consider the special case $Y = \{0,1\}$ where the outputs (but not the inputs) are required to be discrete.

To judge the quality of the predictions, we first introduce a *loss function* $L$ that gives a (nonnegative) quantity $L(y_t, \widehat{y}_t)$ as a measure of discrepancy between the prediction and actual outcome. The square loss given by $L(y, \widehat{y}) = (y - \widehat{y})^2$ is a good example of a loss function suitable for our setting.

In addition to the loss function, it is essential to give a *comparison class* $\mathcal{F}$ of predictors as a reference point. The predictors are mappings from the set of possible inputs $X$ to the set of possible predictions. We then define the *total loss* for an algorithm $A$ that gives the predictions $\widehat{y}_t$ on a sequence $S = ((x_1, y_1), \ldots, (x_\ell, y_\ell))$ as $\mathrm{Loss}_A(S) = \sum_{t=1}^{\ell} L(y_t, \widehat{y}_t)$, and similarly for a predictor $f \in \mathcal{F}$ as $\mathrm{Loss}_f(S) = \sum_{t=1}^{\ell} L(y_t, f(x_t))$. We can measure the performance of our prediction algorithm by considering the additional loss $\mathrm{Loss}_A(S) - \inf_{f \in \mathcal{F}} \mathrm{Loss}_f(S)$ it incurs compared to the best fixed predictor from the comparison class. We call such performance bounds *relative loss bounds*.

In the extreme case that the outcomes $y_t$ are completely random, the algorithm obviously cannot perform better than random guessing, but then neither can the predictors from the comparison class, so the additional loss can still be made small. In the more interesting extreme case that one predictor $f \in \mathcal{F}$ is perfect and we have $L(y_t, f(x_t)) = 0$ for all $t$, the algorithm can still be allowed some initial interval of bad predictions, but to achieve a small additional loss it needs to quickly learn to make good predictions. Usually we are somewhere between these to extremes. Some predictors from the comparison class predict better than others, and the algorithm is required to perform roughly as well as the better ones.

In this paper the comparison classes we use come from the framework of predicting with expert advice [Vov90,CBFH+97]. We assume there are $n$ experts, and the prediction of the $i$th expert for the $t$th outcome is given by $x_{t,i} \in [0,1]$. The vector $x_t$ of all the experts' predictions at trial $t$ is then the $t$th input vector to our algorithm. Hence, if we define $\mathcal{E}_i(x) = x_i$, then $\mathrm{Loss}_{\mathcal{E}_i}(S)$ denotes the loss that the expert $\mathcal{E}_i$ would incur on the sequence $S$. The obvious thing to do now is to take as comparison class the set $\{\mathcal{E}_1, \ldots, \mathcal{E}_n\}$ of expert predictors and thus compare the loss of the algorithm to the loss $\min_i \mathrm{Loss}_{\mathcal{E}_i}(S)$ of the best single expert.

Earlier work on the expert framework by Vovk [Vov90] has shown that for a very general class of loss functions his *Aggregating Algorithm* (AA) achieves the bound

$$\mathrm{Loss}_{\mathrm{AA}}(S) \le \mathrm{Loss}_{\mathcal{E}_i}(S) + c_L \ln n \qquad \text{for all } i \qquad (1)$$

where the constant $c_L$ depends on the loss function. For example, with the square loss we have $c_L = 1/2$. This bound has also been shown to be essentially optimal [HKW98]. (Notice that for the important special case of absolute loss $L(y, \hat{y}) = |y - \hat{y}|$, only bounds of a somewhat weaker form are possible [LW94,Vov90,CBFH$^+$97].) Vovk's Aggregating Algorithm is based on maintaining for each expert a weight that is decreased exponentially as the expert incurs loss. The predictions of the algorithm are of course affected more by the experts with large weights than by those with small weights, but the actual method of obtaining the prediction is somewhat more complicated than just taking a weighted average of the experts' predictions.

The main technical novelty in this paper is considering what happens if we keep using Vovk's algorithm for maintaining the weights but replace the prediction simply by the weighted average of the experts. Considering the optimality of Vovk's algorithm, we cannot hope to outperform it, but it turns out that for the simplified *Weighted Average Algorithm* (WAA) we can still prove the bound

$$\text{Loss}_{\text{WAA}}(S) \leq \text{Loss}_{\mathcal{E}_i}(S) + \tilde{c}_L \ln n \qquad \text{for all } i \qquad (2)$$

where $\tilde{c}_L$ is a constant somewhat greater than $c_L$ in (1). For example, with the square loss we have $\tilde{c}_L = 2$ and $c_L = 1/2$.

The main reason why we want to consider the simplified prediction at the cost of slightly larger additional loss is that the simplified algorithm leads to simplified proofs of the relative loss bounds. Another intuitively appealing aspect of the weighted average as prediction is its probabilistic interpretation. If the negated loss $-L(y_t, x_{t,i})$ can be interpreted as the log likelihood of $y_t$ given model $\mathcal{E}_i$, then the weight of the expert $\mathcal{E}_i$ after the trials can be interpreted as the posterior probability assigned to that expert. The prior probabilities here are the initial weights of the experts. In this setting, the prediction by weighted average correponds to the mean posterior prediction. The log loss, for which the log likelihood interpretation is most obvious, has been analyzed in this context before [Vov90,CBFH$^+$97,FSSW97]. It turns out that in the special case of log loss, the prediction of the Aggregating Algorithm also is the weighted average, so the Weighted Average Algorithm coincides with the original Aggregating Algorithm.

In reducing the algorithm's dependence on the particular loss function, the next step would be Freund and Schapire's Hedge Algorithm [FS97] that needs to assume only that the loss function has a bounded range. They can still prove loss bounds of the same flavor as the bounds here, but in the slightly weaker form of

$$\text{Loss}_{\text{Hedge}}(S) \leq \text{Loss}_{\mathcal{E}_i}(S) + a\sqrt{\text{Loss}_{\mathcal{E}_i}(S)) \ln n} + b \ln n \qquad \text{for all } i$$

for certain $a, b > 0$. Hence, there is a progression of algorithms where Vovk's original Aggregating Algorithm has a weight update that is uniform for all kinds of loss functions, but the prediction method is dependent on $L$. For the Weighted Average Algorithm, the prediction is made by the weighted average regardless of the loss function, but this happens at the cost of slightly worse constants in the loss bounds. Finally, the Hedge Algorithm is even more uniform in its treatment of loss functions, but the loss bounds get worse by more than just a constant.

(Also notice that the bound for the Hedge Algorithm does not work with the unbounded log loss.)

After the technical remarks, consider now relating these results to a larger body of work where the *relative entropy* is the fundamental concept for motivating and analyzing learning algorithms [KW97]. Let $u \in \mathbf{R}^n$ and $v \in \mathbf{R}^n$ be *probability vectors*; i.e., $\sum_i u_i = \sum_i v_i = 1$ and $u_i, v_i \geq 0$ for all $i$. The relative entropy between $u$ and $v$ is then $d_{\mathrm{re}}(u, v) = \sum_{i=1}^{n} u_i \ln(u_i/v_i)$. To introduce relative entropy methods into the present problem, it is useful to start by considering a slightly extended comparison class. We define $\mathrm{Loss}_u^{\mathrm{avg}}(S) = \sum_{t=1}^{\ell} \sum_{i=1}^{n} u_i L(y_t, x_{t,i})$ to be the expected loss if we predict by a random expert chosen according to $u$. We first rewrite Vovk's original proof in order to bring out how the additional loss incurred by the algorithm relates to a relative entropy. The resulting bound is

$$\mathrm{Loss}_{\mathrm{WAA}}(S) \leq \mathrm{Loss}_u^{\mathrm{avg}}(S) + \tilde{c}_L \, d_{\mathrm{re}}(u, v_1) \tag{3}$$

where $v_1$ is the algorithm's initial weigth vector. With $v_1 = (1/n, \ldots, 1/n)$, and $u_i = 1$ and $u_j = 0$ for $j \neq i$, this simplifies to bound (2) where comparison is against the single best expert $\mathcal{E}_i$. Note that since always $\mathrm{Loss}_u^{\mathrm{avg}}(S) \geq \min_i \mathrm{Loss}_{\mathcal{E}_i}(S)$, going from (2) to (3) does not bring any improvement in the first term of the bound. However, improvement in the second term are possible. If there are several expert with nearly optimal performance, then substituting into (3) a comparison vector $u$ that distributes the weight nearly evenly among the good experts gives a significantly sharper bound than (2). As a simple example, assume that $k$ experts all have some small loss $Q$. Then (2) gives the loss bound $Q + \tilde{c}_L \ln n$ while the bound (3) goes down to $Q + \tilde{c}_L \ln(n/k)$. The new method brings out in a more explicit form the feature implicit in earlier proofs (see, e.g., [LW94,Vov90]) that having more than one good expert results in a smaller additional loss. For log loss this feature, with bounds of the form (3) and proofs analogous to ours, was already pointed out in [FSSW97].

Our second use for relative entropy is as a regularizing term in setting up a minimization problem that gives Vovk's rule for updating the weights. The basic idea in such a derivation (see [KW97,HKW95] for other examples) is to see the update as an act of balancing the need to maintain old information by staying close to the old weight vector and the need to learn by moving the weights in the direction of small loss on the last example.

In Sect. 2 we review the basic expert framework and Vovk's algorithm. Sect. 3 gives the new upper bound for the additional loss achieved by the modified algorithm that predicts with the weighted combination of experts. A straightforward proof is given in Sect. 4. In Sect. 5 we restate the bound and proof using a relative entropy, and give a motivation for the algorithm in terms of a relative entropy minimization problem. Finally, in Sect. 6 we generalize the relative loss bounds for the new algorithm to multi-dimensional predictions and outcomes.

## 2 The Setting and the Algorithm

We consider a simple on-line prediction setting, where learning takes place during a sequence of *trials*. At trial $t$, the learner tries to predict a real-valued *outcome* $y_t$. The learner's prediction is denoted by $\hat{y}_t$, and the performance of the learner is measured by using a *loss function* $L$. Loss functions will be discussed in more detail in Sect. 3, but for understanding the algorithm it is sufficient to think of, say, the square loss given by $L(y, \hat{y}) = (y - \hat{y})^2$. The learner bases its prediction $\hat{y}_t$ on an *instance* $x_t$. In the expert-based framework we use here, we imagine there is a set of *experts* $\mathcal{E}_i$, $i = 1, \ldots, n$, and the instance $x_t$ is an $n$-dimensional vector where the $i$th component $x_{t,i}$ of the $t$th instance can be interpreted as the prediction given by expert $\mathcal{E}_i$ for the outcome $y_t$.

We consider here a specific kind of algorithm based on maintaining a weight on each expert. The weight vector $v_t$ is normalized to be a *probability vector* (i.e., $\sum_i v_i = 1$, $v_i \geq 0$), and $v_{t,i}$ can be interpreted as the algorithm's belief in the expert $\mathcal{E}_i$ having the best prediction at the trial $t$. The prediction of the algorithm at trial $t$ is given by the weighted average $\hat{y}_t = v_t \cdot x_t$. After seeing the outcome $y_t$, the algorithm updates its weights. The update method and all other details of the *Weighted Average Algorithm* (WAA) we consider here are given in Figure 1.

Sometimes it is more convenient to express the update in terms of the unnormalized weights

$$w_{t,i} = w_{1,i} \exp\left( -\frac{1}{c} \sum_{j=1}^{t-1} L(y_j, x_{j,i}) \right) \tag{4}$$

where $w_{1,i} = v_{1,i}$. Now $v_{t,i} = w_{t,i}/W_t$ where $W_t = \sum_{i=1}^{n} w_{t,i}$ is the normalization factor. Thus, ignoring the normalization factor, the logarithm of the weight of an expert is proportional to the expert's accumulated loss from preceding trials. We call this the *loss update* to emphasize that only the values of the loss function (and not its gradient etc.) are used.

The loss update of the Weighted Average Algorithm was introduced by Vovk [Vov90] in his Aggregating Algorithm (AA) that generalized the Weighted Majority algorithm [LW94]. However, the prediction of the Aggregating Algorithm is usually given by a function that is non-linear in $v_t$ and depends on the loss function. In contrast, we use the fixed prediction function $\hat{y}_t = v_t \cdot x_t$ for all loss functions. (A notable special case is the log loss, for which the Aggregating Algorithm also predicts with $\hat{y}_t = v_t \cdot x_t$.)

## 3 Basic Loss Bounds

We begin with a short discussion of some basic properties of loss functions. The definitions of the loss functions most interesting to us are given in Table 1. For a loss function $L$, we define $L_y(\hat{y}) = L(y, \hat{y})$ for convenience in writing derivatives with respect to $\hat{y}$. Note that with the exception of the absolute loss, all the loss

**Initialize** the weights to some probability vector $v_{1,i}$;
    set the parameter $c$ to some positive value.
**Repeat** for $t = 1, \ldots, \ell$:
    (i) Receive the instance $x_t$.
    (ii) Output the prediction $\widehat{y}_t = v_t \cdot x_t$.
    (iii) Receive the outcome $y_t$.
    (iv) Update the weights by the *loss update* defined as follows:

$$v_{t+1,i} = v_{t,i} \exp(-L(y_t, x_{t,i})/c)/\text{norm}_t$$

where

$$\text{norm}_t = \sum_{i=1}^{n} v_{t,i} \exp(-L(y_t, x_{t,i})/c) \ .$$

**Fig. 1.** The Weighted Average Algorithm (WAA) for combining expert predictions

functions given in Table 1 are *convex*, i.e., $L_y''(x) > 0$ for all $x$ and $y$, and also satisfy $L_y'(y) = 0$ for $0 < y < 1$. This implies *monotonicity*, i.e., $L_y'(x) < 0$ for $x < y$ and $L_y'(x) > 0$ for $x > y$. We generalize the derivative notation also for the end points by defining $L_0'(0) = L_1'(1) = 0$. The absolute loss $L(y, \widehat{y}) = |y - \widehat{y}|$ (and other loss functions that are not continuously differentiable) is not covered by the bounds given in this paper.

Given some fixed loss function $L$, consider now the total loss

$$\text{Loss}_A(S) = \sum_{t=1}^{\ell} L(y_t, \widehat{y}_t)$$

suffered by some algorithm $A$ on the trial sequence with the instance-outcome pairs $S = ((x_1, y_1), \ldots, (x_\ell, y_\ell))$. We wish to prove upper bounds for this total loss without making statistical or other assumptions about how the instances and outcomes are generated. When no such assumptions are made, one suitable way of measuring the quality of the learner's predictions is to compare it against the losses incurred by the individual experts on the same sequence. Thus, we also define $\text{Loss}_{\mathcal{E}_i}(S) = \sum_{t=1}^{\ell} L(y_t, x_{t,i})$.

Consider first the known bounds for the Aggregating Algorithm, which uses the same weights $v_t$ as the algorithm of Figure 1 but a different prediction $\widehat{y}_t$. To state the optimal constants in the bounds, and the learning rates that lead to them, define for $z, p, q \in [0, 1]$ (where $z$ should be interpreted as a "prediction" and $p$ and $q$ as two possible "outcomes") the ratio

$$R(z, p, q) = \frac{L_p'(z)L_q'(z)^2 - L_q'(z)L_p'(z)^2}{L_p'(z)L_q''(z) - L_q'(z)L_p''(z)} \ ;$$

we define $R(z, p, q) = 0$ in the special case $p = q$. Let further

$$c_L = \sup_{0 \le z, p, q \le 1} R(z, p, q) \ .$$

**Table 1.** Some common loss functions for the domain $[0, 1] \times [0, 1]$

| loss function $L$ | value for $L(y, \widehat{y})$ |
|---|---|
| square loss | $(y - \widehat{y})^2$ |
| relative entropy loss | $(1 - y)\ln((1 - y)/(1 - \widehat{y})) + y\ln(y/\widehat{y})$ |
| Hellinger loss | $\frac{1}{2}\left(\left(\sqrt{1 - y} - \sqrt{1 - \widehat{y}}\right)^2 + \left(\sqrt{y} - \sqrt{\widehat{y}}\right)^2\right)$ |
| absolute loss | $|y - \widehat{y}|$ |

The bound for the Aggregating Algorithm originally given by Vovk [Vov90] can now be stated as follows.

**Theorem 1.** *Let $L$ be a convex monotone twice differentiable loss function and AA be the Aggregating Algorithm with $c \geq c_L$ and initial weights $w_{1,i} = 1$. Then for any sequence $S = ((x_1, y_1), \ldots, (x_\ell, y_\ell))$ we have*

$$\text{Loss}_{\text{AA}}(S) \leq \left(\min_i \text{Loss}_{\mathcal{E}_i}(S)\right) + c\ln n \ . \tag{5}$$

The Aggregating Algorithm was also considered by Haussler et al. [HKW98], who showed the bound (5) optimal in the sense that under some reasonable regularity conditions, for *any* on-line algorithm $A$ there are sequences $S$ such that

$$\text{Loss}_A(S) \geq \left(\min_i \text{Loss}_{\mathcal{E}_i}(S)\right) + c_L \ln n - o(1) \ ,$$

where $o(1)$ approaches 0 as $n$ and $\ell$ approach $\infty$ in a suitable manner.

Vovk and Haussler et al. were mainly interested in the binary case $y_t \in \{0, 1\}$ and actually state (5) only for that case in the form

$$\text{Loss}_{\text{AA}}(S) \leq \left(\min_i \text{Loss}_{\mathcal{E}_i}(S)\right) + c_{L,\text{bin}} \ln n \tag{6}$$

where $c_{L,\text{bin}} = \sup_z R(z, 0, 1)$. The actual proof of Theorem 1 is a simple generalization of the earlier proofs [Vov90,HKW98] for (6); we omit it here. Haussler et al. also use some special techniques to show that for certain loss functions such as the square loss and the relative entropy loss the bound (6) holds even when $y_t$ is allowed to range over the whole interval $[0, 1]$. (The value of the constant for Hellinger loss for continuous-valued outcomes was left open in [HKW98].) The new formulation of Theorem 1 gives a unified method of obtaining bounds in the continuous-valued case. For square, relative entropy, and Hellinger loss a straightforward proof (omitted) shows that we actually have $c_L = c_{L,\text{bin}}$, so the bound is the same for continuous-valued and binary outcomes.

The main content of the bound (5) is that even for a large number of experts, the loss of the algorithm exceeds the loss of the best expert only by a small additive constant, regardless of the number of trials. Thus, the algorithm is good at weeding out the bad experts and then following the good ones. We can

**Table 2.** Comparison of the constants in bounds (5) and (9) for various loss functions.

| loss function $L$ | $c_L$ | $\widetilde{c}_L$ |
|---|---|---|
| relative entropy | 1 | 1 |
| square | $1/2$ | 2 |
| Hellinger | $2^{-1/2} \approx 0.71$ | 1 |

prove a similar bound for the Weighted Average Algorithm that predicts with $\widehat{y}_t = v_t \cdot x_t$. Define

$$\widetilde{R}(z,p) = \frac{L'_p(z)^2}{L''_p(z)} \tag{7}$$

and

$$\widetilde{c}_L = \sup_{0 < z, p < 1} \widetilde{R}(z,p) \ . \tag{8}$$

We can now state the bound for WAA as follows.

**Theorem 2.** *Let $L$ be a monotone convex twice differentiable loss function and WAA be the Weighted Average Algorithm of Figure 1 with uniform initial weights $w_{1,i} = 1$ and with $c \geq \widetilde{c}_L$. Then for any sequence $S = ((x_1, y_1), \ldots, (x_\ell, y_\ell))$ we have*

$$\text{Loss}_{\text{WAA}}(S) \leq \left( \min_i \text{Loss}_{\mathcal{E}_i}(S) \right) + c \ln n \ . \tag{9}$$

A generalization for multi-dimensional predictions and outcomes is given in Sect. 6.

To compare the constants $c_L$ and $\widetilde{c}_L$ in (5) and (9), respectively, recall that $(a + b)/(a' + b') \leq \max\{a/a', b/b'\}$ for any $a, a', b, b' > 0$. From this it is immediate that $c_L \leq \widetilde{c}_L$. For the most usual cases (9) is strictly worse than (5), as can be seen from the comparison in Table 2. For the relative entropy loss the bouds are actually equal, which is no surprise since then also the algorithms are the same (i.e., the Aggregating Algorithm also predicts with $\widehat{y}_t = v_t \cdot x_t$).

## 4 The Basic Upper Bound Proof

We apply to our situation the potential function method commonly used in computer science to analyze on-line algorithms. Thus, we introduce a *potential* $P$, with the value $P_t$ describing the algorithm's state just prior to trial $t$. Then $P_t - P_{t+1}$ is the decrease in the potential due to trial $t$. The key in proving the loss bound for an algorithm $A$ is to show for each trial $t$ that the prediction $\widehat{y}_t$ of $A$ satisfies

$$L(y_t, \widehat{y}_t) \leq P_t - P_{t+1} \ , \tag{10}$$

from which summing over $t = 1, \ldots, \ell$ yields $\text{Loss}_A(S) \leq P_1 - P_{\ell+1}$. That is, the total loss of the algorithm is bounded by the total decrease in potential. The basic question now is, how to choose the potential $P$ such that the equation (10) can be satisfied by a suitable choice of the prediction $\widehat{y}_t$, and the total increase of the potential gives interesting loss bounds. This question was originally answered for general loss functions by Vovk [Vov90] who generalized the potential used in [LW94] for the absolute loss. We shall next review Vovk's method for obtaining total loss bounds from (10) using our notation and then show how (10) can be achieved by the prediction $\widehat{y}_t = v_t \cdot x_t$ with slightly worse constants than with Vovk's original prediction.

First, recall from Sect. 2 that our algorithm has at trial $t$ an $n$-dimensional weight vector $w_t$ defined in (4), and we write $W_t = \sum_{i=1}^n w_{t,i}$. As our potential we now choose

$$P_t = c \ln W_t \tag{11}$$

where $c > 0$ is the same constant that is used in the updates. As it turns out, multiplying the weights by a constant affects neither the algorithm nor our analysis of it. Regarding the potentials in particular, multiplying the weights by a positive constant $a$ translates into adding the constant $c \ln a$ to the potential, which leaves potential differences unaffected. Thus, without loss of generality we can scale the initial weights so that $W_1 = 1$ holds, and $P_1 = 0$.

Elaborating further on our loss bound we get

$$\mathrm{Loss}_A(S) \le P_1 - P_{\ell+1}$$
$$= -c \ln \sum_{i=1}^n w_{1,i} \exp(-\mathrm{Loss}_{\mathcal{E}_i}(S)/c)$$
$$\le -c \ln w_{1,i} \exp(-\mathrm{Loss}_{\mathcal{E}_i}(S)/c)$$
$$= \mathrm{Loss}_{\mathcal{E}_i}(S) - c \ln w_{1,i}$$

for any given expert $i$. In particular, in the absence of any other preference it seems natural to set all the initial weights equal, which gives $w_{1,i} = 1/n$ for all $i$ and thus results in the final bound

$$\mathrm{Loss}_A(S) \le \left( \min_i \mathrm{Loss}_{\mathcal{E}_i}(S) \right) + c \ln n . \tag{12}$$

To prove Theorem 2, it thus remains to show that (10) is satisfied for the Weighted Average Algorithm. This turns out to be true for all $y_t$ and $x_t$ exactly when the constant $c$ satisfies the condition of the theorem.

To prove (10), first write the potential difference in the form

$$P_t - P_{t+1} = -c \ln \frac{W_{t+1}}{W_t} = -c \ln \sum_{i=1}^n v_{t,i} \exp(-L(y_t, x_{t,i})/c)$$

where $v_{t,i} = w_{t,i}/W_t$ is the normalized $i$th weight. We use the normalized weight vector in the prediction by choosing $\widehat{y}_t = v_t \cdot x_t$. Then (10) becomes

$$L(y_t, v_t \cdot x_t) \le -c \ln \sum_{i=1}^n v_{t,i} \exp(-L(y_t, x_{t,i})/c) ,$$

or equivalently

$$\exp(-L(y_t, v_t \cdot x_t)/c) \geq \sum_{i=1}^{n} v_{t,i} \exp(-L(y_t, x_{t,i})/c) \ .$$

If we define $f_y(x) = \exp(-L(y, x)/c)$, (10) therefore is equivalent with

$$f_{y_t}\left(\sum_{i=1}^{n} v_{t,i} x_{t,i}\right) \geq \sum_{i=1}^{n} v_{t,i} f_{y_t}(x_{t,i}) \ .$$

Since $v_t$ is a probability vector, this holds by Jensen's inequality if $f_{y_t}$ is concave. Using the notation $L_y(x) = L(y, x)$, we have

$$f_y'(x) = (-L_y'(x)/c) \exp(-L_y(x)/c)$$

and

$$f_y''(x) = ((L_y'(x)/c)^2 - L_y''(x)/c) \exp(-L_y(x)/c) \ .$$

Hence, since we assume $L_y''(x)$ to be positive, $f_y''(x) \leq 0$ holds if and only if $c \geq L_y'(x)^2/L_y''(x)$. Therefore, (10) holds for the prediction $\hat{y}_t = v_t \cdot x_t$ if the constant $c$ satisfies

$$c \geq \frac{L_{y_t}'(x_{t,i})^2}{L_{y_t}''(x_{t,i})} \qquad \text{for } i = 1, \ldots, n \ .$$

This concludes the proof of Theorem 2.

The result can be generalized to multi-dimensional predictions, as we see in Sect. 6.

## 5   Bounds Based on the Relative Entropy

We now wish to consider bounds in which the loss of the algorithm is compared not to the loss of the best single expert, but the loss of the best *probabilistic combination* of the experts. In particular, assume that at trial $t$ we predict according to the prediction of an expert chosen at random, with expert $\mathcal{E}_i$ having probability $u_i$ of being chosen. For such probabilistic predictions, the expected loss over the whole sequence is given by

$$\text{Loss}_u^{\text{avg}}(S) = \sum_{i=1}^{n} u_i \text{Loss}_{\mathcal{E}_i}(S) = \sum_{t=1}^{\ell} u \cdot L_t, \ ,$$

where $L_t$ denotes the vector of losses of the experts at trial $t$, i.e., $L_{t,i} = L(y_t, x_{t,i})$.

As discussed in the introduction, we wish to bound the loss of the algorithm in terms of the average loss $\text{Loss}_u^{\text{avg}}(S)$ and the distance $d(u, v_1)$ between $u$ and the algorithm's initial weight vector $v_1$ for some natural distance function $d$. For both the Aggregating Algorithm and the Weighted Average Algorithm, the most suitable distance is the *relative entropy* given by $d_{re}(u, v) = \sum_{i=1}^{n} u_i \ln(u_i/v_i)$. Our bound is then as follows.

**Theorem 3.** *Let L be a monotone convex twice differentiable loss function, and let the Weighted Average Algorithm WAA use arbitrary initial weights $v_1$ and parameter $c = \tilde{c}_L$, where $\tilde{c}_L$ is as in (8). Then for any sequence $S = ((x_1, y_1), \ldots, (x_\ell, y_\ell))$ and for all probability vectors $u$ we have*

$$\mathrm{Loss}_{\mathrm{WAA}}(S) \leq \mathrm{Loss}_u^{\mathrm{avg}}(S) + \tilde{c}_L \, d_{\mathrm{re}}(u, v_1) \ . \tag{13}$$

It is easy to see that also in Vovk's original analysis one can use the distance $d_{\mathrm{re}}(u, v_t)$ as done in the above bound. As a result one gets for the Aggregating Algorithm a bound like (13) with $c_L$ instead of $\tilde{c}_L$.

**Proof of Theorem 3:** We express the progress towards the reference vector $u$ as follows:

$$d_{\mathrm{re}}(u, v_t) - d_{\mathrm{re}}(u, v_{t+1}) = \sum_{i=1}^{n} u_i \ln \frac{v_{t+1,i}}{v_{t,i}}$$

$$= \sum_{i=1}^{n} u_i \ln \frac{w_{t+1,i} W_t}{w_{t,i} W_{t+1}}$$

$$= -u \cdot L_t / c + \sum_{i=1}^{n} u_i \ln \frac{W_t}{W_{t+1}}$$

$$= -u \cdot L_t / c + (P_t - P_{t+1}) / c \ . \tag{14}$$

Applying (10) now yields

$$L(y_t, \hat{y}_t) \leq P_t - P_{t+1} = u \cdot L_t + c \left( d_{\mathrm{re}}(u, v_t) - d_{\mathrm{re}}(u, v_{t+1}) \right) \ .$$

Summing over all the trials we obtain

$$\mathrm{Loss}_{\mathrm{WAA}}(S) \leq P_1 - P_{\ell+1} = \mathrm{Loss}_u^{\mathrm{avg}}(S) + c \left( d_{\mathrm{re}}(u, v_1) - d_{\mathrm{re}}(u, v_{\ell+1}) \right) \ . \tag{15}$$

Omitting the non-negative distance $d_{\mathrm{re}}(u, v_{\ell+1})$ gives the bound (13) of the theorem. ∎

To see some interesting details of the proof, notice that in (14), the probability vector $u$ is arbitrary. So in particular we can choose $u = v_t$ and thus obtain

$$-d_{\mathrm{re}}(v_t, v_{t+1}) = -v_t \cdot L_t / c + (P_t - P_{t+1}) / c \ . \tag{16}$$

Combining (14) and (16) gives us the following fundamental connection between distances and average losses:

$$v_t \cdot L_t = u \cdot L_t + c \left\{ d_{\mathrm{re}}(u, v_t) - d_{\mathrm{re}}(u, v_{t+1}) + d_{\mathrm{re}}(v_t, v_{t+1}) \right\} \ .$$

We conclude this section by pointing out a strong relationship between the update of the algorithm and the bound (13). One can show that the probability vector $u$ that minimizes the right-hand side of the bound (13) is $v_{\ell+1}$. With this minimizer $u = v_{t+1}$ the value of the bound equals $P_1 - P_{t+1}$ (which is the constant value of the right-hand side of (15)). Thus, the weight vector $v_{t+1}$ produced by the loss update at the end of trial $t$ is the minimizer of the bound (13) with respect to the first $t$ examples, and with this minimizer the bound on the first $t$ examples becomes $P_1 - P_{t+1}$.

Alternatively, the update of the algorithm can be derived in an on-line fashion as $v_{t+1} = \operatorname{argmin}_v U_t(v)$ where

$$U_t(v) = c\, d_{\mathrm{re}}(v, v_t) + v \cdot L_t$$

and $v$ is constrained to be a probability vector. Again, substituting the minimizing argument into $U_t$ gives a potential difference, namely

$$P_t - P_{t+1} = U_t(v_{t+1}) \leq U_t(v_t) = v_t \cdot L_t \ .$$

Note that the above upper bound for $P_t - P_{t+1}$ is complemented by the lower bound (11) that is central to the relative loss bounds proven for the expert setting.

If we want to compare the loss of the algorithm to $L(y_t, u \cdot x_t)$ instead of $u \cdot L_t$, a better update might result from $v_{t+1} = \operatorname{argmin}_v \hat{U}_t(v)$ where

$$\hat{U}_t(v) = c\, d_{\mathrm{re}}(v, v_t) + L(y_t, v \cdot x_t)$$

and again $v$ is constrained to be a probability vector. If the loss function is convex then $L(y_t, v \cdot x_t) \leq v \cdot L_t$ and $U_t(v)$ bounds $\hat{U}_t(v)$ from above. The bounds that can be obtained for algorithms based on minimizing $\hat{U}_t$ [KW97,HKW95] differ significantly from the style of bounds we have here. When the loss $L(y_t, \hat{y}_t)$ of the algorithm is compared to $L(y_t, u \cdot x_t)$, it is usually impossible to bound the additional loss by a constant (such as $\tilde{c}_L \ln n$ here). However, bounds where the comparison is to $L(y_t, u \cdot x_t)$ are in some sense much stronger than the expert style bounds of this paper.

# 6  Multi-dimensional predictions

We now consider briefly the case of multi-dimensional predictions. In other words, instead of having real numbers as outcomes $y_t$, experts' predictions $x_{t,i}$, and predictions $\hat{y}_t$, we now have vectors from (some subset of) $\mathbf{R}^k$, for some $k \geq 1$. For instance, the experts' predictions and the outcomes might be from the $k$-dimensional unit ball $\{ x \in \mathbf{R}^k \mid \|x\|_2 \leq 1 \}$. Since the prediction of each individual expert at a given time $t$ is a $k$-dimensional vector, all the expert predictions at time $t$ constitute a $k \times n$ matrix $X_t$. The prediction of the algorithm will still be a weighted average (i.e., convex combination) of the experts' predictions: $\hat{y}_t = X_t v_t$ where the weight vector $v_t$ is maintained by multiplicative updates as before. A loss function is now defined on $\mathbf{R}^k \times \mathbf{R}^k$; a simple examples would be $L(y, \hat{y}) = \|y - \hat{y}\|_2^2$.

Consider now the proof of our main result Theorem 2. The only place where we use the fact that the values $y_t$ and $x_{t,i}$ are real numbers is in proving that the function $f_y$ defined by $f_y(x) = \exp(-L(y,x)/c)$ is concave for all $y$. We do this proof by considering the sign of the second derivative of $f_y$.

In the multi-dimensional case, we analogously need to prove that the function $f_y$ defined by $f_y(x) = \exp(-L(y,x)/c)$ is concave. If we find a value for $c$ such that this holds, then the rest of the proof goes as before and we again obtain the familiar bound $\text{Loss}_{\text{WAA}}(S) \le (\min_i \text{Loss}_{\mathcal{E}_i}(S)) + c \ln n$. Alternatively we can use the relative entropy as in Sect. 5 and obtain the bound $\text{Loss}_{\text{WAA}}(S) \le \text{Loss}_u^{\text{avg}}(S) + c\, d_{\text{re}}(u, v_1)$ for any probability vector $u$.

Consider now when $f_y$ is concave. Let us denote the gradient and Hessian of $f_y$ by $\nabla f_y$ and $\text{D}^2 f_y$, respectively. We need to find out when $\text{D}^2 f_y$ is negative semidefinite everywhere. Thus, we have

$$(\nabla f_y(x))_i = \frac{\partial f_y(x)}{\partial x_i} = -\frac{1}{c} f_y(x) \frac{\partial L(y,x)}{\partial x_i}$$

and

$$\left(\text{D}^2 f_y(x)\right)_{ij} = \frac{\partial^2 f_y(x)}{\partial x_i \partial x_j} = \frac{1}{c} f_y(x) \left( \frac{1}{c} \frac{\partial L(y,x)}{\partial x_i} \frac{\partial L(y,x)}{\partial x_j} - \frac{\partial^2 L(y,x)}{\partial x_j \partial x_j} \right) \ .$$

For $z \in \mathbf{R}^k$ we now have $z^{\text{T}} \text{D}^2 f_y(x)\, z \le 0$ if and only if

$$(z \cdot \nabla L_y(x))^2 / c - z^{\text{T}} \text{D}^2 L_y(x)\, z \le 0 \ . \tag{17}$$

Note that in order to have this hold for all $z$ we at least need to have $z^{\text{T}} \text{D}^2 L_y(x)\, z$ positive, i.e., the loss $L(y,x)$ needs to be convex in $x$. In this case we get for $c$ the condition

$$c \ge \sup_{z,y,x} \frac{(z \cdot \nabla L_y(x))^2}{z^{\text{T}} \text{D}^2 L_y(x) z}$$

where $y$ and $x$ in the supremum range over the possible values of outcomes and (single) experts' predictions, respectively, and $z$ ranges over $\mathbf{R}^k$. Comparing this with the constant $\tilde{c}_L$ defined in (8), we see that the first and second derivatives there are here in some sense replaced with first and second derivatives in some direction $z$, where the direction $z$ is chosen as the worst case.

As a first example, consider the square loss $L(y,x) = \|y - x\|_2^2$. Then $\nabla L_y(x) = 2(x - y)$, and $\text{D}^2 L_y(x) = 2I$ where $I$ is the identity matrix. Hence, we get

$$\frac{(z \cdot \nabla L_y(x))^2}{z^{\text{T}} \text{D}^2 L_y(x) z} = \frac{(z \cdot (2x - 2y)^2}{2z^2} \ ,$$

and this expression obtains its maximum value $2(x - y)^2$ when $z$ is parallel to $x - y$. Hence, if the outcomes $y_t$ and the experts' predictions $x_{t,i}$ are from a ball of radius $R$, so $(x - y)^2 \le 4R^2$, we can take $c = 8R^2$, which gets us the bound

$$\text{Loss}_{\text{WAA}}(S) \le \text{Loss}_u^{\text{avg}}(S) + 8R^2 \ln n$$

for any $u$.

Since the square loss in the multi-dimensional case is simply the sum of square losses on individual components, we could try handling the $k$-dimensional case simply by running $k$ copies of the Weighted Average Algorithm and predicting each component independently of each other. Let us denote the resulting algorithm by WAA($k$) and compare this approach to the one analyzed above. It is easy to see that if we allow the experts' predictions and outcomes in the one-dimensional case to range over $[-B, B]$ instead of $[0, 1]$, we must for square loss replace the constant $\widetilde{c}_L = 2$ by $\widetilde{c}_L (2B)^2 = 8B^2$. The bound we get is then

$$\text{Loss}_{\text{WAA}(k)}(S) \leq \sum_{j=1}^{k} \left( \min_i \sum_{t=1}^{\ell} (y_{t,j} - (x_{t,i})_j)^2 \right) + 8kB^2 \ln n .$$

Comparing this with the bound we have for the true multi-dimensional Weighted Average Algorithm (WAA), we see that the first term in the bound for WAA($k$) can be much lower if there are experts that are good for predicting some but not all of the components. This potential for better fit is what WAA($k$) gains by having $kn$ instead of $n$ weights. On the other hand, the second term in the bound for WAA($k$) is linear in $k$, which is where WAA($k$) loses for having so many weights. (Of course, depending on how the vectors $y_t$ and $x_{t,i}$ are located in $R^k$, the factor $8R^2$ in the bound for the true multi-dimensional WAA may also grow linearly in $k$.)

As another example, consider the relative entropy loss $L(y, x) = \sum_{j=1}^{k} y_j \ln(y_j / x_j)$, where we assume that $y$ and $x$ are in the probability simplex: $y_i, x_i \geq 0$ and $\sum_j x_j = \sum_j y_j = 1$. Then

$$\frac{\partial L_y(x)}{\partial x_i} = -\frac{y_i}{x_i}$$

and

$$\frac{\partial^2 L_y(x)}{\partial x_i \partial x_j} = \delta_{ij} \frac{y_i}{x_i^2} ,$$

where $\delta_{ij} = 1$ for $i = j$ and $\delta_{ij} = 0$ otherwise. Now, given $y$, $x$ and a vector $z \in R^k$, let $Q$ be a random variable that for $i = 1, \ldots, k$ takes the value $q_i = z_i / x_i$ with probability $y_i$. We can then write

$$z \cdot \nabla L_y(x) = -\sum_{j=1}^{k} z_i \frac{y_i}{x_i} = -\sum_{j=1}^{k} y_i q_i = -\text{E}[Q] ,$$

and similarly

$$z^{\text{T}} D^2 L_y(x) z = \sum_{j=1}^{k} z_i^2 \frac{y_i}{x_i^2} = \sum_{j=1}^{k} y_i q_i^2 = \text{E}[Q^2] .$$

Thus, we have

$$\frac{(z \cdot \nabla L_y(x))^2}{z^{\text{T}} D^2 L_y(x) z} = \frac{\text{E}[Q]^2}{\text{E}[Q^2]} \leq 1$$

by the usual properties of random variables. Hence, for relative entropy loss we have

$$\text{Loss}_{\text{WAA}}(S) \le \left(\min_i \text{Loss}_{\mathcal{E}_i}(S)\right) + \ln n$$

even in the multi-dimensional case.

# References

[CBFH⁺97] N. Cesa-Bianchi, Y. Freund, D. Haussler, D. P. Helmbold, R. E. Schapire, and M. K. Warmuth. How to use expert advice. *Journal of the ACM*, 44(3):427–485, 1997.

[FS97] Yoav Freund and Robert E. Schapire. A decision-theoretic generalization of on-line learning and an application to boosting. *Journal of Computer and System Sciences*, 55(1):119–139, August 1997.

[FSSW97] Y. Freund, R. E. Schapire, Y. Singer, and M. K. Warmuth. Using and combining predictors that specialize. In *Proc. 29th ACM Symposium on Theory of Computing*, pages 334–343. ACM, 1997.

[HKW95] D. P. Helmbold, J. Kivinen, and M. K. Warmuth. Worst-case loss bounds for sigmoided linear neurons. In *Proc. 1995 Neural Information Processing Conference*, pages 309–315. MIT Press, Cambridge, MA, November 1995.

[HKW98] D. Haussler, J. Kivinen, and M. K. Warmuth. Sequential prediction of individual sequences under general loss functions. *IEEE Transactions on Information Theory*, 44(5):1906–1925, September 1998.

[KW97] J. Kivinen and M. K. Warmuth. Additive versus exponentiated gradient updates for linear prediction. *Information and Computation*, 132(1):1–64, January 1997.

[LW94] N. Littlestone and M. K. Warmuth. The weighted majority algorithm. *Information and Computation*, 108(2):212–261, 1994.

[Vov90] V. Vovk. Aggregating strategies. In *Proc. 3rd Annu. Workshop on Comput. Learning Theory*, pages 371–383. Morgan Kaufmann, 1990.

# On Teaching and Learning Intersection-Closed Concept Classes

Christian Kuhlmann*

Fakultät für Mathematik
Lehrstuhl Mathematik & Informatik
Ruhr-Universität Bochum
D-44780 Bochum
kuhlmann@lmi.ruhr-uni-bochum.de

**Abstract.** We consider the *self-directed learning model* [7] which is a variant of Littlestone's mistake-bound model [9, 10]. We will refute the conjecture of [8, 2] that for intersection-closed concept classes, the self-directed learning complexity is related to the VC-dimension. We show that, even under the assumption of intersection-closedness, both parameters are completely incomparable.

We furthermore investigate the structure of intersection-closed concept classes which are difficult to learn in the self-directed learning model. We show that such classes must contain maximum classes.

We consider the *teacher-directed learning model* [5] in the *worst*, *best* and *average case* performance. While the teaching complexity in the worst case is incomparable to the VC-dimension, large concept classes (e.g. balls) are bounded by VC-dimension with respect to the average case.

We show that the teaching complexity in the best case is bounded by the self-directed learning complexity. It is also bounded by the VC-dimension, if the concept class is intersection-closed. This does not hold for arbitrary concept classes. We find examples which substantiate this gap.

## 1   Introduction

The *self-directed learning model* was first introduced by Goldman et al. [7] as a variant of the *mistake-bound model* of Littlestone [9], [10] and has attracted much attention in the meantime. It was successively studied by [8, 5, 2, 12, 6, 1]. In this model, the learner makes predictions on adaptively chosen instances in order to gain knowledge of the concept to be learnt and is charged with a mistake, if his prediction was wrong.

Goldman and Sloan [8] extensively studied this model with respect to different families of concept classes and investigated the self-directed learning complexity

---

\* The author likes to thank Hans Ulrich Simon, Norbert Klasner, Michael Schmitt, Andreas Birkendorf and unidentified referees for helpful hints and discussions. The author gratefully acknowledges the support of the German-Israeli Foundation for Scientific Research and Development (grant I-403-001.06/95).

in relation to the VC-dimension. They conjectured that for any concept class, the self-directed learning complexity is bounded by its VC-dimension up to a constant factor, and that the upper bound is exactly the VC-dimension, if one requires the concept class to be intersection-closed.

Ben-David et al. [2] refuted both conjectures showing that the self-directed learning complexity is completely incomparable for arbitrary concept classes. They additionally introduced a family of intersection-closed classes with VC-dimension $2d$ and self-directed learning complexity $3d$. They conjectured that $3/2$ is a general maximum ratio of these two parameters for intersection-closed classes.

We will show that, even for intersection-closed concept classes, the self-directed learning complexity is completely incomparable to the VC-dimension introducing a family $\mathcal{C}_m^d$, $d \geq 2, m \geq 1$, with VC-dimension $d$ and self-directed learning complexity at least $m$.

This implies that the minimum size of an unlabeled compression scheme is also not bounded by the VC-dimension, even if the concept class is intersection-closed. Up to now, this was only proved for arbitrary concept classes.

We show that intersection-closed concept classes of VC-dimension 2 with high self-directed learning complexity have a special structure. They contain maximum classes of the same size as the complexity.

The *teacher-directed learning model* introduced by Goldman and Kearns [5] focusses on the minimum number of labeled instances a helpful teacher has to present such that any consistent learner is able to identify the target concept.

They consider the corresponding teaching complexity in the *worst case* scenario, i.e. the minimum number of labeled examples the teacher has to present such that the learner identifies the 'most difficult' concept. The teaching complexity in the worst case is also completely incomparable with the VC-dimension, even if the concept class is intersection-closed.

Here, we consider this model in the average and best case scenario. In the average case, we make a complete analysis for concept classes of VC-dimension 1. Furthermore, we prove that for concept classes $\mathcal{B}^d(c)$ (balls of center $c$ and size $\leq d$), the teaching complexity in the average case is bounded by $2d$, i.e. $2\mathrm{VCD}(\mathcal{B}^d(c))$.

The best case model is obviously stronger than the other teacher-directed models, but we show that it is also stronger than the self-directed model. The teaching complexity is bounded by the VC-dimension, if the concept class admits most specific concepts (which is a superfamily of intersection-closed classes). We present examples substantiating that this is not true for arbitrary concept classes.

## 2 Basic Definitions and Learning Models

Let $X$ be an *instance space* of $n$ *instances* and $\mathcal{C} \subseteq 2^X$. We call $\mathcal{C}$ *concept class*, its elements $c \in \mathcal{C}$ *concepts*. If it is convenient, we regard a concept $c$ as a mapping from $X$ to $\{0, 1\}$ where $c(x) = 1$, iff $x \in c$.

Let $z$ denote a subset of $X$ which we call a *sequence of $X$*. We define $\Pi_{\mathcal{C}}(z) = \{c \cap z : c \in \mathcal{C}\}$ to be the set of intersections of $z$ with all concepts of $\mathcal{C}$. Furthermore, we say that $z$ is *shattered* by $\mathcal{C}$, if $\Pi_{\mathcal{C}}(z) = 2^z$. Let $\Pi_{\mathcal{C}}(d) = \max_{|z|=d} |\Pi_{\mathcal{C}}(z)|$. Then we define the *Vapnik-Chervonenkis Dimension* as the maximum size of a sequence of $X$ shattered by $\mathcal{C}$, i.e.

$$\text{VCD}(\mathcal{C}) = \max\{d : \Pi_{\mathcal{C}}(d) = 2^d\}.$$

Let $\Phi_d(n) = \sum_{i=0}^{d} \binom{n}{i}$. Then Sauer's Lemma [13] implies that the cardinality of a concept class $\mathcal{C}$ with VC-dimension $d$ is bounded by $\Phi_d(n)$, i.e. $|\mathcal{C}| \leq \Phi_d(n)$.

Let $z$ be a sequence of $X$ of size $|z| = m$. Let $f$ be a mapping from subset $z$ into $\{0,1\}$. Then we call $z|f = \{(x, f(x)) : x \in z\}$ a *labeled sequence (of size $m$)*, which consists of a set of $m$ *labeled instances*. If $f$ is constant, i.e. $f \equiv 1$ ($f \equiv 0$, resp.), then we simply write $z|1$ ($z|0$, resp.). If $z$ is labeled according to a concept $c$, then we write $z|c$. A concept $c$ is called *consistent* with $z|f$, iff $z|f = z|c$. According to this, we call $\mathcal{C}_{z|f} = \{c \in \mathcal{C} : c \text{ is consistent with } z|f\}$ the *version space* of $\mathcal{C}$ with respect to $z|f$. Now we define $S(\mathcal{C})$ and $G(\mathcal{C})$, respectively, to be the set of the concepts of minimum and maximum size, respectively, in $\mathcal{C}$. We call a concept *most specific (most general, resp.)* with respect to $z|f$, iff $c \in S(\mathcal{C}_{z|f})$ ($c \in G(\mathcal{C}_{z|f})$, resp.).

We say that $\mathcal{C}$ *admits a unique most specific concept*, formally written as $\mathcal{C} \in$ MSC, iff for every labeled sequence $z|f$, $|S(\mathcal{C}_{z|f})| \leq 1$. We call $\mathcal{C}$ *intersection-closed*, denoted by $\mathcal{C} \in$ IC, iff for all $c_1, c_2 \in \mathcal{C}$, also $c_1 \cap c_2 \in \mathcal{C}$.

Let $X = \{x_1, ..., x_n\}$ and $\mathcal{C} = \{c_1, ..., c_m\}$. Then the *incidence matrix of $\mathcal{C}$* is defined as the binary $n \times m$-matrix, where entry $a_j^i = 1$, iff $x_i \in c_j$. Hence, the columns of the incidence matrix represent the concepts of $\mathcal{C}$. For the sake of simplicity, we will consider $\mathcal{C}$ as its incidence matrix, if it is convenient.

Let $\mathcal{C} \in$ MSC. Then we define $\mathfrak{I}(c)$ as the set containing all subsets $z$ of minimum size with $c$ as their mosts specific concept, i.e. $\mathfrak{I}(c) = \{z : S(\mathcal{C}_{z|1}) = \{c\}\}$. These minimum sets are called *the spanning sets of the concept $c$*. $\mathfrak{I}(\mathcal{C}) = \max_c |\mathfrak{I}(c)|$ denotes the maximum size of the number of spanning sets over all concepts in $\mathcal{C}$.

Let $Ind(\mathcal{C}, x) = |\{c \in \mathcal{C} : x \in c\}|$ be the *index number of $x$* and $Ind(\mathcal{C}) = \min_{x \in X} Ind(\mathcal{C}, x)$ the *index number of $\mathcal{C}$*. Finally, we define the *inverse concept class* $\bar{\mathcal{C}} = \{\bar{c} : \bar{c} = X - c, c \in \mathcal{C}\}$.

**Self-directed model** A *self-directed learning algorithm $L$ for a concept class $\mathcal{C}$* selects labeled instances and presents it to the environment as a prediction . After each prediction, the environment reveals the true labeling of the selected instance with respect to the target concept.

The choice of the labeled instances is adaptive, i.e. it may depend on the classification of the previously seen instances.

Let $\text{M}_{sd}(\mathcal{C}, L, c_t)$ denote the number of wrong predictions (*mistakes*) $L$ made to uniquely identify the target concept $c_t$. Then the *self-directed learning complexity* is defined as

$$M_{sd}(\mathcal{C}) = \min_L \max_{c_t \in \mathcal{C}}(M_{sd}(L, c_t))$$

**Teacher-directed model** We define the *teaching complexity for $\mathcal{C}$ with respect to the target concept $c_t$*, denoted by $M_{td}(\mathcal{C}, c_t)$, as the minimum size of a sequence $z$ which uniquely identifies a target concept $c_t \in \mathcal{C}$, i.e. $|\mathcal{C}_{z|c_t}| = 1$.

This parameter can be regarded as the shortest size of a sequence a helpful teacher has to present as a labeled sequence $z|c_t$ such that *any* consistent learner uniquely identifies the target concept $c_t$.

We call a sequence $z$ of minimum size which uniquely identifies a target concept $c_t \in \mathcal{C}$ *minimum sequence for $c_t$*.

We define the *teaching complexity of $\mathcal{C}$* distinguishing between the *best* and the *worst* and *average case* performance:

$$M_{td\text{-}worst}(\mathcal{C}) = \max_{c_t \in \mathcal{C}}(M_{td}(\mathcal{C}, c_t))$$

$$M_{td\text{-}best}(\mathcal{C}) = \min_{c_t \in \mathcal{C}}(M_{td}(\mathcal{C}, c_t)).$$

In order to define the average case, let $P$ be a distribution over $\mathcal{C}$. Then the average case performance of the *teaching complexity (average case) w.r.t. the distribution $P$* is

$$M_{td\text{-}average}(\mathcal{C}, P) = \sum_{c \in \mathcal{C}} P(c) M_{td}(\mathcal{C}, c).$$

The teaching complexity in the worst case performance is identical to the teaching dimension introduced by Goldman et al. [5].

It is known that $M_{td\text{-}worst}$ can be arbitrarily high, if the VC-dimension is constant - even under the assumption of intersection-closedness [5] (it is easy to see that , e.g., *singleton* $\cup\ \emptyset$ is intersection-closed with VC-dimension 1, but $M_{td\text{-}worst}(\mathcal{C}) = n$).

In the sequel, we will deal with the other two models $M_{td\text{-}average}$ and $M_{td\text{-}best}$ in order to investigate their behaviour with respect to arbitrary and intersection-closed concept classes. Obviously, the hierarchical structure of the learning models is

$$M_{td\text{-}best}(\mathcal{C}) \le M_{td\text{-}average}(\mathcal{C}) \le M_{td\text{-}worst}(\mathcal{C}).$$

But it also holds that

$$M_{td\text{-}best}(\mathcal{C}) \le M_{sd}(\mathcal{C}).$$

We will prove this in section 7 (Lemma 6).

Hence, $M_{td\text{-}best}$ stands hierarchically above all other models which we consider in this context.

## 3  Preliminary Results

A basic tool to apply the property of intersection-closedness is that there exist $d+1$ concepts which witness that the VC-dimension is at least $d$. We can express this observation in terms of the occurrence of a *submatrix*[1] $D_d = (\lambda_j^i)_{j=0...d}^{i=1...d}$ in the incidence matrix of the concept class. $\lambda_j^i = 0$, iff $i = j$. In other words, $D_d$ is a $d \times (d+1)$-matrix which has a diagonal with 0, and all other entries are 1. Now we have the following

**Lemma 1.** *Let $\mathcal{C}$ be an intersection-closed concept class. $\mathcal{C}$ contains a submatrix $D_d$, if and only if $VCD(\mathcal{C})$ is at least $d$.*

**Proof.** Assume the existence of $D_d$. Let $x_1, ..., x_d$ be the instances (rows) and $c_0, ..., c_d$ the concepts (columns) of $D_d$. Then, for every labeling $f$ of the instances, the intersection $c_\cap = \bigcap_{f(x_i)=1} c_i$ is in $\mathcal{C}$ due to the intersection-closedness, and $x_1, ..., x_d | f = x_1, ..., x_d | c_\cap$. This implies that $x_1, ..., x_d$ is shattered by $\mathcal{C}$.
The other direction is evident because the VC-dimension implies the existence of $d$ instances on which every labeling occurs. Hence, $\mathcal{C}$ also contains $D_d$ on the $d$ instances. ∎

Now we briefly investigate the learning properties of concept classes of VC-dimension 1. First, the following structural result holds:

**Lemma 2.** *Let $\mathcal{C}$ be an arbitrary concept class with VC-dimension 1. Then either $Ind(\mathcal{C}) \le 1$ or $Ind(\bar{\mathcal{C}}) \le 1$.*

**Proof. Sketch** Consider a concept $c_0 \in \mathcal{C}$. With respect to this concept we define a new concept class $\mathcal{C}_{[c_0]} = \{\tilde{c} : \tilde{c} = c \triangle c_0, c \in \mathcal{C}\}$. In other words, we invert those entries of rows of the incidence matrix of $\mathcal{C}$ for which $c_0(x) = 1$. This clearly has no influence on the VC-dimension and, obviously, $\mathcal{C}_{[c_0]}$ contains the empty set $\tilde{c}_0 = c_0 \triangle c_0$. We will find an $x$ such that $Ind(\mathcal{C}_{[c_0]}, x) \le 1$. Then, either $x$ is only contained in $c_0$ ($Ind(\mathcal{C}) \le 1$) or $x$ is contained in every other concept but $c_0$ ($Ind(\bar{\mathcal{C}}) \le 1$). This proves the lemma.
In order to show $Ind(\mathcal{C}_{[c_0]}) \le 1$, we assume the contrary, i.e. $Ind(\mathcal{C}_{[c_0]}) \ge 2$. It can be shown by induction that for an arbitrarily large $k$ we can find a sequence of different instances and corresponding concepts $x_1, \tilde{c}_1, ..., x_k, \tilde{c}_k \in (X \times \mathcal{C}_{[c_0]})^k$ with the property that for all $i$ and all $j > i$, $x_1, ..., x_i \in \tilde{c}_i$ and $x_j \notin \tilde{c}_i$. This is a contradiction, since $X$ is finite. ∎

**Lemma 3.** *Let $\mathcal{C}$ be an intersection-closed concept class with VC-dimension 1. Then $Ind(\mathcal{C}) \le 1$.*

**Proof.** The proof is similar to the one of the previous lemma, but this time the construction of $\mathcal{C}_{[c_0]}$ is not necessary. It is a consequence of the intersection-closedness that, with the assumption $Ind(\mathcal{C}) \ge 2$, the empty set is in $\mathcal{C}$. ∎

---

[1] A *submatrix* of a matrix $A$ is obtained by deletion and permutation of arbitrary rows and columns of $A$

Finally we want to mention that Lemma 41 enables us to prove a result of Goldman and Sloan [8] in a alternative, compact way:

**Theorem 1.** *Let $\mathcal{C}$ be a concept class with $VCD(\mathcal{C}) = 1$. Then $M_{sd}(\mathcal{C}) = 1$.*

**Proof.** We introduce a learning strategy which relies on the previous lemma. The self-directed learning strategy goes the 'safest' way and chooses the instance which is covered by one or by all but one concepts of the version space, respectively. Its prediction is the label of the majority. Hence, a mistake identifies uniquely the target concept. ∎

## 4 Self-directed learning of intersection-closed concept classes and the VC-Dimension

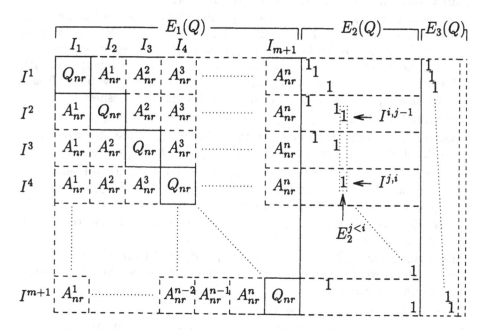

**Fig. 1.** The invariant extension of an intersection-closed incidence matrix $Q$

Repeatedly, it was conjectured that the self-directed learning complexity is bounded by the VC-dimension (up to a constant factor), if the concept class to be learnt is intersection-closed. Goldman and Sloan [8] supposed that $M_{sd}$ is bounded by the VC-dimension for intersection-closed concept classes. Ben-David et al. [2] disproved this by a family of examples where the ratio of the two values is $3/2$. They conjectured that this ratio holds as an upper bound for all intersection-closed concept classes.

In this chapter, we will refute this conjecture showing that there exist intersection-closed concept classes of constant VC-dimension and arbitrarily large self-directed learning complexity.

**Theorem 2.** *For each $m \geq 1$ and each $d \geq 2$, there exists a concept class $\mathcal{C}_m^d$ with the following properties:*   $\mathcal{C}_m^d \in IC$,   $VCD(\mathcal{C}_m^d) = d$,   $M_{sd}(\mathcal{C}_m^d) \geq m$

**Proof.** **Sketch** The basic idea of the proof is to extend a concept class recursively according to a rule which leaves the VC-dimension and the property of intersection-closedness invariant. Then we show that if the concept class is extended $m$ times, for each learner, the adversary is able to save at least the $m-1$ times extended concept class in the version space.

For the extension rule we consider the incidence matrix of the concept classes. Figure 1 illustrates the incidence matrix of the extended concept class.

Formally, let $Q_{nr}$ be an $(n \times r)$-matrix. We furthermore define $A_{nr}^i$ as the $(n \times r)$-matrix where all rows are 0 except the $i$th row which is 1.

Then we consider the $((n+1)n \times (n+1)r)$-matrix $E_1(Q_{nr})$ which contains $n+1$ blocks of $n$ rows and $n+1$ blocks of $r$ columns. We denote the *row blocks* as $I^1, ..., I^{n+1}$ and *column blocks* as $I_1, ..., I_{n+1}$ where $I^{i,k}$ denotes the $k$th instance (row) in the $i$th row block and $I_{j,l}$ denotes the $l$th concept (column) in the $j$th column block, respectively. We further denote the block of row block $I^i$ and column block $I_j$ as $I_j^i$ and the label of the $l$th instance with respect to the $k$th concept in this block as $I_{j,l}^{i,k}$. $E(Q_{nr})$ contains $n+1$ copies of $Q_{nr}$ in its main diagonal $I_i^i$. The other blocks contain the matrices $A_{nr}^i$. More precisely, for all $i < j$ the block $I_j^i$ contains $A_{nr}^i$ and for all $i > j$ the block $I_j^i$ contains $A_{nr}^{i-1}$.

Furthermore we define matrix $E_2(Q_{nr})$ as an $((n+1)n \times \frac{1}{2}n(n+1)$-matrix of columns where, for each two different blocks $I_i, I_j$, $i < j$, of $E_1(Q_{nr})$, there is a concept containing exactly two instances in these blocks at row $I^{i,j-1}$ and $I^{j,i}$.

Now $E_3(Q_{nr})$ is the $((n+1)n \times (n+1)n+1$-matrix which is the identity matrix with an additional column of zeros.

Finally, we obtain $E(Q_{nr}) = E_1(Q_{nr})|E_2(Q_{nr})|E_3(Q_{nr})$ (where $|$ is the matrix-concatenation) which represents the incidence matrix of the extended concept class we want to consider.

**Claim 1** $Q_{nr} \in IC \Rightarrow E(Q_{nr}) \in IC$

**Claim 2** *If $Q_{nr} \in IC$ and $VCD(Q_{nr}) = d \geq 2$, then $VCD(E(Q_{nr})) = d$.*

**Claim 3** *For all labeled instances $(x,l) \in X \times \{0,1\}$, $Q_{nr} \in E(Q_{nr})_{x|l}$*

The claims are proved in the appendix.

Now we complete the proof of the lemma. Let $M_1^d$ be the incidence matrix of an arbitrary concept class $\mathcal{C}_1^d$ with $\mathcal{C}_1^d \in IC$ and $VCD(\mathcal{C}_1^d) = d$. We inductively define $\mathcal{C}_m^d$ as the concept class which corresponds to $E(M_{m-1}^d)$. According to Claim 1 and 2 , $\mathcal{C}_m^d \in IC$ and $VCD(\mathcal{C}_m^d) = d$. Finally, Claim 3 states that the adversary can force the learner to make a mistake and the version space still contains $\mathcal{C}_{m-1}^d$. Hence, after $m$ mistakes the version space still contains at least $\mathcal{C}_1^d$. ∎

Floyd an Warmuth ([4]) establish the relationship between self-directed learning and *unlabeled compression schemes*. An unlabeled compression scheme can be interpreted as a self-directed learner who is restricted to choose his predictions from a particular sequence. Thus, the self-directed learning model is at least as powerful as the unlabeled compression scheme.

With the above result we can formulate the following

**Corollary 1.** *The minimum size of an unlabeled compression scheme is not bounded by any function of the VC-Dimension of intersection-closed concept classes.*

# 5 The structure of intersection-closed concept classes with high learning complexity

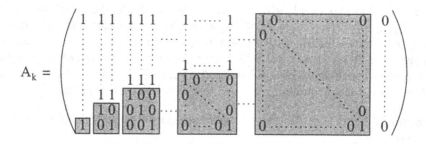

**Fig. 2.** The maximum matrix $A_k$ which is included as a submatrix in the incidence matrix

In the last section we proved that, even under the assumption of intersection-closedness, the self-directed learner can be forced to make arbitrarily many mistakes to learn a concept class with constant VC-dimension.

For these cases, it is sometimes interesting to receive knowledge about the structure of the concept class to be learned. In this chapter, we investigate the structure of concept classes of VC-dimension 2 with self-directed learning complexity $k$ and find out that we can find a *maximum subclass*[2] contained in the concept class.

We define the $k \times \frac{1}{2}k(k+1)$-matrix $A_k = A_k^1, ..., A_k^k \bar{0}$ where $A_k^i$ is a $k \times i$-matrix containing the unit matrix of size $i$ in the last $i$ rows. The other entries are labeled with 1. $\bar{0}$ indicates the zero vector. Figure 2 illustrates the form of this matrix. This matrix represents a maximum class, since it has VC-dimension 2 and the number of labelings on the $k$ instances is maximum size (Sauer's lemma).

---

[2] A *maximum subclass* is maximum in the sense that its VC-dimension increases, if an arbitrary concept is added.

**Theorem 3.** *Let $\mathcal{C} \in IC$ with $VCD(\mathcal{C}) = 2$ and let $M_{sd}(\mathcal{C}) = k$. Then the incidence matrix of $\mathcal{C}$ contains a submatrix $A_k$.*

**Proof. Sketch** We follow the strategy of the learner who always chooses the instances $x_1, x_2, ...$ with the minimum index number of the version space. Exactly the concept class restricted to the subsequence the learner made wrong predictions, has the structure of $A_k$.

For the detailed proof we refer to the extended version of this paper. ∎

## 6 Teacher-directed learning - average case

In this chapter, we investigate how the teaching complexity behaves on a concept class in the average case. Throughout this chapter, $U$ denotes the *uniform distribution* on $\mathcal{C}$. We first observe that the teaching complexity of a concept $c_0$ is related to the existence of concepts which are 'close' to $c_0$.

**Definition** Let $z|f_0$ be a labeled sequence. Then we define the *k-ball with center* $z|f_0$, $\mathcal{B}_z^k(f_0) = \{z|f : d_z(f_0, f) \leq k\}$, where $d_z(f_0, f)$ denotes the Hamming-distance of two labelings with respect to the sequence $z$. If $z = X$ then we simply write $\mathcal{B}^k(c_0)$ the *k-ball with center* $c_0$. We say that $\mathcal{C}$ *contains a k-ball with center* $z|c_0$, iff $\mathcal{B}_z^k(c_0)$ is a subset of $\mathcal{C}|z$. Since the VC-dimension of a $k$-ball is $k$, a concept class containing a $k$-ball has VC-dimension of at least $k$.

**Lemma 4.** *Let $c_t \in \mathcal{C}$. For any minimum sequence $z$ for $c_t$, $\mathcal{C}$ contains a 1-ball with center $z|c_t$.*

**Proof.** Let $z$ be a minimum sequence for $c_t$, i.e. $|\mathcal{C}_{z|c_t}| = 1$. Then for every $i$, $|\mathcal{C}_{z-x_i|c_t}|$ must be at least two, otherwise $z - x_i$ is already a minimum sequence. Therefore, for all $i$, $|\mathcal{C}_{z-x_i|c_t;x_i|\bar{c}_i}|$ is at least one. ∎

**Theorem 4.** *Consider $\mathcal{C} = \{c_0, ..., c_m\}$ with $VCD(\mathcal{C}) = 1$. Then there exist $k_0, ..., k_m \in \mathbb{N}_0$ with $\sum_{i=0}^{m} k_i \leq 2m$ such that*

$$M_{td\text{-}average}(\mathcal{C}, P) = \sum_{i=0}^{m} k_i P(c_i).$$

*In particular, for the uniform distribution $U$, $M_{td\text{-}average}(\mathcal{C}, U) < 2$.*

**Proof. Sketch** Since every concept class with VC-dimension 1 is embeddable into a maximum class [3], we can assume that the instance space has size $m$.

We prove the first part of the lemma by induction over size $m$ of the instance space. For $m = 1$, the lemma holds trivially.

Let us now assume, that the lemma holds for $m - 1$. Now let the instance space $X$ be of $m$ elements. For an instance $x \in X$ define $\mathcal{C}|(X - x)$ as the restriction of $\mathcal{C}$ to $X - x$. We call $(c_1, c_2)_x$ a *pair of $x$*, if $x \notin c_1$ and $c_1 \cup \{x\} = c_2$. We call $c$

*independent*, if it does not belong to any pair. Let $k_c$ be the length of the smallest sequence identifying $c$ in $\mathcal{C}$ (i.e. $k_c = M_{td}(\mathcal{C}, c)$), and let $\tilde{k}_c$ be the smallest sequence identifying the restriction of $c$ on $\mathcal{C}|(X-x)$ (i.e. $\tilde{k}_c = M_{td}(\mathcal{C}|(X-x), c)$). Then, according to the definition, $M_{td\text{-}average}(\mathcal{C}) = \sum_{c \in \mathcal{C}} k_c P(c)$.

**Claim 1** *There exists at most one pair of $x$ in $\mathcal{C}$.*

**Claim 2** *Let $(c_1, c_2)_z$ be a pair in $\mathcal{C}$. Then, up to a permutation, $k_{c_1} = \tilde{k}_{c_1} + 1$ and $k_{c_2} = 1$.*

**Claim 3** *For all independent concepts $c$, $k_c = \tilde{k}_c$.*

We prove the claims in the extended version of this paper.

Since, with the restriction of $\mathcal{C}$ to $X - x$, only $c_2$ of a pair $(c_1, c_2)_x$ is removed, $\mathcal{C} = (\mathcal{C}|(X - x)) \cup \{c_2\}$. Hence, if $\mathcal{C}$ does not contain a pair, then, according to Claim 3,

$$\sum_{c \in \mathcal{C}} k_c = \sum_{c \in \mathcal{C}|(X-x)} \tilde{k}_c \leq 2(m - 1).$$

Otherwise, Claim 1 implies that $\mathcal{C}$ contains exactly one pair and with Claim 2,

$$\sum_{c \in \mathcal{C}} k_c = \sum_{c \in \mathcal{C}|(X-x)} \tilde{k}_c + 2 \leq 2m.$$

This completes the induction.

For the uniform distribution $U$, we obtain $M_{td\text{-}average}(\mathcal{C}, U) \leq \frac{\sum_{i=0}^{m} k_i}{m+1} < 2$. ∎

**Lemma 5.** *For every ball $\mathcal{B}^k(c)$, the measures VCD, $M_{td}$, $M_{td\text{-}average}$ and $M_{td\text{-}best}$ are independent from center $c$.*

**Proof.** This is easy to see, since to different balls $\mathcal{B}^k(c_1)$ and $\mathcal{B}^k(c_2)$ can be transformed into each other by simply inverting those rows of the incidence matrix for which $c_1(x) \neq c_2(x)$. This clearly has no influence on any of the four measures. ∎

**Theorem 5.** *Let $\mathcal{B}^d(c)$ be a ball with an arbitrary center $c$ and $U$ be the uniform distribution over $\mathcal{B}^d(c)$. Then $M_{td\text{-}average}(\mathcal{B}^d(c), U) \leq 2d$.*

**Proof.** Due to the previous lemma, it suffices to the ball with center $\emptyset$, i.e. $\mathcal{B}^d = \{c : |c| \leq d\}$ Partition $\mathcal{B}^d$ into $\mathcal{C}_0, ..., \mathcal{C}_d$, where $\mathcal{C}_i = \{c : |c| = i\}$. Clearly, for all $i < d$ and all $c \in \mathcal{C}_i$, $M_{td}(\mathcal{C}_i, c) \leq n$. For $c \in \mathcal{C}_d$, it holds $M_{td}(\mathcal{C}_d, c) \leq d$, since every sequence is determined by its positive labels. Hence, applying the easy observation that $\Phi_{d-1}(n) \leq \frac{d}{n-d}\Phi_d(n)$,

$$M_{td\text{-}average}(\mathcal{B}^d, U) \leq \frac{n\Phi_{d-1}(n) + d\binom{n}{d}}{\Phi_d(n)} = d + (n - d)\frac{\Phi_{d-1}(n)}{\Phi_d(n)} \leq 2d.$$

∎

# 7   Teacher-directed learning - best case

In the previous sections we demonstrated that neither for the self-directed learning complexity nor for the teaching complexity (worst case) the learnability of intersection-closed concept classes is bounded by any function of their VC-dimension. In this section, we investigate $M_{td\text{-}best}$. We will see that, in fact, the complexity is bounded if $\mathcal{C}$ is intersection-closed. This is not true for arbitrary concept classes as we will see by an example. We introduce a family of concept classes $\mathcal{C}^d$ with $VCD(\mathcal{C}^d) = 2d$ and $M_{td\text{-}best}(\mathcal{C}) = 3d$.

In section 2 we asserted that $M_{td\text{-}best}$ is more powerful than any other learning model considered in this paper. It remains to show that $M_{td\text{-}best}$ is even more powerful than the self-directed learning model.

**Lemma 6.** *For any concept class* $\mathcal{C}$, $M_{td\text{-}best}(\mathcal{C}) \leq M_{sd}(\mathcal{C})$

**Proof.** The idea of the proof is to run the 'greedy' adversary, who provoces the self-directed learner $L_{sd}$ to make mistakes, whenever it is possible. Let $z$ be the sequence $L_{sd}$ presents. Let $\{x_1, ..., x_k\} \subset z$ be the instances on which $L_{sd}$ made a mistake and $\{y_1, ..., y_l\} \subset z$ those for which the adversary was not able to reveal another label but the one issued from the learner. Then $x_1, ..., x_k | c_t$ already uniquely identifies the target concept $c_t$.

Consider $\mathcal{C}_{z|c_t}$ which contains only the target concept $c_t$. If we remove $y_i$ from the sequence then $\mathcal{C}_{z-y_i|c_t}$ still contains only $c_t$ since all concepts of the version space provide $y_i$ with the same labeling. Therefore $y_i$ cannot gain more information. With the same argument, we can remove successively all instances $y_1, ..., y_l$ from the sequence $z$ and, hence, $\mathcal{C}_{x_1,...,x_k|c_t}$ only contains the target concept. ∎

**Theorem 6.** *For every concept class* $\mathcal{C} \in MSC$, $M_{td\text{-}best}(\mathcal{C})$ *is bounded by* $VCD(\mathcal{C})$.

**Proof.** We prove that, for $\mathcal{C} \in MSC$, $M_{td\text{-}best}(\mathcal{C}) \leq \mathcal{I}(\mathcal{C})$.

Let $c_t \in G(\mathcal{C})$ and take $z_t \in \mathcal{I}(c_t)$ which identifies $c_t$ as its most specific concept, i.e., $S(\mathcal{C}_{z|1}) = \{c_t\}$. Since there is no concept $c \in \mathcal{C}$ containing $c_t$, $\mathcal{C}_{z|1} = \{c_t\}$. Hence, $M_{td\text{-}best}(\mathcal{C}) \leq |z| \leq \mathcal{I}(\mathcal{C})$.

Since Natarajan [11] shows that $\mathcal{I}(\mathcal{C})$ is bounded by the VC-dimension of $\mathcal{C}$, the theorem is proved. ∎

The above theorem does not hold for arbitrary concept classes. The property $\mathcal{C} \in MSC$ cannot be dropped to bound the teaching complexity by the VC-dimension. In order to show this, we construct a concept class $E(\mathcal{C})$ with $VCD(E(\mathcal{C})) = 2$ and $M_{td\text{-}best}(E(\mathcal{C})) = 3$. Let $\mathcal{C} = \{c_1, c_2, c_3, c_4\}$ be the powerset of $X = \{x_1, x_2\}$. Clearly $VCD(\mathcal{C}) = 2$. Now let $E(\mathcal{C})$ be the concept class whose incidence matrix consists of $8 \times 8$ blocks of size $2 \times 3$. We use the same notation of the blocks, rows and columns ($I^i, I_j, ...$) as in the proof of Theorem 2. Figure 3 illustrates the extension matrix of $\mathcal{C}$. The entries of the diagonal are those three vectors of $\mathcal{C}$, which are not in the other blocks in the same column. More precisely:

| 1 0 0 | 1 1 1 | 1 1 1 : 1 1 1 | 0 0 0 : 0 0 0 | 0 0 0 : 0 0 0 |
| 0 1 0 | 1 1 1 | 0 0 0 : 0 0 0 | 1 1 1 : 1 1 1 | 0 0 0 : 0 0 0 |
| 1 1 1 | 1 0 0 | 1 1 1 : 1 1 1 | 0 0 0 : 0 0 0 | 0 0 0 : 0 0 0 |
| 1 1 1 | 0 1 0 | 0 0 0 : 0 0 0 | 1 1 1 : 1 1 1 | 0 0 0 : 0 0 0 |
| 1 1 1 : 1 1 1 | 1 0 0 | 1 1 1 | 0 0 0 : 0 0 0 | 0 0 0 : 0 0 0 |
| 1 1 1 : 1 1 1 | 1 1 0 | 0 0 0 | 1 1 1 : 1 1 1 | 0 0 0 : 0 0 0 |
| 1 1 1 : 1 1 1 | 1 1 1 | 1 0 0 | 0 0 0 : 0 0 0 | 0 0 0 : 0 0 0 |
| 1 1 1 : 1 1 1 | 0 0 0 | 1 1 0 | 1 1 1 : 1 1 1 | 0 0 0 : 0 0 0 |
| 1 1 1 : 1 1 1 | 1 1 1 : 1 1 1 | 1 1 0 | 0 0 0 | 0 0 0 : 0 0 0 |
| 1 1 1 : 1 1 1 | 0 0 0 : 0 0 0 | 1 0 0 | 1 1 1 | 0 0 0 : 0 0 0 |
| 1 1 1 : 1 1 1 | 1 1 1 : 1 1 1 | 0 0 0 | 1 1 0 | 0 0 0 : 0 0 0 |
| 1 1 1 : 1 1 1 | 0 0 0 : 0 0 0 | 1 1 1 | 1 0 0 | 0 0 0 : 0 0 0 |
| 1 1 1 : 1 1 1 | 1 1 1 : 1 1 1 | 0 0 0 : 0 0 0 | 1 1 0 | 0 0 0 |
| 1 1 1 : 1 1 1 | 0 0 0 : 0 0 0 | 1 1 1 : 1 1 1 | 1 0 1 | 0 0 0 |
| 1 1 1 : 1 1 1 | 1 1 1 : 1 1 1 | 0 0 0 : 0 0 0 | 0 0 0 | 1 1 0 |
| 1 1 1 : 1 1 1 | 0 0 0 : 0 0 0 | 1 1 1 : 1 1 1 | 0 0 0 | 1 0 1 |

**Fig. 3.** The expansion of powerset $\mathcal{C}$ to a concept class $E(\mathcal{C})$ with $\mathrm{VCD}(E(\mathcal{C})) = 2$ and learning complexity $\mathrm{M}_{td\text{-}best}(E(\mathcal{C})) = 3$

$I_i^i = \mathcal{C} - c_{\lceil i/2 \rceil}$. And for all $i \neq j$ and $k = 1, ..., 3$ $I_j^{i,k} = c_{\lceil i/2 \rceil}$. Note that, on every column block $I_i$, all instances are constant up to those in row block $I^i$.

**Theorem 7.** *There exists a family of concept classes* $(\mathcal{C}^d)$ *with* $\mathrm{VCD}(\mathcal{C}^d) = 2d$ *and*

$$\mathrm{M}_{td\text{-}best}(\mathcal{C}^d) = 3d.$$

**Proof.** For the proof of $\mathrm{VCD}(E(\mathcal{C}^d)) = 2$ and $\mathrm{M}_{td\text{-}best}(E(\mathcal{C})) = 3$, we refer to the extended version of this paper. Given this, the statement is established for the case $d = 1$. From this we easily obtain the case for arbitrary $d$ combining $d$ copies of the concept class, $\tilde{\mathcal{C}} = \mathcal{C} \times ... \times \mathcal{C}$. ∎

## 8 Conclusion and Open Problems

In this paper we discussed the self-directed learning complexity and teaching complexity, respectively, in relation to intersection-closed concept classes. We completely solved the question of the relation between the self-directed learning complexity and the VC-dimension under the assumption of intersection-closedness. We showed that both parameters are completely incomparable.

Knowing that the self-directed learning complexity of intersection-closed concept classes may be arbitrarily large while the VC-dimension is constant, we investigated the structure of such a concept class. We proved, that for concept classes $\mathcal{C}$ with $VCD(\mathcal{C}) = 2$ and $M_{sd}(\mathcal{C}) = k$, the concept class must contain a maximum subclass of size $k$. This raises the question

**Open Problem 1** *Is it possible to extend the structural result given in Theorem 3 to concept classes with higher VC-dimension?*

In section 6 and 7, we investigated the teacher-directed complexity in the average and best case performance. Next to the full analysis of concept classes of VC-dimension 1, we show that in the average case, the teacher-directed complexity of the classes $\mathcal{B}^d(c)$ is bounded by two times the VC-dimension of the class.

**Open Problem 2** *Does Theorem 5 hold for any intersection-closed concept class. i.e. $M_{td\text{-}average}(\mathcal{C}, U) \leq 2d$ for the uniform distribution $U$ over $\mathcal{C}$?*

The best case analysis of teacher-directed complexity establishes a gap between arbitrary and intersection-closed concept classes. For intersection-closed concept classes, the teacher-directed complexity is bounded by the VC-dimension. On the other hand we found a concept class for which the teacher-directed complexity (best case) exceeds the VC-dimension by a ratio of 3/2. This gap is a strong result since we show that $M_{td\text{-}best}$ is the strongest model considered in this paper.

**Open Problem 3** *Are there families of concept classes with constant VC-dimension, but arbitrary $M_{td\text{-}best}$ complexity?*

# A   Appendix

**Proof. (Theorem 2)**

In order to prove the three claims, consider $i \neq j$ the bijective function

$$\mu(i,j) = \begin{cases} i,j & \text{for } i > j \\ i,j-1 & \text{for } i < j. \end{cases}$$

Note that $\mu(i,j)$ indicates the position of the instance labeled by 1 in block $I_j^i$. Also note that, in matrix $E_2(Q_{nr})$, for different blocks $i,j$, there is a concept containing exactly two instances in these blocks at row $I^{\mu(i,j)}$ and $I^{\mu(j,i)}$.

**Claim 1** $Q_{nr} \in IC \Rightarrow E(Q_{nr}) \in IC$

We have to show that, for two concepts $c_1, c_2 \in E(Q_{nr})$, also the intersection belongs to the concept class, i.e. $c_1 \cap c_2 \in E(Q_{nr})$.

Case 1: $c_1, c_2 \in I_i$
Then $c_1 \cap c_2 \in I_i$. This is clear because the concepts in $I_i$ are constant on $I^k$, if $k \neq i$, and $Q_{nr}$ is intersection-closed.

Case 2: $c_1 \in I_i$, $c_2 \in I_j$
Without loss of generality, let $i < j$. The intersection of $c_1$ and $c_2$ is clearly zero on $I^k$ for $k \notin i,j$. As on $I^i$, $c_2$ contains exactly one instance at position $j-1$, and, conversely, on $I^j$, $c_1$ contains exactly one instance at position $i$, $c_1 \cap c_2$ contains

at most two instances which are at position $I^{i,j-1}$ and $I^{j,i}$. These concepts are contained either in $E_2(Q_{nr})$ or in $E_3(Q_{nr})$.

Case 3: $c_1 \in E_1(Q_{nr})$, $c_2 \in E_2(Q_{nr})E_3(Q_{nr})$
If $c_1 \cap c_2 \neq c_2$ then $c_1 \cap c_2$ it contains at most one instance which is clearly in $E_3(Q_{nr})$.

This proves Claim 1.

We see that $E_2(Q_{nr})$ and $E_3(Q_{nr})$ are necessary submatrices in order to assure the intersection-closedness of the extended concept class.

**Claim 2** *If $Q_{nr} \in IC$ and $VCD(Q_{nr}) = d \geq 2$, then $VCD(E(Q_{nr})) = d$.*

Let $VCD(Q_{nr}) = d$. Assume that $VCD(E(Q_{nr})) \geq d+1$ and $x_1...x_{d+1}$ be instances shattered by $E(Q_{nr})$. Then not all instances can be in one row block $I^i$ as otherwise this row block would contain the submatrix $D_{d+1}$ which could only appear in $I_i^i = Q_{nr}$ because more than one instance is labeled positively. This would imply that $VCD(Q_{nr}) \geq d+1$ (see Lemma 1) and, therefore, contradict our assumption.

Hence, at least two row blocks contain shattered instances. Let us consider three of the shattered points $(x_1, x_2, x_3)$ which are contained in different row blocks. We will show that they cannot be shattered.

Case 1: $x_1, x_2 \in I^i$ and $x_3 \in I^j$
Consider concept $c_{123}$ which contains all three instances. $c_{123}$ is in $I_i$ (the only column block which can contain more than one instance of $I^i$) and $x_3 = I^{\mu(i,j)}$. Now we look for the concept $c_{12}$ which contains $x_1, x_2$ but not $x_3$. As it must contain two instances of row block $I^i$, $c_{12}$ must be in $I_i$. This would imply that $x_3$ is contained in $c_{12}$ which is a contradiction.

Case 2: $x_1 \in I^i$, $x_2 \in I^j$ and $x_3 \in I^k$
Consider again the concept $c_{123}$ which contains all three elements. Now without loss of generality, we assume $c_{123}$ to be in $I_i$. Then clearly $x_2 = I^{\mu(i,j)}$ and $x_3 = I^{\mu(i,k)}$. We furthermore consider $c_{12}$ which contains $x_1, x_2$, but not $x_3$. Due to the fixed position of $x_2$, this concept can be either in $I^j$ or in $E_2(Q_{nr})$. Both cases fix $x_1$ on its row position:
If $c_{12}$ is in $I^j$, then clearly $x_1 = I^{\mu(j,i)}$.
If $c_{12}$ is in $E_2(Q_{nr})$, then the concept contains exactly two elements at row $I^{\mu(j,i)}$ and $I^{\mu(i,j)}$, i.e. again, $x_1 = I^{\mu(j,i)}$.
We now look for concept $c_{13}$ which contains $x_1, x_3$ and not $x_2$. This concept fixes $x_1$ on row $I^{\mu(k,i)}$ which is different from $I^{\mu(j,i)}$ as $\mu$ is bijective.

This implies that, in both cases, the three instances are not shattered in contradiction to the assumption that $x_1...x_{d+1}$ are shattered by $E(Q_{nr})$.

**Claim 3** *For all labeled instances $(x, l) \in X \times \{0, 1\}$*

$$Q_{nr} \in E(Q_{nr})_{x|l}$$

Let $x = I^{i,j}$ be an arbitrary instance given out by the learner. If the adversary chooses a target $c_t$ containing $x$, then $I_j$ is part of the version space and therefore block $I_j^j = Q_{nr}$ is a submatrix in the version space. The same holds for the case that $c_t$ does not contain $x$. Here, all $I_k$, $k \neq j$ are part of the version space and at least one $Q_{nr}$ is a submatrix in the version space. ∎

# References

1. S. Ben-David and N. Eiron. Self-directed learning and its relation to the vc-dimension and to teacher-directed learning. *to appear*, 1998.

2. S. Ben-David, N. Eiron, and E. Kushilevitz. On self-directed learning. *Proceedings of the Eighth Annual Conference on Computational Learning Theory*, 8:136–143, 1995.

3. S. Floyd. On space-bounded learning and the vapnik-chervonenkis dimension. *PhD thesis, International Computer Science Institute Technicak Report TR-89061, Berkeley, California*, 1989.

4. S. Floyd and M. Warmuth. Sample compression, learnability, and the vapnik-chervonenkis dimension. *Machine Learning*, 21:269–304, 1995.

5. S. A. Goldman and M. J. Kearns. On the complexity of teaching. *Journal of Computer and System Sciences*, 50:20–31, 1995.

6. S. A. Goldman and D. H. Mathias. Teaching a smarter learner. *Journal of Computer and System Sciences*, 52(20):255–267, 1996.

7. S. A. Goldman, R. L. Rivest, and R. E. Schapire. Learning binary relations and total orders. *SIAM Journal of Computation*, 22(5):1006–1034, 1993.

8. S. A. Goldman and R. H. Sloan. The power of self-directed learning. *Machine Learning*, 14:271–294, 1994.

9. N. Littlestone. Learning with irrelevant attributes abound: A new linear-threshold algorithm. *Machine Learning*, 2:285–318, 1988.

10. N. Littlestone. Mistake bound and logarithmic linear-threshold learning algorithms. *PhD Thesis, U.C. Santa Cruz*, March 1989.

11. B. K. Natarajan. Probabaly approximate learning of sets and functions. *SIAM Journal of Computing*, 20(2):328–351, 1991.

12. R. L. Rivest and Y. L. Yin. Being taught can be faster than asking questions. *Proceedings of the Eighth Annual Conference on Computational Learning Theory*, 8:144–151, 1995.

13. N. Sauer. On the density of families of sets. *Journal of Combinatorial Theory*, 13:145–147, 1972.

# Avoiding Coding Tricks
# by Hyperrobust Learning

Matthias Ott[1] and Frank Stephan[2]

[1] Institut für Logik, Komplexität und Deduktionssysteme, Am Fasanengarten 5,
Universität Karlsruhe, 76128 Karlsruhe, Germany, EU, m_ott@ira.uka.de
[2] Mathematisches Institut, Im Neuenheimer Feld 294, Universität Heidelberg,
69120 Heidelberg, Germany, EU, fstephan@math.uni-heidelberg.de

**Abstract**　The present work introduces and justifies the notion of hyperrobust learning where one fixed learner has to learn all functions in a given class plus their images under primitive recursive operators. The following is shown: This notion of learnability does not change if the class of primitive recursive operators is replaced by a larger enumerable class of operators. A class is hyperrobustly Ex-learnable iff it is a subclass of a recursively enumerable family of total functions. So, the notion of hyperrobust learning overcomes a problem of the traditional definitions of robustness which either do not preserve learning by enumeration or still permit topological coding tricks for the learning criterion Ex. Hyperrobust BC-learning as well as the hyperrobust version of Ex-learning by teams are more powerful than hyperrobust Ex-learning. The notion of bounded totally reliable BC-learning is properly between hyperrobust Ex-learning and hyperrobust BC-learning. Furthermore, the bounded totally reliably BC-learnable classes are characterized in terms of infinite branches of certain enumerable families of bounded recursive trees. A class of infinite branches of a further family of trees separates hyperrobust BC-learning from totally reliable BC-learning.

## 1 Introduction

Self-reference and coding-tricks are an elegant way to prove many separation results in inductive inference. For example, the class of all functions $f$ such that $f(0)$ is a program for $f$ separates finite learning from the criterion Num which contains all classes that are subsets of enumerable families of total functions. Similarly, the class of all functions $f$ where $f(0)$ is a program which computes $f$ on almost all (but not necessarily all) places witnesses that BC-learning is more powerful than Ex-learning [5]. Such coding tricks allow to build simple proofs by using the following method: the less pretentious learner can evaluate the provided self-referential information — it is usually almost the desired output. But the more pretentious learner has to transform the information to information of higher quality (for example a program of a partial function into a program of a total extension) which turns out to be as difficult as well-known unsolvable recursion-theoretic problems

Bārzdiņš proposed several notions of robust learning in order to find a concept of learning, where decoding self-referential information cannot be any longer the essential part of learning. In particular, he was interested into the question whether learning by enumeration is the only type of learning, where coding does not help. His basic hypothesis was that no kind of coding trick was preserved by all recursive operators. So he strengthened the notion of learning by requiring that not only the class $S$ itself but also each image $\Theta(S)$ must be learnable for all suitable operators $\Theta$. Clearly, $\Theta$ has to be recursive, but it was discussed whether $\Theta$ must map total functions to total ones, that is, must be general recursive. Jain, Smith and Wiehagen [8] analyzed this question and discovered that all proposed notions roughly behave like one of the following two cases: (a) The operator is only required to map the functions in $S$ to total functions. Then robust learning does not even preserve Num: Some operator maps some class of constant functions onto the class of all recursive functions which is not learnable. (b) The operator is required to be general recursive, that is, the image of every total function has to be total. Then there is a class outside Num which is still robustly Ex-learnable.

Case (b) looks much more natural, since any notion of learning in the limit should cover Num, in particular, every class of constant functions should be learnable. In his original definition of robust learning, Fulk [7] followed this path and defined that

a class $S$ is *robustly learnable* if $\Theta(S)$ is learnable for all general recursive operators $\Theta$.

Furthermore, he constructed already a class outside Num which is robustly learnable in the limit. Jain, Smith and Wiehagen [8] showed that Fulk's result can even be obtained using some topological kind of self-referential coding trick. They constructed a class of functions $f_1, f_2, \ldots$ which converge pointwise to one function $f$ such that, for every general recursive operator $\Theta$, either almost all $\Theta(f_k)$ are equal to $\Theta(f)$ and the class to be learned is finite or the point where $\Theta(f_k)$ and $\Theta(f)$ become different is, for almost all $k$, an upper bound on a program for $f_k$. Having such an upper bound, one can find a program for $\Theta(f_k)$ in the limit.

So, there is some demand to find a notion of robustness which on the one hand prevents the use of coding tricks and on the other hand preserves at least Num. The main idea to achieve this goal is to force the learner to cope with several images $\Theta(S)$ at the same time while keeping these operators restrictive enough to preserve at least learnability by enumeration. So, given any $S$,

let $[S] = \{\Theta_e(f) : e = 0, 1, \ldots$ and $f \in S\}$ denote the closure of $S$ under all *primitive recursive* operators $\Theta_0, \Theta_1, \ldots$ and define that $S$ is *hyperrobustly* Ex-*learnable* iff $[S]$ is Ex-learnable.

Theorem 3 justifies this definition since it shows that the hyperrobustly learnable classes remain the same if one takes any larger enumerable class of operators instead of the one above. Furthermore, the notion of hyperrobust learning is compatible to standard robust learnability as used in [3,8]: if $S$ is hyperrobustly learnable then $S$ is also robustly learnable. Moreover, if $S$ is closed under finite variants then both notions are equivalent. The set $[S]$ is dense for every nonempty class $S$ of functions, thus, hyperrobust learning cannot respect any bounds on the number of mind changes. Therefore, it is not suitable to look at mind change complexity in the context of hyperrobust learning and so, this paper focuses on the notions Num, Ex, BC and teams of Ex-learners or BC-learners.

This new notion of hyperrobust learning has also a further, more intuitive, motivation: Assume that a learner $M$ can learn all axis-parallel rectangles in the plane. Certainly, one assumes that from $M$ one can build a learner which additionally infers all rotated rectangles. However, clearly one does not want to build, for every different rotation $\Theta$, a learner succeeding just on rectangles mapped by the rotation $\Theta$. But instead one is interested in a learner which learns every image of any axis-parallel rectangle under *any* rotation $\Theta$. The notion of hyperrobustness reflects this situation by requiring that *one* learning machine $M$ learns every image of the functions in a class $S$ under *all* primitive recursive operators.

For the reader's convenience, the definitions of Num, Ex and BC are included here: A learner $M$ is a total recursive machine which receives as input initial segments $\sigma$ of a total function $f$ and outputs for every $\sigma$ a guess for a program which is intended to represent a rule generating the function $f$. $M$ learns $f$ iff almost all guesses are programs computing $f$; $M$ learns a whole class $S$ of functions iff $M$ learns every $f \in S$. The difference between the three criteria Num, Ex and BC is that a BC-learner need not satisfy any further requirements. But an Ex-learner has to converge explicitly, that is, for sufficiently large $x$ the programs $M(f(0)f(1)\ldots f(x))$ have to be the same. Num contains every class which is a subclass of an enumerable family of total recursive functions. One can infer the classes in Num by an easy algorithm called "learning by enumeration": the Ex-learner outputs always an index for the first function in the given family which is consistent with the data yet seen. "Num" stands for classes contained in a numbering. "Ex" stands for explanatory learning, that is, the learner converges to an explanation or program for $f$. "BC" stands for behaviourally correct learning, that is, the learner outputs almost always correct conjectures but the learner does not necessarily converge syntactically to one single program for $f$.

The notions of robustness can directly be transferred from Ex to BC: $S$ is hyperrobustly BC-learnable iff $[S]$ is BC-learnable. For the ease of notation, if a result holds for explanatory learning as well as for behaviourally correct learning, then just the notion "learnable" is used in place of Ex-learnable and BC-learnable, respectively. If a result holds only for one of these two notions, then this notion is mentioned explicitly. Of course, when using the simplified notion "learnable", one has always to replace every occurrence of "learnable" consistently by either "Ex-learnable" or "BC-learnable", but one must not mix both notions.

The interested reader can find background information on recursion theory in the book of Odifreddi [11] and on inductive inference in the book of Osherson, Stob and Weinstein [12].

## 2 General Results

Hyperrobust learning differs from robust learning in the way that a hyperrobust learner succeeds on a class of functions $S$ only if it succeeds on all images of $S$ under primitive recursive operators. On the other hand, in the case of robust learning, it is only required that for every general recursive operator there is a learner succeeding with the data translated by this single operator.

Before defining robust and hyperrobust learning, the notions of operators are made more precise. An operator $\Theta$ is *general recursive* iff there is a program $e$ such that, for every function $f$ and every $x$, the program $\varphi_e^f$ computes $\Theta(f)(x)$ by accessing $f$ via builtin oracle calls and terminates. So, $\Theta$ maps every total function to a total function. Furthermore, the family $\Theta_0, \Theta_1, \ldots$ is *enumerable* iff there is a single general recursive operator $\Theta$ with $\Theta_e(f)(x) = \Theta(f)(e, x)$. On $\{0, 1\}$-valued functions, truth-table operators and general recursive operators mapping every total function to a total one coincide. In the general case, they are different as the example of the operator $\Theta(f)(x) = f(f(x))$ shows. Nevertheless, for the purposes of the present paper, it suffices to use the more restrictive variant and define primitive recursive operators as truth-table operators, that is, $\Theta$ is primitive recursive iff there are two primitive recursive functions $g, h$ such that

$$\Theta(f)(x) = g(x, f(0)f(1) \ldots f(h(x)))$$

for all $f$ and $x$.

**Definition 1.** *Let $S$ be a class of recursive functions.*
(a) *$S$ is robustly learnable iff, for every general recursive operator $\Theta$, there is a learner $M$ which learns $\Theta(S) = \{\Theta(f) : f \in S\}$.*
(b) *$S$ is hyperrobustly learnable iff there is one learner $M$ which learns every function in $[S] = \{\Theta_e(f) : e = 0, 1, \ldots$ and $f \in S\}$ where $\Theta_0, \Theta_1, \ldots$ is an enumeration of all primitive recursive operators.*

Note that in this general definition, one can define robust and hyperrobust learnability for all common notions of learning, like explanatory learning, behaviourally correct learning and so on. Hyperrobust learning satisfies two easy observations.

**Fact 1** (a) *$[S]$ contains all primitive recursive functions since for every primitive recursive function $g$ there is a primitive recursive operator $\Theta$ with $\Theta(f) = g$ for all functions $f$.*

(b) *No class S is hyperrobustly learnable with any bound on the number of mind changes, since [S] is dense and dense classes cannot satisfy mind change bounds.*

These two facts establish a real difference to robust learning because there are classes of recursive functions which are even robustly learnable with at most one mind change [8]. On the other hand, for hyperrobust learning, the notions Ex, BC and their team-versions are the most interesting ones.

The definition of the mapping $S \to [S]$ and thus, also the definition of hyper-robustness is based on the class of primitive recursive operators. The decision to choose the class of primitive recursive operators may seem to be just arbitrary and one may wonder how other choices for the class of operators effect the notion of hyperrobustness. The next two results justify the definition: First it is shown that every hyperrobustly learnable class is bounded in the following sense.

**Definition 2.** *A class S is bounded iff there is a total recursive function g which dominates every $f \in S$: $(\forall f \in S)\,(\exists x)\,(\forall y \geq x)\,[f(y) \leq g(y)]$.*

Second it is shown that if, in the definition of hyperrobust learning, the enumeration $\Theta_0, \Theta_1, \ldots$ of all primitive recursive operators is replaced by a larger enumerable class of operators, then one still gets the same learning notion.

**Theorem 2.** *If S is hyperrobustly learnable then S is bounded.*

**Proof.** It is sufficient to show the result for the more powerful notion of hyperrobust BC-learning. For function learning, it is convenient to represent the BC-learner as an NV''-learner $M$ which predicts the function to be learned almost everywhere but which may be undefined at finitely many places as well as on any invalid data [15].

Now one defines inductively, for every $f$, the following function $\theta(f) = \lim_x \sigma_x$ starting with $\sigma_0 = \lambda$ and using $M_s(\sigma_x)$ as a notation for the result of $M(\sigma_x)$ after $s$ computational steps (which is either undefined or $M(\sigma_x)$):

$$\sigma_{x+1} = \begin{cases} \sigma_x 1 & \text{if } M_s(\sigma_x)\!\downarrow = 0 \text{ for some } s \leq f(0) + f(1) + \ldots + f(x); \\ \sigma_x 0 & \text{otherwise.} \end{cases}$$

Since $\theta$ is a primitive recursive operator, $M$ has to infer $\theta(f)$ for every $f \in S$. But whenever $\theta(f)(x)$ is 1, then $M$ has made a prediction mistake and so, $\theta(f)$ takes only finitely often a value different from 0. Since $M$ has to infer every primitive recursive function by Fact 1, $M$ learns in particular all functions of the form $\sigma 0^\infty$. Thus the following function $g$ is recursive:

$$g(x) = \max\{\min\{s : (\exists t < s)\,[M_s(\sigma 0^t)\!\downarrow = 0]\} : \sigma \in \{0,1\}^x\}.$$

Whenever $f(x) > g(x)$ then one finds within $f(x)$ stages some $t < f(x)$ such that $M(\sigma_x 0^t)\!\downarrow = 0$. So, the inductive definition of $\Theta$ diagonalizes for some $y \in \{x, x+1, \ldots, x+f(x)\}$ against the learner $M$, that is, $\sigma_{y+1} = \sigma_y 1$ while $M(\sigma_y) = 0$. Thus there exist at most finitely many $x$ with $f(x) > g(x)$ and, therefore, $g$ dominates $f$. Since the construction of $g$ does not depend on the actual choice of $f$, $g$ dominates every function in $S$. ∎

The next result shows that one does not change the notion of hyperrobust learning if one uses a more powerful enumerable family of general recursive operators instead of the family of all primitive recursive operators. As already mentioned above, this result provides an important justification of the model: the definition of hyperrobust learning does not depend on the actual choice of the class of operators as long as this class is "sufficiently rich" (for example, if the class contains all primitive recursive operators, or, all polynomial time computable operators). Clearly, if the class of operators contains only the identity operator, then hyperrobust and ordinary Ex-learning coincide and so, "sufficiently rich" is a necessary and natural postulate.

**Theorem 3.** *If $S$ is hyperrobustly learnable then $S$ is also hyperrobustly learnable with respect to any given enumerable family $\Theta_0, \Theta_1, \ldots$ of general recursive operators.*

**Proof.** The main idea is the following: there is a function $h$ with primitive recursive graph such that the operator $\Theta$ given by

$$f \to 0^{h(0)} f(0) 0^{h(1)} f(1) 0^{h(2)} f(2) \ldots$$

is primitive recursive and maps the function $\Theta_e(f)$ into $[S]$ for all $f \in S$ and every operator $\Theta_e$. Then any hyperrobust learner $M$ also infers every function $\Theta(\Theta_e(f))$ and can thus be translated into a learner succeeding on all functions $\Theta_e(f)$ by ignoring the zeros pasted into $\Theta_e(f)$ by $\Theta$.

So, the main part of the proof is to show that $h$ exists and that the concatenation $\Theta(\Theta_e)$ is primitive recursive for every operator $\Theta_e$.

Given $S$, there exists a recursive function $g$ which dominates all $f \in S$ by Theorem 2. Now, $g$ is used in order to define the desired function $h$:

$h(x)$ is the smallest number of computational steps $s$ such that, for all $y \leq x$, all $e \leq x$ and all functions $f$ with $f(z) \leq g(z)+x$, the computation $\Theta_e(f)(y)$ terminates within $s$ steps.

The function $h$ is well-defined since every operator $\Theta_e$ maps every total (not necessarily recursive) function onto a total function. The verification that $h$ is recursive uses similar ideas like the proof of the folklore result that a Turing reduction which gives a total function for every oracle can be turned effectively into a truth-table reduction. Furthermore, one can primitive recursively check whether some computation halts within $s$ stages if $s$ is a lower bound for the input. So the graph of $h$ is primitive recursive. To compute $\Theta(\Theta_e)(f)(x)$ one first checks whether $x$ is of the form $h(0) + 1 + h(1) + 1 + \ldots + h(y)$. If so, one can compute $\Theta_e(f)(y)$ within $\max\{h(e), h(y)\}$ steps and output this value; in particular $f$ is also only queried at places below $\max\{h(e), h(y)\}$. Otherwise, $\Theta(\Theta_e(f))(x) = 0$ and neither any computations nor any queries are necessary. So, $\Theta(\Theta_e)$ is a primitive recursive operator. ∎

**Corollary 1.** (a) *If $S$ is hyperrobustly learnable then $S$ is also robustly learnable in the sense that $\Theta(S)$ is learnable for every general recursive operator $\Theta$.*
(b) *If $S$ is closed under finite variants then $S$ is hyperrobustly learnable iff $S$ is robustly learnable.*

**Proof.** *Part (a) and the identical direction ($\Rightarrow$) of part (b) are a direct corollary of the preceding theorem. The direction ($\Leftarrow$) of part (b) is due to coding the index of $\Theta_e$ into the first argument of the function. Let $e' = \langle e, f(0) \rangle$ and define*

$$\Theta(e' f(1) f(2) \ldots) = \Theta_e(f(0) f(1) f(2) \ldots)$$

*where $\Theta_0, \Theta_1, \ldots$ is an enumeration of all primitive recursive operators. Then $\Theta$ is a general recursive operator. Furthermore, $[S] = \Theta(S)$, since, for every $f \in S$, the function $\Theta_e(f)$ is the image of the finite variant $e' f(1) f(2) \ldots$ which is also in $S$. So, $[S]$ has to be learnable and $S$ is hyperrobustly learnable.* ∎

Corollary 1 shows that hyperrobust learning is a natural generalization of robust learning: it is equivalent to first taking the closure under all finite variants and then applying a suitable general recursive operator $\Theta$.

The notion of robustness was designed to destroy every numerical coding trick: for example, if $f(2x)$ is a program for $f$ for almost all $x$, then the general recursive operator mapping $f$ to $f(1)f(3)f(5) \ldots$ destroys this coding trick. Jain, Smith and Wiehagen [8] showed that topological coding — like, for example, coding the index into the branching points where the functions to be learned branch away from a fixed recursive function — cannot be destroyed by using a single general recursive operator. However, topological coding is destroyed by adding all finite variants of the functions in $S$ to the class to be learned. Combining these two methods, that is, considering robust learning of classes closed under finite variants, one might hope that no coding tricks are left. Indeed, this hope is confirmed by the following characterization result which shows that the hyperrobustly Ex-learnable classes coincide with the classes in Num.

The criterion Num is quite prominent — Bārzdiņš, Leeuwen and Zeugmann [1, 17] showed that it coincides with further natural criteria: PEx-learning where the learner outputs only programs of total functions; NV-learning where the learner is total and predicts every $f \in S$ almost everywhere correctly; robustly totally reliable Ex-learning where a totally reliable Ex-learner either infers a function or diverges on it. Minicozzi [2, 10] introduced the notion of reliable learning; the difference between reliable Ex-learning and totally reliable Ex-learning is that in the second case the learner has also to diverge on nonrecursive functions while an ordinary reliable Ex-learner may behave arbitrarily on nonrecursive functions.

The next result adds hyperrobust learning to this list of characterizations of Num. So, every hyperrobust learnable class $S$ can be learned by enumeration where the learner always outputs an index for the first recursive function, from a list of total recursive functions, which is consistent with the data seen so far.

**Theorem 4.** *A class $S$ is hyperrobustly Ex-learnable iff it is in Num.*

190

**Proof.** One direction is straightforward: If $S$ is in Num, so is $[S]$. That is, if $S \subseteq \{f_0, f_1, \ldots\}$ for an enumeration $f_0, f_1, \ldots$ of total functions then $[S]$ is contained in the enumeration of all $g_{e,e'} = \Theta_{e'}(f_e)$ where $\Theta_0, \Theta_1, \ldots$ is an enumeration of all primitive recursive operators.

The converse direction is proven similar to Theorem 3. Assume that $M$ Ex-learns $[S]$. Then $M$ infers all functions of the form $\sigma 0^\infty$. Since $M$ is an Ex-learner, one knows that, for every $\sigma$, either $\varphi_{M(\sigma)}(x)$ is defined for the first value $x \notin \text{dom}(\sigma)$ or $M(\sigma 0^t) \neq M(\sigma)$ for almost all $t$. Let $g$ be again a strictly increasing recursive function dominating every $f \in S$. Using $g$ one defines inductively a function $h$ with primitive recursive graph such that, for every $\sigma \in \{0, 1, \ldots, g(x)\}^{h(0)+1+h(1)+1+\ldots+h(x-1)}$, either $\varphi_{M(\sigma),h(x)}(h(0)+1+h(1)+1+\ldots+h(x-1))$ has converged or $M(\sigma y 0^{h(x)}) \neq M(\sigma)$ for all $y \leq g(x)$. The function $h$ is total since $M$ has to infer every function which is almost everywhere 0. Now one defines again a primitive recursive operator $\Theta$ by

$$f \to 0^{h(0)} f(0) 0^{h(1)} f(1) 0^{h(2)} f(2) \ldots$$

and uses $\Theta$ to get an upper bound on the computation time of every $f \in S$: The learner $M$ learns $\Theta(f)$ and its guesses $M(0^{h(0)} f(0) 0^{h(1)} f(1) 0^{h(2)} f(2) \ldots 0^{h(x)})$ are, for almost all $x$, equal to some value $e$. From the definition of $h$ it follows that the computation $\varphi_e(h(0)+1+h(1)+1+h(2)+1+\ldots+h(x))$ converges within $h(x+1)$ steps to $f(x)$ for almost all $x$. Thus the function $x \to h(x+1)$ dominates the computation time for all $f \in S$, which implies that the class $S$ is in Num. ∎

## 3  Hyperrobust BC-Learning is not Trivial

Within this section, it is shown that hyperrobust BC-learning does not collapse to Num as hyperrobust Ex-learning and attempts are made to characterize hyperrobust BC. A major tool in this research is the use of recursively bounded recursive trees [11, page 509], just called bounded recursive trees from now on. These trees are a generalization of binary recursive trees: for a bounded recursive tree $T$ one can compute for every $\sigma \in T$ a complete list of the immediate successors in $T$ which is impossible in the general case, even if $\sigma$ has only finitely many successors. But it is still true when a recursive function bounds the size of the successors, that is, whenever $\sigma a \in T$ then $a \leq b(|\sigma|)$ for some fixed recursive function $b$. So, one can define a bounded recursive tree as a recursive function $c$ which associates with every $\sigma \in T$ a finite and explicit list of all nodes $\sigma a \in T$. If $c$ is primitive recursive then $T$ is called a bounded primitive recursive tree.

A learning machine $M$ is said to be *reliable* if $M$ either converges to a correct program for the input function, or outputs infinitely often a signal for divergence, which, in the case of Ex-learning, can just be a mind change. Producing semantic mind changes alone is not sufficient to get a reliable version of BC-learning that differs from ordinary BC, as the following fact shows. This fact is based on two observations: First, behavioural correct learners can be made consistent.

That is, the new consistent learner outputs for every input a hypothesis which is correct on the data seen so far [1, 6]. Second, consistent learners either converge semantically to the desired function or make infinitely many semantic mind changes.

**Fact 5** *For every BC-learnable class $S$ there is a BC-learner which either converges semantically or makes infinitely many semantic mind changes.*

**Proof.** A given BC-learner $M$ for $S$ can be easily transformed into a new BC-learner $N$ such that

$$\varphi_{N(\sigma)}(x) = \begin{cases} \sigma(x) & \text{if } x \in \text{dom}(\sigma); \\ \varphi_{M(\sigma)}(x) & \text{otherwise.} \end{cases}$$

If $M$ learns a function $f$, so does $N$ since $N$ changes the guess of $M$ only on already known arguments by using the given values. If $N$ semantically converges on $f$ and almost always outputs some program of a fixed function $\psi$ then $\psi = f$: for every $x$, there is a $\sigma \preceq f$ such that $N(\sigma)$ computes $\psi$ and $x \in \text{dom}(\sigma)$. It follows that $\psi(x) \downarrow = \sigma(x) = f(x)$. So, $N$ learns a function $f$ iff $N$ converges semantically on $f$. ∎

Looking a bit closer, it even holds that $N$ learns a function $f$ iff $N$ outputs infinitely often the same program during the inference of $f$. Therefore, the analogue of reliable learning for BC must signal divergence more explicitly. A suitable definition is the following: The reliable BC-learner indicates divergence either by outputting a special value like "?" or by making a definitely wrong prediction where the underlying BC-learner is given by an NV''-prediction machine $M$ [5, 15], which, by definition, is successful on $f$ if

$$(\forall f \in S)\,(\forall^\infty x)\,[M(f(0)f(1)\dots f(x)) \downarrow = f(x+1)].$$

A more restrictive variant is *totally reliable learning* [2, 10] where the learner has to signal divergence not only on all recursive functions not learned but also on all nonrecursive function which cannot be learned by definition.

**Definition 3.** *$M$ is a reliable BC-learner iff, for every recursive function $f$, either $M$ BC-learns $f$ by predicting almost always the correct value (that is, for almost all $x$, $M(f(0)f(1)\dots f(x)) \downarrow = f(x+1)$) or $M$ diverges on $f$ by infinitely often outputting either ? or a defined but wrong prediction. $M$ is a totally reliable BC-learner if $M$ diverges also on every nonrecursive function.*

Zeugmann [17] observed that robustly totally reliably Ex-learnable classes are just those in Num. A related result is that, for bounded classes, Num is equal to totally reliable Ex. Together with Theorem 4, one obtains the following equivalence.

**Fact 6** *For a bounded class $S$ the following statements are equivalent.*
(a) $S$ is in Num.
(b) $S$ is totally reliably Ex-learnable.
(c) $S$ is hyperrobustly Ex-learnable.

The central question of this section is to what extent the equivalence above transfers to BC. The next characterization of bounded totally reliably BC-learnable classes is an important tool to attack this question.

**Theorem 7.** *A bounded class $S$ is totally reliably BC-learnable iff there is a family $T_0, T_1, \ldots$ of bounded recursive trees such that every tree has only finitely many infinite branches and every $f \in S$ is the infinite branch of such a tree.*

**Proof.** ($\Rightarrow$): Assume that $g$ bounds $S$ and $M$ is an NV''-predictor for $S$ which in addition signals infinitely often divergence on every function $f$ which $M$ does not learn. Now let the tree $T_\sigma$ contain all prefixes of $\sigma$ plus all $\eta \succeq \sigma$ such that

- $\eta(x) \leq g(x)$ for all $x \in \text{dom}(\eta) - \text{dom}(\sigma)$ and
- there are no $\tau, a$ with $\sigma \preceq \tau a \prec \eta$ and $M_{|\eta|}(\tau)\downarrow \neq a$

where, of course, the special symbol "?" is different from $a$.

Clearly, the $T_\sigma$ form a recursive family of trees bounded by $g$. Assume now that $T_\sigma$ has infinitely many infinite branches. As a consequence of König's Lemma and the fact that $T_\sigma$ is finitely branching, there is an infinite branch $f$ which is not isolated. This implies that $M$ cannot predict $f$ at almost all points correctly. So, on input $f$, divergence must also be signaled above $\sigma$ by $M$, which contradicts the fact that $f$ is an infinite branch of $T_\sigma$.

For every $f \in S$, there is a prefix $\sigma \preceq f$ such that $M$ predicts $f$ correctly after seeing $\sigma$ and all $x$ with $f(x) > g(x)$ are in $\text{dom}(\sigma)$. Then it follows from the definition that $f$ is an infinite branch of $T_\sigma$ and direction ($\Rightarrow$) is completed.

($\Leftarrow$): Let $T_0, T_1, \ldots$ be a family of bounded recursive trees such that every tree has only finitely many infinite branches and every function in $S$ is branch of such a tree. Without loss of generality, the family is dense in the sense that for every $\sigma$ there is a tree containing $\sigma$. This can be achieved by adding all finite trees of the form $\{\tau : \tau \preceq \sigma\}$ to the list. The new family is still enumerable and the class of functions on trees in the family remains the same. Let $T[\tau]$ denote all nodes of the tree $T$ which are comparable to $\tau$. Now the totally reliable BC-learner works as follows:

$M(\sigma)$ finds the first tree $T_e$ with $\sigma \in T_e$.
If there was a recent change of the tree, that is, if there is $e' < e$ with $\tau \in T_{e'}$ for all $\tau \prec \sigma$ then $M(\sigma) = ?$ in order to signal divergence.
Otherwise $M(\sigma)$ searches for an $a$ such that $T_e[\sigma b]$ is finite for all $b \neq a$ and $M(\sigma) = a$ if such an $a$ is found.

The first step of the algorithm is well-defined since every $\sigma$ is node of some tree $T_e$.

If $f$ is not infinite branch of any tree $T_e$ then, during the inference of $f$, $M$ signals infinitely often divergence, since $M$ has infinitely often to change the tree.

If $f$ is infinite branch of some tree then there is a first such tree $T_e$ in the enumeration. For sufficiently large $\sigma = f(0)f(1)\ldots f(x)$, $f$ is the only infinite branch of $T_e[\sigma]$ and $\sigma \notin T_{e'}$ for any $e' < e$. Now $f(x+1)$ is the unique value $a$ with $T_e[\sigma a]$ being infinite. Since the trees $T_e$ are uniformly bounded recursive, a suitable search algorithm finds the value $f(x+1)$. Therefore, $M$ predicts $f$ almost everywhere, that is, $M(f(0)f(1)\ldots f(x))\!\downarrow\, = f(x+1)$ for almost all $x$.

So, for every function $f$, $M$ either BC-learns $f$ (in the prediction model) or $M$ signals infinitely often divergence. ∎

The next theorem establishes some compatibility between the various notions of reliable learning. It shows that reliable Ex-learning and totally reliable BC-learning are generalizations of totally reliable Ex-learning in two disjoint directions.

**Theorem 8.** *A class $S$ is totally reliably Ex-learnable iff $S$ is reliably Ex-learnable and totally reliably BC-learnable.*

**Proof.** The direction ($\Rightarrow$) is clear, for the converse direction ($\Leftarrow$) note that one can count in the limit the number of signals for divergence. So, there is a recursive function $H$ such that $H$ converges on $f$ to $c$, if the totally reliable BC-learner, on input $f$, signals exactly $c$ times divergence, and such that $H$ converges on $f$ to $\infty$, if the totally reliable BC-learner signals infinitely often divergence. Let $M$ be a reliable Ex-learner and let $pad$ be an injective padding function. Now the new learner $N$ is given by

$$N(\sigma) = pad(M(\sigma), H(\sigma)).$$

If $f \in S$ then $N$ converges to $pad(e, c)$ where $e$ is the program to which $M$ converges on $f$ and $c$ is the finite number of (false) signals for divergence produced the totally reliable BC-learner for $S$ on $f$. If $N$ converges on $f$, then $H$ converges on $f$ to a finite number and thus $f$ is recursive. Furthermore, also $M$ must converge to a program $e$ and since $M$ is reliable and $f$ is recursive, $pad(e, c)$ is a program for $f$. Thus $N$ is totally reliable. ∎

Case, Kaufmann, Kinber and Kummer [4] showed that there is a family of binary recursive trees of width 2 whose infinite branches are not Ex-learnable. This yields a class $S$ which is totally reliably BC-learnable but not reliably Ex-learnable. For bounded classes, the concept of totally reliable BC-learning is also a proper generalization of Num. Together with the next result one obtains that the three notions from Fact 6 become all different for BC: Num is properly included in bounded totally reliable BC, which is properly included in hyperrobust BC.

**Theorem 9.** *If $S$ is a bounded and totally reliably BC-learnable class then $S$ is also hyperrobustly BC-learnable. But the converse implication does not hold.*

**Proof.** For the first statement, let $S$ be bounded and totally reliably BC-learnable. There is a uniformly recursive family $T_0, T_1, \ldots$ of trees such that every tree has only finitely many infinite branches and every function in $S$ is infinite branch of some tree $T_e$. Without loss of generality, one can assume that for every $e$ and every primitive recursive operator $\Theta$ there is some $e'$ such that $T_{e'} = \Theta(T_e)$. Otherwise, $T_0, T_1, \ldots$ can be replaced by another uniformly recursive family of trees which contains the trees $T_i$ and which is closed under all primitive recursive operators. So, whenever $f \in S$ and $\Theta$ is a primitive recursive operator then there is some tree $T_e$ such that $f$ is infinite branch of $T_e$ and also of some further tree $T_{e'} = \Theta(T_e)$. This implies that $\Theta(f)$ is an infinite branch of $T_{e'}$. So, the class $S'$ of all infinite branches of $T_0, T_1, \ldots$ contains $[S]$. By Theorem 7 there is a totally reliable BC-learner $M$ for $S'$. Now $M$ is also a BC-learner for $[S]$ and, thus, already a hyperrobust BC-learner for $S$.

The second statement can be proven using the following idea: one constructs a family of binary trees $T_0, T_1, \ldots$ such that, for every tree $T_e$ and every primitive recursive operator $\Theta_i$, the infinite branches of the image tree $\Theta_i(T_e)$ are either isolated or nonrecursive. Furthermore, $T_e$ diagonalizes against the learner $M_e$ from an enumerable list $M_0, M_1, \ldots$ of all learners in such a way that whenever $M_e$ is a totally reliable BC-learner then $T_e$ has only one infinite branch on which $M_e$ infinitely often signals divergence. The class

$$S = \{\Theta_i(f) : \Theta_i(f) \text{ is recursive and } f \text{ is on } T_e \text{ for some } i, e\}$$

witnesses the separation. The details of the construction of the $T_e$ and the verification that $S$ is hyperrobustly BC-learnable but not totally reliable BC-learnable are omitted due to space constraints. ∎

Zeugmann [17] showed that a totally reliably Ex-learnable class $S$ is also robustly learnable under this criterion iff $S$ is in Num. One can deduce from it that $S$ is robustly totally reliably Ex-learnable iff $S$ is bounded. The same holds for robust totally reliably BC-learnability based on Zeugmann's diagonalization strategy for unbounded classes $S$ and on an adaptation of the implication "bounded totally reliable BC $\Rightarrow$ hyperrobust BC" for bounded classes $S$.

**Theorem 10.** *A totally reliably BC-learnable class $S$ is also robustly learnable under this criterion iff $S$ is bounded.*

## 4 Team-Learning and the Union-Theorem

Bārzdiņš [1, 2] showed that there are explanatory learnable classes $S_1, S_2$ such that their union is not explanatorily learnable. This result easily generalizes to the fact that there are unions of $n + 1$ learnable classes which are not contained in the union of $n$ learnable classes [16]. Pitt and Smith [13, 14] showed, that these unions can also be characterized in terms of probabilistic learners and teams of learners, that is, the following statements are equivalent for Ex-learning as well as for BC-learning.

- $S$ is contained in the union of $n$ learnable classes.
- Some probablistic machine learns $S$ with some probability $p$ where $p > \frac{1}{n+1}$.
- A $(h, k)$-team with $\frac{h}{k} > \frac{1}{n+1}$ learns $S$ in the sense that there are $k$ learners such that, for every $f \in S$, at least $h$ of them learn $f$.

Note that the probability and the fraction $\frac{h}{k}$ of successful machines in the team have to be really greater than $\frac{1}{n+1}$ and cannot be equal to this value, since a team of $k = h \cdot (n + 1)$ learners, where $h$ learners have to succeed, can already infer the union of $n + 1$ learnable classes: the first $h$ learners follow the algorithm to learn $S_1$, the second $h$ learners follow the algorithm to learn $S_2$, ..., the last $h$ learners follow the algorithm to learn $S_{n+1}$.

For hyperrobust Ex-learning, one can show that this connection between team-learning on the one side and unions on the other side does no longer hold. The hyperrobustly Ex-learnable classes are closed under union but teams of $n+1$ hyperrobust Ex-learners are more powerful than teams of $n$ learners. An intuitive explanation for this fact is that if $[S_1 \cup S_2]$ needs a team of two Ex-learners then so does $[S_1]$ or $[S_2]$. So, the closure operation does not permit to split a class of functions into two classes which are really easier to learn.

**Fact 11** *If $S_1$ and $S_2$ are hyperrobustly Ex-learnable, so is $S_1 \cup S_2$.*

The result follows from the equivalence of hyperrobust Ex-learning and Num and from the fact that Num is closed under union. The next result establishes that the team hierarchies for hyperrobust Ex-learning and hyperrobust BC-learning are proper.

**Theorem 12.** *The team hierarchy for hyperrobust learning is proper.*

**Proof.** Let $S_k$ be the set of all functions which are infinite branch of some bounded primitive recursive tree of rank up to $k$.

Given $f$, the learning algorithm first finds (in the limit) a tree $T$ such that $f$ is an infinite branch of $T$. Having found this tree $T$, one uses the algorithm of Case, Kaufmann, Kinber and Kummer [4] who showed that knowing an index of the tree and having a primitive recursive function majorizing all infinite branches, one can learn the function by a team of $k+1$ Ex-learners or $k$ BC-learners, respectively. The team-size is also optimal. The class $S_k$ is closed, that is, $[S_k] = S_k$. So, it follows that $S_k$ is learnable by a team of hyperrobust learners of size $k$ (BC) and $k + 1$ (Ex), respectively, but not by a smaller team. ∎

Furthermore, for hyperrobust Ex-learning, one can even show that there exists a proper team hierarchy *within* the class of all hyperrobustly BC-learnable functions. The $n$-th level of this hierarchy is given by the class of all infinite branches of bounded primitive recursive trees of width up to $n$, that is, of trees which have in every depth at most $n$ nodes.

# 5 Conclusion

The research on robust learning has the goal to investigate whether there are learning notions which make it impossible to learn a function by evaluating self-referential coding-information in the graph of the function. The previous approaches to consider all classes $\Theta(S)$ either still allowed some topological kind of coding [7,8] or permitted partial operators which already destruct the basic algorithm "learning by enumeration". The authors believe that such a basic algorithm should be preserved and therefore propose a new approach: the learner has to deal with all images of general recursive operators $\Theta(S)$ simultaneously. The collection of operators used must nevertheless be restricted since permitting all operators would mean to postulate the learning of all recursive functions. It is shown that using all primitive recursive operators is a reasonable choice. In particular, the following two results justify this notion: first, all sufficiently powerful families of operators give the same notion of learning; second, a class $S$ is hyperrobustly learnable with respect to this choice of operators iff the closure of $S$ under finite variants is robustly learnable with respect to the traditional definition. Hyperrobust Ex-learning meets Bārzdiņš' hypothesis since it collapses to Num. But the hyperrobust versions of BC-learning and team-learning permit the inference of classes outside Num. There are relations between hyperrobust BC-learning and totally reliable BC-learning. Furthermore, families of bounded recursive trees turn out to be a useful tool for investigating hyperrobust learning and for characterizing totally reliable BC-learning of bounded classes.

**Acknowledgment**  Frank Stephan is supported by the Deutsche Forschungsgemeinschaft (DFG) grant Am 60/9-2.

# References

1. Janis Bārzdiņš. Two theorems on the limiting synthesis of functions. *In Theory of Algorithms and Programs, Latvian State University, Riga*, 210:82–88, 1974.
2. Leonard Blum and Manuel Blum. Towards a mathematical theory of inductive inference. *Information and Control*, 28:125–155, 1975.
3. John Case, Sanjay Jain, Matthias Ott, Arun Sharma and Frank Stephan. Robust learning aided by context. In *Proceedings of Eleventh Annual Conference on Computational Learning Theory* (COLT), pages 44–55, ACM Press, New York, 1998.
4. John Case, Susanne Kaufmann, Efim Kinber and Martin Kummer. Learning recursive functions from approximations. *Journal of Computer and System Sciences*, 55:183–196, 1997.
5. John Case and Carl Smith. Comparison of identification criteria for machine inductive inference. *Theoretical Computer Science*, 25:193–220, 1983.
6. Jerome Feldmann. Some decidability results on grammatical inference and complexity. *Information and Control*, 20:244–262, 1972.
7. Marc Fulk. Robust separations in inductive inference. In *Proceedings of the 31st Annual Symposium on Foundations of Computer Science* (FOCS), pages 405–410, St. Louis, Missouri, 1990.

8. Sanjay Jain, Carl Smith and Rolf Wiehagen. On the power of learning robustly. In *Proceedings of Eleventh Annual Conference on Computational Learning Theory* (COLT), pages 187–197, ACM Press, New York, 1998.

9. Wolfgang Merkle and Frank Stephan. Trees and learning. *Proceedings of the Ninth Annual Conference on Computational Learning Theory* (COLT), pages 270–279, ACM Press, New York, 1996.

10. Eliana Minicozzi. Some natural properties of strong-identification in inductive inference. *Theoretical Computer Science*, 2:345–360, 1976.

11. Piergiorgio Odifreddi. *Classical Recursion Theory*. North-Holland, Amsterdam, 1989.

12. Daniel Osherson, Michael Stob and Scott Weinstein. *Systems that Learn*. MIT Press, Cambridge, Massachusetts, 1986.

13. Lenny Pitt. Probablistic inductive inference. *Journal of the Association of Computing Machinery*, 36:383–433, 1989.

14. Lenny Pitt and Carl Smith. Probability and plurality for aggregations of learning machines. *Information and Computation*, 77:77–92, 1998.

15. Karlis Podnieks. Comparing various concepts of function prediction, Part 1. *Theory of Algorithms and Programs, Latvian State University, Riga*, 210:68–81, 1974.

16. Carl Smith. The power of pluralism for automatic program synthesis *Journal of the Association of Computing Machinery*, 29:1144–1165, 1982.

17. Thomas Zeugmann. On Bārzdiņš' conjecture. In K. P. Jantke, editor, *Proceedings of the International Workshop on Analogical and Inductive Inference* (AII'86), volume 265 of LNCS, pages 220–227. Springer, 1986.

# Mind Change Complexity of Learning Logic Programs *

Sanjay Jain[1] and Arun Sharma[2]

[1] School of Computing
National University of Singapore
Singapore 119260, Republic of Singapore
Email: sanjay@comp.nus.edu.sg
[2] School of Computer Science and Engineering
The University of New South Wales
Sydney, NSW 2052, Australia
Email: arun@cse.unsw.edu.au

**Abstract.** The present paper motivates the study of mind change complexity for learning minimal models of length-bounded logic programs. It establishes ordinal mind change complexity bounds for learnability of these classes both from positive facts and from positive and negative facts.

Building on Angluin's notion of finite thickness and Wright's work on finite elasticity, Shinohara defined the property of bounded finite thickness to give a sufficient condition for learnability of indexed families of computable languages from positive data. This paper shows that an effective version of Shinohara's notion of bounded finite thickness gives sufficient conditions for learnability with ordinal mind change bound, both in the context of learnability from positive data and for learnability from complete (both positive and negative) data.

More precisely, it is shown that if a language defining framework yields a uniformly decidable family of languages and has effective bounded finite thickness, then for each natural number $m > 0$, the class of languages defined by formal systems of length $\leq m$:

- is identifiable in the limit from positive data with a mind change bound of $\omega^m$;
- is identifiable in the limit from both positive and negative data with an ordinal mind change bound of $\omega \times m$.

The above sufficient conditions are employed to give an ordinal mind change bound for learnability of minimal models of various classes of length-bounded Prolog programs, including Shapiro's linear programs, Arimura and Shinohara's depth-bounded linearly-covering programs, and Krishna Rao's depth-bounded linearly-moded programs. It is also noted that the bound for learning from positive data is tight for the example classes considered.

* The research of Arun Sharma is supported by Australian Research Council Grant A49803051.

# 1 Motivation and Introduction

Machine learning in the context of first-order logic and its subclasses can be traced back to the work of Plotkin [Plo71] and Shapiro [Sha81]. In recent years, this work has evolved into the very active field of Inductive Logic Programming (ILP). Numerous practical systems have been built to demonstrate the feasibility of learning logic programs as descriptions of complex concepts. The utility of these systems has been demonstrated in many domains including drug design, protein secondary structure prediction, and finite element mesh design (see Muggleton and DeRaedt [MDR94], Lavrac and Dzeroski [LD94], Bergadano and Gunetti [BG96], and Nienhuys-Cheng and de Wolf [NCdW97] for a survey of this field).

Together with practical developments, there has also been some interest in deriving learnability results for ILP. Several results in the PAC setting have been established; we refer the reader to Dzeroski, Muggleton, and Russell [DMR92a] [DMR92b], Cohen [Coh95a,Coh95b,Coh95c], De Raedt and Dzeroski [DRD94], Haussler [Hau89], Frisch and Page [FP91], Yamamoto [Yam93], Kietz [Kie93], and Maass and Turán [MT96].

Insights about which classes of logic programs are suitable as hypothesis spaces from the learnability perspective are likely to be very useful to ILP. Unfortunately, the few positive results that have been demonstrated in the PAC setting are for very restricted classes of logic programs. Hence, it is useful to consider more general models to analyze learnability of logic programs.[1] In the present paper, we develop tools to investigate identifiability in the limit with "mind change bounds" of minimal models of logic programs.

The first identification in the limit result about learnability of logic programs is due to Shapiro [Sha81]. He showed that the class of $h$-easy models is identifiable in the limit from both positive and negative facts. Adapting the work on learnability of subclasses of elementary formal systems[2], Shinohara [Shi91] showed that the class of minimal models of *linear* Prolog programs consisting of at most $m$ clauses is identifiable in the limit from only positive facts. Unfortunately, linear logic programs are very restricted as they do not even allow local variables (i.e., each variable in the body must appear in the head). Arimura and Shinohara [AS94] introduced a class of *linearly-covering* logic programs that allows local variables in a restricted sense. They showed that the class of minimal

---

[1] The learnability analysis of ILP in the learning by query model is able to overcome some of the restrictive nature of the PAC model by allowing the learner queries to an oracle. For examples of such analysis, see Khardon [Kha98] and Krishna-Rao and Sattar [KRS98].

[2] Arikawa [Ari70] adapted Smullyan's [Smu61] elementary formal systems (EFS) for investigation of formal languages. Later, Arikawa et al. [ASY92] showed that EFS can be viewed as a logic programming language over strings. Recently, various subclasses of EFS have been investigated in the context of learnability (e.g., see Shinohara [Shi91,Shi94]).

models of linearly-covering Prolog programs consisting of at most $m$ clauses of bounded body length is identifiable in the limit from only positive facts. Krishna Rao [KR96] noted that the class of linearly-covering programs is very restrictive as it did not even include the standard programs for reverse, merge, split, partition, quick-sort, and merge-sort. He proposed the class of *linearly-moded* programs that included all these standard programs and showed the class of minimal models of such programs consisting of at most $m$ clauses of bounded body length to be identifiable in the limit from positive facts.

While the above results are positive, it may be argued that the model is too general as the number of mind changes allowed is unbounded. Some authors have considered a polynomial time bound on the update of hypotheses in the identification in the limit setting. However, this restriction may not be very meaningful if the number of mind changes (and consequently the number of updates) is unbounded. The present paper considers learnability of logic programs in the identification in the limit setting with a bound on the mind change complexity. Recently, a number of approaches for modeling mind change bounds have been proposed [FS93,JS97,AJS97,Amb95,SSV97,AFS96]. In the present paper, we employ constructive ordinals as bounds for mind changes. We illustrate this notion in the context of identification in the limit of languages from positive data.

**TxtEx** denotes the collection of language classes that can be identified in the limit from positive data. An obvious approach to bounding the number of mind changes is to require that the learning machine make no more than a constant number of mind changes. This approach of employing natural numbers as mind change bounds was first considered by Bārzdiņš and Podnieks [BP73] (see also Case and Smith [CS83]). For each natural number $m$, **TxtEx$_m$** denotes the set of language classes that can be identified in the limit from positive data with no more than $m$ mind changes. However, a constant mind change bound has several drawbacks:

- it places the same bound on each language in the class irrespective of its "complexity";
- it does not take into account scenarios in which a learner, after examining an element of the language, is in a position to issue a bound on the number of mind changes (i.e., the learner computes and updates mind change bounds based on the incoming data).

To model situations where a mind change bound can be derived from data and updated as more data becomes available, constructive ordinals have been employed as mind change counters by Freivalds and Smith [FS93], and by Jain and Sharma [JS97]. We describe this notion next.

**TxtEx$_\alpha$** denotes the set of language classes that can be identified in the limit from positive data with an ordinal mind change bound $\alpha$. We illustrate the interpretation of this notion with a few examples. Let $\omega$ denote a notation for the least limit ordinal. Then a mind change bound of $\alpha \prec \omega$ is the earlier notion of mind change identification where the bound is a natural number. For $\alpha = \omega$, **TxtEx**$_\omega$ denotes learnable classes for which there exists a machine that, after examining some element(s) of the language, can announce an upper bound on the number of mind changes it will make before the onset of successful convergence. Angluin's [Ang80b,Ang80a] class of pattern languages is a member of **TxtEx**$_\omega$. Proceeding on, the class **TxtEx**$_{\omega \times 2}$ contains classes for which there is a learning machine that after examining some element(s) of the language announces an upper bound on the number of mind changes, but reserves the right to revise its upper bound once. **TxtEx**$_{\omega^2}$ contains classes for which the machine announces an upper bound on the number of times it may revise its conjectured upper bound on the number of mind changes, and so on.

The notion of ordinal mind change bound has been employed to give learnability results for unions of pattern languages and subclasses of elementary formal systems (see [JS97,AJS97]). In the present paper, we generalize these results to establish two sufficient conditions for learnability with ordinal mind change bounds and apply the results to obtain mind change bounds for learning subclasses of length-bounded logic programs. We discuss these two sufficient conditions briefly.

Let $U$ be an enumerable set of objects. A *language* is any subset of $U$; a typical variable for languages is $L$. Let $R$ be an enumerable set of rules[3]. A finite subset of $R$ is referred to as a *formal system*; a typical variable for formal systems is $\Gamma$. Let **Lang** be a mapping from the set of formal systems to languages.[4] We call the triple $\langle U, R, \mathbf{Lang} \rangle$ a *language defining framework*. In the sequel, we only consider those language defining frameworks for which the class $\{\mathbf{Lang}(\Gamma) \mid \Gamma$ is a finite subset of $R\}$ is a uniformly decidable family of computable languages. Furthermore, we suppose that a decision procedure for **Lang**$(\Gamma)$ can be found effectively from $\Gamma$.

A semantic mapping from formal systems to languages is *monotonic* just in case $\Gamma \subset \Gamma'$ implies $\mathbf{Lang}(\Gamma) \subseteq \mathbf{Lang}(\Gamma')$. A formal system $\Gamma$ is said to be reduced with respect to a finite $X \subseteq U$ just in case $X$ is contained in **Lang**$(\Gamma)$ but not in any language defined by a proper subset of $\Gamma$. We assume, without loss of generality for this paper, that for all finite sets $X \subseteq U$, there exists a finite $\Gamma \subseteq R$, such that $X \subseteq \mathbf{Lang}(\Gamma)$. Building on the work of Angluin [Ang80b] on finite thickness and of Wright [Wri89] on finite elasticity, Shinohara [Shi91] defined a language defining framework to have *bounded finite thickness* just in case

(a) it is monotonic and

(b) for each finite $X \subseteq U$ and for each natural number $m > 0$, the set of languages defined by formal systems that
   (i) are reduced with respect to $X$ and
   (ii) that are of cardinality $\leq m$,

---

[3] These could be productions in the context of formal languages or clauses in the context of logic programs.

[4] For technical convenience, we assume that **Lang**$(\emptyset) = \emptyset$.

is finite. He showed that if a language defining framework has bounded finite thickness, then for each $m > 0$, the class of languages definable by formal systems of cardinality $\leq m$ is identifiable in the limit from positive data.

The present paper places a further requirement on Shinohara's notion of bounded finite thickness to derive sufficient conditions for learnability with mind changes bounds. A language defining framework is said to have *effective bounded finite thickness* just in case the set of formal systems that are reduced with respect to $X$ in the definition of bounded finite thickness can be obtained effectively in $X$. We show that the notion of effective bounded finite thickness gives an ordinal mind change bound for both learnability from positive data and for learnability from positive and negative data. In particular, we establish that if a language defining framework has effective bounded finite thickness, then for each natural number $m > 0$, the class of languages defined by formal systems of cardinality $\leq m$:

- is identifiable in the limit from positive data with a mind change bound of $\omega^m$;
- is identifiable in the limit from both positive and negative data with an ordinal mind change bound of $\omega \times m$.

We employ the above results to give mind change bounds for the following classes of Prolog programs:

(a) Shapiro's linear logic programs (similar result can be shown for the class of hereditary logic programs [MSS91,MSS93] and reductive logic programs [KR96]);
(b) Krishna Rao's linearly-moded logic programs with bounded body length (similar result holds for Arimura and Shinohara's linearly-covering logic programs with bounded body length [AS94]).

In the sequel we proceed as follows. Section 2 introduces the preliminaries of ordinal mind change identification. Section 3 establishes sufficient conditions for learnability with ordinal mind change bound for both positive data and positive and negative data. In Section 4, we introduce preliminaries of logic programming and apply the results from Section 3 to establish mind change bounds for learnability of minimal models of various subclasses of length-bounded Prolog programs.

## 2  Ordinal Mind Change Identification

$N$ denotes the set of natural numbers, $\{0, 1, 2, \ldots\}$. Any unexplained recursion theoretic notation is from [Rog67]. Cardinality of a set $S$ is denoted $\text{card}(S)$. The maximum and minimum of a set are represented by $\max(\cdot)$ and $\min(\cdot)$, respectively. The symbols $\subseteq, \supseteq, \subset, \supset$, and $\emptyset$ respectively stand for subset, superset, proper subset, proper superset, and the emptyset. $\Lambda$ denotes the empty sequence.

**Definition 1.** A class of languages $\mathcal{L} = \{L_i \mid i \in N\}$ is a *uniformly decidable family of computable languages* just in case there exists a computable function $f$ such that for each $i \in N$ and for each $x \in U$,

$$f(i, x) = \begin{cases} 1, & \text{if } x \in L_i, \\ 0, & \text{otherwise.} \end{cases}$$

As noted in the introduction, we only consider uniformly decidable families of computable languages. In the next three definitions we introduce texts (positive data presentation), informants (positive and negative data presentation), and learning machines.

**Definition 2.** [Gol67]

(a) A *text* $T$ is a mapping from $N$ into $U \cup \{\#\}$. (The symbol $\#$ models pauses in data presentation.)
(b) content($T$) denotes the intersection of $U$ and the range of $T$.
(c) A text $T$ is for a language $L$ iff $L = $ content($T$).
(d) The initial sequence of text $T$ of length $n$ is denoted $T[n]$.
(e) The set of all finite initial sequences of $U$ and $\#$'s is denoted SEQ. We let $\sigma$ and $\tau$ range over SEQ.

**Definition 3.** [Gol67]

(a) An *informant* $I$ is an infinite sequence over $U \times \{0, 1\}$ such that for each $x \in U$ either $(x, 1)$ or $(x, 0)$ (but not both) appear in the sequence.
(b) An informant $I$ is for $L$ iff $(x, 1)$ appears in $I$ if $x \in L$ and $(x, 0)$ appears in $I$ if $x \notin L$.
(c) $I[n]$ denotes the initial sequence of informant $I$ with length $n$.
(d) content($I$) = $\{(x, y) \mid (x, y)$ appears in sequence $I\}$; content($I[n]$) is defined similarly.
(e) PosInfo($I[n]$) = $\{x \mid (x, 1) \in $ content($I[n]$)$\}$; NegInfo($I[n]$) = $\{x \mid (x, 0) \in $ content($I[n]$)$\}$.
(f) InfSEQ = $\{I[n] \mid I$ is an informant for some $L \subseteq U\}$. We let $\sigma$ and $\tau$ also range over InfSEQ.

**Definition 4.** Let $\mathcal{F}$ denote the set of all formal systems.

(a) A learning machine from texts (informants) is an algorithmic mapping from SEQ (InfSEQ) into $\mathcal{F} \cup \{?\}$. A typical variable for learning machines is **M**.
(b) **M** is said to *converge* on text $T$ to $\Gamma$ (written: **M**($T$) converges to $\Gamma$ or **M**($T$)$\downarrow$ = $\Gamma$) just in case for all but finitely many $n$, **M**($T[n]$) = $\Gamma$. A similar definition for informants holds.

A conjecture of "?" by a machine is interpreted as "no guess at this moment." This is useful to avoid biasing the number of mind changes of a machine. For this paper, we assume, without loss of generality, that $\sigma \subseteq \tau$ and $\mathbf{M}(\sigma) \neq ?$ implies $\mathbf{M}(\tau) \neq ?$.

We next introduce ordinals as models for mind change counters. We assume a fixed notation system, $O$, and partial ordering of ordinal notations as used by, for example, Kleene [Kle38,Rog67,Sac90]. $\preceq, \prec, \succeq$ and $\succ$ on ordinal notations below refer to the partial ordering of ordinal notations in this system. We do not go into the details of the notation system used, but instead refer the reader to [Kle38,Rog67,Sac90,CJS95,FS93]. In the sequel, we are somewhat informal and use $+$, $\times$, and for all $m \in N$ as notation for the same.

**Definition 5.** $\mathbf{F}$, an algorithmic mapping from SEQ (or InfSEQ) into ordinal notations, is an *ordinal mind change counter function* just in case $(\forall \sigma \subseteq \tau)[\mathbf{F}(\sigma) \succeq \mathbf{F}(\tau)]$.

**Definition 6.** [FS93,JS97] Let $\alpha$ be an ordinal notation.

(a) We say that $\mathbf{M}$, with associated ordinal mind change counter function $\mathbf{F}$, $\mathbf{TxtEx}_\alpha$-*identifies* a text $T$ just in case the following three conditions hold:
   (i) $\mathbf{M}(T)\!\downarrow = \Gamma$ and $\mathbf{Lang}(\Gamma) = \text{content}(T)$,
   (ii) $\mathbf{F}(\Lambda) = \alpha$, and
   (iii) $(\forall n)[? \neq \mathbf{M}(T[n]) \neq \mathbf{M}(T[n+1]) \Rightarrow \mathbf{F}(T[n]) \succ \mathbf{F}(T[n+1])]$.
(b) $\mathbf{M}$, with associated ordinal mind change counter function $\mathbf{F}$, $\mathbf{TxtEx}_\alpha$-*identifies* $L$ (written: $L \in \mathbf{TxtEx}_\alpha(\mathbf{M},\mathbf{F})$) just in case $\mathbf{M}$, with associated ordinal mind change counter function $\mathbf{F}$, $\mathbf{TxtEx}_\alpha$-identifies each text for $L$.
(c) $\mathbf{TxtEx}_\alpha = \{\mathcal{L} \mid (\exists \mathbf{M},\mathbf{F})[\mathcal{L} \subseteq \mathbf{TxtEx}_\alpha(\mathbf{M},\mathbf{F})]\}$.

**Definition 7.** [FS93,AJS97] Let $\alpha$ be an ordinal notation.

(a) We say that $\mathbf{M}$, with associated ordinal mind change counter function $\mathbf{F}$, $\mathbf{InfEx}_\alpha$-*identifies* an informant $I$ just in case the following three conditions hold:
   (i) $\mathbf{M}(I)\!\downarrow = \Gamma$ and $\mathbf{Lang}(\Gamma) = \text{PosInfo}(I)$.
   (ii) $\mathbf{F}(\Lambda) = \alpha$, and
   (iii) $(\forall n)[? \neq \mathbf{M}(I[n]) \neq \mathbf{M}(I[n+1]) \Rightarrow \mathbf{F}(I[n]) \succ \mathbf{F}(I[n+1])]$.
(b) $\mathbf{M}$, with associated ordinal mind change counter function $\mathbf{F}$, $\mathbf{InfEx}_\alpha$-*identifies* $L$ (written: $L \in \mathbf{InfEx}_\alpha(\mathbf{M},\mathbf{F})$) just in case $\mathbf{M}$, with associated ordinal mind change counter function $\mathbf{F}$, $\mathbf{InfEx}_\alpha$-identifies each informant for $L$.
(c) $\mathbf{InfEx}_\alpha = \{\mathcal{L} \mid (\exists \mathbf{M},\mathbf{F})[\mathcal{L} \subseteq \mathbf{InfEx}_\alpha(\mathbf{M},\mathbf{F})]\}$.

We refer the reader to Ambainis [Amb95] for a discussion on how the learnability classes depend on the choice of the ordinal notation.

# 3 Conditions for learnability with mind change bound

We now formally define what it means for a language defining framework to have the property of *effective bounded finite thickness*. Recall that a semantic mapping **Lang** is *monotonic* just in case for any two formal systems $\Gamma$ and $\Gamma'$, $\Gamma \subseteq \Gamma' \Rightarrow \textbf{Lang}(\Gamma) \subseteq \textbf{Lang}(\Gamma')$. Also, recall from the introduction that we only consider language defining frameworks that yield uniformly decidable families of computable languages.

**Definition 8.** Let $\langle U, R, \textbf{Lang} \rangle$ be a language defining framework such that **Lang** is monotonic. For any finite $X \subseteq U$, let

$$\mathsf{Gen}_X \stackrel{\text{def}}{=} \{\Gamma \mid \Gamma \subseteq R \ \wedge \ \text{card}(\Gamma) < \infty \ \wedge \ X \subseteq \textbf{Lang}(\Gamma)\}$$

and let

$$\mathsf{Min}_X \stackrel{\text{def}}{=} \{\Gamma \in \mathsf{Gen}_X \mid (\forall \Gamma' \in \mathsf{Gen}_X)[\Gamma' \not\subseteq \Gamma]\}.$$

Then $\langle U, R, \textbf{Lang} \rangle$ is said to have *effective bounded finite thickness* just in case for all finite $X \subseteq U$, $\mathsf{Min}_X$ is finite and can be obtained effectively in $X$ (i.e. there are recursive functions (in $X$) for enumerating $\mathsf{Min}_X$, and for finding cardinality of $\mathsf{Min}_X$).

## 3.1 Learnability from positive data

We now show that if a language defining framework has effective bounded finite thickness then the class of languages defined by formal systems of cardinality $\leq m$ can be $\textbf{TxtEx}_{\omega^m}$-identified. This result is a generalization of a lemma from [JS97]. To state this lemma, we need some technical machinery which we describe next.

**Definition 9.** A *search tree* is a finite labeled rooted tree. We denote the label of node, $v$, in search tree $H$ by $C_H(v)$.

Intuitively, the label on the nodes are interpreted as decision procedures. We abuse the notation slightly and by $\textbf{Lang}(C_H(v))$, we mean the language decided by $C_H(v)$. We next introduce a partial order on search trees.

**Definition 10.** Suppose $H_1$ and $H_2$ are two search trees. We say that $H_1 \preceq H_2$ just in case the following properties are satisfied:

(A) root of $H_1$ has the same label as root of $H_2$;

(B) $H_1$ is a labeled subgraph of $H_2$; and

(C) all nodes of $H_1$, except the leaves, have exactly the same children in both $H_1$ and $H_2$.

Essentially, $H_1 \preceq H_2$ means that $H_2$ is obtained by attaching some (possibly empty) trees to some of the leaves of the search tree $H_1$. It is helpful to formalize the notion of *depth* of a search tree as follows: depth of root is 0; depth of a child is $1 +$ depth of parent; and depth of a search tree is depth of its deepest leaf.

$Q$, a mapping from SEQ to search trees, is called an $m$-Explorer iff the following properties are satisfied:

(A) $\sigma \subseteq \tau \Rightarrow Q(\sigma) \preceq Q(\tau)$;

(B) $(\forall \sigma)[\text{depth}(Q(\sigma)) \le m]$; and

(C) for all $T$, $Q(T){\downarrow}$, i.e., $(\overset{\infty}{\forall} n)[Q(T[n]) = Q(T[n+1])]$.

(The reader should note that C is actually implied by A and B; C has been included to emphasize the point.)

We can now state the lemma from [JS97] that links the existence of an $m$-Explorer to $\mathbf{TxtEx}_{\omega^m}$-identification.

**Lemma 1.** *Suppose $Q$ is an $m$-Explorer. Then there exists a machine $\mathbf{M}$ and an associated ordinal mind change counter $\mathbf{F}$ such that the following properties are satisfied:*

*(A) $(\forall \text{ texts } T)[\mathbf{M}(T){\downarrow}]$;*

*(B) $\mathbf{F}(\Lambda) = \omega^m$; and*

*(C) if there exists a node $v$ in $Q(T)$ such that $C_{Q(T)}(v)$ is a decision procedure for $\text{content}(T)$, then $\mathbf{M}$, with associated mind change counter $\mathbf{F}$, $\mathbf{TxtEx}_{\omega^m}$-identifies $T$.*

We now establish a theorem that bridges Lemma 1 with the notion of effective bounded finite thickness and $\mathbf{TxtEx}_{\omega^m}$-identifiability.

**Theorem 1.** *Let $\langle U, R, \mathbf{Lang} \rangle$ be a language defining framework with effective bounded finite thickness. For each $m > 0$, let*

$$\mathcal{L}^m \overset{\text{def}}{=} \{\mathbf{Lang}(\Gamma) \mid \Gamma \subseteq R \wedge \text{card}(\Gamma) \le m\}.$$

*Then for each $m > 0$, there exists an $m$-Explorer $Q$ such that for any text $T$ for any $L \in \mathcal{L}^m$, there is a node $v$ in $Q(T)$ which is labelled by the decision procedure for $\text{content}(T) = L$.*

**Proof.** We construct an $m$-Explorer $Q$ as follows. Let $T$ be a text. Let $Q(\Lambda) =$ just a root with label $\emptyset$. $Q(T[n+1])$ is obtained as follows. For each leaf $v$ in $Q(T[n])$ such that $\text{depth}(v) < m$ and $\text{content}(T[n+1]) \not\subseteq \mathbf{Lang}(C_H(v))$ do the following:

For each $\Gamma \in \text{Min}_{\text{content}(T[n+1])}$, add a child to $v$ with label of the decision procedure for $\mathbf{Lang}(\Gamma)$.

It is easy to verify that $Q$ is an $m$-Explorer. ∎

## 3.2 Learnability from positive and negative data

In this section we show that if a language defining framework has effective bounded finite thickness then the class of languages defined by formal systems of cardinality $\leq m$ can be **InfEx**-identified with an ordinal mind change bound of $\omega \times m$. This result is a generalization of a result about unions of pattern languages from [AJS97]. We first introduce some technical machinery.

Let $\mathsf{Pos} \subseteq U$ and $\mathsf{Neg} \subseteq U$ be two disjoint finite sets such that $\mathsf{Pos} \neq \emptyset$. Then let

$$X_i^{\mathsf{Pos,Neg}} \stackrel{\text{def}}{=} \{\Gamma \subseteq R \mid \mathrm{card}(\Gamma) = i \wedge [\mathsf{Pos} \subseteq \mathbf{Lang}(\Gamma)] \wedge [\mathsf{Neg} \subseteq U - \mathbf{Lang}(S)]\}.$$

The next lemma and corollary shed light on computation of $X_i^{\mathsf{Pos,Neg}}$.

**Lemma 2.** *Let $\langle U, R, \mathbf{Lang} \rangle$ be a language defining framework with effective bounded finite thickness. Let $\mathsf{Pos} \neq \emptyset$ and $\mathsf{Neg}$ be two disjoint finite subsets of $U$ and let $i \in N$. Suppose $(\forall j \leq i)[X_j^{\mathsf{Pos,Neg}} = \emptyset]$. Then, $X_{i+1}^{\mathsf{Pos,Neg}}$ can be computed effectively in $\mathsf{Pos}$, $\mathsf{Neg}$, and $i$. (Note that $X_{i+1}^{\mathsf{Pos,Neg}}$ must be finite in this case!)*

**Proof.** Let $\mathsf{Pos}$, $\mathsf{Neg}$, and $i$ be as given in the hypothesis of the lemma. From the effective bounded finite thickness property of $\langle U, R, \mathbf{Lang} \rangle$ it easily follows that for each $x \in U$, $H_x \stackrel{\text{def}}{=} \{\Gamma \subseteq R \mid x \in \mathbf{Lang}(\Gamma) \wedge \mathrm{card}(\Gamma) < \infty \wedge (\forall \Gamma' \subset \Gamma)[x \notin \mathbf{Lang}(\Gamma')]\}$ is finite and effective in $x$.

Let $X \stackrel{\text{def}}{=} \{\Gamma \subseteq R \mid \mathrm{card}(\Gamma) = i+1 \wedge (\forall x \in \mathsf{Pos})(\exists \Gamma_x \in H_x)[\Gamma_x \subseteq \Gamma] \wedge (\mathsf{Neg} \cap \mathbf{Lang}(\Gamma) = \emptyset)\}$.

It is easy to verify that $X = X_{i+1}^{\mathsf{Pos,Neg}}$. Also, since $H_x$ is finite and effective in $x$ for each $x \in U$, $X$ is finite and can be obtained effectively from $\mathsf{Pos}$, $\mathsf{Neg}$ and $i$. ∎

**Corollary 1.** *Let $\mathsf{Pos} \neq \emptyset$ and $\mathsf{Neg}$ be two disjoint finite subsets of $U$. Then there exists an $i$, effective in $\mathsf{Pos}$ and $\mathsf{Neg}$, such that $i = \min(\{j \mid X_j^{\mathsf{Pos,Neg}} \neq \emptyset\})$.*

**Proof.** Note that $\mathbf{Lang}(\emptyset)$ is empty. The corollary now follows by repeated use of Lemma 2 until one finds an $i$ such that $X_i^{\mathsf{Pos,Neg}} \neq \emptyset$. ∎

**Theorem 2.** *Let $\langle U, R, \mathbf{Lang} \rangle$ be a language defining framework with effective bounded finite thickness. For each $m > 0$, let*

$$\mathcal{L}^m \stackrel{\text{def}}{=} \{\mathbf{Lang}(\Gamma) \mid \Gamma \subseteq R \wedge \mathrm{card}(\Gamma) \leq m\}.$$

*Then $(\forall m > 0)[\mathcal{L}^m \in \mathbf{InfEx}_{\omega \times m}]$.*

**Proof.** Fix $m$. Let $I$ be an informant. Then for $n \in N$, $\mathbf{M}(I[n])$ and $\mathbf{F}(I[n])$ are defined as follows.

Let Pos $=$ PosInfo($I[n]$) and Neg $=$ NegInfo($I[n]$).

If Pos $= \emptyset$, then $\mathbf{M}(I[n]) =?$ and $\mathbf{F}(I[n]) = \omega \times m$.

If Pos $\neq \emptyset$, then let $j = \min(\{j' \mid X_{j'}^{\text{Pos,Neg}} \neq \emptyset\})$. Note that $j$ (and corresponding $X_j^{\text{Pos,Neg}}$) can be found effectively in $I[n]$, using Corollary 1.

If $j > m$, then let $\mathbf{M}(I[n]) = \mathbf{M}(I[n-1])$.

If $j \leq m$, then let $\mathbf{M}(I[n]) = \Gamma$, where $\Gamma$ is the lexicographically least element in $X_j^{\text{Pos,Neg}}$, and let $\mathbf{F}(I[n]) = \omega \times k + \ell$, where $k = m - j$, and $\ell = \text{card}(X_j^{\text{Pos,Neg}}) - 1$.

It is easy to verify that $\mathbf{M}, \mathbf{F}$ witness the theorem. ∎

# 4 Classes of logic programs

We next describe the preliminaries from logic programming; the reader is referred to Lloyd [Llo87] for any unexplained notation.

Let $\Pi, \Sigma, \mathcal{X}$ be mutually disjoint sets such that $\Pi$ and $\Sigma$ are finite. $\Pi$ is the set of *predicate symbols*, $\Sigma$ is the set of *function symbols*, and $\mathcal{X}$ is the set of *variables*. The arity of a function or a predicate symbol $p$ is denoted arity($p$). The set of terms constructed from the function symbols in $\Sigma$ and variables in $\mathcal{X}$ is denoted Terms($\Sigma, \mathcal{X}$). Atoms($\Pi, \Sigma, \mathcal{X}$) denotes the set of atoms formed from predicate symbols in $\Pi$ and terms in Terms($\Sigma, \mathcal{X}$). The set of ground atoms for a predicate symbol $p$, then is Atoms($\{p\}, \Sigma, \emptyset$); we denote this set by $B(p)$. The size of a term $t$, denoted $|t|$, is the number of symbols other than punctuation symbols in $t$. The *body length* of a definite clause is the number of literals in its body. The *length of a logic program* $P$, denoted Length($P$), is just the number of clauses in $P$.

Following the treatment of [KR96], we take the least Herbrand model semantics of logic programs as our monotonic semantic mapping in the present paper. We will refer to the target predicate being learned by the symbol $p$. Then our language defining frameworks will be of the form $\langle B(p), LP, M_p \rangle$, where $LP$ is the class of Prolog clauses being considered and $M_p$ denotes the semantic mapping such that $M_p(P)$ is the set of all atoms of the target predicate $p$ in the least Herbrand model of $P$.

We next describe linear Prolog programs introduced by Shapiro [Sha81].

**Definition 11.** [Sha81] A definite clause $p(t_1, \ldots, t_n) \leftarrow q_1(s_{1_1}, \ldots, s_{1_{n_1}}), \ldots,$ $q_k(s_{k_1}, \ldots, s_{k_{n_k}})$ is called *linear* just in case for each $i$, $1 \leq i \leq k$, $|t_1\sigma| + \cdots + |t_n\sigma| \geq |s_{i_1}\sigma| + \cdots + |s_{i_{n_i}}\sigma|$ for any substitution $\sigma$. A logic program $P$ is said to be *linear* just in case each clause in $P$ is linear.

**Theorem 3.** [Shi91] *The class of least Herbrand models of linear Prolog programs is a uniformly decidable family of computable languages.*

Let LC denote the class of all linear clauses and $M_p$ be a semantic mapping such that $M_p(P)$ is the set of all atoms of the target predicate $p$ in the least Herbrand model of $P$. Then we have the following.

**Theorem 4.** *The language defining framework* $\langle B(p), \mathsf{LC}, M_p \rangle$ *has effective bounded finite thickness.*

**Proof.** Shinohara's proof of $\langle B(p), \mathsf{LC}, M_p \rangle$ having bounded finite thickness can easily be modified to show that it is effective. ∎

We note that a similar result can be shown for the class of hereditary logic programs [MSS91,MSS93] and reductive logic programs [KR96].

The above results were for classes of logic programs that did not allow local variables. We now turn our attention to the classes of logic programs that allow local variables. We show that the language defining frameworks associated with the class of linearly-covering Prolog prorgams of Arimura and Shinohara and the class of linearly-moded Prolog programs of Krishna Rao have effective bounded finite thickness if the body length of the clauses is bounded. Since the class of linearly-covering programs are subsumed by the class of linearly-moded programs, we show the result for only the latter class. But, first we introduce some terminology about multisets, parametric size of terms, and moded logic programs.

For a multiset $X$ and an object $o$, $\mathrm{Occ}(o, X)$ denotes the number of occurrences of $o$ in $X$. The inclusion $\subseteq$ between multisets $X$ and $Y$ is defined as $X \subseteq Y$ just in case $\mathrm{Occ}(o, X) \leq \mathrm{Occ}(o, Y)$ for any object $o$. The sum of two multisets $X$ and $Y$, denoted $X + Y$, is defined as the multiset for which $\mathrm{Occ}(o, X + Y) = \mathrm{Occ}(o, X) + \mathrm{Occ}(o, Y)$ for any object $o$. Let $\langle\,\rangle$ denote an empty list.

**Definition 12.** The *parametric size* of a term $t$, denoted $\mathrm{Psize}(t)$, is defined inductively as follows:

(a) if $t$ is a variable $x$ then $\mathrm{Psize}(t)$ is the linear expression $x$;
(b) if $t$ is the empty list, then $\mathrm{Psize}(t)$ is 0;
(c) if $t = f(t_1, \ldots, t_n)$ and $f \in \Sigma - \{\langle\,\rangle\}$, then $\mathrm{Psize}(t)$ is the linear expression $1 + \mathrm{Psize}(t_1) + \cdots + \mathrm{Psize}(t_n)$.

We usually denote a sequence of terms $t_1, \ldots, t_n$ by $\mathbf{t}$. The parametric size of a sequence of terms $t_1, \ldots, t_n$ is the sum $\mathrm{Psize}(t_1) + \cdots + \mathrm{Psize}(t_n)$.

The definition of linearly-covering programs requires the notion of modes associated with each argument in a predicate.

**Definition 13.** (a) A *mode declaration* for an $n$-ary predicate $p$ is a mapping from $\{1,\ldots,n\}$ to the set $\{+,-\}$. (b) Let md be a mode declaration for the predicate $p$. Then the sets $+(p) = \{j \mid \mathsf{md}(j) = +\}$ and $-(p) = \{j \mid \mathsf{md}(j) = -\}$ are the sets of input and output positions of $p$, respectively.

If each predicate in a logic program has a unique mode declaration, the program is referred to as a moded program. In dealing with moded programs, it is useful to group together the input and output arguments, i.e., $p(\mathbf{s}; \mathbf{t})$ is an atom with input terms $\mathbf{s}$ and output terms $\mathbf{t}$.

The definition of linearly-moded logic programs requires the following technical notion.

**Definition 14.** [KR96] Let $P$ be a moded logic program and let $I$ be a mapping from the set of predicates occurring in $P$ to sets of input positions such that $I(p) \subseteq +(p)$ for each predicate $p$ in $P$. Then for an atom $A = p(\mathbf{s}; \mathbf{t})$, the following linear inequality is denoted $\mathsf{LI}(A, I)$.

$$\Sigma_{i \in I(p)}\mathsf{Psize}(s_i) \geq \Sigma_{j \in -(p)}\mathsf{Psize}(t_j).$$

We now define Krishna Rao's notion of what it means for a logic program to be linearly-moded.

**Definition 15.** [KR96]

(a) Let $P$ be a moded logic program and let $I$ be a mapping from the set of predicates in $P$ to the sets of input positions satisfying $I(p) \subseteq +(p)$ for each predicate $p$ in $P$. $P$ is said to be *linearly-moded with respect to $I$* if each clause

$$p_0(\mathbf{s}_0; \mathbf{t}_0) \leftarrow p_1(\mathbf{s}_1; \mathbf{t}_1), \ldots, p_k(\mathbf{s}_k; \mathbf{t}_k)$$

in $P$ satisfies the following two conditions:
  (i) $\mathsf{LI}(A_1, I), \ldots, \mathsf{LI}(A_{j-1}, I)$ together imply $\mathsf{Psize}(\mathbf{s}_0) \geq \mathsf{Psize}(\mathbf{s}_j)$ for each $j \geq 1$, and
  (ii) $\mathsf{LI}(A_1, I), \ldots, \mathsf{LI}(A_k, I)$ together imply $\mathsf{LI}(A_0, I)$,
  where $A_j$ is the atom $p_1(\mathbf{s}_j; \mathbf{t}_j)$ for each $j \geq 0$.
(b) A logic program $P$ is said to be *linearly-moded* just in case it is linearly-moded with respect to some mapping $I$.

We now introduce the language defining framework of linearly-moded clauses. For $k > 0$, let $\mathsf{LMC}_k$ denote the set of all linearly-moded clauses of body length at most $k$. Then the language defining framework associated with linearly-moded clauses is $\langle B(p), \mathsf{LMC}_k, M_p \rangle$.

**Theorem 5.** [KR96] *For $k \geq 1$, the class of least Herbrand models of logic programs with clauses in $\mathsf{LMC}_k$ is an indexed family of recursive languages.*

**Theorem 6.** *For $k \geq 1$, the language defining framework $\langle B(p), \mathsf{LMC}_k, M_p \rangle$ has effective bounded finite thickness.*

**Proof.** Krishna Rao's [KR96] proof of $\langle B(p), \mathsf{LMC}_k, M_p \rangle$ having bounded finite thickness can easily be made effective. ∎

As a consequence of the above theorem and the results in Section 3 for each $m \geq 1$, for each $k \geq 1$, the class of languages $\mathcal{L}_m^k = \{M_p(P) \mid P \in \mathsf{LMC}_k \wedge \mathrm{Length}(P) \leq m\}$ is a member of $\mathbf{TxtEx}_{\omega^m}$ and of $\mathbf{InfEx}_{\omega \times m}$. The reader should note that the bound $k$ on the body length of clauses is crucial for the effective bounded thickness property. It can be shown that without such a restriction the class of least Herbrand models of length-bounded linearly-moded programs contains a superfinite subclass, thereby ruling out its learnability from positive data. Krishna Rao [KR96] has shown that both the classes of linear clauses and the class of linearly-covering clauses is included is the class of linearly-moded clauses, but the classes of linear clauses and linearly-covering clauses are incomparable to each other.

# 5 Conclusion

A natural question is whether the bounds of $\omega^m$ and $\omega \times m$ are tight. It can be shown for the example classes in this paper that for identification from positive data, the ordinal bound of $\omega^m$ is tight. For identification from both positive and negative data, it is still open if the bound of $\omega \times m$ is tight. However, we can show an improvement on the bound $\omega \times m$ under certain conditions if a restricted version of the language equivalence problem is decidable. In particular we can show that if for some fixed $k \leq m$, the equivalence of $\mathbf{Lang}(\Gamma)$ and $\mathbf{Lang}(\Gamma')$ is decidable for $\mathrm{card}(\Gamma) = \mathrm{card}(\Gamma') \leq k$, then $\mathcal{L}^m \in \mathbf{InfEx}_{\omega \times (m-k)+(k \dot{-} 1)}$.

# References

[AFS96] A. Ambainis, R. Freivalds, and C. Smith. General inductive inference types based on linearly-ordered sets. In *Proceedings of Symposium on Theoretical Aspects of Computer Science*, volume 1046 of *Lecture Notes in Computer Science*, pages 243–253. Springer-Verlag, 1996.

[AJS97] A. Ambainis, S. Jain, and A. Sharma. Ordinal mind change complexity of language identification. In S. Ben-David, editor, *Third European Conference on Computational Learning Theory*, volume 1208 of *Lecture Notes in Artificial Intelligence*, pages 301–315. Springer-Verlag, 1997.

[Amb95] A. Ambainis. Power of procrastination in inductive inference: How it depends on used ordinal notations. In Paul Vitányi, editor, *Second European Conference on Computational Learning Theory*, volume 904 of *Lecture Notes in Artificial Intelligence*, pages 99–111. Springer-Verlag, 1995.

[Ang80a] D. Angluin. Finding patterns common to a set of strings. *Journal of Computer and System Sciences*, 21:46–62, 1980.

[Ang80b]  D. Angluin. Inductive inference of formal languages from positive data. *Information and Control*, 45:117–135, 1980.

[Ari70]   S. Arikawa. Elementary formal systems and formal languages—simple formal systems. *Memoirs of the Faculty of Science, Kyushu University Series A*, 24:47–75, 1970.

[AS94]    H. Arimura and T. Shinohara. Inductive inference of Prolog programs with linear data dependency from positive data. In H. Jaakkola, H. Kangassalo, T. Kitahashi, and A. Markus, editors, *Proc. Information Modelling and Knowledge Bases V*, pages 365–375. IOS Press, 1994.

[ASY92]   S. Arikawa, T. Shinohara, and A. Yamamoto. Learning elementary formal systems. *Theoretical Computer Science*, 95:97–113, 1992.

[BG96]    F. Bergadano and G. Gunetti. *Inductive Logic Programming: from Machine Learning to Software Engineering*. MIT Press, 1996.

[BP73]    J. Bārzdiņš and K. Podnieks. The theory of inductive inference. In *Second Symposium on Mathematical Foundations of Computer Science*, pages 9–15. Math. Inst. of the Slovak Academy of Sciences, 1973.

[CJS95]   J. Case, S. Jain, and M. Suraj. Not-so-nearly-minimal-size program inference. In K. Jantke and S. Lange, editors, *Algorithmic Learning for Knowledge-Based Systems*, volume 961 of *Lecture Notes in Artificial Intelligence*, pages 77–96. Springer-Verlag, 1995.

[Coh95a]  W. W. Cohen. PAC-Learning non-recursive Prolog clauses. *Artificial Intelligence*, 79:1–38, 1995.

[Coh95b]  W. W. Cohen. PAC-Learning recursive logic programs: Efficient algorithms. *Journal of Artificial Intelligence Research*, 2:501–539, 1995.

[Coh95c]  W. W. Cohen. PAC-Learning recursive logic programs: Negative results. *Journal of Artificial Intelligence Research*, 2:541–573, 1995.

[CS83]    J. Case and C. Smith. Comparison of identification criteria for machine inductive inference. *Theoretical Computer Science*, 25:193–220, 1983.

[DMR92a]  S. Dzeroski, S. Muggleton, and S. Russell. PAC-Learnability of constrained nonrecursive logic programs. In *Proceedings of the Third International Workshop on Computational Learning Theory and Natural Learning Systems*, 1992. Wisconsin, Madison.

[DMR92b]  S. Dzeroski, S. Muggleton, and S. Russell. PAC-Learnability of determinate logic programs. In *Proceedings of the Fifth Annual Workshop on Computational Learning Theory*, pages 128–135. ACM Press, July 1992.

[DRD94]   L. De Raedt and S. Dzeroski. First-order $jk$-clausal theories are PAC-learnable. *Artificial Intelligence*, 70:375–392, 1994.

[FP91]    A. Frisch and C.D. Page. Learning constrained atoms. In *Proceedings of the Eighth International Workshop on Machine Learning*. Morgan Kaufmann, 1991.

[FS93]    R. Freivalds and C. Smith. On the role of procrastination in machine learning. *Information and Computation*, pages 237–271, 1993.

[Gol67]   E. M. Gold. Language identification in the limit. *Information and Control*, 10:447–474, 1967.

[Hau89]   D. Hausler. Learning conjunctive concepts in structural domains. *Machine Learning*, 4(1), 1989.

[JS97]    S. Jain and A. Sharma. Elementary formal systems, intrinsic complexity, and procrastination. *Information and Computation*, 132:65–84, 1997.

[Kha98]   R. Khardon. Learning first order universal Horn expressions. In *Proceedings of the Eleventh Annual Conference on Computational Learning Theory*, pages 154–165. ACM Press, 1998.

[Kie93]   J-U. Kietz. Some computational lower bounds for the computational complexity of inductive logic programming. In *Proceedings of the 1993 European Conference on Machine Learning*, 1993. Vienna.

[Kle38]  S. Kleene. Notations for ordinal numbers. *Journal of Symbolic Logic*, 3:150–155, 1938.

[KR96]  M. Krishna Rao. A class of Prolog programs inferable from positive data. In A. Arikawa and A. Sharma, editors, *Algorithmic Learning Theory: Seventh International Workshop (ALT '96)*, volume 1160 of *Lecture Notes in Artificial Intelligence*, pages 272–284. Springer-Verlag, 1996.

[KRS98]  M. Krishna Rao and A. Sattar. Learning from entailment of logic programs with local variables. In M. Richter, C. Smith, R. Wiehagen, and T. Zeugmann, editors, *Algorithmic Learning Theory: Ninth International Workshop (ALT '97)*, Lecture Notes in Artificial Intelligence. Springer-Verlag, 1998. To appear.

[LD94]  N. Lavarač and S. Džeroski. *Inductive Logic Programming*. Ellis Horwood, New York, 1994.

[Llo87]  J.W. Lloyd. *Foundation of Logic Programming (Second Edition)*. Springer, New York, 1987.

[MDR94]  S. Muggleton and L. De Raedt. Inductive Logic Programming: Theory and Methods. *Journal of Logic Programming*, 19(20):629–679, 1994.

[MSS91]  S Miyano, A. Shinohara, and T. Shinohara. Which classes of elementary formal systems are polynomial-time learnable? In *Proceedings of the Second Workshop on Algorithmic Learning Theory*, pages 139–150, 1991.

[MSS93]  S. Miyano, A. Shinohara, and T. Shinohara. Learning elementary formal systems and an application to discovering motifs in proteins. Technical Report RIFIS-TRCS-37, RIFIS, Kyushu University, 1993.

[MT96]  W. Maass and Gy. Turán. On learnability and predicate logic. Technical Report NC-TR-96-023, NeuroCOLT Technical Report, 1996.

[NCdW97]  S.H. Nienhuys-Cheng and R. de Wolf. *Foundations of Inductive Logic Programming*. LNAI Tutorial 1228. Springer-Verlag, 1997.

[Plo71]  G. Plotkin. *Automatic Methods of Inductive Inference*. PhD thesis, University of Edinburgh, 1971.

[Rog67]  H. Rogers. *Theory of Recursive Functions and Effective Computability*. McGraw-Hill, 1967. Reprinted, MIT Press 1987.

[Sac90]  G. Sacks. *Higher Recursion Theory*. Springer-Verlag, 1990.

[Sha81]  E. Shapiro. Inductive inference of theories from facts. Technical Report 192, Computer Science Department, Yale University, 1981.

[Shi91]  T. Shinohara. Inductive inference of monotonic formal systems from positive data. *New Generation Computing*, 8:371–384, 1991.

[Shi94]  T. Shinohara. Rich classes inferable from positive data: Length–bounded elementary formal systems. *Information and Computation*, 108:175–186, 1994.

[Smu61]  R. Smullyan. *Theory of Formal Systems, Annals of Mathematical Studies, No. 47.* Princeton, NJ, 1961.

[SSV97]  A. Sharma, F. Stephan, and Y. Ventsov. Generalized notions of mind change complexity. In *Proceedings of the Tenth Annual Conference on Computational Learning Theory*, pages 96–108. ACM Press, 1997.

[Wri89]  K. Wright. Identification of unions of languages drawn from an identifiable class. In R. Rivest, D. Haussler, and M. Warmuth, editors, *Proceedings of the Second Annual Workshop on Computational Learning Theory*, pages 328–333. Morgan Kaufmann, 1989.

[Yam93]  A. Yamamoto. Generalized unification as background knowledge in learning logic programs. In K. Jantke, S. Kobayashi, E. Tomita, and T. Yokomori, editors, *Algorithmic Learning Theory: Fourth International Workshop (ALT '93)*, volume 744 of *Lecture Notes in Artificial Intelligence*, pages 111–122. Springer-Verlag, 1993.

# Regularized Principal Manifolds*

Alex J. Smola[1], Robert C. Williamson[2],
Sebastian Mika[1], Bernhard Schölkopf[1]

[1] GMD FIRST, Rudower Chaussee 5, 12489 Berlin, Germany
[2] Department of Engineering, Australian National University, Canberra, Australia

**Abstract.** Many settings of unsupervised learning can be viewed as quantization problems — the minimization of the expected quantization error subject to some restrictions. This allows the use of tools such as regularization from the theory of (supervised) risk minimization for unsupervised settings. Moreover, this setting is very closely related to both principal curves and the generative topographic map.
We explore this connection in two ways: 1) we propose an algorithm for finding principal manifolds that can be regularized in a variety of ways. Experimental results demonstrate the feasibility of the approach. 2) We derive uniform convergence bounds and hence bounds on the learning rates of the algorithm. In particular, we give good bounds on the covering numbers which allows us to obtain a nearly optimal learning rate of order $O(m^{-\frac{1}{2}+\alpha})$ for certain types of regularization operators, where $m$ is the sample size and $\alpha$ an arbitrary positive constant.

## 1 Introduction

The problems of unsupervised learning are much less precisely defined than those of supervised learning. Usually no explicit cost function exists by which the hypthesis can be compared with training data. Instead, one has to make assumptions on the data, with respect to which questions may be asked.

A possible goal would be to look for reliable feature extractors, a setting that can be shown to lead to Kernel Principal Component Analysis [8]. Another option is to look for properties that represent the data best. This means leads to a *descriptive* model of the data (and possibly also a quite crude model of the underlying probability distribution). Principal Curves [6], the Generative Topographic Mapping [2], several linear Gaussian models, or also simple vector quantizers [1] are examples thereof.

We will study this type of models in the present paper. As many problems of unsupervised learning can be formalized in a quantization functional setting, this will allow to use techniques from regularization theory. In particular this

---

* This work was supported in part by grants of the ARC and the DFG (Ja 379/71 and Ja 379/51). Moreover we thank Balazs Kégl and Adam Krzyżak for helpful comments and discussions.

leads to a natural generalization (to higher dimensionality and different criteria of regularity) of the principal curves algorithm with a length constraint [7]. See also [4] for an overview and background on principal curves. Experimental results demonstrate the feasibility of this approach.

In the second part we use the quantization functional approach to give uniform convergence bounds. In particular we derive a bound on the covering/entropy number, using functional analytic tools with respect to the $L_\infty(\ell_2^d)$ metric. This allows us to give a bound on the rate of convergence by $O(m^{-\frac{1}{2}+\alpha})$ for arbitrary positive $\alpha$ where $m$ is the number of examples seen. For specific kernels this improves on the rate in [7] which is $O(m^{-\frac{1}{3}})$. Curiously, using our approach and a regularization operator equivalent to that implicitly used in [7] results in a weaker bound of $O(m^{-\frac{1}{4}})$. We suggest a possible reason for this in the penultimate section of the paper.

## 2 The Quantization Error Functional

Denote by $\mathcal{X}$ a vector space and $X := \{x_1, \ldots, x_m\} \subset \mathcal{X}$ a dataset drawn iid from an underlying probability distribution $\mu(x)$. Moreover consider index sets $\mathcal{Z}$, maps $f : \mathcal{Z} \to \mathcal{X}$, and classes $\mathcal{F}$ of such maps (with $f \in \mathcal{F}$).

Here the map $f$ is supposed to describe some basic properties of $\mu(x)$. In particular one seeks such $f$ that the so-called quantization error

$$R[f] := \int_{\mathcal{X}} \min_{z \in \mathcal{Z}} \|x - f(z)\|^2 d\mu(x) \tag{1}$$

is minimized. Unfortunately, this is unsolvable, as $\mu$ is generally unknown. Hence one replaces $\mu$ by the empirical density $\mu_m(x) := \frac{1}{m} \sum_{i=1}^m \delta(x - x_i)$ and instead of (1) analyzes the empirical quantization error

$$R_{\text{emp}}[f] := \frac{1}{m} \sum_{i=1}^m \min_{z \in \mathcal{Z}} \|x_i - f(z)\|^2. \tag{2}$$

Many problems of unsupervised learning can be cast in the form of finding a minimizer of (1) or (2). Let us consider some practical examples.

*Example 1 (Sample Mean).* Define $\mathcal{Z} := \{1\}$, $f : 1 \to f_1$ with $f_1 \in \mathcal{X}$, and $\mathcal{F}$ to be the set of all such functions. Then the minimum of

$$R[f] := \int_{\mathcal{X}} \|x - f_1\|^2 d\mu(x) \tag{3}$$

denotes the variance of the data and the minimizers of the quantization functionals can be determined analytically by

$$\operatorname*{argmin}_{f \in \mathcal{F}} R[f] = \int_{\mathcal{X}} x d\mu(x) \quad \text{and} \quad \operatorname*{argmin}_{f \in \mathcal{F}} R_{\text{emp}}[f] = \frac{1}{m} \sum_{i=1}^m x_i. \tag{4}$$

This is the (empirical) sample mean. Via the law of large numbers $R_{emp}[f]$ and its minimizer converge to $R[f]$ and the corresponding minimizer (which is already a uniform convergence statement).

*Example 2 (k–Vectors Quantization).* Define $\mathcal{Z} := \{1, \ldots, k\}$, $f : i \to f_i$ with $f_i \in \mathcal{X}$, and $\mathcal{F}$ to be the set of all such functions. Then

$$R[f] := \int_{\mathcal{X}} \min_{z \in \{1, \ldots, k\}} \|x - f_z\|^2 d\mu(x) \qquad (5)$$

denotes the canonical distortion error of a vector quantizer. In practice one uses the $k$–means algorithm to find a set of vectors $\{f_1, \ldots, f_k\}$ minimizing $R_{emp}[f]$. Also here [1], one can prove convergence properties of (the minimizer) of $R_{emp}[f]$ to (the one of) $R[f]$.

Instead of discrete quantization one can also consider a mapping onto a manifold of lower dimensionality than the input space. PCA can also be viewed in this way [6]:

*Example 3 (Principal Components).* Define $\mathcal{Z} := \mathbb{R}$, $f : z \to f_0 + z \cdot f_1$ with $f_0, f_1 \in \mathcal{X}$, $\|f_1\| = 1$, and $\mathcal{F}$ to be the set of all such line segments. Then the minimizer of

$$R[f] := \int_{\mathcal{X}} \min_{z \in [0,1]} \|x - f_0 - z \cdot f_1\|^2 d\mu(x) \qquad (6)$$

yields a line parallel to the direction of largest variance in $\mu(x)$ [6].

Based on the properties of the current example, Hastie & Stuetzle [6] carried this idea further by also allowing other than linear functions $f(z)$.

*Example 4 (Principal Curves and Surfaces).* Denote $\mathcal{Z} := [0,1]^D$ (with $D > 1$ for principal surfaces), $f : z \to f(z)$ with $f \in \mathcal{F}$ be a class of continuous $\mathbb{R}^d$-valued continuous functions (possibly with further restrictions). The minimizer of

$$R[f] := \int_{\mathcal{X}} \min_{z \in [0,1]^D} \|x - f(z)\|^2 d\mu(x) \qquad (7)$$

is not well defined, unless $\mathcal{F}$ is a compact set. Moreover, even the minimizer of $R_{emp}[f]$ is not well defined either, in general. In fact, it is an ill posed problem in the sense of Arsenin and Tikhonow [10]. Until recently [7], no convergence properties of $R_{emp}[f]$ to $R[f]$ could be stated.

Kégl et al. [7] modified the original "principal–curves" algorithm, in order to prove bounds on $R[f]$ in terms of $R_{emp}[f]$ and to show that the resulting estimate is well defined. The changes imply a restriction of $\mathcal{F}$ to polygonal lines with a fixed number of knots and, most importantly, *fixed* length $L$.[1] Instead of the latter

---

[1] In practice Kegl et al. use a constraint on the angles of a polygonal curve rather than the actual length constraint to achieve sample complexity rates on the training time. For the uniform convergence part, however, the length constraint is used.

we now consider smoothness constraints on the estimated curve $f(x)$. This is done via a regularization operator. As well as allowing greater freedom in the choice of regularizer (which, as we show, can lead to faster convergence), the regularization operator framework can be extended to situations where $D > 1$. Thus we can provide theoretical insight into principal manifold algorithms.

## 3 Invariant Regularizers

As a first step we will show that the class of admissible operators can be restricted to scalar ones, provided some basic assumption about scaling behavior and permutation symmetry are imposed.

**Proposition 1 (Homogeneous Invariant Regularization).** *Any regularizer* $Q[f]$ *that is both homogeneous quadratic and invariant under an irreducible orthogonal representation* $\rho$ *of the group* $\mathcal{G}$ *on* $\mathcal{X}$, *i.e. satisfies*

$$Q[f] \geq 0 \text{ for all } f \in \mathcal{F} \tag{8}$$

$$Q[af] = a^2 Q[f] \text{ for all scalars } a \tag{9}$$

$$Q[\rho(g)f] = Q[f] \text{ for all } \rho(g) \in \mathcal{G} \tag{10}$$

*is of the form* $Q[f] = \langle Pf, Pf \rangle$ *where* $P$ *is a "scalar" operator.*

**Proof.** It follows directly from (9) and Euler's "homogeneity property", that $Q[f]$ is a quadratic form, thus $Q[f] = \langle f, Mf \rangle$ for some operator $M$. Moreover $M$ can be written as $P^*P$ as it has to be positive (cf. (8)).

Finally from $\langle Pf, Pf \rangle = \langle P\rho(g)f, P\rho(g)f \rangle$ and the polarization equation it follows that $P^*P\rho(g) = \rho(g)P^*P$ has to hold for any $\rho(g) \in \mathcal{G}$. Thus, by virtue of Schur's lemma (cf. e.g. [5]) $P^*P$ only may be a scalar operator. Without loss of generality, also $P$ may be assumed to be scalar. ∎

A consequence is that there exists no "vector valued" regularization operator satisfying the invariance conditions. Hence it is useless to look for other operators $P$ in the presence of a sufficiently strong invariance.

Under the assumptions of proposition 1 both the canonical representation of the permutation group in a finite dimensional vector space $\mathcal{X}$ and the group of orthogonal transformations on $\mathcal{X}$ enforce scalar operators $P$. This follows immediately from the fact that these groups are unitary and irreducible on $\mathcal{X}$ by construction. Thus in the following we will only consider scalar operators $P$.

## 4 A Regularized Quantization Functional

We now propose a variant to minimizing the empirical quantization functional which leads to an algorithm that is more amenable to implementation. Moreover, uniform convergence bounds can be obtained for the classes of smooth curves induced by this approach. For this purpose, a regularized version of the empirical quantization functional is needed.

$$R_{\text{reg}}[f] := R_{\text{emp}}[f] + \frac{\lambda}{2}\|Pf\|^2 = \sum_{i=1}^{m} \min_{z \in \mathcal{Z}} \|x_i - f(z)\|^2 + \frac{\lambda}{2}\|Pf\|^2. \quad (11)$$

Here $P$ is a *scalar* regularization operator in the sense of Arsenin and Tikhonov, penalizing unsmooth functions $f$ (see [9] for details). (See some examples in section 4.2.) For the sake of finding principal manifolds, utilizing a scalar regularization operator simply means all curves or surfaces which can be transformed into each other by rotations should be penalized equally.

Using the results of [9] regarding the connection between regularization operators and kernels it appears suitable to choose a kernel expansion of $f$ matching the regularization operator $P$, i.e. $\langle Pk(x_i, \cdot), Pk(x_j, \cdot)\rangle = k(x_i, x_j)$. Finally assume $P^*Pf_0 = 0$, i.e. constant functions are not regularized. For an expansion like

$$f(z) = f_0 + \sum_{i=1}^{M} \alpha_i k(z_i, z) \text{ with } z_i \in \mathcal{Z}, \ \alpha_i \in \mathcal{X}, \text{ and } k : \mathcal{Z}^2 \to \mathbb{R} \quad (12)$$

with some previously chosen nodes $z_1, \ldots, z_M$ (of which one takes as many as one may afford in terms of computational cost) the regularization term can be written as

$$\|Pf\|^2 = \sum_{i,j=1}^{M} \langle \alpha_i, \alpha_j \rangle k(z_i, z_j). \quad (13)$$

What remains is to find an algorithm that minimizes $R_{\text{reg}}$. This is achieved by coordinate descent. In the following we will assume the data to be centered and therefore drop the term $f_0$. This greatly simplifies the notation.

## 4.1  An Algorithm for minimizing $R_{\text{reg}}[f]$

Minimizing the regularized quantization functional for a given kernel expansion is equivalent to solving

$$\min_{\substack{\{\alpha_1,\ldots,\alpha_M\} \subset \mathcal{X} \\ \{\zeta_1,\ldots,\zeta_m\} \subset \mathcal{Z}}} \left[ \sum_{i=1}^{m} \left\| x_i - \sum_{j=1}^{M} \alpha_j k(\zeta_i, z_j) \right\|^2 + \frac{\lambda}{2} \sum_{i,j=1}^{M} \langle \alpha_i, \alpha_j \rangle k(z_i, z_j) \right]. \quad (14)$$

This is achieved in an iterative fashion analogously to how the EM algorithm operates. One iterates over minimizing (14) with respect to $\{\zeta_1, \ldots, \zeta_m\}$, equivalent to the projection step, and $\{\alpha_1, \ldots, \alpha_M\}$, which corresponds to the expectation step. This is repeated until convergence, in practice, until the regularized quantization functional does not decrease significantly any further. One obtains:
Projection: For each $i \in \{1, \ldots, m\}$ choose $\zeta_i := \text{argmin}_{\zeta \in \mathcal{Z}} \|f(\zeta) - x_i\|^2$. Clearly,

for fixed $\alpha_i$, the so chosen $\zeta_i$ minimizes the term in (14), which in turn is equal to $R_{\text{reg}}[f]$ for given $\alpha_i$ and $X$. Adaptation: Now the parameters $\zeta_i$ are fixed and $\alpha_i$ is adapted such that $R_{\text{reg}}[f]$ decreases further. For fixed $\zeta_i$ differentiation of (14) with respect to $\alpha_i$ yields

$$\left(\frac{\lambda}{2}K_z + K_\zeta^\top K_\zeta\right)\alpha = K_\zeta^\top X \tag{15}$$

where $(K_z)_{ij} := k(z_i, z_j)$ is an $M \times M$ matrix and $(K_\zeta)_{ij} := k(\zeta_i, z_j)$ is $m \times M$. Moreover, with slight abuse of notation, $\alpha$, and $X$ denote the *matrix* of all parameters, and samples, respectively. The term in (14) keeps on decreasing until the algorithm converges to a (local) minimum. What remains is to find good starting values. Initialization If not dealing, as assumed, with centered data, set $f_0$ to the sample mean, i.e. $f_0 = \frac{1}{m}\sum_{i=1}^m x_i$. Moreover, choose the coefficients $\alpha_i$ such that $f$ approximately points into the directions of the first $D$ principal components given by the matrix $V := (v_1, \ldots, v_D)$. This is done as follows, analogously to the initialization in the generative topographic map [2, eq. (2.20)].

$$\min_{\{\alpha_1,\ldots,\alpha_M\}\subset\mathcal{X}}\left[\sum_{i=1}^M\left\|V(z_i - z_0) - \sum_{j=1}^M\alpha_j k(z_i, z_j)\right\|^2 + \frac{\lambda}{2}\sum_{i,j=1}^M\langle\alpha_i, \alpha_j\rangle k(z_i, z_j)\right]. \tag{16}$$

Thus $\alpha$ is given by the solution of $\left(\frac{\lambda}{2}\mathbf{1} + K_z\right)\alpha = V(Z - Z_0)$ where $Z$ denoted the matrix of $z_i$, $z_0$ the mean of $z_i$, and $Z_0$ the matrix of $z_0$ correspondingly.

The derivation of this algorithm was quite ad hoc, however, there are similar precursors in the literature. An example are principal curves with a length constraint. We will show below that for a particular choice of a regularizer, minimizing (11) is equivalent to the latter.

## 4.2 Examples of Regularizers

By choosing $P := \partial_z$, i.e. the differentiation operator, $\|Pf\|^2$ becomes an integral over the squared "speed" of the curve. Reparameterizing $f$ to constant speed leaves the empirical quantization error unchanged, whereas the regularization term is minimized. This can be seen as follows: by construction $\int_{[0,1]}\|\partial_z f(z)\|dz$ does not depend on the (re)parameterization. The variance, however, is minimal for a constant function, hence $\|\partial_z f(z)\|$ has to be constant over interval $[0, 1]$. Thus $\|Pf\|^2$ equals the squared length $L^2$ of the curve at the optimal solution.

One can show that minimizing the empirical quantization error plus a regularizer is equivalent to minimizing the empirical quantization error for a fixed value of the regularization term (for $\lambda$ adjusted suitably). Hence the proposed algorithm is equivalent to finding the optimal curve with a length constraint, i.e. it is equivalent to the algorithm proposed by [7].[2]

---

[2] The reasoning is slightly incorrect — $f$ *cannot* be completely reparameterized to constant speed, as it is an expansion in terms of a *finite* number of nodes. However the basic properties still hold, provided the number of kernels is sufficiently high.

In the experiments we chose a Gaussian RBF kernel $k(x, x') = \exp(-\frac{\|x-x'\|^2}{2\sigma^2})$. This corresponds to a regularizer penalizing all orders of derivatives simultaneously. In particular [14] show that this kernel corresponds to the pseudodifferential operator defined by

$$\|Pf\|^2 = \int dx \sum_{n=0}^{\infty} \frac{\sigma^{2n}}{n!2^n} (O^n f(x))^2 \tag{17}$$

with $O^{2n} = \Delta^n$ and $O^{2n+1} = \nabla\Delta^n$, $\Delta$ being the Laplacian and $\nabla$ the gradient operator. This means that one is looking not only for smooth functions but also curves whose curvature and other higher-order properties change very slowly. For more details on regularization operators see e.g. [9].

### 4.3   The Connection to the GTM

Just considering the basic algorithm of the GTM (without the Bayesian framework), one can observe that it minimizes a rather similar quantity to $R_{\text{reg}}[f]$. It differs in its choice of $\mathcal{Z}$, which is chosen to be a grid, identical with the points $z_i$ in our setting, and the different regularizer (called Gaussian prior in that case) which is of $\ell_2$ type. In other words instead of using $\|Pf\|^2$ Bishop et al. [2] choose $\sum_i \|\alpha_i\|^2$ as a regularizer. Finally in the GTM several $\zeta_i$ may take on "responsibility" for having generated a data-point $x_i$ (this follows naturally from the generative model setting in the latter case).

Note that unlike in the GTM (cf. [2, sec. 2.3]) the number of nodes (for the kernel expansion) is not a critical parameter. This is due to the fact that there is a *coupling* between the single centers of the basis functions $k(z_i, z_j)$ via the regularization operator. If needed, one could also see the proposed algorithm in a Gaussian Process context (see [12]) — the data $X$ then should be interpreted as created by a homogeneous process mapping from $\mathcal{Z}$ to $\mathcal{X}$. Finally the use of periodical kernels (cf. [9]) allows one to model circular structures in $\mathcal{X}$.

## 5   Experiments

In order to show that the basic idea of the proposed algorithm is sound, we ran several toy experiments (cf. figure 1). In all cases Gaussian rbf kernels, as discussed in section 4.2, were used. We generated different data sets in 2 and 3 dimensions from 1 or 2 dimensional parameterizations. Then we applied our algorithm using the prior knowledge about the original parameterization dimension of the data set in choosing the latent variable space to have the appropriate size. For almost any parameter setting ($\lambda$, $M$, and width of basis functions) we obtained reasonable results.

We found that for a suitable choice of the regularization factor $\lambda$ a very close match to the original distribution can be achieved. The number and width of the basis functions had of course an effect on the solution, too. But their influence on the basic characteristics is quite small.

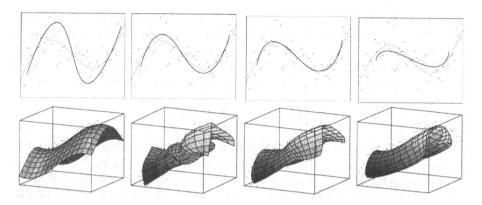

**Fig. 1.** Upper 4 images. We generated a dataset (small dots) by adding noise to a distribution indicated by the dotted line. The resulting manifold generated by our approach is given by the solid line (over a parameter range of $\mathcal{Z} = [-1, 1]$). From left to right we used different values for the regularization parameter $\lambda = 0.1, 0.5, 1, 4$. The width and number of basis function was constant 1, and 10 respectively. Lower 4 images. Here we generated a dataset by sampling (with noise) from a distribution depicted in the left most image (small dots are the sampled data). The remaining three images show the manifold yielded by our approach over the parameter space $\mathcal{Z} = [-1, 1]^2$ for $\lambda = 0.001, 0.1, 1$. The width and number of basis functions was constant (1 and 36).

Finally, figure 2 shows the convergence properties of the algorithm. One can clearly observe that the overall regularized quantization error decreases for each step, while both the regularization term and the quantization error term are free to vary. This experimentally shows that the algorithm finds a (local) minimum of $R_{reg}[f]$.

## 6 Uniform Convergence Bounds

We now proceed to an analysis of the rate of convergence of the above algorithm. To avoid several technicalities (like boundedness of some moments of the

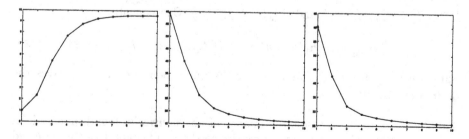

**Fig. 2.** Left: regularization term, middle: empirical quantization error, right: regularized quantization error vs. number of iterations.

distribution $\mu(x)$ [11]) we will assume that there exists a ball of radius $r$ such that $\Pr\{\|x\| \le r\} = 1$ for all $x$. Kégl et al. [7] showed that under these assumptions also the prinicial manifold $f$ is contained in the ball $U_r$ of radius $r$, hence the quantization error will be no larger than $(2r)^2$ for all $x$. In order to derive uniform convergence bounds let us introduce the $L_\infty(\ell_2^d)$ norm on $\mathcal{F}$ (assumed continuous)

$$\|f\|_{L_\infty(\ell_2^d)} := \sup_{z \in \mathcal{Z}} \|f(z)\|_{\ell_2^d} \tag{18}$$

where the $\|\cdot\|_{\ell_2^d}$ denotes the Euclidean norm in $d$ dimensions. The metric is induced by the norm in the usual fashion. Given a metric $\rho$ and a set $\mathcal{F}$, the $\epsilon$ covering number of $\mathcal{F}$, denoted $\mathcal{N}(\epsilon, \mathcal{F}, \rho)$ (also $\mathcal{N}_\epsilon$ when the dependency is obvious), is the smallest number of $\rho$-balls of radius the union of which contains $\mathcal{F}$.

The next two results are similar in their style to the bounds obtained in [7], however slightly streamlined, as they are independent of some technical conditions on $\mathcal{F}$ as needed in [7].

**Proposition 2 ($L_\infty(\ell_2^d)$ bounds for Principal Manifolds).**
*Denote by $\mathcal{F}$ a class of continuous functions from $\mathcal{Z}$ into $\mathcal{X} \subseteq U_r$ and let $\mu$ be a distribution over $\mathcal{X}$. If $m$ points are drawn i.i.d. from $\mu$, then for all $\eta > 0, \epsilon \in (0, \eta/2)$*

$$\Pr\left\{\sup_{f \in \mathcal{F}} \left|R_{\text{emp}}^m[f] - R[f]\right| > \eta\right\} \le 2\mathcal{N}\left(\tfrac{\epsilon}{8r}, \mathcal{F}, L_\infty(\ell_2^d)\right) e^{-m(\eta-\epsilon)^2/(2r^2)}.$$

**Proof.** By definition of $R_{\text{emp}}^m[f] = \sum_{i=1}^m \min_z \|f(z) - x_i\|^2$ the empirical quantization functional is a sum of $m$ iid random variables which are each bounded by $4r^2$ due to the fact that $x$ is contained in a ball of radius $r$. Hence we may apply Hoeffding's inequality to obtain

$$\Pr\left\{\left|R_{\text{emp}}^m[f] - R[f]\right| \ge \eta\right\} \le 2e^{-m\eta^2/(2r^2)}. \tag{19}$$

By the Lipschitz property of the $\ell_2^d$ norm (the 'target' values are bounded by $r$), a $\frac{\epsilon}{8r}$ cover of $\mathcal{F}$ is an $\frac{\epsilon}{2}$ cover of the loss function induced class: For every $f \in \mathcal{F}$ there exists some $f_i \in \mathcal{N}_{\epsilon/8r}$ such that $\|f_i - f\|_{L_\infty^{2m}(\ell_2^d)}^2 \le \frac{\epsilon}{2}$. Hence also $|R_{\text{emp}}^m[f] - R_{\text{emp}}^m[f_i]| \le \frac{\epsilon}{2}$ and $|R[f] - R[f_i]| \le \frac{\epsilon}{2}$. Consequently

$$\Pr\left\{\left|R_{\text{emp}}^m[f] - R[f]\right| \ge \eta\right\} \le \Pr\left\{\left|R_{\text{emp}}^m[f_i] - R[f_i]\right| \ge \eta - \epsilon\right\} \tag{20}$$

Substituting (20) into (19) and taking the union bound over $\mathcal{N}_{\epsilon/8r}$ gives the desired result. ∎

This result is useful to assess the quality of an *empirically* found manifold. In order to obtain rates of convergence we also need a result connecting the expected quantization error of the principal manifold $f_{\text{emp}}^*$ minimizing $R_{\text{emp}}^m[f]$ and the manifold $f^*$ with minimal quantization error $R[f^*]$.

**Proposition 3 (Rates of Convergence for Optimal Estimates).**
*With the definitions of Proposition 2 and the definition of $f^*_{emp}$ and $f^*$ one has*

$$\Pr\left\{\sup_{f\in\mathcal{F}}\left|R[f^*_{emp}]-R[f^*]\right|>\eta\right\}\leq 2\left(\mathcal{N}\left(\tfrac{\varepsilon}{4r},\mathcal{F},L_\infty(\ell_2^d)\right)+1\right)e^{-\frac{m(\eta-\varepsilon)^2}{8r^2}}.$$

**Proof.** The proof is similar to the one of proposition 2, however uses $\mathcal{N}_{\varepsilon/4r}$ and $\eta/2$ to bound $R[f^*_{emp}]$

$$R[f^*_{emp}]-R[f^*] = R[f^*_{emp}]-R_{emp}[f^*_{emp}]+R_{emp}[f^*_{emp}]-R[f^*] \quad (21)$$
$$\leq \varepsilon + R[f_i]-R_{emp}[f_i]+R_{emp}[f^*_{emp}]-R[f^*] \quad (22)$$
$$\leq \varepsilon + 2\max_{f\in\mathcal{N}_\varepsilon\cup\{f^*\}}|R[f]-R_{emp}[f]| \quad (23)$$

where $f_i\in\mathcal{N}_\varepsilon$ and clearly $R_{emp}[f^*_{emp}]\leq R_{emp}[f^*]$. Now apply Hoeffding's inequality, the union bound and change $\eta+\varepsilon$ into $\eta$ to prove the claim. ∎

After that we provided a number of uniform convergence bounds it is now necessary to bound $\mathcal{N}$ in a suitable way.

# 7  Covering and Entropy Numbers

Before going into details let us briefly review what already exists in terms of bounds on the covering number $\mathcal{N}$ for $L_\infty(\ell_2^d)$ metrics. Kégl et al. [7] essentially show that

$$\log\mathcal{N}(\varepsilon,\mathcal{F}) = O(\tfrac{1}{\varepsilon}) \quad (24)$$

under the following assumptions: They consider polygonal curves $f(\cdot)$ of length $L$ in a sphere $U_r$ of radius $r$ in $\mathcal{X}$. The distance measure (no metric!) for $\mathcal{N}(\varepsilon)$ is defined as $\sup_{x\in U_r}|\Delta(x,f)-\Delta(x,f')|\leq\varepsilon$. Here $\Delta(x,f)$ is the minimum distance between a curve $f(\cdot)$ and $x\in U_r$.

By using functional analytic tools [13] one can obtain more general results, which then, in turn, can replace (24) to obtain better bounds on the expected quantization error by using the properties of the regularization operator.

Denote by $\mathcal{L}(E,F)$ the set of all bounded linear operators $T$ between two normed spaces $(E,\|\cdot\|_E)$, $(F,\|\cdot\|_F)$. The $n$th *entropy number* of a set $M\subset E$ relative to a metric $\rho$, for $n\in\mathbf{N}$, is

$$\epsilon_n(M) := \inf\{\epsilon\colon\mathcal{N}(\varepsilon,M,\rho)\leq n\}$$

The *entropy numbers of an operator* $T\in\mathcal{L}(E,F)$ are defined as

$$\epsilon_n(T) := \epsilon_n(T(U_E)). \quad (25)$$

Note that $\epsilon_1(T)=\|T\|$, and that $\epsilon_n(T)$ certainly is well defined for all $n\in\mathbf{N}$ if $T$ is a *compact operator*, i.e. if $T(U_E)$ is compact.

What will be done in the following is to bound the entropy number of parametrized curves in $L_\infty(\ell_2^d)$ satisfying the constraint $\|Pf(\cdot)\|^2 \leq \Lambda$ by viewing

$$\mathcal{F}_\Lambda := \{f : \mathcal{Z} \ni z \mapsto f(z) \in \mathbb{R}^d : f \text{ is continuous, } \|Pf\| \leq \Lambda\}$$

as the image of the unit ball under an operator $T$. A key tool in bounding the relevant entropy number is the following factorization result.

**Lemma 1 (Carl and Stephani [3, p. 11]).** *Let $E, F, G$ be Banach spaces, $R \in \mathcal{L}(F, G)$, and $S \in \mathcal{L}(E, F)$. Then, for $n, t \in \mathbb{N}$,*

$$\epsilon_{nt}(RS) \leq \epsilon_n(R)\epsilon_t(S), \quad \epsilon_n(RS) \leq \epsilon_n(R)\|S\|, \quad \epsilon_n(RS) \leq \epsilon_n(S)\|R\|. \tag{26}$$

As one is dealing with vector valued functions $\mathcal{F}_\Lambda$, it handy to view $f(\cdot)$ as generated by a linear $d = \dim \mathcal{X}$ dimensional operator in feature space, i.e. $f(z) = W\Phi(z) = (\langle w_1, \Phi(z)\rangle, \ldots, \langle w_d, \Phi(z)\rangle)$ with $\|W\|^2 := \sum_{i=1}^d \|w\|^2$. Here the inner product $\langle \cdot, \cdot \rangle$ is given by the regularization operator $P$ as

$$\langle f, g \rangle := \langle Pf, Pg \rangle_{L_2} = \int (Pf)(x)dx \tag{27}$$

where the latter was described in section 3. In practice $w$ is expanded in terms of kernel functions $k(x_i, \cdot)$. The latter can be shown to represent the map from $\mathcal{Z}$ into the associated Reproducing Kernel Hilbert Space (RKHS) [9] (sometimes called feature space). Hence $\Phi(x) = k(x_i, \cdot)$, where the dot product is given by (27). These techniques may be used to give uniform convergence bounds, which are stated in terms of the eigenvalues $\lambda_i$ of the RKHS.

**Proposition 4 (Williamson, Smola, and Schölkopf [13]).** *Let $\Phi(\cdot)$ be the map onto the eigensystem introduced by a Mercer kernel $k$ with eigenvalues $\lambda_i$, $C_k$ a constant of the kernel, and $A$ be the diagonal map*

$$A : \mathbb{R}^N \to \mathbb{R}^N, \qquad A : (x_j)_j \mapsto A(x_j)_j = (a_j x_j)_j. \tag{28}$$

*Then $A^{-1}$ maps $\Phi(\mathcal{X})$ into a ball of finite radius $R_A = C_k \|(\sqrt{\lambda_j} a_j)_j\|_{\ell_2}$, centered at the origin if and only if $(\sqrt{\lambda_j} a_j)_j \in \ell_2$.*

The evaluation operator $S$ plays a crucial role to deal with entire classes of functions (instead of just a single $f(\cdot)$). It is defined as

$$S_{\Phi(z)} : (\ell_2)^d \to L_\infty(\ell_2^d) \text{ and } S_{\Phi(z)} : W \mapsto (\langle w_1, \Phi(\mathcal{Z})\rangle, \ldots, \langle w_d, \Phi(\mathcal{Z})\rangle). \tag{29}$$

By a technical argument one can see that it is possible to replace $(\ell_2)^d$ by $\ell_2$ without further worry — simply reindex the coefficients by

$$\begin{aligned} I_d &: (\ell_2)^d \to \ell_2 \\ I_d &: \begin{array}{l} ((w_{11}, w_{12}, \ldots), (w_{21}, w_{22}, \ldots), \ldots, (w_{d1}, w_{d2}, \ldots)) \to \\ (w_{11}, w_{21}, \ldots, w_{d1}, w_{12}, w_{22}, \ldots, w_{d2}, w_{13}, \ldots) \end{array} \end{aligned} \tag{30}$$

By construction $I_d U_{(\ell_2)^d} = U_{\ell_2}$ and vice versa, thus $\|I_d\| = \|I_d^{-1}\| = 1$. Before proceeding to the actual theorem one has to define a scaling operator $A_d$ for the multi output case as the $d$ times tensor product of A, i.e.

$$A_d : (\ell_2)^d \to (\ell_2)^d \text{ and } A_d := \underbrace{A \times A \times \ldots \times A}_{d\text{-times}} \tag{31}$$

**Theorem 1 (Bounds for Principal Curves Classes).** *Let $k$ be a Mercer kernel, be $\Phi$ the corresponding map into feature space, and let $T := S_{\Phi(Z)}\Lambda$ where $S_{\Phi(Z)}$ is given by (29) and $\Lambda \in \mathbb{R}^+$. Let A be defined by (28) and $A_d$ by (31). Then the entropy numbers of $T$ satisfy the following inequality:*

$$\epsilon_n(T) \leq \Lambda\epsilon_n(A_d) \tag{32}$$

**Proof.** As pointed out before one has to use a factorization argument. In particular one uses the following property.

$$\begin{array}{ccc}
U_{\ell_2} & \xrightarrow{\quad T \quad} & L_\infty(\ell_2^d) \\
I_d^{-1} \downarrow & \quad S_{\Phi(Z)} \nearrow \quad & \uparrow S_{(A^{-1}\Phi(Z))} \\
U_{(\ell_2)^d} & \xrightarrow{\Lambda} \Lambda U_{(\ell_2)^d} \xrightarrow{A_d} & \Lambda\mathcal{E}_d
\end{array} \tag{33}$$

In other words one exploits

$$\epsilon_n\left(S_{\Phi(Z)}\left(\Lambda U_{(\ell_2)^d}\right)\right) = \epsilon_n\left(S_{(A^{-1}\Phi(Z))}A_d\Lambda I_d^{-1}\right) \tag{34}$$

$$\leq \left\|S_{(A^{-1}\Phi(Z))}\right\|\epsilon_n(A_d)\Lambda\left\|I_d^{-1}\right\| \leq \Lambda\epsilon_n(A_d). \tag{35}$$

Here we have relied on Proposition 4 which says $A^{-1}\Phi(Z) \subset U$ and thus by Cauchy-Schwarz, $\|S_{(A^{-1}\Phi(Z))}\| \leq 1$. ∎

The price for dealing with vector valued functions is a degeneracy in the eigenvalues of $A_d$ — scaling factors appear $d$ times, instead of only once in the single output situation. From a theorem for degenerate eigenvalues of scaling operators [13] one immediately obtains the following corollary.

**Corollary 1 (Entropy numbers for the vector valued case).** *Let $k$ be a Mercer kernel, let A be defined by (28) and $A_d$ by (31). Then*

$$\epsilon_n(A_d: \ell_2 \to \ell_2) \leq \inf_{(a_s)_s: \left(\frac{\sqrt{\lambda_s}}{a_s}\right)_s \in \ell_2} \sup_{j \in \mathbb{N}} 6C_k\sqrt{d}\left\|\left(\frac{\sqrt{\lambda_s}}{a_s}\right)_s\right\|_{\ell_2} n^{-\frac{1}{j \cdot d}}(a_1 a_2 \cdots a_j)^{\frac{1}{j}}.$$

Note that the dimensionality of $Z$ does not affect these considerations directly, however it has to be taken into account implicitly by the decay of the eigenvalues [13] of the integral operator induced by $k$. $d$ appears twice — once due to the increased operator norm (the $\sqrt{d}$ term) for the scaling operator $A_d$, and secondly due to the slower decay properties (each scaling factor $a_i$ appears $d$ times).

The same techniques that led to the bounds on entropy numbers in [13] can also be applied here. As this is rather technical, we only sketch a similar result for the case of principal manifolds, for dim $\mathcal{Z} = 1$ and exponential polynomial decay of the eigenvalues $\lambda_i$ of the kernel $k$.

**Proposition 5 (Exponential–Polynomial decay).** *Suppose $k$ is a Mercer kernel with $\lambda_j = \beta^2 e^{-\alpha j^p}$ for some $\alpha, \beta, p > 0$. Then*

$$\ln \epsilon_n^{-1}(A_d \colon \ell_2 \to \ell_2) = O(\ln^{\frac{p}{p+1}} n) \tag{36}$$

**Proof.** We use a series $(a_j)_j = e^{-\tau/2 j^p}$. Then we bound

$$\sqrt{d} \left\| \left( \frac{\sqrt{\lambda_j}}{a_j} \right) \right\|_{j \ell_2} = \sqrt{d}\beta \left( \sum_{j=0}^{\infty} e^{(\tau-\alpha)j^p} \right)^{\frac{1}{2}} \le \sqrt{d}\beta \sqrt{1 + \int_0^{\infty} e^{(\tau-\alpha)t^p} dt}$$
$$= \sqrt{d}\beta \sqrt{1 + \frac{\Gamma(1/p)}{p(\alpha-\tau)^{1/p}}}$$

and $(a_1 a_2 \ldots a_j)^{\frac{1}{j}} = e^{-\frac{1}{2j}\tau \sum_{s=1}^{j} s^p} \le e^{-\tau \phi j^p}$ for some positive number $\phi$. For the purpose of finding an upper bound, $\sup_{j \in \mathbb{N}}$ can be replaced by $\sup_{j \in [1,\infty]}$. One computes $\sup_{j \in [1,\infty]} n^{-\frac{1}{dj}} e^{-\tau \phi j^p}$ which is obtained for some $j = \phi' \ln^{\frac{1}{p+1}} n$ and some $\phi' > 0$. Resubstitution yields the claimed rate of convergence for any $\tau \in (0, \alpha)$ which proves the theorem.[3] ∎

Possible kernels for which proposition 5 applies are Gaussian rbf, i.e. $k(x, x') = \exp(-\|x - x'\|^2)$ $(p = 2)$ and the "Damped Harmonic Oscillator", i.e. $k(x, x') = \frac{1}{1+\|x-x'\|^2}$ with $p = 1$. For more details on this issue see [13]. Finally one has to invert (36) to obtain a bound on $\mathcal{N}(\epsilon, \mathcal{F}_\Lambda)$. We have:

$$\ln \mathcal{N}\left( \frac{\epsilon}{\Lambda}, \mathcal{F}_\Lambda, L_\infty(\ell_2^d) \right) = O(-\ln^{\frac{p+1}{p}} \epsilon) \tag{37}$$

A similar result may be obtained for the case of polynomial decay in the eigenvalues of the Mercer kernel. Following [13] one gets:

**Proposition 6 (Polynomial decay).** *Suppose $k$ is a Mercer kernel with $\lambda_j = \beta^2 j^{-\alpha-1}$ for some $\alpha, \beta > 0$. Then $\epsilon_n^{-1}(A_d : \ell_2 \to \ell_2) = O(\ln^{\frac{\alpha}{2}} n)$.*

## 8  Rates of Convergence

It is of theoretical interest how well Principal Manifolds can be learned. Kégl et al. [7] have show a $O(m^{-1/3})$ result for principal curves $(D = 1)$ with length

---

[3] See [13] how exact constants can be obtained instead of solely asymptotical rates.

contraint regularizer. We show that if one utilizes a more powerful regularizer (as one can do using our algorithm) one can obtain a bound of the form $O(m^{-\frac{\alpha}{2(\alpha+1)}})$ for polynomial rates of decay of the eigenvalues of $k$ ($\alpha+1$ is the rate of decay); or $O(m^{-1/2+\alpha})$ for exponential rates of decay ($\alpha$ is an arbitrary positive constant). The latter is nearly optimal, as supervised learning rates are no better than $O(m^{-1/2})$.

## Proposition 7 (Learning Rates for Principal Manifolds).

*For any fixed $\mathcal{F}_\Lambda$ the learning rate of principal manifolds can be lower bounded by $O(m^{-1/2+\alpha})$ where $\alpha$ is an arbitrary positive constant, i.e.*

$$R[f^*_{\text{emp}}] - R[f^*] \leq O(m^{-1/2+\alpha}) \text{ for } f^*_{\text{emp}}, f^* \in \mathcal{F}_\Lambda \tag{38}$$

*if the eigenvalues of $k$ decay exponentially. Moreover the learning rate can be bounded by $O(m^{-\frac{\alpha}{2(\alpha+1)}})$ in the case of polynomially decaying eigenvalues with rate $\alpha + 1$. We obtain*

$$R[f^*_{\text{emp}}] - R[f^*] \leq O(m^{-\frac{\alpha}{2(\alpha+1)}}) \text{ for } f^*_{\text{emp}}, f^* \in \mathcal{F}_\Lambda \tag{39}$$

**Proof.** We use a clever trick from [7], however without the difficulty of also having to bound the approximation error. Proposition 3 will be useful.

$$
\begin{aligned}
R[f^*_{\text{emp}}] - R[f^*] &= \int_0^\infty \Pr\left\{ R[f^*_{\text{emp}}] - R[f^*] > \eta \right\} d\eta \\
&\leq u + \epsilon + 2(\mathcal{N}(\epsilon/4r) + 1) \int_{u+\epsilon}^\infty e^{-\frac{m(\eta-\epsilon)^2}{8r^2}} d\eta \\
&\leq u + \epsilon + \frac{8r^2}{um}(\mathcal{N}(\epsilon/4r) + 1)e^{-\frac{mu^2}{8r^2}} \\
&\leq \sqrt{\frac{8r^2 \ln(\mathcal{N}(\epsilon/4r)+1)}{m}} + \epsilon + \sqrt{\frac{8r^2}{m\ln(\mathcal{N}(\epsilon/4r)+1)}}
\end{aligned}
\tag{40}
$$

Here we used $\int_x^\infty \exp(-t^2/2)dt \leq \exp(-x^2/2)/x$ in the second step. The third inequality was derived by substituting $u^2 = \frac{8r^2}{m}\log(\mathcal{N}(\epsilon/4r) + 1)$.

Setting $\epsilon = \sqrt{1/m}$ and exploiting (37) yields

$$R[f^*_{\text{emp}}] - R[f^*] = O\left(\sqrt{\ln^{\frac{p+1}{p}} m/m}\right) + O(m^{-\frac{1}{2}}). \tag{41}$$

As $\ln^{\frac{p+1}{p}} m$ can be bounded by any $c_\alpha m^\alpha$ for suitably large $c_\alpha$ and $\alpha > 0$ one obtains the desired result. For polynomially decaying eigenvalues one obtains from proposition 6 that for a sufficiently large constant $c \ln \mathcal{N}\left(\epsilon/4r, \mathcal{F}, L_\infty(\ell_2^d)\right) \leq c\epsilon^{-\frac{2}{\alpha}}$. Substituting this into (40) yields

$$R[f^*_{\text{emp}}] - R[f^*] \leq \sqrt{\frac{2^{3-\frac{4}{\alpha}}r^{2-\frac{2}{\alpha}}c}{m}}\varepsilon^{-\frac{1}{\alpha}} + 2\epsilon + O(m^{-\frac{1}{2}}). \tag{42}$$

The minimum is obtained for $\epsilon = c'm^{-\frac{\alpha}{2(\alpha+1)}}$ for some $c' > 0$. Hence $m^{-\frac{1}{2}}\varepsilon^{-\frac{1}{\alpha}}$ is of order $O(m^{-\frac{\alpha}{2(\alpha+1)}})$, which proves the theorem. ∎

Interestingly the above result is slightly weaker than the result in [7] for the case of length constraints, as the latter corresponds to the differentiation operator, thus polynomial eigenvalue decay of order 2, i.e. $\alpha = 1$ and therefore to a rate $\frac{\alpha}{2(\alpha+1)} = \frac{1}{4}$ (Kégl et al. [7] obtain $\frac{1}{3}$). It is unclear, whether this is due to a (possibly) not optimal bound on the entropy numbers induced by $k$, or the fact that our results were stated in terms of the (stronger) $L_\infty(\ell_2^d)$ metric. This yet to be fully understood weakness should not detract from the fact that we *can* get better rates by using stronger regularizers, *and* our algorithm can utilize such regularizers.

## 9    Summing Up

We proposed a framework for unsupervised learning that can draw on the techniques available in minimization of risk functionals in supervised learning. This yielded an algorithm suitable to deal with principal manifolds. The expansion in terms of kernel functions and the treatment by regularization operators made it easier to decouple the algorithmic part (of finding a suitable manifold) from the part of specifying a class of manifolds with desirable properties. In particular, our algorithm does not crucially depend on the number of nodes used.

Sample size dependent bounds for principal manifolds were given which depend on the underlying distribution $\mu$ in a very mild way. These may be used to perform capacity control more effectively. Moreover our calculations have shown that regularized principal manifolds are a feasible way to perform unsupervised learning. The proofs largely rest on a connection between functional analysis and entropy numbers [13]. This fact also allowed us to give good bounds on the learning rate.

## References

1. P. Bartlett, T. Linder, and G. Lugosi. The minimax distortion redundancy in empirical quantizer design. *IEEE Transactions on Information Theory*, 44(5):1802–1813, 1998.
2. C.M. Bishop, M. Svensén, and C.K.I. Williams. GTM: The generative topographic mapping. *Neural Computation*, 10(1):215–234, 1998.
3. B. Carl and I. Stephani. *Entropy, compactness, and the approximation of operators.* Cambridge University Press, Cambridge, UK, 1990.
4. R. Der, U. Steinmetz, B. Balzuweit, and G. Schüürmann. Nonlinear principal component analysis. University of Leipzig, Preprint, http://www.informatik.uni-leipzig.de/der/Veroeff/npcafin.ps.gz, 1998.
5. M. Hamermesh. *Group theory and its applications to physical problems.* Addison Wesley, Reading, MA, 2 edition, 1962. Reprint by Dover, New York, NY.
6. T. Hastie and W. Stuetzle. Principal curves. *Journal of the American Statistical Association*, 84(406):502–516, 1989.
7. B. Kégl, A. Krzyżak, T. Linder, and K. Zeger. Learning and design of principal curves. *IEEE Transactions on Pattern Analysis and Machine Intelligence*, 1999. http://magenta.mast.queensu.ca/linder/psfiles/KeKrLiZe97.ps.gz.

8. B. Schölkopf, A. Smola, and K.-R. Müller. Nonlinear component analysis as a kernel eigenvalue problem. *Neural Computation*, 10:1299 – 1319, 1998.
9. A.J. Smola, B. Schölkopf, and K.-R. Müller. The connection between regularization operators and support vector kernels. *Neural Networks*, 11:637–649, 1998.
10. A. N. Tikhonov and V. Y. Arsenin. *Solution of Ill-Posed Problems*. Winston, Washington, DC, 1977.
11. V. N. Vapnik. *Estimation of Dependences Based on Empirical Data*. Springer-Verlag, Berlin, 1982.
12. C.K.I. Williams. Prediction with gaussian processes: From linear regression to linear prediction and beyond. *Learning and Inference in Graphical Models*, 1998.
13. R.C. Williamson, A.J. Smola, and B. Schölkopf. Generalization performance of regularization networks and support vector machines via entropy numbers of compact operators. NeuroCOLT NC-TR-98-019, Royal Holloway College, 1998.
14. A. Yuille and N. Grzywacz. The motion coherence theory. In *Proceedings of the International Conference on Computer Vision*, pages 344–354, Washington, D.C., December 1988. IEEE Computer Society Press.

# Distribution-Dependent Vapnik-Chervonenkis Bounds

Nicolas Vayatis[1,2,3] and Robert Azencott[1]

[1] Centre de Mathématiques et de Leurs Applications (CMLA),
Ecole Normale Supérieure de Cachan,
61, av. du Président Wilson - 94 235 Cachan Cedex, France
[2] Centre de Recherche en Epistémologie Appliquée (CREA),
Ecole Polytechnique,
91 128 Palaiseau Cedex, France
[3] Nicolas.Vayatis@cmla.ens-cachan.fr,
WWW home page: http://www.cmla.ens-cachan.fr/Utilisateurs/vayatis

**Abstract.** Vapnik-Chervonenkis (VC) bounds play an important role in statistical learning theory as they are the fundamental result which explains the generalization ability of learning machines. There have been consequent mathematical works on the improvement of VC rates of convergence of empirical means to their expectations over the years. The result obtained by Talagrand in 1994 seems to provide more or less the final word to this issue as far as universal bounds are concerned. Though for fixed distributions, this bound can be practically outperformed. We show indeed that it is possible to replace the $2\epsilon^2$ under the exponential of the deviation term by the corresponding Cramér transform as shown by large deviations theorems. Then, we formulate rigorous distribution-sensitive VC bounds and we also explain why these theoretical results on such bounds can lead to practical estimates of the effective VC dimension of learning structures.

## 1 Introduction and motivations

One of the main parts of statistical learning theory in the framework developed by V.N. Vapnik [23], [25] is concerned with non-asymptotic rates of convergence of empirical means to their expectations.

The historical result obtained originally by Vapnik and Chervonenkis (VC) (see [21], [22]) has provided the qualitative form of these rates of convergences and it is a remarkable fact that this result holds with no assumption on the probability distribution underlying the data. Consequently, VC-theory of bounds is considered as a Worst-Case theory.

This observation is the source of most of the criticisms addressed to VC-theory. It has been argued (see e.g. [4], [5], [9], [17]) that VC bounds are loose in general. Indeed, there is an infinite number of situations in which the observed learning curves representing the generalization error of some learning structure are not well described by theoretical VC bounds.

In [17], D. Schuurmans criticizes the *worst-case-argument* by pointing out that there is no practical evidence that pathological probability measures must be taken into account. This is the open problem we want to tackle : **the distribution-sensitivity of VC bounds.**

Another question which motivates our work (Vapnik *et al.* [24]) is the measure of effective VC dimension. The idea to use a VC bound as an estimate of the error probability tail, and to simulate this probability to identify the constants and to estimate the VC dimension "experimentally".

We will show how to improve these results by computing new accurate VC bounds for fixed families of distributions.

It is thus possible to provide a deeper understanding for VC theory and its main concepts. We also want to elaborate a practical method for measuring empirically the VC dimension of a learning problem. This part is still work in progress (see forthcoming [26] for examples and effective simulations).

## 2  Classical VC bounds

We first present universal VC bounds. For simplicity, we consider the particular case of deterministic pattern recognition with noiseless data. The set-up is standard :

Consider a device $T$ which transforms any input $X \in \mathbb{R}^d$ in some binary output $Y \in \{0,1\}$. Let us denote $P$ the distribution of the random variable $(X,Y)$, $\mu$ the distribution of $X$ and $R$ the Borel set in $\mathbb{R}^d$ of all $X$'s associated to the label $Y = 1$.

The goal of learning is to select an appropriate model of the device $T$ among a fixed set $\Gamma$ of models $C$ on the basis of a sample of empirical data $(X_1, Y_1)$, ..., $(X_n, Y_n)$. Here, $\Gamma$ is a family[1] of Borel sets of $\mathbb{R}^d$ with finite VC dimension $V$. The VC dimension is a complexity index which characterizes the capacity of any given family of sets to *shatter* a set of points.

The error probability associated to the selection of $C$ in $\Gamma$ is :

$$L(C) = \mu(C\Delta R) \qquad (\textit{true error})$$
$$\hat{L}_n(C) = \frac{1}{n}\sum_{k=1}^n \mathbb{1}_{C\Delta R}(X_k) = \mu_n(C\Delta R) \ (\textit{empirical error})$$

where $\mu_n$ is the empirical measure $\mu_n = \frac{1}{n}\sum_{k=1}^n \delta_{X_k}$.

The problem of model selection consists in minimizing the (unknown) risk functional $L(C) = \mu(C\Delta R)$, problem usually replaced by a tractable one which is the minimization of the empirical risk $\hat{L}_n(C) = \mu_n(C\Delta R)$ (this principle is known as ERM for Empirical Risk Minimization). But then, one has to guarantee that the

---

[1] $\Gamma$ satisfies some technical, but unimportant for our purpose, measurability condition. In order to avoid such technicalities, we will assume that $\Gamma$ is countable.

minimum of the empirical risk is "close" to the theoretical minimum. This is precisely the point where Vapnik-Chervonenkis bound drops in. Their fundamental contribution is the upper bound of the quantity

$$Q(n, \epsilon, \Gamma, \mu) = \Pr \left\{ \sup_{C \in \Gamma} |\mu_n(C) - \mu(C)| > \epsilon \right\} .$$

*Remark 1.* Note that

$$\Pr \left\{ \sup_{C \in \Gamma} |\hat{L}_n(C) - L(C)| > \epsilon \right\} = \Pr \left\{ \sup_{C \in \Gamma} |\mu_n(C \Delta R) - \mu(C \Delta R)| > \epsilon \right\} ,$$

and by a slight notational abuse without any consequence on the final result[2], we take $C := C \Delta R$ and $\Gamma := \Gamma \Delta R = \{C \Delta R : C \in \Gamma\}$.

We recall here this result :

**Theorem 1 (Vapnik-Chervonenkis [21]).** *Let $\Gamma$ be a class of Borel sets of $\mathbb{R}^d$ with finite VC dimension $V$. Then, for $n\epsilon^2 \geq 2$,*

$$\sup_{\mu \in \mathcal{M}_1(\mathbb{R}^d)} \Pr \left\{ \sup_{C \in \Gamma} |\mu_n(C) - \mu(C)| > \epsilon \right\} \leq 4 \left( \frac{2en}{V} \right)^V e^{-n\epsilon^2/8} .$$

*Remark 2.* For a very readable proof, see [7].

This bound actually provides an estimate of the worst rate of convergence of the empirical estimator to the true probability.

To comment on the form of the previous upper bound, we notice that the exponential term quantifies the worst deviation for a single set $C$ and the polynomial term characterizes the richness of the family $\Gamma$.

There have been several improvements for this type of bound since the pioneering work of Vapnik and Chervonenkis [21](see Vapnik [23], Devroye[6], Pollard[16] , Alexander[1], Parrondo-Van den Broek [15], Talagrand[19], Lugosi [13]).

Many of these improvements resulted from theory and techniques in empirical processes (see Pollard[16], Alexander[1], Talagrand[19]), and these works indicated that the proper variable is $\epsilon\sqrt{n}$ (or $n\epsilon^2$). Keeping this in mind, we can summarize the qualitative behavior of VC-bounds by the following expression :

$$K(\epsilon, V) \cdot \underbrace{(n\epsilon^2)^{\tau(V)}}_{capacity} \cdot \underbrace{e^{-n\gamma\epsilon^2}}_{deviation} \quad \text{for} \quad n\epsilon^2 \geq M ,$$

with $M$ constant, $\tau$ an affine function of V, $\gamma \in [0, 2]$, and $K(\epsilon, V)$ constant independent of $n$, possibly depending on $\epsilon$ and $V$ (ideally $K(\epsilon, V) \leq K(V)$).

Once we have stated this general form for VC-bounds, we can address the following issues (both theoretically and practically) :

---

[2] Indeed, for a fixed set $R$, we have $VCdim(\Gamma) = VCdim(\Gamma \Delta R)$. For a proof, see e.g. [11].

(a) What is the best exponent $\gamma$ in the deviation term ?
(b) What is the correct power $\tau(V)$ of $n$ in the capacity term ?
(c) What is the order of the constant term $K(V)$ for the bound to be sharp ?

In Table 1, we provide the theoretical answers brought by previous studies, in a distribution-free framework.

**Table 1.** Universal bounds

| | $M$ | $K(\epsilon, V)$ | $\tau(V)$ | $\gamma$ |
|---|---|---|---|---|
| Pollard (1984) | 2 | $8\left(\frac{\epsilon}{V}\frac{1}{\epsilon^2}\right)^V$ | $V$ | $1/32$ |
| Vapnik-Chervonenkis (1971) | 2 | $4\left(\frac{2\epsilon}{V}\frac{1}{\epsilon^2}\right)^V$ | $V$ | $1/8$ |
| Vapnik (1982) | 2 | $6\left(\frac{2\epsilon}{V}\frac{1}{\epsilon^2}\right)^V$ | $V$ | $1/4$ |
| Parrondo-Van den Broeck (1993) | 2 | $6e^{2\epsilon}\left(\frac{2\epsilon}{V}\frac{1}{\epsilon^2}\right)^V$ | $V$ | $1$ |
| Devroye (1982) | 1 | $4e^{4\epsilon+4\epsilon^2}\left(\frac{\epsilon}{V}\frac{1}{\epsilon^2}\right)^V$ | $2V$ | $2$ |
| Lugosi (1995) | $\frac{V}{2}$ | $4e(V+1)\left(\frac{32e^5}{V^2}\frac{1}{\epsilon}\right)^V$ | $2V$ | $2$ |
| Alexander (1984) | 64 | $16$ | $2048V$ | $2$ |
| Talagrand (1994) | 0 | $K(V)$ | $V-\frac{1}{2}$ | $2$ |

to conclude this brief review, we point out that in the above distribution-free results, the optimal value for the exponent $\gamma$ is 2 (which actually is the value in Hoeffding's inequality), and the best power achieved for the capacity term is the one obtained by Talagrand $V - \frac{1}{2}$ (see also the discussion about this point in [19]). In most of the results, the function $K(\epsilon, V)$ is not bounded as $\epsilon$ goes to zero, and only Alexander's and Talagrand's bounds satisfy the requirement $K(\epsilon, V) \leq K(V)$.

Our point in the remainder of this paper is that the $2\epsilon^2$ term under the exponential can be larger in particular situations.

## 3 Rigorous distribution-dependent results

In the continuity of the results evoked in the previous section, one issue of interest is the construction of bounds taking into account the characteristics of the underlying probability measure $\mu$.

There are some works tackling this problem but with very different perspectives (see Vapnik [25], Bartlett-Lugosi [3], in a learning theory framework; Schuurmans [17], in a PAC-learning framework; Pollard [16], Alexander [1], Massart [14], who provide the most significant results in empirical processes).

We note that :

- in learning theory, the idea of distribution-dependent VC-bounds led to other expressions for the capacity term, involving different concepts of entropy as VC-entropy, annealed entropy or metric entropy, depending on the probability measure.
- while in the theory of empirical processes, a special attention was given to refined exponential rates for restricted families of probability distributions (see [1], [14]).

Our purpose is to formulate a distribution-dependent result preserving the structure of universal VC bounds with an optimal exponential rate and with some nearly optimal power $\tau(V)$, though we will keep the concept of VC dimension unchanged[3].

Indeed, we would like to point out that if we consider a particular case where the probability measure $\mu$ underlying the data belongs to a restricted set $\mathcal{P} \subset \mathcal{M}_1(\mathbb{R}^d)$, then the deviation term can be fairly improved. Our argument is borrowed from large deviations results which provide asymptotically exact estimates of probability tails on a logarithmic scale. A close look at the proof of the main theorem in the case of real random variables (Cramér's theorem, for a review, see [2] or [18]) will reveal that the result holds as a non-asymptotical upper bound. Thanks to this result, we obtain the *exact* term under the exponential quantifying the worst deviation.

In order to formulate our result, we need to introduce the Cramér transform (see the appendix) of a Bernoulli law with parameter $p$ given by : $\Lambda_p(x) = x \log \left(\frac{x}{p}\right) + (1 - x) \log \left(\frac{1-x}{1-p}\right)$, for $x$ in $[0,1]$.

Then, the uniform deviation of the empirical error from its expectation, for a fixed family of probability distributions, can be estimated according to the following theorem (a sketch of its proof is given in Sect. 6) :

**Theorem 2.** *Let $\Gamma$ be a family of measurable sets $C$ of $\mathbb{R}^d$ with finite VC dimension $V$, and $\mathcal{P} \subset \mathcal{M}_1(\mathbb{R}^d)$ a fixed family of probability distributions $\mu$.*

*Let $\Lambda_p$ be the Cramér transform of a Bernoulli law with parameter $p$, let $J = \{q : q = \mu(C), (\mu, C) \in \mathcal{P} \times \Gamma\}$ and set $p = \arg\min_{q \in J} |q - \frac{1}{2}|$. For every $\beta > 0$, there exists $M(\beta, p, V)$ and $\epsilon_0(\beta, p, V) > 0$ such that if $\epsilon < \epsilon_0(\beta, p, V)$ and $n\epsilon^2 > M(\beta, p, V)$, we have :*

$$\sup_{\mu \in \mathcal{P}} \mathbf{Pr} \left\{ \sup_{C \in \Gamma} |\mu_n(C) - \mu(C)| > \epsilon \right\} \leq K(V)(n\epsilon^2)^V \, e^{-n \cdot (1-\beta) \cdot \Lambda_p(\epsilon + p)} .$$

*Remark 3.* The corrective term $\beta$ can be chosen to be as small as possible at the cost of increasing $M(\beta, p, V)$.

---

[3] However, we could use alternatively effective VC dimension which is a distribution-dependent index (see [26] for details).

*Remark 4.* Here we achieved $\tau(V) = V$ instead of the optimal $V - \frac{1}{2}$ found by Talagrand in [19]. However, refining the proof by using a smart partitioning of the family $\Gamma$ should lead to this value.

*Remark 5.* Note that the result above can be extended to the other fundamental problems of statistics as regression or density estimation.

# 4  Comparison with Universal VC Bounds

To appreciate the gain in considering distribution-dependent rates of convergence instead of universal rates, we provide a brief discussion in which we compare the $\Lambda_p(\epsilon + p)$ in our result with the universal $\gamma\epsilon^2$.

First, we point out that even in the worst-case situation (take $\mathcal{P} = \mathcal{M}_1(\mathbb{R}^d)$) where $p = \frac{1}{2}$, we have a better result since $\Lambda = \Lambda_{\frac{1}{2}}(\epsilon + \frac{1}{2}) \geq 2\epsilon^2$ (see Fig. 1).

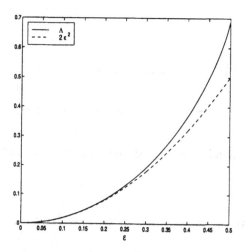

**Fig. 1.** Comparison between $\Lambda = \Lambda_{\frac{1}{2}}(\epsilon + \frac{1}{2})$ and $2\epsilon^2$.

In the general case when $p \neq \frac{1}{2}$, we claim that the distribution-dependent VC bound obtained in Theorem 2 is of the same type of universal bounds listed in Sect. 2. In order to make the comparison, we recall a result proved by W. Hoeffding :

**Proposition 1 (Hoeffding [10]).** *For any $p \in [0,1]$, the following inequality holds :*

$$\frac{\Lambda_p(\epsilon + p)}{\epsilon^2} \geq g(p) \geq 2 \ ,$$

where the function $g$ is defined by :

$$g(p) = \begin{cases} \dfrac{1}{1-2p} \log\left(\dfrac{1-p}{p}\right) & \text{, if } p < \tfrac{1}{2} \\[3mm] \dfrac{1}{2p(1-p)} & \text{, if } p \geq \tfrac{1}{2} \end{cases}.$$

With the help of Fig. 2, the comparison between $g(p)$ and the values of $\gamma$ becomes quite explicit. Indeed, it is clear that, as soon as $p \neq 1/2$, we have a better bound than in the universal case.

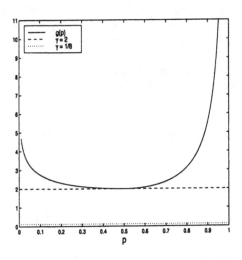

**Fig. 2.** Comparison between *distribution-dependent* $g(p)$ and *universal* $\gamma$'s.

## 5 PAC-Learning Application of the Result

A PAC-learning formulation of distribution-dependent VC bounds in terms of sample complexity can easily be deduced from the main result :

**Corollary 1.** *Under the same assumptions as in Theorem 2. The sample complexity* $N(\epsilon, \delta)$*, that guarantees :*

$$\mathbf{Pr}\left\{ \sup_{C \in \Gamma} |\mu_n(C) - \mu(C)| > \epsilon \right\} \leq \delta$$

*for* $n \geq N(\epsilon, \delta)$*, is bounded by :*

$$N(\epsilon, \delta) \leq max\left( \frac{2V}{\Lambda} \log\left(\frac{2V\epsilon^2}{\Lambda}\right), \frac{2}{\Lambda} \log\left(\frac{K(V)}{\delta}\right) \right)$$

*where* $\Lambda = (1 - \beta) \cdot \Lambda_p(\epsilon + p)$.

*Remark 6.* In order to appreciate this result, one should consider that $\Lambda_p(\epsilon+p) \simeq g(p)\epsilon^2$.

**Proof.** Consider $n$ such that : $(n\epsilon^2)^V \leq e^{n\Lambda/2}$. Then , taking the log and multiplying by $\epsilon^2$, we obtain : $n\epsilon^2 \geq \frac{2V\epsilon^2}{\Lambda}\log(n\epsilon^2)$. Thus, taking the log again, we have $\log(n\epsilon^2) \geq \log(\frac{2V\epsilon^2}{\Lambda})$ which we inject in the last inequality. We get : $n \geq \frac{2V}{\Lambda}\log\left(\frac{2V\epsilon^2}{\Lambda}\right)$. If $n$ satisfies the previous condition, we have : $(n\epsilon^2)^V e^{-n\Lambda} \leq e^{-n\Lambda/2}$, and we want $K(V)e^{-n\Lambda/2}$ to be smaller than $\delta$. Hence, $n$ should also satisfy : $n \geq \frac{2}{\Lambda}\log\left(\frac{K(V)}{\delta}\right)$. ∎

As a matter of fact, Theorem 2 provides an appropriate theoretical foundation for computer simulations. Indeed, in practical situations, *a priori* informations about the underlying distribution and about realistic elements $C$ of the family $\Gamma$ turn distribution-dependent VC bounds in an operational tool for obtaining estimates of the effective VC dimension $V$ and of the constant $K(V)$ as well (see [26] for examples).

# 6 Elements of proof for Theorem 2

In this section, we provide a sketch of the proof of Theorem 2 (for a complete and general proof, see [26]). It relies on some results from empirical processes theory. The line of proof is inspired from the direct approximation method exposed by D. Pollard [16] while most of the techniques and intermediate results used in this proof are due to M. Talagrand and come from [19], [20].

First, note that if the family $\Gamma$ is finite, the proof is a straightforward consequence of Chernoff's bound (see the appendix) together with the union-of-events bound. In the case of a countable family, we introduce a finite approximation $\Gamma_\lambda$ which is a $\lambda$-net[4] for the symmetric difference associated to the measure $\mu$, with cardinality $N(\Gamma, \mu, \lambda) = N(\lambda)$. We shall take $\lambda = \frac{1}{n\epsilon^2}$.

The first step of the proof is to turn the global supremum of the empirical process $G_n(C) = \mu_n(C) - \mu(C)$ into a more tractable expression like the sum of a maximum over a finite set and some local supremum. Then, the tail $Q(n, \epsilon, \Gamma, \mu)$ is bounded by $A + B$, where $A$ is the tail of the maximum of a set of random variables which can be bounded by :

$$A \leq N(\lambda) \max_{C^* \in \Gamma_\lambda} \mathbf{Pr}\left\{|G_n(C^*)| > (1 - \frac{\beta}{2})\epsilon\right\}, \tag{1}$$

---

[4] If $\Gamma$ is totally bounded, by definition, it is possible, for every $\lambda > 0$, to cover $\Gamma$ by a finite number of balls of radius $\lambda$ centered in $\Gamma$. Consider a minimal cover of $\Gamma$, then a $\lambda$-net will be the set of all the centers of the balls composing this cover.

and $B$ is the tail of the local supremum of a family of random variables bounded as follows :

$$B \leq N(\lambda) \max_{C^* \in \Gamma_\lambda} \mathbf{Pr} \left\{ \sup_{C \in \mathcal{B}(C^*,\lambda)} |G_n(C) - G_n(C^*)| > \frac{\beta\epsilon}{2} \right\} , \qquad (2)$$

where $\mathcal{B}(C^*,\lambda) = \{C \in \Gamma : \mu(C \Delta C^*) \leq \lambda\}$.

The probability tail in (1) can be bounded by large deviations estimates according to Chernoff's bound :

$$\mathbf{Pr} \left\{ |G_n(C^*)| > (1 - \frac{\beta}{2})\epsilon \right\} \leq 2e^{-n \cdot \Lambda_p((1-\frac{\beta}{2})\epsilon+p)} ,$$

where $p = \arg\min_{q \,:\, q=\mu(C),\, (\mu,C)\in \mathcal{P}\times\Gamma} |q - \frac{1}{2}|$.

The estimation of (2) requires the use of technical results on empirical processes mainly from [19] and [20] : symmetrization of the empirical processes with Rademacher random variables, decomposition of the conditional probability tail using the median, application of the chaining technique. In the end, we introduce the parameter $u$ to obtain the bound :

$$B \leq 4N(\lambda) \left( 2e^{-\frac{\beta^2\epsilon^2}{1024u}} + e^{-\frac{1}{2}n^2 u \log\left(\frac{nu}{64m_1}\right)} + e^{-\frac{n\beta\epsilon}{64}\log\left(\frac{\beta\epsilon}{128m_2}\right)} \right)$$
$$= 4N(\lambda)\,(D + F + G) , \qquad (3)$$

where $m_1 = k_1(V) \cdot (1/n\epsilon^2) \cdot \log(k_2\,n\epsilon^2))$, and $m_2 = k_3(V) \cdot (1/n\epsilon) \cdot \log(k_2\,n\epsilon^2))$. The meaning of each of the terms in (3) is the following : $D$ measures the deviation of the symmetric process from the median, $F$ controls its variance and $G$ bounds the tail of the median which can be controlled thanks to the chaining technique.

To get the proper bound from (3), one has to consider the constraint on $u$ :

$$u \in \mathcal{I} = \left[ \frac{k_5(\beta,p,V)}{n\log(n\epsilon^2)} , \; k_4(\beta,p) \cdot \frac{1}{n} \right] ,$$

which leads to the condition : $n\epsilon^2 > M(\beta,p,V)$.

To get the desired form of the bound, we eventually apply a result due to D. Haussler [8]:

$$N(\lambda) \leq e(V + 1) \left( \frac{2e}{\lambda} \right)^V ,$$

and set $\lambda = \frac{1}{n\epsilon^2}$, $u \in \mathcal{I}$, which ends the proof.

# 7 Appendix - Chernoff's bound on large deviations

We remind the setting for Chernoff's bound (see [2] for further results).

Consider $\nu$ a probability measure over $\mathbb{R}$. $\hat{\nu} : \mathbb{R} \longrightarrow ]0, +\infty]$ is the Laplace transform of $\nu$, defined by $\hat{\nu}(t) = \int_{\mathbb{R}} e^{tx} \nu(dx)$.

The Cramér transform $\Lambda : \mathbb{R} \longrightarrow [0, +\infty]$ of the measure $\nu$ is defined, for $x \in \mathbb{R}$, by

$$\Lambda(x) = \sup_{t \in \mathbb{R}} (tx - \log \hat{\nu}(t)) \ .$$

If we go through the optimization of the function of $t$ inside the *sup* (it is a simple fact that this function is infinitely differentiable, cf. e.g. [18]), we can compute exactly the optimal value of $t$. Let $t(x)$ be that value. Then, we write

$$\Lambda(x) = t(x)x - \log \hat{\nu}(t(x)) \ .$$

**Proposition 2 (Chernoff's bound).** *Let $U_1, ..., U_n$ be real i.i.d. random variables. Denote their sum by $S_n = \sum_{i=1}^{n} U_i$. Then, for every $\epsilon > 0$, we have :*

$$\mathbf{Pr}\left\{|S_n - \mathbf{E}S_n| > \epsilon\right\} \leq 2e^{-n\Lambda(\epsilon + \mathbf{E}U_1)}$$

*where $\Lambda$ is the Cramér Transform of the random variable $U_1$.*

# References

1. Alexander, K.: Probability Inequalities for Empirical Processes and a Law of the Iterated Logarithm. Annals of Probability **4** (1984) 1041-1067
2. Azencott, R.: Grandes Déviations, in Hennequin, P.L. (ed.): Ecole d'Eté de Probabilités de Saint-Flour VIII-1978. Lecture Notes in Mathematics, Vol. **774**. Springer-Verlag, Berlin Heidelberg New York (1978)
3. Bartlett, P., Lugosi, G.: An Inequality for Uniform Deviations of Sample Averages from their Means. To appear (1998)
4. Cohn, D., Tesauro, G.: How Tight Are the Vapnik-Chervonenkis Bounds ? Neural Computation **4** (1992) 249-269
5. Cohn, D.: Separating Formal Bounds from Practical Performance in Learning Systems. PhD thesis, University of Washington (1992)
6. Devroye, L.: Bounds for the Uniform Deviation of Empirical Measures. Journal of Multivariate Analysis **12** (1982) 72-79
7. Devroye, L., Györfi, L., Lugosi, G.: A Probabilistic Theory of Pattern Recognition. Springer-Verlag, Berlin Heidelberg New York (1996)
8. Haussler, D.: Sphere Packing Numbers for Subsets of the Boolean n-Cube with Bounded Vapnik-Chervonenkis Dimension. Journal of Combinatorial Theory, Series A **69** (1995) 217-232
9. Haussler, D., Kearns, M., Seung, H.S., Tishby, N.: Rigorous Learning Curve Bounds from Statistical Mechanics. Machine Learning (1996) 195-236
10. Hoeffding, W.: Probability Inequalities for Sums of Bounded Random Variables. Journal of the American Statistical Association **58** (1963) 13-30

11. Kearns, M.J., Vazirani, U.V.: An Introduction to Computational Learning Theory. MIT Press, Cambridge Massachussets (1994)
12. Ledoux, M., Talagrand, M.: Probability in Banach Spaces. Springer-Verlag, Berlin Heidelberg New York (1992)
13. Lugosi, G.: Improved Upper Bounds for Probabilities of Uniform Deviations. Statistics and Probability Letters **25** (1995) 71-77
14. Massart, P.: Rates of Convergence in the Central Limit Theorem for Empirical Processes. Annales de l'Institut Henri Poincaré, Vol. 22, No. 4 (1986) 381-423
15. Parrondo, J.M.R., Van den Broeck, C.: Vapnik-Chervonenkis Bounds for Generalization. J. Phys. A : Math. Gen. **26** (1993) 2211-2223
16. Pollard, D.: Convergence of Stochastic Processes. Springer-Verlag, Berlin Heidelberg New York (1984)
17. Schuurmans, D. E.: Effective Classification Learning. PhD thesis, University of Toronto (1996)
18. Stroock, D.W.: Probability Theory, an Analytic View. Cambridge University Press (1993)
19. Talagrand, M.: Sharper Bounds for Gaussian and Empirical Processes. The Annals of Probability, Vol. 22, No. 1 (1994) 28-76
20. van der Vaart, A. W., Wellner, J. A.: Weak Convergence and Empirical Processes. Springer-Verlag, Berlin Heidelberg New York (1996)
21. Vapnik, V. N., Chervonenkis, A. Ya.: On the Uniform Convergence of Relative Frequencies of Events to their Probabilities. Theory of Probability and its Applications, Vol. XVI, No. 2 (1971) 264-280
22. Vapnik, V. N., Chervonenkis, A. Ya.: Necessary and Sufficient Conditions for the Uniform Convergence of Means to their Expectations. Theory of Probability and its Applications, Vol. XXVI, No. 3 (1981) 532-553
23. Vapnik, V. N.: Estimation of Dependences Based on Empirical Data. Springer-Verlag, Berlin Heidelberg New York (1982)
24. Vapnik, V. N., Levin, E., Le Cun, Y.: Measuring the VC Dimension of a Learning Machine. Neural Computation **6** (1994) 851-876
25. Vapnik, V. N.: The Nature of Statistical Learning Theory. Springer-Verlag, Berlin Heidelberg New York (1995)
26. Vayatis, N.: Learning Complexity and Pattern Recognition. PhD thesis, Ecole Polytechnique. To appear (1999)

# Lower Bounds on the Rate of Convergence of Nonparametric Pattern Recognition [*]

András Antos[1]

Informatics Laboratory, Computer and Automation Research Institute of the
Hungarian Academy of Sciences, H-1111 Lágymányosi u. 11, Budapest, Hungary,
email: antos@inf.bme.hu,
WWW home page: http://www.szit.bme.hu/~antos/

**Abstract.** We show that there exist individual lower bounds corresponding to the upper bounds on the rate of convergence of nonparametric pattern recognition which are arbitrarily close to Yang's minimax lower bounds, if the a posteriori probability function is in the classes used by Stone and others. The rates equal to the ones on the corresponding regression estimation problem. Thus for these classes classification is not easier than regression estimation either in individual sense.

## 1  Introduction

Let $(X, Y)$, $(X_1, Y_1)$, $(X_2, Y_2), \ldots$ be independent identically distributed $\mathcal{R}^d \times \{0, 1\}$ –valued random variables. In pattern recognition (or classification) one wishes to decide whether the value of $Y$ (the label) is 0 or 1 given the ($d$–dimensional) value of $X$ (the observation), i.e., one wants to find a decision function $g$ defined on the range of $X$ taking values 0 or 1 so that $g(X)$ equals to $Y$ with high probability. Assume that the main aim of the analysis is to minimize the probability of error :

$$\min_g L(g) \stackrel{\text{def}}{=} \min_g \mathbf{P}\{g(X) \neq Y\} \ . \tag{1}$$

Let $\eta(x) \stackrel{\text{def}}{=} \mathbf{P}\{Y = 1 | X = x\} = \mathbf{E}\{Y | X = x\}$ be the a posteriori probability (or regression) function, let

$$g^*(x) \stackrel{\text{def}}{=} \begin{cases} 1 \text{ if } \eta(x) > 1/2, \\ 0 \text{ else} \end{cases}$$

be the Bayes-decision, let

$$L^* \stackrel{\text{def}}{=} L(g^*) = \mathbf{P}\{g^*(X) \neq Y\}$$

[*] The author's work was supported by a grant from the Hungarian Academy of Sciences (MTA SZTAKI).

be the Bayes-error and denote the distribution of $X$ by $\mu$. Introduce $\|f\|_q \overset{\text{def}}{=} (\int |f|^q \, d\mu)^{1/q}$. It is well-known, that for each measurable function $g : \mathcal{R}^d \mapsto \{0,1\}$ the relation

$$L(g) - L^* = 2 \int \left| \eta - \frac{1}{2} \right| I_{\{g \neq g^*\}} \, d\mu \qquad (2)$$

holds. Therefore the function $g^*$ achieves the minimum in (1) and the minimum is $L^*$.

For the classification problem, the distribution of $(X, Y)$ (and so $\eta$ and $g^*$) is unknown. Given only a sample $D_n = \{(X_1, Y_1), \ldots, (X_n, Y_n)\}$ of the distribution of $(X, Y)$, one wants to construct a decision rule $g_n(x) = g_n(x, D_n) : \mathcal{R}^d \times (\mathcal{R}^d \times \{0,1\})^n \mapsto \{0,1\}$ such that

$$L_n \overset{\text{def}}{=} L(g_n) = \mathbf{P}\{g_n(X) \neq Y | D_n\}$$

is close to $L^*$. In this paper we study asymptotic properties of $\mathbf{E}L_n - L^*$.

If we have an estimate $\eta_n$ of the regression function $\eta$ and we derive a plug-in rule $g_n$ from $\eta_n$ quite naturally by

$$g_n(x) = \begin{cases} 1 \text{ if } \eta_n(x) > 1/2, \\ 0 \text{ else,} \end{cases}$$

then from (2) we get easily

$$L_n - L^* \leq 2\|\eta_n - \eta\|_1 \leq 2\|\eta_n - \eta\|_2$$

(see Devroye, Györfi and Lugosi [6]). This shows that if $\|\eta_n - \eta\|_1 \to 0$ then $L_n \to L^*$ in the same sense, and the latter has at least the same rate, i.e., classification is not more complex than regression estimation.

It is well-known, that there exist regression estimates, and so classification rules, which are universally consistent, i.e., which satisfy

$$\mathbf{E}L_n \to L^* \quad (n \to \infty)$$

for all distributions of $(X, Y)$. This was first shown in Stone [8] for nearest neighbor estimates (see also [6] for a list of references).

Classification is actually easier than regression estimation in the sense that if $\mathbf{E}\|\eta_n - \eta\|_1 \to 0$, then for the plug-in rule

$$\frac{\mathbf{E}L_n - L^*}{\sqrt{\mathbf{E}\{\|\eta_n - \eta\|_2^2\}}} \to 0 . \qquad (3)$$

(see [6] Chapter 6), i.e. the relative expected error of $g_n$ decreases faster than the expected $\mathcal{L}_2(\mu)$ error of $\eta_n$. (Moreover, if $\|\eta_n - \eta\|_1 \to 0$ a.s., then for the plug-in rule

$$\frac{L_n - L^*}{\|\eta_n - \eta\|_2} \to 0 \quad \text{a.s.}$$

(see Antos [1]), i.e. the relation also holds for strong consistency.) However the value of the ratio above can not be universally bounded, the convergence can be arbitrary slow. It depends on the behavior of $\eta$ near $1/2$ and the rate of convergence of $\eta_n$.

## 2 Lower Bounds

Unfortunately, there do not exist rules for which $EL_n - L^*$ tends to zero with a guaranteed rate of convergence for all distributions of $(X, Y)$. Theorem 7.2 and Problem 7.2 in [6] imply the following slow rate of convergence result: Let $\{a_n\}$ be a sequence of positive numbers converging to zero with $1/16 \geq a_1 \geq a_2 \geq \ldots$. For every sequence of decision rules $\{g_n\}$, there exists a distribution of $(X, Y)$, such that $X$ is uniformly distributed on $[0, 1]$, $\eta \in \{0, 1\}$ $(L^* = 0)$ and

$$EL_n \geq a_n$$

for all $n$.

Therefore one has to restrict the class of distributions, which one considers, in order to obtain nontrivial rate of convergence results. Then it is natural to ask what the fastest achievable rate is for a given class of distributions. This is usually done by considering minimax rate of convergence results, where one derives lower bounds according to the following definition.

**Definition 1.** *A sequence of positive numbers $a_n$ is called* lower rate of convergence *for a class $\mathcal{D}$ of distributions of $(X, Y)$, if*

$$\varliminf_{n \to \infty} \inf_{g_n} \sup_{(X,Y) \in \mathcal{D}} \frac{EL_n - L^*}{a_n}.$$

Yang [10] pointed out that while (3) holds for every fixed *distribution* for which $\eta_n$ is consistent, the optimal rates of convergence for many usual *classes* are the same in classification and regression estimation. He shows many examples and some counterexamples to this phenomenon with rates of convergence in term of metric entropy. Classification seems to have the same complexity as regression estimation for classes which contain functions with many values near 1/2. (See also Mamman and Tsybakov [7].)

E.g. it was shown in [10] that for Lipschitz classes $\mathcal{D}^{(p,M)}$ below, the optimal lower rate of convergence is $n^{-\frac{p}{2p+d}}$, the same as for regression estimation (see also Stone [9]). For lower bound results on other types of distribution classes (e.g. Vapnik-Chevonenkis classes) see [6] and the references there.

**Definition 2.** *Let $\mathcal{F}^{(p,M)}$ be the set of functions $f : \mathcal{R}^d \to \mathcal{R}$ such that for $p = k + \beta$, $k \in \mathcal{N}_0$, $0 < \beta \leq 1$*

$$|D^\alpha f(x) - D^\alpha f(z)| \leq M \|x - z\|^\beta,$$

*where $D^\alpha$ denotes the partial derivatives for $\alpha = (\alpha_1, \ldots, \alpha_d)$, $\alpha_i \in \mathcal{N}_0$, $\sum_{j=1}^d \alpha_j = k$.*

**Definition 3.** *Let $\mathcal{D}^{(p,M)}$ be the class of distributions of $(X, Y)$ such that*
*(i) $X$ is uniformly distributed on $[0, 1]^d$,*
*(ii) $\eta \in \mathcal{F}^{(p,M)}$.*

It is well–known, that there exist regression estimates $\eta_n$, which satisfy

$$\varlimsup_{\substack{n \to \infty \\ (X,Y) \in \mathcal{D}^{(p,M)}}} \sup \frac{\sqrt{\mathbf{E}\{\|\eta_n - \eta\|_2^2\}}}{n^{-\frac{p}{2p+d}}} < \infty \tag{4}$$

(see, e.g., Barron, Birge and Massart [4]), thus for the plug-in rules $g_n$

$$\varlimsup_{\substack{n \to \infty \\ (X,Y) \in \mathcal{D}^{(p,M)}}} \sup \frac{\mathbf{E}L_n - L^*}{n^{-\frac{p}{2p+d}}} < \infty, \tag{5}$$

i.e., $\sup_{(X,Y) \in \mathcal{D}^{(p,M)}} (\mathbf{E}L_n - L^*) = O\left(n^{-\frac{p}{2p+d}}\right)$. (This remains true leaving condition (i) from Definition 3. Note that the rate does not depend on $M$.)

**Theorem 1.** (YANG [10]) *The sequence*

$$a_n = n^{-\frac{p}{2p+d}}$$

*is a lower rate of convergence for the class $\mathcal{D}^{(p,M)}$.*

In some sense, such lower bounds are not satisfactory. They do not tell us anything about the way the probability of error decreases as the sample size is increased for a given classification problem. These bounds, for each $n$, give information about the maximal probability of error within the class, but not about the behavior of the probability of error for a single fixed distribution as the sample size $n$ increases. In other words, the "bad" distribution, causing the largest probability of error for a decision rule, may be different for each $n$. For example, the lower bound for the class $\mathcal{D}^{(p,M)}$ does not exclude the possibility that there exists a sequence of rules $\{g_n\}$ such that for *every* distribution in $\mathcal{D}^{(p,M)}$, the expected probability of error $\mathbf{E}L_n - L^*$ decreases at an exponential rate in $n$.

In this paper, we are interested in "individual" minimax lower bounds that describe the behavior of the probability of error for a fixed distribution $(X,Y)$ as the sample size $n$ grows.

**Definition 4.** *A sequence of positive numbers $a_n$ is called* individual lower rate *of convergence for a class $\mathcal{D}$ of distributions of $(X,Y)$, if*

$$\inf_{\{g_n\}} \sup_{(X,Y) \in \mathcal{D}} \varlimsup_{n \to \infty} \frac{\mathbf{E}L_n - L^*}{a_n} > 0,$$

*where the infimum is taken over all sequences $\{g_n\}$ of decision rules.*

The concept of individual lower rate has been introduced in Birgé [5] concerning density estimation. For individual lower rate results concerning pattern recognition see Antos and Lugosi [3].

We will show that for every sequence $\{b_n\}$ tending to zero, $b_n n^{-\frac{p}{2p+d}}$ is an individual lower rate of convergence of the class $\mathcal{D}^{(p,M)}$. Hence there exist individual lower rates of these classes, which are arbitrarily close to the optimal lower rates.

These rates are the same as the individual lower rates for the expected $\mathcal{L}_2(\mu)$ error of regression estimation for these classes in Antos, Györfi and Kohler [2]. (Actually the results here imply some results there.) Both individual lower rates are optimal by (4) and (5), hence we extended Yang's observation for the individual rates for these classes.

Our results also imply that the ratio $\dfrac{EL_n - L^*}{\sqrt{E\{\|\eta_n - \eta\|_2^2\}}}$ can tend to zero arbitrary slowly (even for a fixed sequence $\{\eta_n\}$).

**Theorem 2.** *Let $\{b_n\}$ be an arbitrary positive sequence tending to zero. Then the sequence*

$$b_n a_n = b_n n^{-\frac{2p}{2p+d}}$$

*is an individual lower rate of convergence for the class $\mathcal{D}^{(p,M)}$.*

REMARK 1. Applying for the sequence $\{\sqrt{b_n}\}$, Theorem 2 implies that for all $\{g_n\}$ there is $(X,Y) \in \mathcal{D}^{(p,M)}$ such that

$$\varlimsup_{n\to\infty} \frac{EL_n - L^*}{b_n a_n} = \infty .$$

REMARK 2. Certainly Theorems 1 and 2 hold if we increase the class by leaving condition (i) from Definition 3.

Call a sequence $c_n$ an *upper rate of convergence* for a class $\mathcal{D}$, if there exist rules $g_n$ which satisfy

$$\varlimsup_{n\to\infty} \sup_{(X,Y)\in\mathcal{D}} \frac{EL_n - L^*}{c_n} < \infty,$$

i.e., $\sup_{(X,Y)\in\mathcal{D}}(EL_n - L^*) = O(c_n)$, and call it an *individual upper rate of convergence for a class $\mathcal{D}$*, if there exist rules $g_n$ which satisfy

$$\sup_{(X,Y)\in\mathcal{D}} \varlimsup_{n\to\infty} \frac{EL_n - L^*}{c_n} < \infty .$$

This implies only that for every distribution in $\mathcal{D}$, $EL_n - L^* = O(c_n)$, possible with different constants. Then (5) implies that $n^{-\frac{p}{2p+d}}$ is an upper rate of convergence, and thus also an individual upper rate of convergence for $\mathcal{D}^{(p,M)}$. While Theorem 1 shows only that there is no upper rate of convergence for $\mathcal{D}^{(p,M)}$ better than $n^{-\frac{p}{2p+d}}$, it follows from Theorem 2 that $n^{-\frac{p}{2p+d}}$ is even the optimal individual upper rate for $\mathcal{D}^{(p,M)}$ in the sense, that there doesn't exist an individual upper rate $c_n$ of convergence for $\mathcal{D}^{(p,M)}$, which satisfies

$$\lim_{n\to\infty} \frac{c_n}{n^{-\frac{p}{2p+d}}} = 0 .$$

Moreover (3) and (4) imply

$$\inf_{\{g_n\}} \sup_{(X,Y)\in\mathcal{D}^{(p,M)}} \varlimsup_{n\to\infty} \frac{EL_n - L^*}{n^{-\frac{p}{2p+d}}} = 0, \tag{6}$$

which shows that Theorem 2 can not be improved by dropping $b_n$. This shows the strange nature of individual lower bounds, that while every sequence tending to zero faster than $n^{-\frac{p}{2p+d}}$ is an individual lower rate for $\mathcal{D}^{(p,M)}$, $n^{-\frac{p}{2p+d}}$ itself is not that.

## 3  Proofs

The proofs of the theorems apply the following lemma:

**Lemma 1.** *Let $u = (u_1, \ldots, u_l)$ be a $l$-dimensional real vector taking values in $[-1/4, 1/4]^l$, let $C$ be a zero mean random variable taking values in $\{-1, +1\}$, and let $Y_1, \ldots, Y_l$ be indepedent binary variables given $C$ with*

$$\mathbf{P}\{Y_i = 1|C\} = \frac{1}{2} + Cu_i \quad i = 1, \ldots, l .$$

*Then for the error probability of the Bayes decision for $C$ based on $Y = (Y_1, \ldots, Y_l)$*

$$L^* \geq \frac{1}{4} e^{-10\sqrt{\sum_i u_i^2 + 4\sum_{i \neq i'} u_i^2 u_{i'}^2}} .$$

PROOF.  The Bayes decision is 1 if $\mathbf{P}\{C = 1|Y\} \geq \frac{1}{2}$ and $-1$ otherwise, therefore

$$L^* = \mathbf{E}\{\min(\mathbf{P}\{C = 1|Y\}, \mathbf{P}\{C = -1|Y\})\} = \mathbf{E}\{\pi\} .$$

One can verify that

$$\mathbf{P}\{C = 1|Y\} = \frac{T}{T+1},$$

where

$$T \stackrel{\text{def}}{=} \prod_{i \leq l} \left( \frac{\frac{1}{2} + u_i}{\frac{1}{2} - u_i} I_{\{Y_i = 1\}} + \frac{\frac{1}{2} - u_i}{\frac{1}{2} + u_i} I_{\{Y_i = 0\}} \right) = \prod_{i \leq l} \left( \frac{\frac{1}{2} + u_i}{\frac{1}{2} - u_i} \right)^{2Y_i - 1}$$

$$= e^{\sum_{i \leq l} (2Y_i - 1) \log \frac{1 + 2u_i}{1 - 2u_i}} = e^{\sum_{i \leq l} Z_i},$$

where $Z_i \stackrel{\text{def}}{=} (2Y_i - 1) \log((1 + 2u_i)/(1 - 2u_i))$. For arbitrary $0 < q < 1/2$, $\pi \geq q$ if and only if $|\log T| \leq \log \frac{1-q}{q}$, therefore

$$\mathbf{E}\{\pi\} \geq q\mathbf{P}\{\pi \geq q\} = q\mathbf{P}\left\{ |\log T| \leq \log \frac{1-q}{q} \right\} .$$

By Markov's inequality

$$\mathbf{P}\left\{ |\log T| \leq \log \frac{1-q}{q} \right\} \geq 1 - \frac{\mathbf{E}|\log T|}{\log \frac{1-q}{q}} .$$

Moreover because of $|\log T| = \left|\sum_{i \leq l} Z_i\right|$ we get

$$\mathbf{E}|\log T| = \mathbf{E}\left|\sum_{i \leq l} Z_i\right| \leq \sqrt{\mathbf{E}\left(\sum_{i \leq l} Z_i\right)^2} = \sqrt{\mathbf{E}\sum_i Z_i^2 + \sum_{i \neq i'} Z_i Z_{i'}}$$

$$= \sqrt{\sum_i \mathbf{E}\{Z_i^2\} + \sum_{i \neq i'} \mathbf{E}\{Z_i Z_{i'}\}} \ .$$

Using the inequality for $-1/4 \leq x \leq 1/4$

$$\left|\log \frac{1+2x}{1-2x}\right| = |\log(1+2x) - \log(1-2x)| = \log(1+2|x|) - \log(1-2|x|)$$

$$\leq 2|x| + \log 4 \cdot 2|x| \leq 5|x|,$$

on the one hand

$$\mathbf{E}\{Z_i^2\} = \log^2 \frac{1+2u_i}{1-2u_i} \leq 25 u_i^2$$

and on the other hand

$$\mathbf{E}\{(2Y_i - 1)(2Y_{i'} - 1)\} = 4\mathbf{E}\{Y_i Y_{i'}\} - 2\mathbf{E}\{Y_i\} - 2\mathbf{E}\{Y_{i'}\} + 1$$
$$= 4(\mathbf{E}\{Y_i Y_{i'}|C=1\}\mathbf{P}\{C=1\} + \mathbf{E}\{Y_i Y_{i'}|C=-1\}\mathbf{P}\{C=-1\}) - 1$$
$$= 4\left(\left(\frac{1}{2}+u_i\right)\left(\frac{1}{2}+u_{i'}\right)\frac{1}{2} + \left(\frac{1}{2}-u_i\right)\left(\frac{1}{2}-u_{i'}\right)\frac{1}{2}\right) - 1 = 4u_i u_{i'},$$

so

$$\mathbf{E}\{Z_i Z_{i'}\} = \mathbf{E}\{(2Y_i - 1)(2Y_{i'} - 1)\}\log\frac{1+2u_i}{1-2u_i}\log\frac{1+2u_{i'}}{1-2u_{i'}}$$

$$= 4u_i u_{i'} \log\frac{1+2u_i}{1-2u_i}\log\frac{1+2u_{i'}}{1-2u_{i'}}$$

$$\leq 4|u_i|\left|\log\frac{1+2u_i}{1-2u_i}\right||u_{i'}|\left|\log\frac{1+2u_{i'}}{1-2u_{i'}}\right| \leq 100 u_i^2 u_{i'}^2 \ .$$

Hence

$$\mathbf{E}|\log T| \leq \sqrt{25\sum_i u_i^2 + 100\sum_{i \neq i'} u_i^2 u_{i'}^2} \ .$$

Thus

$$\mathbf{E}\{\pi\} \geq q\left(1 - \frac{\mathbf{E}|\log T|}{\log\frac{1-q}{q}}\right) \geq q\left(1 - \frac{5\sqrt{\sum_i u_i^2 + 4\sum_{i \neq i'} u_i^2 u_{i'}^2}}{\log\frac{1-q}{q}}\right) \ .$$

By choosing $q = \left(1 + \exp\left(1 + 5\sqrt{\sum_i u_i^2 + 4\sum_{i \neq i'} u_i^2 u_{i'}^2}\right)\right)^{-1}$,

$$E\{\pi\} \geq \frac{1}{1 + \exp(1 + 5\sqrt{\sum_i u_i^2 + 4\sum_{i \neq i'} u_i^2 u_{i'}^2})} \frac{1}{1 + 5\sqrt{\sum_i u_i^2 + 4\sum_{i \neq i'} u_i^2 u_{i'}^2}}$$

$$\geq \frac{1}{(e+1)e^{10\sqrt{\sum_i u_i^2 + 4\sum_{i \neq i'} u_i^2 u_{i'}^2}}} \geq \frac{1}{4} e^{-10\sqrt{\sum_i u_i^2 + 4\sum_{i \neq i'} u_i^2 u_{i'}^2}}.$$

∎

PROOF OF THEOREM 1. This proof differs from that of Yang, it can be easily modified to individual lower bound in Theorem 2. First we define a subclass of distributions $(X, Y)$ contained in $\mathcal{D}^{(p,M)}$. We pack infinitely many disjoint cubes into $[0, 1]^d$ in the following way: For a given probability distribution $\{p_j\}$, let $\{B_j\}$ be a partition of $[0, 1]$ such that $B_j$ is an interval of length $p_j$. We pack disjoint cubes of volume $p_j^d$ into the rectangle

$$B_j \times [0, 1]^{d-1}.$$

Denote these cubes by $A_{j,1}, \ldots, A_{j,S_j}$, where $S_j = \left\lfloor \frac{1}{p_j} \right\rfloor^{d-1}$. Let $a_{j,k}$ be the center of $A_{j,k}$. Choose a function $m : \mathcal{R}^d \to [0, 1/4]$ such that
(I) the support of $m$ is a subset of $[-\frac{1}{2}, \frac{1}{2}]^d$,
(II) $\int m(x)\, dx > 0$,
(III) $m \in \mathcal{F}^{(p, M2^{\beta-1})}$.
The class of a posteriori probability functions is indexed by a vector

$$c = (c_{1,1}, c_{1,2}, \ldots, c_{1,S_1}, c_{2,1}, c_{2,2}, \ldots, c_{2,S_2}, \ldots)$$

of $+1$ or $-1$ components. Denote the set of all such vectors by $\mathcal{C}$. For $c \in \mathcal{C}$ define the function

$$\eta^{(c)}(x) = \frac{1}{2} + \sum_{j=1}^{\infty} \sum_{k=1}^{S_j} c_{j,k} m_{j,k}(x),$$

where $m_{j,k}(x) = p_j^p m(p_j^{-1}(x - a_{j,k}))$. Then it is easy to check (cf. [9], p. 1045) that $\eta^{(c)}(x) \in [0, 1]$ for all $x \in [0, 1]^d$ and because of (III)

$$\eta^{(c)} \in \mathcal{F}^{(p,M)}.$$

Hence, each distribution $(X, Y)$ with $Y \in \{0, 1\}$ and $E\{Y|X = x\} = P\{Y = 1|X = x\} = \eta^{(c)}(x)$ for all $x \in [0, 1]^d$ for some $c \in \mathcal{C}$ is contained in $\mathcal{D}^{(p,M)}$, which implies

$$\varliminf_{n \to \infty} \inf_{g_n} \sup_{(X,Y) \in \mathcal{D}^{(p,M)}} \frac{EL_n - L^*}{a_n}$$

$$\geq \varliminf_{n \to \infty} \inf_{g_n} \sup_{(X,Y):E\{Y|X=x\}=\eta^{(c)}(x), c \in \mathcal{C}} \frac{EL_n - L^*}{a_n}. \tag{7}$$

Let $g_n$ be an arbitrary rule. By definition, $\{I_{A_{j,k}}/2 : j, k\}$ is an orthogonal system in $\mathcal{L}_2(\nu)$ for the measure $\nu(A) = \int_A \sum_{j,k} m_{j,k} \, d\mu$, therefore the projection $\hat{g}_n - \frac{1}{2}$ of $g_n - \frac{1}{2}$ is given by

$$\hat{g}_n(x) - \frac{1}{2} = \sum_{j,k} \hat{c}_{n,j,k} \frac{I_{A_{j,k}}(x)}{2},$$

where

$$\hat{c}_{n,j,k} = \frac{\int (g_n - 1/2) I_{A_{j,k}}/2 \, d\nu}{\int \left(I_{A_{j,k}}/2\right)^2 d\nu} = 2 \frac{\int\limits_{A_{j,k}} (g_n - 1/2) \, d\nu}{\int\limits_{A_{j,k}} 1 \, d\nu}$$

$$= 2 \frac{\int\limits_{A_{j,k}} (g_n(x) - 1/2) m_{j,k}(x) \, dx}{\int\limits_{A_{j,k}} m_{j,k}(x) \, dx} = 2 \frac{\int\limits_{A_{j,k}} g_n(x) m_{j,k}(x) \, dx}{\int\limits_{A_{j,k}} m_{j,k}(x) \, dx} - 1 .$$

(Note that $\hat{c}_{n,j,k} \in [-1,1]$.) Let $c \in \mathcal{C}$ be arbitrary. Note that $g^* = \frac{1}{2} + \sum_{j,k} c_{j,k} \frac{I_{A_{j,k}}}{2}$. Then by (2)

$$L_n - L^* = 2 \int \left| \eta^{(c)} - \frac{1}{2} \right| I_{\{g_n \neq g^*\}} \, d\mu = 2 \int \sum_{j,k} m_{j,k} (g_n - g^*)^2 \, d\mu$$

$$= 2 \int \left( \left(g_n - \frac{1}{2}\right) - \left(g^* - \frac{1}{2}\right) \right)^2 d\nu$$

$$\geq 2 \int \left( \left(\hat{g}_n - \frac{1}{2}\right) - \left(g^* - \frac{1}{2}\right) \right)^2 d\nu$$

$$= 2 \int \sum_{j,k} m_{j,k} (\hat{g}_n - g^*)^2 \, d\mu = 2 \sum_{j,k} \frac{(\hat{c}_{n,j,k} - c_{j,k})^2}{4} \int\limits_{A_{j,k}} m_{j,k} \, d\mu$$

$$= \frac{1}{2} \|m\|_1 \sum_{j,k} (\hat{c}_{n,j,k} - c_{j,k})^2 p_j^{p+d} .$$

Let $\tilde{c}_{n,j,k}$ be 1 if $\hat{c}_{n,j,k} \geq 0$ and $-1$ otherwise. Because of $|\hat{c}_{n,j,k} - c_{j,k}| \geq \frac{|\tilde{c}_{n,j,k} - c_{j,k}|}{2} = I_{\{\tilde{c}_{n,j,k} \neq c_{j,k}\}}$, we get

$$L_n - L^* \geq \frac{1}{2} \|m\|_1 \sum_{j,k} I_{\{\tilde{c}_{n,j,k} \neq c_{j,k}\}} p_j^{p+d} .$$

This proves

$$\mathbf{E} L_n - L^* \geq \frac{1}{2} \|m\|_1 R_n(c), \qquad (8)$$

where

$$R_n(c) = \sum_{j:np_j^{2p+d} \leq 1} \sum_{k=1}^{S_j} p_j^{p+d} \cdot \mathbf{P}\{\tilde{c}_{n,j,k} \neq c_{j,k}\} . \qquad (9)$$

Equations (7) and (8) imply

$$\varliminf_{n \to \infty} \inf_{g_n} \sup_{(X,Y) \in \mathcal{D}(p,M)} \frac{EL_n - L^*}{a_n} \geq \frac{1}{2} \|m\|_1 \varliminf_{n \to \infty} \inf_{g_n} \sup_{c \in \mathcal{C}} \frac{R_n(c)}{a_n} . \qquad (10)$$

To bound the last term, we fix the rules $g_n$ and choose $c \in \mathcal{C}$ randomly. Let

$$C = (C_{1,1}, \dots, C_{1,S_1}, C_{2,1}, \dots, C_{2,S_2}, \dots)$$

be a sequence of independent identically distributed random variables independent of $X_1, X_2, \dots$, which satisfy $\mathbf{P}\{C_{1,1} = 1\} = \mathbf{P}\{C_{1,1} = -1\} = 1/2$. Next we derive a lower bound for

$$ER_n(C) = \sum_{j:np_j^{2p+d} \leq 1} \sum_{k=1}^{S_j} p_j^{p+d} \cdot \mathbf{P}\{\tilde{c}_{n,j,k} \neq C_{j,k}\} .$$

$\tilde{c}_{n,j,k}$ can be interpreted as a decision on $C_{j,k}$ using $D_n$. Its error probability is minimal for the Bayes decision $\bar{C}_{n,j,k}$, which is 1 if $\mathbf{P}\{C_{j,k} = 1 | D_n\} \geq \frac{1}{2}$ and $-1$ otherwise, therefore

$$\mathbf{P}\{\tilde{c}_{n,j,k} \neq C_{j,k}\} \geq \mathbf{P}\{\bar{C}_{n,j,k} \neq C_{j,k}\} .$$

Let $X_{i_1}, \dots, X_{i_l}$ be those $X_i \in A_{j,k}$. Then given $X_1, \dots, X_n$, $(Y_{i_1}, \dots, Y_{i_l})$ is distributed as $(Y_1, \dots, Y_l)$ in the conditions of Lemma 1 with $u_r = m_{j,k}(X_{i_r})$, while

$$(Y_1, \dots, Y_n) \setminus (Y_{i_1}, \dots, Y_{i_l})$$

depends only on $C \setminus \{C_{j,k}\}$ and on $X_r$'s with $r \notin \{i_1, \dots, i_l\}$, therefore is independent of $C_{j,k}$ given $X_1, \dots, X_n$. Now conditioning on $X_1, \dots, X_n$, the error of the conditional Bayes decision for $C_{j,k}$ based on $(Y_1, \dots, Y_n)$ depends only on $(Y_{i_1}, \dots, Y_{i_l})$, hence Lemma 1 implies

$$\mathbf{P}\{\bar{C}_{n,j,k} \neq C_{j,k} | X_1, \dots, X_n\} \geq \frac{1}{4} e^{-10\sqrt{\sum_i m_{j,k}^2(X_i) + 4 \sum_{i \neq i'} m_{j,k}^2(X_i) m_{j,k}^2(X_{i'})}} .$$

By Jensen-inequality

$$\mathbf{P}\{\bar{C}_{n,j,k} \neq C_{j,k}\} = \mathbf{E}\{\mathbf{P}\{\bar{C}_{n,j,k} \neq C_{j,k} | X_1, \dots, X_n\}\}$$

$$\geq \frac{1}{4} \mathbf{E} \left\{ e^{-10\sqrt{\sum_i m_{j,k}^2(X_i) + 4 \sum_{i \neq i'} m_{j,k}^2(X_i) m_{j,k}^2(X_{i'})}} \right\}$$

$$\geq \frac{1}{4} e^{-10\sqrt{\sum_i \mathbf{E}\{m_{j,k}^2(X_i)\} + 4 \sum_{i \neq i'} \mathbf{E}\{m_{j,k}^2(X_i) m_{j,k}^2(X_{i'})\}}}$$

$$= \frac{1}{4} e^{-10\sqrt{\int m^2 \, d\mu \cdot np_j^{2p+d} + 4(\int m^2 \, d\mu)^2 \cdot n(n-1) p_j^{4p+2d}}}$$

independently of $k$. Thus if $np_j^{2p+d} \leq 1$

$$\mathbf{P}\{\bar{C}_{n,j,k} \neq C_{j,k}\} \geq \frac{1}{4} e^{-10\|m\|_2\sqrt{1+4\|m\|_2^2}} > 0,$$

and

$$\mathbf{E}R_n(C) \geq \sum_{j:np_j^{2p+d}\leq 1} S_j p_j^{p+d} \cdot \mathbf{P}\{\bar{C}_{n,j,1} \neq C_{j,1}\}$$

$$\geq \frac{1}{4}e^{-10\|m\|_2\sqrt{1+4\|m\|_2^2}} \sum_{j:np_j^{2p+d}\leq 1} S_j p_j^{p+d} \geq K_1 \sum_{j:np_j^{2p+d}\leq 1} p_j^{p+1}, \quad (11)$$

where $K_1 = \frac{1}{4}e^{-10\|m\|_2\sqrt{1+4\|m\|_2^2}}(1/2)^{d-1}$. Setting $p_j = p_{j,n} = (1/n)^{\frac{1}{2p+d}}$ for $j \leq n^{\frac{1}{2p+d}}$,

$$\mathbf{E}R_n(C) \geq K_1 \lfloor n^{\frac{1}{2p+d}} \rfloor n^{-\frac{p+1}{2p+d}} = K_1 a_n(1 - o(1)),$$

so

$$\varliminf_{n\to\infty} \inf_{g_n} \sup_{c\in\mathcal{C}} \frac{R_n(c)}{a_n} \geq \varliminf_{n\to\infty} \inf_{g_n} \frac{\mathbf{E}R_n(C)}{a_n} \geq K_1 > 0 . \quad (12)$$

This together with (10) implies the assertion. ∎

PROOF OF THEOREM 2. We use the notations and results of the proof of Theorem 1. Now we have by (8)

$$\inf_{\{g_n\}} \sup_{(X,Y)\in\mathcal{D}(p,M)} \varlimsup_{n\to\infty} \frac{EL_n - L^*}{b_n a_n} \geq \frac{1}{2}\|m\|_1 \inf_{\{g_n\}} \sup_{c\in\mathcal{C}} \varlimsup_{n\to\infty} \frac{R_n(c)}{b_n a_n} . \quad (13)$$

In this case we have to choose $\{p_j\}$ independently from $n$. Since $b_n$ and $a_n$ tend to zero we can take a subsequence $\{n_t\}_{t\in\mathcal{N}}$ of $\{n\}_{n\in\mathcal{N}}$ with $b_{n_t} \leq 2^{-t}$ and $a_{n_t}^{1/p} \leq 2^{-t}$. Define $q_t$ such that

$$\frac{2^{-t}}{q_t} = \left\lceil \frac{2^{-t}}{a_{n_t}^{1/p}} \right\rceil,$$

and choose $\{p_j\}$ as

$$q_1, \ldots, q_1, q_2, \ldots, q_2, \ldots, q_t, \ldots, q_t, \ldots,$$

where $q_t$ is repeated $2^{-t}/q_t$ times. So

$$\sum_{j:np_j^{2p+d}\leq 1} p_j^{p+1} = \sum_{t:nq_t^{2p+d}\leq 1} \frac{2^{-t}}{q_t} q_t^{p+1} \geq \sum_{t:nq_t^{2p+d}\leq 1} b_{n_t} q_t^p$$

$$= \sum_{t:\lceil 2^{-t}a_{n_t}^{-1/p}\rceil \geq 2^{-t}a_n^{-1/p}} b_{n_t} \left(\frac{2^{-t}}{\left\lceil \frac{2^{-t}}{a_{n_t}^{1/p}} \right\rceil}\right)^p \geq \sum_{t:a_{n_t}\leq a_n} b_{n_t} \left(\frac{2^{-t}}{\frac{2^{-t}}{a_{n_t}^{1/p}} + 1}\right)^p$$

$$= \sum_{t:n_t\geq n} b_{n_t} \left(\frac{a_{n_t}^{1/p}}{1 + 2^t a_{n_t}^{1/p}}\right)^p \geq \sum_{t:n_t\geq n} \frac{b_{n_t} a_{n_t}}{2^p}$$

by $a_{n_t}^{1/p} \leq 2^{-t}$, and specially for $n = n_s$ (11) implies

$$\mathrm{ER}_{n_s}(C) \geq K_1 \sum_{j:n_s p_j^{2p+d} \leq 1} p_j^{p+1} \geq \frac{K_1}{2^p} \sum_{t \geq s} b_{n_t} a_{n_t} \geq \frac{K_1}{2^p} b_{n_s} a_{n_s} . \qquad (14)$$

Using (14) one gets

$$\inf_{\{g_n\}} \sup_{c \in \mathcal{C}} \varlimsup_{n \to \infty} \frac{R_n(c)}{b_n a_n} \geq \inf_{\{g_n\}} \sup_{c \in \mathcal{C}} \varlimsup_{s \to \infty} \frac{R_{n_s}(c)}{b_{n_s} a_{n_s}}$$

$$\geq \frac{K_1}{2^p} \inf_{\{g_n\}} \sup_{c \in \mathcal{C}} \varlimsup_{s \to \infty} \frac{R_{n_s}(c)}{\mathrm{ER}_{n_s}(C)} \geq \frac{K_1}{2^p} \inf_{\{g_n\}} \mathrm{E} \left( \varlimsup_{s \to \infty} \frac{R_{n_s}(C)}{\mathrm{ER}_{n_s}(C)} \right) .$$

Because of (11) and the fact that for all $c \in \mathcal{C}$

$$R_n(c) \leq \sum_{j:np_j^{2p+d} \leq 1} S_j p_j^{p+d} \leq \sum_{j:np_j^{2p+d} \leq 1} p_j^{p+1},$$

the sequence $R_{n_s}(C)/\mathrm{ER}_{n_s}(C)$ is uniformly bounded, so we can apply Fatou's lemma to get

$$\inf_{\{g_n\}} \sup_{c \in \mathcal{C}} \varlimsup_{n \to \infty} \frac{R_n(c)}{b_n a_n} \geq \frac{K_1}{2^p} \inf_{\{g_n\}} \varliminf_{s \to \infty} \mathrm{E} \left( \frac{R_{n_s}(C)}{\mathrm{ER}_{n_s}(C)} \right) = \frac{K_1}{2^p} > 0 .$$

This together with (13) implies the assertion. ∎

# References

1. Antos, A.: *Függvényosztályok tulajdonságai és szerepe az alakfelismerésben* (in Hungarian) (Properties of classes of functions and their roles in pattern recognition). M.Sc. Thesis, Technical University of Budapest, Budapest, Hungary (1995)
2. Antos, A., Györfi, L. and Kohler, M.: Lower bounds on the rate of convergence of nonparametric regression estimates. Preprint No. 98-11 (1998), Universität Stuttgart. Submitted
3. Antos, A. and Lugosi, G.: Strong minimax lower bounds for learning. *Machine Learning* 30 (1998) 31–56
4. Barron, A. R., Birgé, L. and Massart, P.: Risk bounds for model selection via penalization. Technical Report No. 95.54 (1995), Université Paris Sud. To appear in *Probability Theory and Related Fields*
5. Birgé, L.: On estimating a density using Hellinger distance and some other strange facts. *Probability Theory and Related Fields* 71 (1986) 271–291
6. Devroye, L. , Györfi, L. and Lugosi, G. : *A Probabilistic Theory of Pattern Recognition* Springer Verlag (1996)
7. Mammen, E. and Tsybakov, A. B.: Smooth discrimination analysis. Submitted
8. Stone, C. J.: Consistent nonparametric regression. *Annals of Statistics* 5 (1977) 595–645
9. Stone, C. J. : Optimal global rates of convergence for nonparametric regression. *Annals of Statistics* 10 (1982) 1040–1053
10. Yang, Y.: Minimax nonparametric classification — Part I: Rates of convergence. Submitted

# On Error Estimation for the Partitioning Classification Rule

Márta Horváth

Dept. of Computer Science and Information Theory,
Technical University of Budapest
1521 Stoczek u. 2, Budapest, Hungary.
marti@szit.bme.hu

**Abstract.** The resubstitution and the deleted error estimates for the partitioning
classification rule from a sample
$(X_1, Y_1), \ldots, (X_n, Y_n)$ are studied. The random part of the resubstitution
estimate is shown to be small for arbitrary partition and for any distribution of $(X, Y)$. If we assume that $X$ has a density $f$ and the partitions
consist of rectangles, then the difference between the expected value of
the estimate and the Bayes error restricted to the partition is less than
a constant times $1/\sqrt{n}$. The main result of the paper is that, under the
same conditions, the deleted estimate is asymptotically normal.

## 1  Introduction

Let $X$ be the $d$-dimensional feature vector with distribution $\mu$, and let $Y$ be the
binary valued label. Throughout the paper it is assumed that $X$ takes its value
in a bounded region $\mathcal{X} \subset \mathcal{R}^d$. Denote the aposteriori probabilities by

$$P_i(x) = \mathbf{P}\{Y = i | X = x\}, \ i = 0, 1.$$

In pattern recognition the value of the label $Y$ is to be predicted upon observing
the feature vector $X$. The prediction rule or classifier $g$ is a function $\mathcal{X} \to \{0, 1\}$,
whose performance is measured by the probability of error

$$L(g) = \mathbf{P}\{g(X) \neq Y\}.$$

The Bayes classifier

$$g^*(x) = \begin{cases} 0, & \text{if } P_1(x) < 1/2 \\ 1, & \text{otherwise.} \end{cases}$$

is well-known to have minimal probability of error among all possible classifiers.
Its error probability $L(g^*)$ is called the Bayes error, and is denoted by $L^*$.

$$L^* = \mathbf{E}\{\min(P_0(X), P_1(X))\}.$$

Assume that $n$ independent copies of $(X, Y)$ form the available data sequence:

$$D_n = ((X_1, Y_1), \ldots, (X_n, Y_n)).$$

These data may be used to design the classification rule $g_n(x)$, whose probability of error is the random variable

$$L_n = L(g_n) = \mathbf{P}\{g_n(X) \neq Y | D_n\}.$$

Many important classification rules partition $\mathcal{X}$ into disjoint cells and classify in each cell according to the majority vote among the labels of the $X_i$'s falling in the same cell. Let $\mathcal{P}_n = \{A_{nj}, j = 1, 2, \ldots\}$ be a partition of $\mathcal{X}$, let $m_n$ denote the number of cells in the partition, and let $A_n(x)$ denote the cell in the partition that includes $x$, then the partitioning classification rule becomes:

$$g_n(x) = \begin{cases} 0 \text{ if } \sum_{i=1}^n I_{\{Y_i=1\}} I_{\{X_i \in A_n(x)\}} \\ \quad \leq \sum_{i=1}^n I_{\{Y_i=0\}} I_{\{X_i \in A_n(x)\}} \\ 1 \text{ otherwise} \end{cases}$$

Estimating the error probability of a classification rule $g_n$ is of great importance. The designer always wants to know what performance can be expected from a classifier. Since the distribution of the data is unknown, it is important to find and analyze error estimation methods that work well independently from the distribution of $(X, Y)$.

## 2 Resubstitution estimate

The resubstitution estimate $\hat{L}_n$ counts the number of errors committed on the training sequence $(X_1, Y_1), (X_2, Y_2), \ldots, (X_n, Y_n)$ by the classification rule, i.e. for a classifier $g_n$ it is defined as

$$\hat{L}_n = \frac{1}{n} \sum_{i=1}^n I_{\{g_n(X_i) \neq Y_i\}},$$

which for the partitioning classification rule can be written in the following form:

$$\hat{L}_n = \sum_{j=1}^{m_n} \min\{\nu_n(A_{nj}), \mu_n(A_{nj}) - \nu_n(A_{nj})\},$$

where

$$\nu_n(A) = \frac{1}{n} \sum_{i=1}^n I_{\{X_i \in A\}} Y_i \quad \text{and} \quad \mu_n(A) = \frac{1}{n} \sum_{i=1}^n I_{\{X_i \in A\}}.$$

$\hat{L}_n$ is an estimate of the Bayes error $R_n^*$ restricted to the partition $\mathcal{P}_n$:

$$R_n^* = \sum_{j=1}^{m_n} \min\{\nu(A_{nj}), \mu(A_{nj}) - \nu(A_{nj})\},$$

where

$$\nu(A) = \mathbf{E}\nu_n(A).$$

Concerning the resubstitution error estimate for partitioning rule, the following inequalities are known (see Sec. 23.2 in Devroye, Györfi and Lugosi (1996)): for an arbitrary partition $\mathcal{P}_n$,

$$Var(\hat{L}_n) \leq \frac{1}{n}$$

and

$$\mathbf{E}\hat{L}_n \leq R_n^*.$$

For a finite partition of size $m_n$

$$R_n^* - \mathbf{E}\hat{L}_n \leq \sqrt{\frac{2m_n}{n}}. \tag{1}$$

The resubstitution estimate for the partitioning rule is asymptotically normal under certain conditions:

**Lemma 1.** *(Györfi,Horváth (1998)) Consider the partitions where $A_{nj}$ are $d$-dimensional rectangles. Let $a_n^i(x)$, $i = 1, 2, ..., d$, denote the sidelengths of $A_n(x)$. Assume that for all $x$ there exists a $K(x)$ so that $\frac{a_n^i(x)}{a_n^j(x)} \leq K(x)$ for all $1 \leq i, j \leq d$ and $n$. Assume that*

$$\lim_{n \to \infty} \sup_{A_{nj}} diam(A_{nj}) = 0$$

*and*

$$\lim_{n \to \infty} \frac{m_n^2}{n} = 0 \tag{2}$$

*and*

$$\lim_{n \to \infty} \frac{\log n}{n\lambda(A_n(x))} = 0,$$

*where $\lambda$ is the Lebesgue measure. If $\mu$ has a density $f$ and there is a constant $c$ such that*

$$|\mu(A_{nj}) - 2\nu(A_{nj})| > c\mu(A_{nj}) \tag{3}$$

*for all $n$ and $j$, then*

$$n^{1/2} \left( \hat{L}_n - R_n^* \right) / \sqrt{L^*/2} \xrightarrow{\mathcal{D}} N(0, 1).$$

REMARK. For cubic partitions with size $h_n$ these conditions mean $h_n \to 0$, $nh_n^{2d} \to \infty$ and $nh_n^d/\log n \to \infty$ as $n \to \infty$.

The random part of the estimate $\hat{L}_n$ is small for arbitrary partition and for any distribution of $(X, Y)$:

**Theorem 1.** *For the resubstitution estimate for the partitioning rule, and for all $n$ and $\epsilon > 0$,*

$$\mathbf{P}\{n^{1/2}|\hat{L}_n - \mathbf{E}\hat{L}_n| > \epsilon\} \leq 2e^{-2\epsilon^2}.$$

Using this result we can remove $m_n$ from the upper bound in (1).

**Theorem 2.** *For any distribution of* $(X, Y)$ *and for $n$ large enough for the estimate $\hat{L}_n$ of the error probability of a partitioning rule satisfying the conditions of Lemma 1*

$$R_n^* - \mathbf{E}\hat{L}_n \leq \frac{1.18}{\sqrt{n}}.$$

## 3  Deleted estimate

The deleted estimate or cross-validation attempts to avoid the bias present in the resubstitution estimate. The method deletes $(X_i, Y_i)$ from the training data and creats a classifier $g_{n-1}$ using the remaining $n - 1$ pairs. It tests for an error on $(X_i, Y_i)$, and repeats this procedure for all $n$ pairs of the training data $D_n$. Formally denote the training set with $(X_i, Y_i)$ deleted by

$$D_{n,i} = ((X_1, Y_1), \ldots, (X_{i-1}, Y_{i-1}), (X_{i+1}, Y_{i+1}), \ldots, (X_n, Y_n)).$$

Then define

$$\bar{L}_n = \frac{1}{n} \sum_{i=1}^{n} I_{\{g_{n-1}(X_i, D_{n,i}) \neq Y_i\}}.$$

Clearly, the deleted estimate is almost unbiased in the sense that

$$\mathbf{E}\bar{L}_n = \mathbf{E}L_{n-1}.$$

Concerning the deleted error estimate for partitioning rule the following is known (see Sec. 24.5 in Devroye, Györfi and Lugosi (1996)): for an arbitrary partition $\mathcal{P}_n$,

$$\mathbf{E}\left\{ (\bar{L}_n - L_n)^2 \right\} \leq \frac{1 + 6/e}{n} + \frac{6}{\sqrt{\pi(n-1)}}.$$

The resubstitution estimate for any partitioning classification rule is smaller than the deleted estimate:

$$\bar{L}_n \geq \hat{L}_n, \tag{4}$$

since if $(X_i, Y_i)$ is a mistake w.r.t. $\hat{L}_n$, i.e. $Y_i \neq g_n(X_i)$, then the label $Y_i$ is in the minority among the labels of the data falling into its cell. Then, of course, $Y_i$ is in the minority of its cell w.r.t. $D_{n,i} = D_n \setminus \{X_i, Y_i\}$, which implies that $(X_i, Y_i)$ is a mistake w.r.t. $\bar{L}_n$.

The main aim of the paper is to derive the asymptotic normality of the distribution of $\bar{L}_n$.

**Theorem 3.** *Under the conditions of Lemma 1,*

$$n^{1/2} \left( \bar{L}_n - R_n^* \right) / \sqrt{L^*/2} \overset{\mathcal{D}}{\to} N(0, 1).$$

The deleted estimate for partitioning classification rule is asymptotically normal under similar conditions as the resubstitution estimate.

# 4  Proofs

PROOF OF THEOREM 1

The result comes from a straightforward application of McDiarmid's inequality:

**Lemma 2.** *(McDiarmid (1989), for the proof see Devroye, Györfi and Lugosi (1996)) Let $Z_1, \ldots, Z_n$ be independent random variables taking values in a set $A$, and assume that the measurable function $F : A^n \to \mathcal{R}$ satisfies*

$$\sup_{z_1, \ldots, z_n, z_i'} |F(z_1, \ldots, z_i, \ldots, z_n) - F(z_1, \ldots, z_i', \ldots, z_n)| \leq c_i, \ 1 \leq i \leq n.$$

*Then for all $\epsilon > 0$*

$$\mathbf{P}\{|F(Z_1, \ldots, Z_n) - \mathbf{E}F(Z_1, \ldots, Z_n)| > \epsilon\} \leq 2e^{-2\epsilon^2/(\sum_{i=1}^n c_i^2)}.$$

Let $Z_i = (X_i, Y_i)$ and the set $A$ is $(\mathcal{R}^d \times 0, 1)^n$. It can be easily seen that in case of the resubstitution estimate for partitioning rule $c_i = \frac{1}{n}$. ∎

PROOF OF THEOREM 2

From the result on the asymptotic normality

$$\mathbf{P}\{n^{1/2}|\hat{L}_n - R_n^*| > \epsilon\} \to 1 - 2\Phi\left(\frac{\epsilon}{\sqrt{L^*/2}}\right),$$

where $\Phi$ is the standard normal distribution function. Since $R_n^* - \mathbf{E}\hat{L}_n$ is not random

$$\begin{aligned}
I_{\{\sqrt{n}|R_n^* - \mathbf{E}\hat{L}_n| > \epsilon\}} &= \mathbf{P}\{\sqrt{n}|R_n^* - \mathbf{E}\hat{L}_n| > \epsilon\} \\
&\leq \mathbf{P}\{\sqrt{n}(|\hat{L}_n - \mathbf{E}\hat{L}_n| + |\hat{L}_n - R_n^*|) > \epsilon\} \\
&\leq \mathbf{P}\{\sqrt{n}|\hat{L}_n - \mathbf{E}\hat{L}_n| > \epsilon/2\} \\
&\quad + \mathbf{P}\{\sqrt{n}|\hat{L}_n - R_n^*| > \epsilon/2\}
\end{aligned}$$

therefore

$$\varlimsup_{n\to\infty} I_{\{\sqrt{n}|R_n^* - \mathbf{E}\hat{L}_n| > \epsilon\}} \leq 2e^{-\epsilon^2/2} + 1 - 2\Phi\left(\frac{\epsilon}{\sqrt{2L^*}}\right).$$

Obviously there exist such $\epsilon_0$ for which the righthand side of the inequality is strictly smaller than 1, and then

$$I_{\{\sqrt{n}|R_n^* - \mathbf{E}\hat{L}_n| > \epsilon_0\}} = 0$$

for sufficiently large $n$. Using the trivial upper bound

$$\Phi(\epsilon/\sqrt{2L^*}) \geq 1/2,$$

$\epsilon_0 = \sqrt{2\ln 2} \approx 1.18$ is a valid choice. ∎

## PROOF OF THEOREM 3

It is easy to see that if $U_n$ and $V_n$ are random variables and $U_n \overset{\mathcal{D}}{\to} N(0,1)$ and $V_n \to 0$ in probability, then $U_n + V_n \overset{\mathcal{D}}{\to} N(0,1)$.

So, since the conditions are the same as for Lemma 1, it suffices to show that

$$\sqrt{n}\left(\bar{L}_n - \hat{L}_n\right) \to 0$$

in probability as $n \to \infty$.

It is well known that if, for a nonnegative random variable $Z_n$, $\mathbf{E}Z_n \to 0$, then $Z_n \to 0$ in probability. Thus, since from (4) $\bar{L}_n - \hat{L}_n \geq 0$, we have to prove that

$$\sqrt{n}\mathbf{E}(\bar{L}_n - \hat{L}_n) \to 0$$

as $n \to \infty$.

For the partitioning classification rule the deleted estimate can be written in the following form:

$$\bar{L}_n = \sum_{j=1}^{m_n} \left( \nu_n(A_{nj}) I_{\{n\nu_n(A_{nj})-1 \leq n(\mu_n(A_{nj})-\nu_n(A_{nj}))\}} \right.$$

$$\left. + (\mu_n(A_{nj}) - \nu_n(A_{nj})) I_{\{n(\mu_n(A_{nj})-\nu_n(A_{nj}))-1 < n\nu_n(A_{nj})\}} \right).$$

Therefore

$$\sqrt{n}\mathbf{E}(\bar{L}_n - \hat{L}_n)$$

$$= \sqrt{n}\mathbf{E}\left\{ \sum_{j=1}^{m_n} (\min\{\nu_n(A_{nj}), \mu_n(A_{nj}) - \nu_n(A_{nj})\} \right.$$

$$- \left( \nu_n(A_{nj}) I_{\{n\nu_n(A_{nj})-1 \leq n(\mu_n(A_{nj})-\nu_n(A_{nj}))\}} \right.$$

$$\left. \left. + (\mu_n(A_{nj}) - \nu_n(A_{nj})) I_{\{n(\mu_n(A_{nj})-\nu_n(A_{nj}))-1 < n\nu_n(A_{nj})\}} \right)\right) \right\}$$

$$= \sqrt{n}\mathbf{E}\left\{ \sum_{j=1}^{m_n} \left( \nu_n(A_{nj}) I_{\{n\nu_n(A_{nj}) \leq n(\mu_n(A_{nj})-\nu_n(A_{nj}))\}} \right. \right.$$

$$+ (\mu_n(A_{nj}) - \nu_n(A_{nj})) I_{\{n(\mu_n(A_{nj})-\nu_n(A_{nj})) < n\nu_n(A_{nj})\}}$$

$$- \left( \nu_n(A_{nj}) I_{\{n\nu_n(A_{nj})-1 \leq n(\mu_n(A_{nj})-\nu_n(A_{nj}))\}} \right.$$

$$\left. \left. + (\mu_n(A_{nj}) - \nu_n(A_{nj})) I_{\{n(\mu_n(A_{nj})-\nu_n(A_{nj}))-1 < n\nu_n(A_{nj})\}} \right)\right) \right\}$$

$$= \sqrt{n}\mathbf{E}\left\{ \sum_{j=1}^{m_n} \left( \nu_n(A_{nj}) I_{\{n\nu_n(A_{nj})-1 \leq n(\mu_n(A_{nj})-\nu_n(A_{nj})), n\nu_n(A_{nj}) > n(\mu_n(A_{nj})-\nu_n(A_{nj}))\}} \right. \right.$$

$$\left. \left. + (\mu_n(A_{nj}) - \nu_n(A_{nj})) I_{\{n(\mu_n(A_{nj})-\nu_n(A_{nj}))-1 < n\nu_n(A_{nj}), n(\mu_n(A_{nj})-\nu_n(A_{nj})) \geq n\nu_n(A_{nj})\}} \right) \right\}$$

$$= \sqrt{n}\mathbf{E}\left\{ \sum_{j=1}^{m_n} \left( \nu_n(A_{nj}) I_{\{n\nu_n(A_{nj})-1 \leq n(\mu_n(A_{nj})-\nu_n(A_{nj})) < n\nu_n(A_{nj})\}} \right. \right.$$

$$+(\mu_n(A_{nj}) - \nu_n(A_{nj}))I_{\{n(\mu_n(A_{nj})-\nu_n(A_{nj}))-1<n\nu_n(A_{nj})\le n(\mu_n(A_{nj})-\nu_n(A_{nj}))\}}\Big)\Big\}$$

$$= \sqrt{n}\mathbf{E}\left\{\sum_{j=1}^{m_n}\left(\nu_n(A_{nj})I_{\{n\nu_n(A_{nj})=n(\mu_n(A_{nj})-\nu_n(A_{nj}))+1\}}\right.\right.$$

$$\left.\left.+(\mu_n(A_{nj}) - \nu_n(A_{nj}))I_{\{n(\mu_n(A_{nj})-\nu_n(A_{nj}))=n\nu_n(A_{nj})\}}\right)\right\}$$

$$= \sqrt{n}\sum_{j=1}^{m_n}\mathbf{E}\left\{\nu_n(A_{nj})I_{\{n\nu_n(A_{nj})=n(\mu_n(A_{nj})-\nu_n(A_{nj}))+1\}}\right.$$

$$\left.+(\mu_n(A_{nj}) - \nu_n(A_{nj}))I_{\{n(\mu_n(A_{nj})-\nu_n(A_{nj}))=n\nu_n(A_{nj})\}}\right\}$$

$$= \sqrt{n}\sum_{j=1}^{m_n}\left(\mathbf{E}\left\{\nu_n(A_{nj})I_{\{n\nu_n(A_{nj})=n(\mu_n(A_{nj})-\nu_n(A_{nj}))+1\}}\right\}\right.$$

$$\left.+\mathbf{E}\left\{(\mu_n(A_{nj}) - \nu_n(A_{nj}))I_{\{n(\mu_n(A_{nj})-\nu_n(A_{nj}))=n\nu_n(A_{nj})\}}\right\}\right). \tag{5}$$

Consider the first term of the sum for the cell $A = A_{nj}$:

$$\mathbf{E}\left\{\nu_n(A)I_{\{n\nu_n(A)=n(\mu_n(A)-\nu_n(A))+1\}}\right\}$$

$$= \sum_{k=0}^{n}\mathbf{E}\left\{\nu_n(A)I_{\{n\nu_n(A)=n(\mu_n(A)-\nu_n(A))+1\}}|n\mu_n(A) = k\right\}\mathbf{P}\{n\mu_n(A) = k\}$$

$$= \sum_{k=0}^{n/2}\mathbf{E}\left\{\nu_n(A)I_{\{n\nu_n(A)=n(\mu_n(A)-\nu_n(A))+1\}}|n\mu_n(A) = 2k+1\right\}\mathbf{P}\{n\mu_n(A) = 2k+1\}$$

$$= \sum_{k=0}^{n/2}\frac{k+1}{n}\binom{2k+1}{k+1}\left(\frac{\nu(A)}{\mu(A)}\right)^{k+1}\left(\frac{\mu(A)-\nu(A)}{\mu(A)}\right)^{k}$$

$$\binom{n}{2k+1}\mu(A)^{2k+1}(1-\mu(A))^{n-(2k+1)}$$

$$= \sum_{k=0}^{n/2}\frac{k+1}{n}\binom{2k+1}{k+1}\nu(A)^{k+1}(\mu(A)-\nu(A))^{k}\binom{n}{2k+1}(1-\mu(A))^{n-(2k+1)}$$

$$= \sum_{k=0}^{n/2}\frac{2k+1}{n}\binom{2k}{k}\nu(A)^{k+1}(\mu(A)-\nu(A))^{k}\binom{n}{2k+1}(1-\mu(A))^{n-(2k+1)}$$

$$= \sum_{k=0}^{n/2}\binom{2k}{k}\nu(A)^{k+1}(\mu(A)-\nu(A))^{k}\binom{n-1}{2k}(1-\mu(A))^{n-(2k+1)}$$

$$\le \sum_{k=0}^{n/2}2^{2k}\nu(A)^{k+1}(\mu(A)-\nu(A))^{k}\binom{n}{2k}(1-\mu(A))^{n-(2k+1)}$$

$$= \frac{\nu(A)}{1-\mu(A)}\sum_{k=0}^{n/2}2^{2k}\nu(A)^{k}(\mu(A)-\nu(A))^{k}\binom{n}{2k}(1-\mu(A))^{n-2k}$$

$$
= \frac{\nu(A)}{1-\mu(A)} \sum_{k=0}^{n/2} \binom{n}{2k} \left(2\sqrt{\nu(A)(\mu(A)-\nu(A))}\right)^{2k} (1-\mu(A))^{n-2k}
$$

$$
\leq \frac{\nu(A)}{1-\mu(A)} \sum_{k=0}^{n} \binom{n}{k} \left(2\sqrt{\nu(A)(\mu(A)-\nu(A))}\right)^{k} (1-\mu(A))^{n-k}
$$

$$
= \frac{\nu(A)}{1-\mu(A)} \left(2\sqrt{\nu(A)(\mu(A)-\nu(A))}+1-\mu(A)\right)^{n}
$$

$$
\leq \frac{\mu(A)}{1-\mu(A)} \left(2\sqrt{\nu(A)(\mu(A)-\nu(A))}+1-\mu(A)\right)^{n} \tag{6}
$$

The second term in (5) can be bounded similarly:

$$
\mathbf{E}\left\{(\mu_n(A)-\nu_n(A))I_{\{n(\mu_n(A)-\nu_n(A))=n\nu_n(A)\}}\right\}
$$

$$
= \sum_{k=0}^{n} \mathbf{E}\left\{(\mu_n(A)-\nu_n(A))I_{\{n(\mu_n(A)-\nu_n(A))=n\nu_n(A)\}}\big|n\mu_n(A)=k\right\}\mathbf{P}\{n\mu_n(A)=k\}
$$

$$
= \sum_{k=0}^{n/2} \mathbf{E}\left\{(\mu_n(A)-\nu_n(A))I_{\{n(\mu_n(A)-\nu_n(A))=n\nu_n(A)\}}\big|n\mu_n(A)=2k\right\}\mathbf{P}\{n\mu_n(A)=2k\}
$$

$$
= \sum_{k=0}^{n/2} \frac{k}{n}\binom{2k}{k}\left(\frac{\nu(A)}{\mu(A)}\right)^{k}\left(\frac{\mu(A)-\nu(A)}{\mu(A)}\right)^{k}\binom{n}{2k}\mu(A)^{2k}(1-\mu(A))^{n-2k}
$$

$$
= \sum_{k=0}^{n/2} \frac{k}{n}\binom{2k}{k}\nu(A)^{k}(\mu(A)-\nu(A))^{k}\binom{n}{2k}(1-\mu(A))^{n-2k}
$$

$$
\leq \frac{1}{n}\sum_{k=0}^{n/2} 2k2^{2k}\nu(A)^{k}(\mu(A)-\nu(A))^{k}\binom{n}{2k}(1-\mu(A))^{n-2k}
$$

$$
= \frac{1}{n}\sum_{k=0}^{n/2} 2k\binom{n}{2k}\left(2\sqrt{\nu(A)(\mu(A)-\nu(A))}\right)^{2k}(1-\mu(A))^{n-2k}
$$

$$
\leq \frac{1}{n}\sum_{k=0}^{n} k\binom{n}{k}\left(2\sqrt{\nu(A)(\mu(A)-\nu(A))}\right)^{k}(1-\mu(A))^{n-k}
$$

$$
= \frac{1}{n}\left(2\sqrt{\nu(A)(\mu(A)-\nu(A))}+1-\mu(A)\right)^{n}\frac{1}{\left(2\sqrt{\nu(A)(\mu(A)-\nu(A))}+1-\mu(A)\right)^{n}}
$$

$$
\sum_{k=0}^{n} k\binom{n}{k}\left(2\sqrt{\nu(A)(\mu(A)-\nu(A))}\right)^{k}(1-\mu(A))^{n-k}
$$

$$
= \frac{1}{n}\left(2\sqrt{\nu(A)(\mu(A)-\nu(A))}+1-\mu(A)\right)^{n}
$$

$$
\mathbf{E}\left\{Binom\left(n,\frac{2\sqrt{\nu(A)(\mu(A)-\nu(A))}}{2\sqrt{\nu(A)(\mu(A)-\nu(A))}+1-\mu(A)}\right)\right\}
$$

$$= \frac{1}{n} \frac{n2\sqrt{\nu(A)(\mu(A) - \nu(A))}}{2\sqrt{\nu(A)(\mu(A) - \nu(A))} + 1 - \mu(A)} \left(2\sqrt{\nu(A)(\mu(A) - \nu(A))} + 1 - \mu(A)\right)^n$$

$$\leq \frac{\mu(A)}{1 - \mu(A)} \left(2\sqrt{\nu(A)(\mu(A) - \nu(A))} + 1 - \mu(A)\right)^n$$

From this upper bound and from (5) and (6)

$$\sqrt{n}\mathbf{E}(\bar{L}_n - \hat{L}_n)$$

$$\leq \sqrt{n} \sum_{j=1}^{m_n} 2 \frac{\mu(A_{nj})}{1 - \mu(A_{nj})} \left(2\sqrt{\nu(A_{nj})(\mu(A_{nj}) - \nu(A_{nj}))} + 1 - \mu(A_{nj})\right)^n$$

$$\leq \sqrt{n} \sum_{j=1}^{m_n} 2\mu(A_{nj}) e^{-n\left(\mu(A_{nj}) - 2\sqrt{\nu(A_{nj})(\mu(A_{nj}) - \nu(A_{nj}))}\right)}$$

$$= \sqrt{n} \sum_{j=1}^{m_n} 2\mu(A_{nj}) e^{-n\mu(A_{nj})\left(1 - 2\sqrt{\frac{\nu(A_{nj})}{\mu(A_{nj})}\left(1 - \frac{\nu(A_{nj})}{\mu(A_{nj})}\right)}\right)},$$

where the second inequality comes from the fact that $1 - z \leq e^{-z}$ if $z > 0$, and clearly $\mu(A_{nj}) - 2\sqrt{\nu(A_{nj})(\mu(A_{nj}) - \nu(A_{nj}))} > 0$, and we can assume that $\mu(A_{nj}) < 1/2$.

The condition (3) means that

$$\left|\frac{1}{2} - \frac{\nu(A_{nj})}{\mu(A_{nj})}\right| > \frac{c}{2},$$

and because of this

$$\frac{\nu(A_{nj})}{\mu(A_{nj})} \left(1 - \frac{\nu(A_{nj})}{\mu(A_{nj})}\right) \leq \frac{1}{4} - \frac{c^2}{4}.$$

Thus, if we denote $1 - 2\sqrt{\frac{1}{4} - \frac{c^2}{4}} = 1 - \sqrt{1 - c^2}$ by $\delta(c)$ then

$$\sqrt{n}\mathbf{E}(\bar{L}_n - \hat{L}_n) \leq \sqrt{n} \sum_{j=1}^{m_n} 2\mu(A_{nj}) e^{-n\mu(A_{nj})\left(1 - 2\sqrt{\frac{\nu(A_{nj})}{\mu(A_{nj})}\left(1 - \frac{\nu(A_{nj})}{\mu(A_{nj})}\right)}\right)}$$

$$\leq \sqrt{n} \sum_{j=1}^{m_n} 2\mu(A_{nj}) e^{-\delta(c)n\mu(A_{nj})}$$

$$= \sqrt{n} \sum_{j=1}^{m_n} \frac{2}{\delta(c)n} \delta(c)n\mu(A_{nj}) e^{-\delta(c)n\mu(A_{nj})}$$

$$\leq \sqrt{n} \sum_{j=1}^{m_n} \frac{2}{\delta(c)n} \max_z z e^{-z}$$

$$\leq \sqrt{n} m_n \frac{2}{\delta(c)n} = \frac{2m_n}{\delta(c)\sqrt{n}} \to 0$$

because of condition (2). ∎

# References

1. Devroye, L., Györfi, L. and Lugosi, G. (1996). *Probabilistic Theory of Pattern Recognition*. Springer Verlag, New York.
2. Györfi, L. and Horváth, M. (1998) On the asymptotic normality of the resubstitution error estimate for partitioning classification rule, In *Advances in Data Science and Classification*, A. Rizza, M. Vichi, H. H. Bock (Eds.), Springer, p. 197-204.
3. McDiarmid, C. (1989) On the method of bounded differences, In *Surveys in Combinatorics 1989*, p. 148-188. Cambridge University Press, Cambridge.

# Margin Distribution Bounds on Generalization

John Shawe-Taylor and Nello Cristianini

Royal Holloway, University of London
University of Bristol
j.shawe-taylor@dcs.rhbnc.ac.uk, nello.cristianini@bristol.ac.uk

**Abstract.** A number of results have bounded generalization of a classifier in terms of its margin on the training points. There has been some debate about whether the minimum margin is the best measure of the distribution of training set margin values with which to estimate the generalization. Freund and Schapire [6] have shown how a different function of the margin distribution can be used to bound the number of mistakes of an on-line learning algorithm for a perceptron, as well as an expected error bound. We show that a slight generalization of their construction can be used to give a pac style bound on the tail of the distribution of the generalization errors that arise from a given sample size. We also derive an algorithm for optimizing the new measure for general kernel based learning machines. Some preliminary experiments are presented.

## 1 Introduction

The idea that a large margin classifier might be expected to give good generalization is certainly not new [5, 14]. Despite this insight it was not until comparatively recently [10] that such a conjecture has been placed on a firm footing in the probably approximately correct (pac) model of learning. Learning in this model entails giving a bound on the generalization error which will hold with high confidence over randomly drawn training sets. In this sense it can be said to ensure robust learning, something that cannot be guaranteed by bounds on the expected error of a classifier.

Despite successes in extending this style of analysis to the agnostic case [1] and applying it to neural networks [1], boosting algorithms [9] and Bayesian algorithms [4], there has been concern that the measure of the distribution of margin values attained by the training set is largely ignored in a bound that depends only on its minimal value. Intuitively, there appeared to be something lost with a bound that depended so critically on the positions of possibly a small proportion of the training set, ignoring the margin attained by the majority of the points.

Freund and Schapire [6] (a similar technique was employed by Klasner and Simon [8] for rendering a real valued function learning algorithm noise tolerant) developed a measure of the margin distribution which they showed could be used to bound the expected generalization error more tightly than the minimal margin. The aim of this paper is to show that the same measure can also be used to provide a pac style bound on the generalization error. We will also develop an algorithm for a modified kernel based linear machine which directly optimises the new measure.

## 2   Background Results

We first give some necessary definitions.

**Definition 1.** *Let $H$ be a set of binary valued functions. We say that a set of points $X$ is shattered by $H$ if for all binary vectors $b$ indexed by $X$, there is a function $f_b \in H$ realising $b$ on $X$. The Vapnik-Chervonenkis (VC) dimension, VCdim($H$), of the set $H$ is the size of the largest shattered set, if this is finite or infinity otherwise.*

**Definition 2.** *Let $H$ be a set of real valued functions. We say that a set of points $X$ is $\gamma$-shattered by $H$ if there are real numbers $r_x$ indexed by $x \in X$ such that for all binary vectors $b$ indexed by $X$, there is a function $f_b \in H$ satisfying*

$$f_b(x) \begin{cases} \geq r_x + \gamma \text{ if } b_x = 1 \\ \leq r_x - \gamma \text{ otherwise.} \end{cases}$$

*The* fat shattering dimension *$\text{fat}_H$ of the set $H$ is a function from the positive real numbers to the integers which maps a value $\gamma$ to the size of the largest $\gamma$-shattered set, if this is finite or infinity otherwise.*

We will make critical use of the following result contained in Shawe-Taylor et al [10] which involves the fat shattering dimension of the space of functions.

**Theorem 1.** *Consider a real valued function class $\mathcal{H}$ having fat shattering function bounded above by the function $\text{afat} : \mathbf{R} \to \mathbf{N}$ which is continuous from the right. Fix $\theta \in \mathbf{R}$. Then with probability at least $1 - \delta$ a learner who correctly classifies $m$ independently generated examples $z$ with $h = T_\theta(f) \in T_\theta(\mathcal{H})$ such that $\text{er}_z(h) = 0$ and $\gamma = \min |f(\mathbf{x}_i) - \theta|$ will have error of $h$ bounded from above by*

$$\epsilon(m, k, \delta) = \frac{2}{m} \left( k \log_2 \left( \frac{8em}{k} \right) \log_2(32m) + \log_2 \left( \frac{8m}{\delta} \right) \right),$$

*where $k = \text{afat}(\gamma/8) \leq em$.*

Note how the fat shattering dimension at scale $\gamma/8$ plays the role of the VC dimension in this bound. This result motivates the use of the term effective VC dimension for this value. In order to make use of this theorem, we must have a bound on the fat shattering dimension and then calculate the margin of the classifier. We begin by considering bounds on the fat shattering dimension. The first bound on the fat shattering dimension of bounded linear functions in a finite dimensional space was obtained by Shawe-Taylor *et al.* [10]. Gurvits [7] generalised this to infinite dimensional Banach spaces. We will quote an improved version of this bound for Hilbert spaces which is contained in [2] (slightly adapted here for an arbitrary bound on the linear operators).

**Theorem 2.** *[2] Consider a Hilbert space and the class of linear functions L of norm less than or equal to B restricted to the sphere of radius R about the origin. Then the fat shattering dimension of L can be bounded by*

$$\text{fat}_L(\gamma) \le \left(\frac{BR}{\gamma}\right)^2.$$

In order to apply Theorems 1 and 2 we need to bound the radius of the sphere containing the points and the norm of the linear functionals involved. Clearly, scaling by these quantities will give the margin appropriate for application of the theorem.

## 3   Main Result

Let $X$ be a Hilbert space. We define the following Hilbert space derived from $X$.

**Definition 3.** *Let $L_f(X)$ be the set of real valued functions $f$ on $X$ with support* supp($f$) *finite, that is functions in $L_f(X)$ are non-zero only for finitely many points. We define the inner product of two functions $f, g \in L_f(X)$, by*

$$\langle f \cdot g \rangle = \sum_{x \in \text{supp}(f)} f(x)g(x).$$

Note that the sum which defines the inner product is well-defined since the functions have finite support. Clearly the space is closed under addition and multiplication by scalars.

Now for any fixed $\Delta > 0$ we define an embedding of $X$ into the Hilbert space $X \times L_f(X)$ as follows.

$$\tau_\Delta : x \mapsto X_\Delta = (x, \Delta\delta_x),$$

where $\delta_x \in L_f(X)$ is defined by

$$\delta_x(y) = \begin{cases} 1; & \text{if } y = x; \\ 0; & \text{otherwise.} \end{cases}$$

We begin by considering the case where $\Delta$ is fixed. In practice we wish to choose this parameter in response to the data. In order to obtain a bound over different values of $\Delta$ it will be necessary to apply the following theorem several times. For a linear classifier $\mathbf{u}$ on $X$ and threshold $b \in \mathbf{R}$ we define

$$d((\mathbf{x}, y), (\mathbf{u}, b), \gamma) = \max\{0, \gamma - y(\langle \mathbf{u} \cdot \mathbf{x} \rangle - b)\}.$$

This quantity is the amount by which $\mathbf{u}$ fails to reach the margin $\gamma$ on the point $(\mathbf{x}, y)$ or 0 if its margin is larger than $\gamma$. Similarly for a training set $S$, we define

$$D(S, (\mathbf{u}, b), \gamma) = \sqrt{\sum_{(\mathbf{x}, y) \in S} d((\mathbf{x}, y), (\mathbf{u}, b), \gamma)^2}.$$

**Theorem 3.** *Fix $\Delta > 0$, $b \in \mathbf{R}$. Consider a fixed but unknown probability distribution on the input space $X$ with support in the ball of radius $R$ about the origin. Then with probability $1 - \delta$ over randomly drawn training sets $S$ of size $m$ for all $\gamma > 0$ the generalization of a linear classifier $\mathbf{u}$ on $X$ thresholded at $b$ is bounded by*

$$\epsilon(m, k, \delta) = \frac{2}{m} \left( k \log_2 \left( \frac{8em}{k} \right) \log_2(32m) + \log_2 \left( \frac{8m}{\delta} \right) \right),$$

*where*

$$k = \left\lceil \frac{64.5(R^2 + \Delta^2)(\|\mathbf{u}\|^2 + D(S, (\mathbf{u}, b), \gamma)^2/\Delta^2)}{\gamma^2} \right\rceil,$$

*provided $m \geq 2/\epsilon$ and $k \leq em$.*

**Proof:** Consider the fixed mapping $\tau_\Delta$ and the augmented linear functional over the space $X \times L_f(X)$,

$$\hat{\mathbf{u}} = \left( \mathbf{u}, \frac{1}{\Delta} \sum_{(\mathbf{x}, y) \in S} d((\mathbf{x}, y), (\mathbf{u}, b), \gamma) y \delta_\mathbf{x} \right).$$

We claim that

(a) for $\mathbf{x} \notin S$, $\langle \mathbf{u} \cdot \mathbf{x} \rangle = \langle \hat{\mathbf{u}} \cdot \tau_\Delta(\mathbf{x}) \rangle$, and
(b) the margin of $\hat{\mathbf{u}}$ with threshold $b$ on the training set $\tau_\Delta(S)$ is $\gamma$.

Hence, the behaviour of the linear classifier $(\mathbf{u}, b)$ can be characterised by the behaviour of $(\hat{\mathbf{u}}, b)$, while $(\hat{\mathbf{u}}, b)$ is a large margin classifier in the space $X \times L_f(X)$. Since for $x \in S$, $\|\tau(\mathbf{x})\|^2 \leq R^2 + \Delta^2$ and $\|\hat{\mathbf{u}}\|^2 = \|\mathbf{u}\|^2 + D(S, (\mathbf{u}, b), \gamma)^2/\Delta^2$, the result will then follow from an application of Theorems 1 and 2. Note that we have replaced the constant 64 by 64.5 to ensure the continuity from the right required by Theorem 1.

(a) The first claim follows immediately from the observation that for $\mathbf{z} \notin S$,

$$\left\langle \sum_{(\mathbf{x}, y) \in S} d((\mathbf{x}, y), (\mathbf{u}, b), \gamma) y \delta_\mathbf{x} \cdot \delta_\mathbf{z} \right\rangle = 0.$$

(b) For $(\mathbf{x}', y') \in S$, we have

$$y'(\langle \hat{\mathbf{u}}, \tau_\Delta(\mathbf{x}') \rangle - b) = y'(\langle \mathbf{u}, \mathbf{x}' \rangle - b) + y' \left\langle \sum_{(\mathbf{x}, y) \in S} d((\mathbf{x}, y), \mathbf{u}, \gamma) y \delta_\mathbf{x} \cdot \delta_{\mathbf{x}'} \right\rangle$$

$$\geq \gamma - d((\mathbf{x}', y'), \mathbf{u}, \gamma) + d((\mathbf{x}', y'), \mathbf{u}, \gamma) = \gamma.$$

The theorem follows. ∎

We now apply this theorem several times to allow a choice of $\Delta$ which approximately minimises the expression for $k$. Note that the minimum of the expression (ignoring the constant and suppressing the denominator $\gamma^2$) is $(R+D)^2$ attained when $\Delta = \sqrt{RD}$.

**Theorem 4.** *Fix $b \in \mathbb{R}$. Consider a fixed but unknown probability distribution on the input space $X$ with support in the ball of radius $R$ about the origin. Then with probability $1 - \delta$ over randomly drawn training sets $S$ of size $m$ for all $\gamma > 0$ such that $d((\mathbf{x}, y), (\mathbf{u}, b), \gamma) = 0$, for some $(\mathbf{x}, y) \in S$, the generalization of a linear classifier $\mathbf{u}$ on $X$ satisfying $\|\mathbf{u}\| \leq 1$ is bounded by*

$$\epsilon(m, k, \delta) = \frac{2}{m} \left( k \log_2 \left( \frac{8em}{k} \right) \log_2(32m) + \log_2 \left( \frac{2m(28 + \log_2(m))}{\delta} \right) \right),$$

*where*

$$k = \left\lfloor \frac{65[(R + D)^2 + 2.25RD]}{\gamma^2} \right\rfloor,$$

*for $D = D(S, (\mathbf{u}, b), \gamma)$, and provided $m \geq \max\{2/\epsilon, 6\}$ and $k \leq em$.*

**Proof:** Consider a fixed set of values for $\Delta$, $\Delta_1 = R\lfloor 2m^{0.25} - 1 \rfloor$, $\Delta_{i+1} = \Delta_i/2$, for $i = 2, \ldots, t$, where $t$ satisfies, $R/32 \geq \Delta_t > R/64$. Hence, $t \leq \log_2(128m^{0.25}) = 7 + 0.25 \log_2(m)$. We apply Theorem 3 for each of these values of $\Delta$, using $\delta' = \delta/t$ in each application. For a given value of $\gamma$ and $D = D(S, \mathbf{u}, \gamma)$, it is easy to check that the value of $k$ is minimal for $\Delta = \sqrt{RD}$ and is monotonically decreasing for smaller values of $\Delta$ and monotonically increasing for larger values. Note that $\sqrt{RD} \leq R\sqrt{2\sqrt{m-1}}$, as the largest absolute difference in the values of the linear function on two training points is $2R$ and since $d((\mathbf{x}, y), (\mathbf{u}, b), \gamma) = 0$, for some $(\mathbf{x}, y) \in S$, we must have $d((\mathbf{x}', y'), (\mathbf{u}, b), \gamma) \leq 2R$, for all $(\mathbf{x}', y') \in S$. Hence, as $2m^{0.25} - 1 > \sqrt{2}(m-1)^{0.25}$ for $m \geq 6$, we can find a value of $\Delta_i$ satisfying $\sqrt{RD}/2 \leq \Delta_i \leq \sqrt{RD}$, provided $\sqrt{RD} \geq R/32$. The value of the expression

$$(R^2 + \Delta^2)(1 + D(S, \mathbf{u}, \gamma)^2/\Delta^2)$$

at the value $\Delta_i$ will be upper bounded by its value at $\Delta = \sqrt{RD}/2$. A routine calculation confirms that for this value of $\Delta$, the expression is equal to $(R + D)^2 + 2.25RD$. Now suppose $\sqrt{RD} < R/32$. In this case we will show that

$$(R^2 + \Delta_t^2)(1 + D^2/\Delta_t^2) \leq \frac{130}{129} \{(R + D)^2 + 2.25RD\},$$

so that the application of Theorem 3 with $\Delta = \Delta_t$ covers this case once the constant 64.5 is replaced by 65. Recall that $R/32 \geq \Delta_t > R/64$ and note that $\sqrt{D/R} < 1/32$. We therefore have

$$(R^2 + \Delta_t^2)(1 + D^2/\Delta_t^2) \leq R^2(1 + 1/32^2)(1 + 64^2 D^2/R^2)$$

$$\leq R^2 \left( 1 + \frac{1}{1024} \right) \left( 1 + \frac{64^2}{32^4} \right)$$

$$\leq R^2 \left(1 + \frac{1}{1024}\right)\left(1 + \frac{1}{256}\right)$$

$$< \frac{130}{129} R^2 \leq \frac{130}{129} \left\{(R+D)^2 + 2.25RD\right\}$$

as required. The result follows. ∎

## 4  Algorithmics

Theorem 4 suggests a different learning goal from the maximal margin hyperplane sought by the Support Vector Machine [3]. We should instead seek to minimise $D(S, (\mathbf{u}, b), \gamma)$ for a given fixed value of $\gamma$ and subsequently minimise over different choices of $\gamma$. Vapnik has posed this problem in a slightly more general form [13, Section 5.5.1] as follows.

For non-negative variables $\xi_i \geq 0$, we minimise the function

$$F_\sigma(\xi) = \sum_{j=1}^{m} \xi_j^\sigma,$$

subject to the constraints:

$$y_j[\langle \mathbf{u} \cdot \mathbf{x}_j \rangle - b] \geq 1 - \xi_j, \quad j = 1, \ldots, m \tag{1}$$
$$\langle \mathbf{u} \cdot \mathbf{u} \rangle \leq C. \tag{2}$$

Note that throughout this section we will use a standard inner product but the same analysis and algorithm will apply if we use a kernel based inner product. Vapnik is most interested in values of $\sigma$ close to 0 when $F$ approximates the number of training set errors. If, however, we take $\sigma = 2$ and make the constraint (2) an equality constraint, the problem corresponds exactly to minimising $D(S, (\mathbf{u}, b), \gamma)$, where $\gamma = 1/\sqrt{C}$. This follows from considering the hyperplane $(\mathbf{u}', b') = (\mathbf{u}/\sqrt{C}, b/\sqrt{C})$ which has norm 1 and classifies the point $(\mathbf{x}_j, y_j)$ such that $d((\mathbf{x}_j, y_j), (\mathbf{u}', b'), \gamma) = \xi_j/\sqrt{C}$, so that $D(S, (\mathbf{u}', b'), \gamma) = \sqrt{F_2(\xi)/C}$. We now consider converting to the dual problem by introducing Lagrange multipliers $\alpha_0$ for constraint (2) and $\alpha_j \geq 0$, $j = 1, \ldots, m$, for constraints (1). Setting the derivatives to zero and solving for $\mathbf{u}$ gives

$$\mathbf{u} = \frac{1}{2\alpha_0} \sum_{j=1}^{m} \alpha_j y_j \mathbf{x}_j.$$

Substituting into the other expressions and simplifying results in the following Lagrangian,

$$F(\alpha_0, \alpha) = -\frac{1}{4} \sum_{j=1}^{m} \alpha_j^2 + \sum_{j=1}^{m} \alpha_j - \frac{1}{4\alpha_0} \sum_{i,j=1}^{m} \alpha_i \alpha_j y_i y_j \langle \mathbf{x}_i \cdot \mathbf{x}_j \rangle - \alpha_0 C,$$

which must be maximised subject to the constraints, $\alpha_j \geq 0$, $j = 0, \ldots, m$, and $\sum_{j=1}^{m} \alpha_j y_j = 0$. It is convenient to use vector notation, with $\alpha$ denoting the vector of $\alpha_j$, $j = 1, \ldots, m$, $G$ the matrix with entries, $G_{ij} = y_i y_j \langle \mathbf{x}_i \cdot \mathbf{x}_j \rangle$, and $\mathbf{1}$ the $m$ vector with entries equal to 1. Using this notation we can write

$$F(\alpha_0, \alpha) = -\frac{1}{4}\alpha^T \alpha + \mathbf{1}^T \alpha - \frac{1}{4\alpha_0}\alpha^T G \alpha - \alpha_0 C.$$

We can optimise with respect to $\alpha_0$ by computing $\frac{\partial F}{\partial \alpha_0}$ and setting it equal to zero.

$$\frac{\partial F(\alpha_0, \alpha)}{\partial \alpha_0} = \frac{1}{4\alpha_0^2}\alpha^T G \alpha - C = 0.$$

Hence, $\alpha_0 = \sqrt{\frac{1}{4C}\alpha^T G \alpha}$ and resubstituting

$$F(\alpha) = F(\alpha_0, \alpha) = -\frac{1}{4}\alpha^T \alpha + \mathbf{1}^T \alpha - \sqrt{C \alpha^T G \alpha} \tag{3}$$

$$\mathbf{u} = \sqrt{\frac{C}{\alpha^T G \alpha}} \sum_{j=1}^{m} \alpha_j y_j \mathbf{x}_j \tag{4}$$

Note that we can ignore the constant factor in the formula for $\mathbf{u}$ as this will not affect the classification, and in fact $\alpha^T G \alpha = \|\mathbf{u}\|^2 = C$ once the optimal value has been found. The value of $b$ can also be determined from the values of $\alpha$. We wish to confirm that this optimisation problem is concave. We can evaluate the Hessian $H(F)$ of the function $F$ as follows:

$$\text{grad}(F) = -\frac{1}{2}\alpha + 1 - \frac{\sqrt{C}G\alpha}{\sqrt{\alpha^T G \alpha}}.$$

$$\text{Hence} \quad H(F) = -\frac{1}{2}I - \frac{\sqrt{C}[(\alpha^T G \alpha)G - G\alpha\alpha^T G]}{(\alpha^T G \alpha)^{1.5}}.$$

We wish to verify that $H(F)$ is concave, that is $\mathbf{x}^T H(F)\mathbf{x} \leq 0$ for all $\mathbf{x}$.

$$\mathbf{x}^T H(F)\mathbf{x} = -0.5\|\mathbf{x}\|^2 - C'[\|\alpha\|_G^2\|\mathbf{x}\|_G^2 - \langle \mathbf{x} \cdot \alpha \rangle_G^2]$$

where $C'$ is a positive constant and $\langle \cdots \rangle_G$ and $\|.\|_G$ are the inner product and norm defined by the semi-definite matrix $G$. By the Cauchy-Schwartz inequality the expression in square brackets is non-negative, making the overall expression negative as required. Hence, the optimal solution can be found in polynomial time by applying a gradient based central path algorithm following $\text{grad}(F)$ with an appropriate learning rate $\eta$.

Note further that a small change in $\gamma > 0$ only changes the value of $D(S, (\mathbf{u}, b), \gamma)$ by a small amount for a fixed $(\mathbf{u}, b)$. Hence, the optimal value of $k$ can also only change by a small amount. Hence, solving the problem for a fine enough grid of values of $\gamma$ and choosing the value which minimises $k$ will give a value which will be within an arbitrarily small margin of the overall optimum.

Finally, note that the computation described in equation (3) can be performed using a kernel inner product in place of the input space inner product, the technique that is used in the Support Vector Machine. Indeed even if the kernel function is not positive definite, the problem remains concave provided its eigenvalues are not too negative and $C$ is not chosen too large.

## 5 Experiments

A preliminary experiment was performed with the algorithm described in the previous section. The Boston housing data [12] was chosen for the experiments. Since this data is not linearly separable, we selected a subset of the data reaching a subnode of a decision tree produced by OC1. There were 225 examples (with 13 features each) while the target function was taken as the decision boundary generated by OC1. Hence, the data was guaranteed to be linearly separable. We selected just 15 examples for training. The standard maximal margin algorithm generated a margin of $\gamma = 0.0284$ once the data had been normalised in each coordinate. Hence, the maximal possible value of the parameter $C$ would be $1239 = 1/\gamma^2$. The maximal margin hyperplane had an error rate of 0.2619 on the remaining 210 examples.

The algorithm described above was run for a range of values of the parameter $C$ and the training error, test error, and value of the indicator $(R + D)^2/\gamma^2$ were computed. The algorithm was implemented in matlab using a gradient based approach. Convergence was fast, but this was to be expected with such a small sample size. Larger sample sizes have not been tested. The $\alpha$'s computed for one value of $C$ were taken as initial values of the iterations for the next value of $C$. Table 1 gives the resulting values obtained.

| $C$ | 50 | 75 | 100 | 125 | 150 | 175 | 200 | 225 |
|---|---|---|---|---|---|---|---|---|
| Training error | 0.0667 | 0.0667 | 0 | 0 | 0 | 0 | 0 | 0 |
| Test error | 0.119 | 0.095 | 0.062 | 0.071 | 0.071 | 0.071 | 0.086 | 0.110 |
| Indicator | 25.70 | 31.79 | 37.78 | 43.65 | 49.39 | 55.03 | 60.59 | 66.10 |
| $C$ | 250 | 275 | 300 | 325 | 350 | 375 | 400 | 1239 |
| Training error | 0 | 0 | 0 | 0 | 0 | 0 | 0 | 0 |
| Test error | 0.114 | 0.114 | 0.129 | 0.124 | 0.138 | 0.152 | 0.162 | 0.262 |
| Indicator | 71.58 | 77.01 | 82.40 | 87.76 | 93.08 | 98.38 | 103.66 | 274.98 |

**Table 1.** Values of the error and indicator for different $C$

The test error goes though a clear minimum of 6.2% at $C = 100$ (see Figure 1). This is extremely impressive when we consider that the maximal margin hyperplane has a test error of 26.2% (see last column of the table). Even for values of $C$ where the training error is non-zero the test error is still significantly better than that achieved by the maximal margin hyperplane. This suggests that the algorithmic strategy proposed is worthy of further investigation.

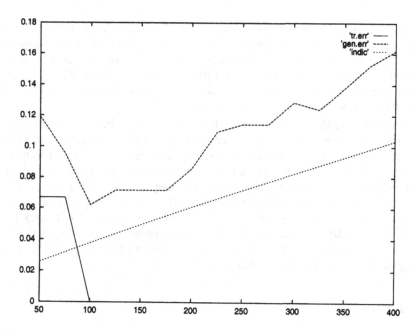

**Fig. 1.** Test error, training error and indicator for different values of $C$

The indicator results are less satisfactory as the indicator does not go through a minimum at or near the best value of $C$. In checking the values involved in the calculation it was verified that the ratio $D^2/\gamma^2$ does reduce with increasing $C$, but the value of $R$ causes the overall expression to increase. Initially it was vainly hoped that by optimising $R$ to be the radius of the minimum ball containing the data (the indicator values shown here were computed with this value for $R$) a minimum would occur. We conjecture that the effect results from the degenerate eigenvalues of the inner product matrix considered. Recent results [11] suggest that this will significantly reduce the "effective" VC dimension and hence the true $R$ should be replaced by a smaller "effective" $R$, when the inner product matrix has a large proportion of small eigenvalues.

## 6 Conclusion

We have shown how an approach developed by Freund and Schapire [6] for mistake bounded learning can be adapted to give pac style bounds which depend on the margin distribution rather than the margin of the closest point to the hyperplane. The bounds obtained can be significantly better than previously obtained bounds, particularly when some of the points are misclassified and agnostic bounds would need to be applied were a classical analysis to be adopted in which the square root of the sample size replaces the sample size in the denominator. The bound is also more robust that that derived for the maximal margin hyperplane where a single point can have a dramatic effect on the hyperplane produced.

We have gone on to show how the measure of the margin distribution that appears in the bound can be optimised by expressing the optimisation problem as a concave dual problem. This formulation also allows the problem to be solved in kernel spaces such as those used with the Support Vector Machine. Preliminary experiments provide evidence that the approach may improve practical classification performance on real world data.

We believe that this paper presents the first pac style bound for a margin distribution measure that is neither critically dependent on the nearest points to the hyperplane nor is an agnostic version of that approach. In addition, we believe it is the first paper to give a provably optimal algorithm for optimizing the generalization performance of agnostic learning with hyperplanes, by showing that the criterion to be minimised should not be the number of training errors, but rather a more flexible criterion which could be termed a 'soft margin'. The problem of finding a more informative and theoretically well-founded measure of the margin distribution has been an open problem for some time. This paper suggests one candidate for such a measure.

# References

1. Peter Bartlett, Pattern Classification in Neural Networks, IEEE Transactions on Information Theory, to appear.
2. Peter Bartlett and John Shawe-Taylor, Generalization Performance of Support Vector Machines and Other Pattern Classifiers, In 'Advances in Kernel Methods - Support Vector Learning', Bernhard Schölkopf, Christopher J. C. Burges, and Alexander J. Smola (eds.), MIT Press, Cambridge, USA, 1998.
3. C. Cortes and V. Vapnik, Support-Vector Networks, *Machine Learning*, 20(3):273-297, September 1995
4. Nello Cristianini, John Shawe-Taylor, and Peter Sykacek, Bayesian Classifiers are Large Margin Hyperplanes in a Hilbert Space, in Shavlik, J., ed., *Machine Learning: Proceedings of the Fifteenth International Conference*, Morgan Kaufmann Publishers, San Francisco, CA.
5. R.O. Duda and P.E. Hart, Pattern Classification and Scene Analysis, New York: Wiley, 1973.
6. Yoav Freund and Robert E. Schapire, Large Margin Classification Using the Perceptron Algorithm, Proceedings of the Eleventh Annual Conference on Computational Learning Theory, 1998.
7. Leonid Gurvits, A note on a scale-sensitive dimension of linear bounded functionals in Banach spaces. In *Proceedings of Algorithm Learning Theory, ALT-97*, and as NECI Technical Report, 1997.
8. Norbert Klasner and Hans Ulrich Simon, From Noise-Free to Noise-Tolerant and from On-line to Batch Learning, *Proceedings of the Eighth Annual Conference on Computational Learning Theory, COLT'95*, 1995, pp. 250-257.
9. R. Schapire, Y. Freund, P. Bartlett, W. Sun Lee, Boosting the Margin: A New Explanation for the Effectiveness of Voting Methods. In D.H. Fisher, Jr., editor, *Proceedings of International Conference on Machine Learning, ICML'97*, pages 322-330, Nashville, Tennessee, July 1997. Morgan Kaufmann Publishers.
10. John Shawe-Taylor, Peter L. Bartlett, Robert C. Williamson, Martin Anthony, Structural Risk Minimization over Data-Dependent Hierarchies, to appear in *IEEE Trans. on Inf. Theory*, and NeuroCOLT Technical Report NC-TR-96-053, 1996. (ftp://ftp.dcs.rhbnc.ac.uk/pub/neurocolt/tech_reports).

11. John Shawe-Taylor and Robert C. Williamson, Generalization Performance of Classifiers in Terms of Observed Covering Numbers, Submitted to EuroCOLT'99, 1998.
12. University of California, Irvine - Machine Learning Repository, http://www.ics.uci.edu/ mlearn/MLRepository.html
13. Vladimir N. Vapnik, *The Nature of Statistical Learning Theory*, Springer-Verlag, New York, 1995.
14. Vladimir N. Vapnik, *Estimation of Dependences Based on Empirical Data*, Springer-Verlag, New York, 1982.
15. Vladimir N. Vapnik, Esther Levin and Yann Le Cunn, Measuring the VC-dimension of a learning machine, *Neural Computation*, 6:851–876, 1994.

# Generalization Performance of Classifiers in Terms of Observed Covering Numbers*

John Shawe-Taylor[1] and Robert C. Williamson[2]

[1] Department of Computer Science
Royal Holloway
University of London
Egham, TW20 0EX, UK
jst@dcs.rhbnc.ac.uk
[2] Department of Engineering
Australian National University
Canberra 0200
Australia
Bob.Williamson@anu.edu.au

**Abstract.** It is known that the covering numbers of a function class on a double sample (length $2m$) can be used to bound the generalization performance of a classifier by using a margin based analysis. In this paper we show that one can utilize an analogous argument in terms of the *observed* covering numbers on a single $m$-sample (being the actual observed data points). The significance of this is that for certain interesting classes of functions, such as support vector machines, there are new techniques which allow one to find good estimates for such covering numbers in terms of the speed of decay of the eigenvalues of a Gram matrix. These covering numbers can be much less than *a priori* bounds indicate in situations where the particular data received is "easy". The work can be considered an extension of previous results which provided generalization performance bounds in terms of the VC-dimension of the class of hypotheses restricted to the sample, with the considerable advantage that the covering numbers can be readily computed, and they often are small.

## 1  Introduction

The PAC framework (sometimes known as the Statistical Learning framework) for analysing the generalization of a learning system bases its analysis on the complexity of the class of hypotheses that can be output by the learning algorithm. Typically this leads to poor estimates of generalization as the class must be chosen large enough to solve a wide range of possible tasks. Structural Risk Minimisation counters this problem by placing an *a priori* hierarchy on the class of functions and allowing the learner to seek a function starting in the simpler classes. If a satisfactory function is found in a simple class the corresponding

* This work was supported by the Australian Research Council and the European Commission under the Working Group Nr. 27150 (NeuroCOLT2).

bound on the generalization error is that much tighter. In this sense the estimate is obtained *a posteriori* based on the class determined by the training algorithm.

Only recently have techniques for bounding the tails of the distribution of a data-dependent estimator been proposed [6, 7, 5]. Initially Shawe-Taylor *et al.* [7] showed that the maximal margin hyperplane algorithm used for the support vector machine of Cortes and Vapnik [3] can be analysed in this way using the size of the margin as the predictor of generalization. This should be distinguished from classical Structural Risk Minimisation since the assignment of hypothesis to complexity class depends on the data and also the target function. The large margin approach has been extended to general neural networks by Bartlett [2]. The line taken in this paper is based on a more general framework developed in [7] which allows inference of good generalization from different measures of performance other than the margin of the classifier.

Our main result is Theorem 1 which bounds the generalization error in terms of the covering numbers observed on the training set at a scale determined by the margin of the classifier. Roughly speaking, the role of the VC dimension in the traditional bound on classifier generalization performance is taken by the log of the covering number of the class when restricted to the observed data sample. The scale at which the covering number is measured depends on the observed margin.

The idea of bounding generalization in terms of the VC dimension measured on the training sample was considered in [7]. The problem with the result there is that there is no simple way of estimating the VC dimension of a set of hypotheses. The approach would also not apply to bounding the generalization of large margin classifiers, since in that case the role of the VC dimension is played by the fat-shattering dimension at a scale dictated by the size of the margin. The present paper is motivated by the recently discovered [10] fact that empirical covering numbers can be readily determined for interesting classes of machines, such as SV machines. We will give one way of using those results as an example towards the end of the paper, though this will not represent the optimal use of the bound in general.

## 2 Background Results

We will assume that a fixed number $m$ of labelled examples are given as a vector $\mathbf{z} = (\mathbf{x}, t(\mathbf{x}))$ to the learner, where $\mathbf{x} = (x_1, \ldots, x_m)$, and $t(\mathbf{x}) = (t(x_1), \ldots, t(x_m))$. We use $\mathrm{Er}_{\mathbf{z}}(h) = |\{i : h(x_i) \neq t(x_i)\}|$ to denote the *number* of errors that $h$ makes on $\mathbf{z}$, and $\mathrm{er}_P(h) = P\{x : h(x) \neq t(x)\}$ to denote the *expected error* when $x$ is drawn according to $P$. In what follows we will often write $\mathrm{Er}_{\mathbf{x}}(h)$ (rather than $\mathrm{Er}_{\mathbf{z}}(h)$) when the target $t$ is obvious from the context. If $\mathbf{x}, \mathbf{y} \in X^m$, we denote by $\mathbf{xy}$ their concatenation $(x_1, \ldots, x_m, y_1, \ldots, y_m)$.

The key concept introduced in Shawe-Taylor *et al.* [7] is 'luckiness'. The main idea is to fix in advance some simplifying assumption about the target function and distribution, and encode this assumption in a real-valued function defined on the space of training samples and hypotheses. The value of the function indicates the extent to which the assumption has been upheld for that sample and hypothesis.

We will not use this theory directly but will follow the spirit of the luckiness approach in bounding the probability that the covering numbers on the first half of the sample differ significantly from those on the double sample. This result can then be used to bound the generalization of a classifier with an observed margin.

We give the definition of the fat-shattering dimension, which was first introduced in [4], and has been used for several problems in learning since [1].

**Definition 1.** *Let $\mathcal{F}$ be a set of real valued functions. We say that a set of points $X$ is $\gamma$-shattered by $\mathcal{F}$ relative to $r = (r_x)_{x \in X}$ if there are real numbers $r_x$ indexed by $x \in X$ such that for all binary vectors $b$ indexed by $X$, there is a function $f_b \in \mathcal{F}$ satisfying*

$$f_b(x) \begin{cases} > r_x + \gamma \text{ if } b_x = 1 \\ \leq r_x - \gamma \text{ otherwise} \end{cases}$$

*The fat-shattering dimension $\mathrm{fat}_{\mathcal{F}}$ of the set $\mathcal{F}$ is a function from the positive real numbers to the integers which maps a value $\gamma$ to the size of the largest $\gamma$-shattered set, if this is finite, or infinity otherwise.*

Note that in our definition of the fat-shattering dimension we have used a slightly unconventional strict inequality for the value on a positive example. This will prove useful in the technical detail, but also ensures that the definition reduces to the Pollard dimension for $\gamma = 0$.

We begin with a technical lemma which analyses the probabilities under the swapping group of permutations used in the symmetrisation argument. The group $\Sigma$ consists of all $2^m$ permutations which exchange corresponding points in the first and second halves of the sample, i.e. $x_j \leftrightarrow y_j$ for $j \in \{1, \ldots, m\}$.

**Lemma 1.** *[7] Let $\Sigma$ be the swapping group of permutations on a $2m$ sample of points* **xy***. Consider any fixed set $z_1, \ldots, z_d$ of the points. For $3k < d$ the probability $P_{d,k}$ under the uniform distribution over permutations that exactly $k$ of the points $z_1, \ldots, z_d$ are in the first half of the sample is bounded by*

$$P_{d,k} \leq \binom{d}{k} 2^{-d}.$$

Before we can quote the next lemma, we need another definition.

**Definition 2.** *Let $(X, d)$ be a (pseudo-) metric space, let $A$ be a subset of $X$ and $\epsilon > 0$. A set $B \subseteq X$ is an $\epsilon$-cover for $A$ if, for every $a \in A$, there exists $b \in B$ such that $d(a, b) \leq \epsilon$. The $\epsilon$-covering number of $A$, $\mathcal{N}_d(\epsilon, A)$, is the minimal cardinality of an $\epsilon$-cover for $A$ (if there is no such finite cover then it is defined to be $\infty$). We will say the cover is proper if $B \subseteq A$.*

We have used a somewhat unconventional less than or equal to in the definition of a cover, as this will prove technically useful in the proofs. We next define the covering numbers that we are concerned with.

**Definition 3.** *Let $\mathcal{F}$ be a class of real-valued functions on the space $X$. For any $m \in \mathbf{N}$ and $\mathbf{x} \in X^m$, we define the pseudo-metric*

$$d_{\mathbf{x}}(f,g) = \max_{1 \leq i \leq m} |f(x_i) - g(x_i)|.$$

*This is referred to as the $l^\infty$ distance over a finite sample $\mathbf{x} = (x_1, \ldots, x_m)$. We write $\mathcal{N}(\epsilon, \mathcal{F}, \mathbf{x}) = \mathcal{N}_{d_{\mathbf{x}}}(\epsilon, \mathcal{F})$. Note that the cover is not required to be proper. Observe that $\mathcal{N}(\epsilon, \mathcal{F}, \mathbf{x}) = \mathcal{N}_{l^\infty}(\epsilon, \mathcal{F}_{\mathbf{x}})$, the $l^\infty$ covering number of*

$$\mathcal{F}_{\mathbf{x}} := \{(f(x_1), \ldots, f(x_m)) : f \in \mathcal{F}\},$$

*the class $\mathcal{F}$ restricted to the sample $\mathbf{x}$.*

We now quote a lemma from [7] which follows directly from a result of Alon *et al.* [1].

**Corollary 1.** *[7] Let $\mathcal{F}$ be a class of functions $X \to [a, b]$ and $P$ a distribution over $X$. Choose $0 < \epsilon < 1$ and let $d = \text{fat}_{\mathcal{F}}(\epsilon/4)$. Then*

$$\sup_{\mathbf{x} \in X^m} \mathcal{N}(\epsilon, \mathcal{F}, \mathbf{x}) \leq 2 \left( \frac{4m(b-a)^2}{\epsilon^2} \right)^{d \log(2em(b-a)/(d\epsilon))}.$$

Let $\pi_\gamma(\alpha)$ be the identity function in the range $[\theta - 2.01\gamma, \theta]$, with output $\theta$ for larger values and $\theta - 2.01\gamma$ for smaller ones, and let $\pi_\gamma(\mathcal{F}) = \{\pi_\gamma(f) : f \in \mathcal{F}\}$. The choice of the threshold $\theta$ is arbitrary but will be fixed before any analysis is made.

We will need some compactness properties of the class of functions which will hold in all cases usually considered. We formalise the requirement in the following definition.

**Definition 4.** *Let*

$$\tilde{\mathbf{x}} : \mathcal{F} \longrightarrow \mathbf{R}^m, \quad \tilde{\mathbf{x}} : f \mapsto (f(x_1), f(x_2), \ldots, f(x_m))$$

*denote the multiple evaluation map induced by $\mathbf{x} = (x_1, \ldots, x_m) \in X^m$. We say that a class of functions $\mathcal{F}$ is sturdy if for all $m \in \mathbf{N}$ and all $\mathbf{x} \in X^m$ the image $\tilde{\mathbf{x}}(\mathcal{F})$ of $\mathcal{F}$ under $\tilde{\mathbf{x}}$ is a compact subset of $\mathbf{R}^m$.*

**Lemma 2.** *Let $\mathcal{F}$ be a sturdy class of functions. Then for each $N \in \mathbf{N}$ and any fixed sequence $\mathbf{x} \in X^m$, the infimum $\gamma_N = \inf\{\gamma : N(\gamma, \mathcal{F}, \mathbf{x}) = N\}$, is attained.*

**Proof:** We first show that for any fixed sequence of functions $\tilde{f} = (f_1, \ldots, f_N)$ the infimum

$$\gamma_{\tilde{f}} = \inf\{\gamma : \cup_j B_\gamma(f_j) = \mathcal{F}\}$$

is attained, where $B_\gamma(f_j) = \{f : d_{\mathbf{x}}(f, f_j) \leq \gamma\}$ is the closed ball centred at $f_j$ of radius $\gamma$ in the $d_{\mathbf{x}}$ metric. For any $m \in \mathbf{N}$, the multiple evaluation map

$$\tilde{\mathbf{x}} : \mathcal{F} \longrightarrow \mathbf{R}^m, \quad \tilde{\mathbf{x}} : f \mapsto (f(x_1), \ldots, f(x_m))$$

has as its image a closed compact subset of $\mathbb{R}^m$ by the definition of sturdiness. The function $f_j$ maps to a point in this subset and the functions in $B_\gamma(f_j)$ are precisely those functions whose image lies in the rectangle with sides $2\gamma$ centred at $\tilde{x}(f_j)$. If we create the Voronoi diagram $V = \bigcup_{j=1}^N V_j$ about the points $\tilde{x}(f_j)$, $j = 1, \ldots, N$ relative to the $l^\infty$ metric in $\mathbb{R}^m$ then $\tilde{x}(\mathcal{F}) \cap V_j$ is closed and compact for $j = 1, \ldots, N$. Thus there is a point $z_j \in \tilde{x}(\mathcal{F}) \cap V_j$ which is a maximum distance from $\tilde{x}(f_j)$ $(j = 1, \ldots, N)$. We can thus define

$$\gamma_{f_j} = \max_{z \in V_j \cap \tilde{x}(\mathcal{F})} \|z - \tilde{x}(f_j)\|_{l^\infty}.$$

With $\gamma_{\bar{f}} = \max_j \{\gamma_{f_j}\}$ we have $\bigcup_j B_{\gamma_{\bar{f}}}(f_j) = \mathcal{F}$ as required. To complete the proof observe that the mapping

$$\gamma : \tilde{x}(\mathcal{F}) \subseteq \mathbb{R}^m \to \mathbb{R}, \quad \gamma : \tilde{x}(f_j) \mapsto \gamma_{f_j}$$

is continuous. Hence the mapping

$$\gamma^N : (\tilde{x}(\mathcal{F}))^N \subseteq (\mathbb{R}^m)^N \to \mathbb{R}$$
$$\gamma^N : (\tilde{x}(f_1), \ldots, \tilde{x}(f_N)) \mapsto \gamma_{\bar{f}} = \max_j \gamma(\tilde{x}(f_j))$$

is too. Since $\tilde{x}(\mathcal{F})$ is compact, $(\tilde{x}(\mathcal{F}))^N$ is too and so $\gamma^N$ attains its minimum $\gamma_N$. ∎

We will use the following lemma, which in the form below is given by Vapnik [8, page 168].

**Lemma 3.** *Let $X$ be a set and $S$ a system of sets on $X$, and $P$ a probability measure on $X$. For $\mathbf{x} \in X^m$, $\mathbf{y} \in X^m$, and $A \in S$, define $\nu_{\mathbf{x}}(A) := |\mathbf{x} \cap A|/m$. If $m > 2/\epsilon$, then*

$$P^m \left\{ \mathbf{x} : \sup_{A \in S} |\nu_{\mathbf{x}}(A) - P(A)| > \epsilon \right\} \leq 2P^{2m} \left\{ \mathbf{xy} : \sup_{A \in S} |\nu_{\mathbf{x}}(A) - \nu_{\mathbf{y}}(A)| > \epsilon/2 \right\}.$$

## 3 Covering Numbers on a Double Sample

We begin by presenting a key proposition that shows with high probability the covering numbers on a sample provide a good estimate of the covering numbers on a double sample. Although the result contains no reference to the fat-shattering dimension, it does play a key role in the proof. It is the combinatorial properties of the fat-shattering dimension which make it possible to infer the properties of the second half of the sample from the first. The probabilistic inference of the fat-shattering dimension on the double sample in terms of its value on the first half involves a multiplicative factor slightly larger than three. Its precise form is given in the following definition.

**Definition 5.** *For $U \in \mathbb{N}$ and $\delta \in \mathbb{R}^+$, we define the function*

$$\alpha(U, \delta) = 3.08 \left( 1 + \frac{1}{U} \ln \frac{1}{\delta} \right).$$

**Proposition 1.** *For fixed $U \in \mathbb{N}$ we have for all $\epsilon > 0$, $\delta \in (0,1)$ and $m \in \mathbb{N}$,*

$$P^{2m}\Big\{\mathbf{xy} : \Big(\lfloor\log\mathcal{N}(\epsilon/4,\mathcal{F},\mathbf{x})\rfloor = U \text{ and}$$

$$2\mathcal{N}(\epsilon,\mathcal{F},\mathbf{x})2^{\alpha(U,\delta)U\log(17m)\log(5em/U)} < \mathcal{N}(\epsilon,\pi_\epsilon(\mathcal{F}),\mathbf{xy})\Big)\Big\} \leq \delta,$$

**Proof: Part 1.** If $B_\mathbf{x}$ is an $\epsilon$-cover of $\mathcal{F}_\mathbf{x}$ for the function class $\mathcal{F}$ and $B_\mathbf{y}$ is an $\epsilon$-cover for $\mathcal{F}_\mathbf{y}$, we can form an (improper) cover $B$ of $\mathcal{F}_\mathbf{xy}$ by simply choosing a function which agrees with each pair of functions from $B_\mathbf{x} \times B_\mathbf{y}$ on their respective domains. If the sequence $\mathbf{y}$ contains common points with $\mathbf{x}$ delete all such common points from $\mathbf{y}$. The size of the cover required for $\mathbf{y}$ will decrease as a result. Hence, $|B| \leq |B_\mathbf{x}||B_\mathbf{y}|$. It follows that

$$\mathcal{N}(\epsilon,\mathcal{F},\mathbf{xy}) \leq \mathcal{N}(\epsilon,\mathcal{F},\mathbf{x})\mathcal{N}(\epsilon,\mathcal{F},\mathbf{y}). \tag{1}$$

Next observe that the fat-shattering dimension $\text{fat}_{\mathcal{F}_\mathbf{x}}(\epsilon)$ satisfies

$$\text{fat}_{\mathcal{F}_\mathbf{x}}(\epsilon) \leq \lfloor\log\mathcal{N}(\epsilon,\mathcal{F},\mathbf{x})\rfloor, \tag{2}$$

since any pair of functions realising a distinct dichotomy with margin $\epsilon$ must differ by more than $2\epsilon$ at some point in $\mathbf{x}$ and hence cannot be covered by the same function in any cover.

**Part 2.** For any $\epsilon > 0$ let

$$A_\mathbf{xy}^\epsilon := \{\mathbf{xy}\colon \alpha(\text{fat}_{\mathcal{F}_\mathbf{x}}(\epsilon),\delta)\text{fat}_{\mathcal{F}_\mathbf{x}}(\epsilon) < \text{fat}_{\mathcal{F}_\mathbf{xy}}(\epsilon)\}.$$

Following an argument similar to one in [7] we will show that for any $\epsilon > 0$, $P^{2m}(A_\mathbf{xy}^\epsilon) \leq \delta$. Let $d = \text{fat}_{\mathcal{F}_\mathbf{xy}}(\epsilon)$ and suppose $\mathbf{z} = (z_1,\ldots,z_d) \subset \mathbf{xy}$ are $\epsilon$-shattered by $\mathcal{F}$. We use the usual permutation argument. Let

$$E_k := \{\mathbf{xy}\colon k = \text{fat}_{\mathcal{F}_\mathbf{x}}(\epsilon),\ \alpha(k,\delta)k < d\}$$

and observe that $A_\mathbf{xy}^\epsilon = \bigcup_k E_k$. Since if $|\mathbf{z} \cap \mathbf{x}| = k$, $\text{fat}_{\mathcal{F}_\mathbf{x}}(\epsilon) \geq k$, we have

$$E_k \subset G_k := \{\mathbf{xy}\colon |\mathbf{z} \cap \mathbf{x}| = k, \alpha(k,\delta)k < d\}$$

and by the union bound,

$$P^{2m}(A_\mathbf{xy}^\epsilon) \leq \sum_k P^{2m}(G_k) = \sum_{k:\alpha(k,\delta)k<d} P^{2m}\{\mathbf{xy}\colon |\mathbf{z} \cap \mathbf{x}| = k\}$$

But $\alpha(k,\delta)k < d \Rightarrow 3k < d$ for all $\delta \in (0,1)$. Thus by setting $U$ to satisfy $\alpha(U,\delta)U = d = \alpha U$ we can write

$$P^{2m}(A_\mathbf{xy}^\epsilon) \leq \sum_{k=0}^{U} P_{d,k} \leq \sum_{k=0}^{U} \binom{d}{i}2^{-d} \leq 2^{-d}\left(\frac{ed}{U}\right)^U = 2^{-\alpha U}(e\alpha)^U,$$

where we have used Lemma 1. One can readily check that for all $\delta \in (0,1)$ and all $U \in \mathbb{N}$, $2^{-\alpha(U,\delta)U}(e\alpha(U,\delta))^U \leq \delta$. Thus $P^{2m}(A_\mathbf{xy}^\epsilon) \leq \delta$, for all $\epsilon > 0$.

**Part 3.** Let $B_{xy}^\epsilon$ be the event in the statement of the proposition. We will show that $B_{xy}^\epsilon \subseteq A_{xy}^{\epsilon/4}$ and thus $P^{2m}(B_{xy}^\epsilon) \leq P^{2m}(A_{xy}^{\epsilon/4}) \leq \delta$. We do this by showing that "$B_{xy}^\epsilon$ is true" $\Rightarrow$ "$A_{xy}^{\epsilon/4}$ is true". Now

$$2\mathcal{N}(\epsilon, \mathcal{F}, x)2^{\alpha(U,\delta)U\log(17m)\log(5em/U)} < \mathcal{N}(\epsilon, \pi_\epsilon(\mathcal{F}), xy)$$

$$\Rightarrow 2\mathcal{N}(\epsilon, \mathcal{F}, x)2^{\alpha(U,\delta)U\log(17m)\log(5em/U)} < \mathcal{N}(\epsilon, \pi_\epsilon(\mathcal{F}), x)\mathcal{N}(\epsilon, \pi_\epsilon(\mathcal{F}), y) \quad (3)$$

$$\Rightarrow 2\mathcal{N}(\epsilon, \mathcal{F}, x)2^{\alpha(U,\delta)U\log(17m)\log(5em/U)}$$

$$< \mathcal{N}(\epsilon, \pi_\epsilon(\mathcal{F}), x)2\left(\frac{4m(2.01\epsilon)^2}{\epsilon^2}\right)^{\mathrm{fat}_{\mathcal{F}_{xy}}(\frac{\epsilon}{4})\log\left(\frac{2\epsilon m2.01\epsilon}{\epsilon\mathrm{fat}_{\mathcal{F}_{xy}}(\frac{\epsilon}{4})}\right)} \quad (4)$$

$$\Rightarrow 2\mathcal{N}(\epsilon, \mathcal{F}, x)2^{\alpha(\mathrm{fat}_{\mathcal{F}_x}(\epsilon/4),\delta)\mathrm{fat}_{\mathcal{F}_x}(\epsilon/4)\log(17m)\log(5em/\mathrm{fat}_{\mathcal{F}_x}(\epsilon/4))}$$

$$< \mathcal{N}(\epsilon, \mathcal{F}, x)2(17m)^{\mathrm{fat}_{\mathcal{F}_{xy}}(\epsilon/4)\log(5em/\mathrm{fat}_{\mathcal{F}_{xy}}(\epsilon/4))} \quad (5)$$

$$\Rightarrow \alpha(\mathrm{fat}_{\mathcal{F}_x}(\epsilon/4),\delta)\mathrm{fat}_{\mathcal{F}_x}(\epsilon/4)\log(17m)\log(5em/\mathrm{fat}_{\mathcal{F}_x}(\epsilon/4)) + 1$$

$$< \mathrm{fat}_{\mathcal{F}_{xy}}(\epsilon/4)\log(5em/\mathrm{fat}_{\mathcal{F}_{xy}}(\epsilon/4))\log(17m) + 1 \quad (6)$$

$$\Rightarrow \alpha(\mathrm{fat}_{\mathcal{F}_x}(\epsilon/4),\delta)\mathrm{fat}_{\mathcal{F}_x}(\epsilon/4) < \mathrm{fat}_{\mathcal{F}_{xy}}(\epsilon/4) \quad (7)$$

where (3) follows from (1); (4) follows from the fact that $\mathrm{fat}_{\mathcal{F}_y}(\epsilon/4) \leq \mathrm{fat}_{\mathcal{F}_{xy}}(\epsilon/4)$, that the range of functions in $\pi_\epsilon(\mathcal{F})$ is an interval $[a, b]$ with $b - a = 2\epsilon$ and Corollary 1; (5) follows from (2) and the fact that $\mathcal{N}(\epsilon, \pi_\epsilon(\mathcal{F}), x) \leq \mathcal{N}(\epsilon, \mathcal{F}, x)$; (6) follows by dividing both sides of the inequality by $\mathcal{N}(\epsilon, \mathcal{F}, x)$ and taking logs; (7) follows from the fact that $\mathrm{fat}_{\mathcal{F}_x}(\epsilon/4) \leq \mathrm{fat}_{\mathcal{F}_{xy}}(\epsilon/4)$ and dividing out common terms on both sides. Now (7) defines the event $A_{xy}^{\epsilon/4}$ as required. ∎

**Lemma 4.** *Suppose $\mathcal{F}$ is a sturdy set of functions that map from $X$ to $\mathbb{R}$. Then for any distribution $P$ on $X$, and any $U \in \mathbb{N}$ and any $\theta \in \mathbb{R}$*

$$P^{2m}\left\{xy: \left(\exists f \in \mathcal{F}, \ r = \max_j\{f(x_j)\}, \ 2\gamma < \theta - r, \ \lfloor\log\mathcal{N}(\gamma/4, \mathcal{F}, x)\rfloor = U, \right.\right.$$

$$\left.\left. \frac{1}{m}|\{i : f(y_i) \geq \theta\}| > \epsilon(m, k, \delta)\right)\right\} < \delta,$$

*where $\epsilon(m, k, \delta) = \frac{1}{m}(U(\log\frac{5em}{U}\log(17m)\alpha(U, \delta/2) + 1) + \log\frac{4}{\delta})$.*

**Proof:** Using the standard permutation argument (as in [9]), we may fix a sequence $xy$ and bound the probability under the uniform distribution on swapping permutations that the permuted sequence satisfies the condition stated. Let

$$\gamma_U := \min\{\gamma': \lfloor\log\mathcal{N}(\gamma'/4, \mathcal{F}, x)\rfloor = U\}.$$

By Lemma 2 and the sturdiness of $\mathcal{F}$, the minimum is attained by some choice of $2^U$ functions from $\mathcal{F}$. The probability above is no greater than

$$P^{2m}\left\{xy : \exists\gamma \in \mathbb{R}^+, \lfloor\log\mathcal{N}(\gamma'/4, \mathcal{F}, x)\rfloor = U, \exists f \in \mathcal{F}, A_f(2\gamma_U)\right\},$$

where $A_f(\gamma)$ is the event that $f(y_i) > \max_j\{f(x_j)\} + \gamma$ for at least $m\epsilon(m, k, \delta)$ points $y_i$ in $y$. Note that $r + 2\gamma < \theta$. Consider a minimal $\gamma_U$-cover $B_{xy}$ of $\pi_{\gamma_U}(\mathcal{F})$

in the pseudo-metric $d_{\mathbf{xy}}$. In the remainder we will suppress the $\gamma_U$ subscript to the function $\pi$ to simplify the notation. We have that for any $f \in \mathcal{F}$, there exists $\tilde{f} \in B_{\mathbf{xy}}$, with $|\pi(f)(x) - \pi(\tilde{f})(x)| \leq \gamma_U$ for all $x \in \mathbf{xy}$. Thus since for all $x \in \mathbf{x}$, by the definition of $r$, $f(x) \leq r < \theta - 2\gamma$, $\pi(f)(x) < \max\{\theta - 2\gamma, \theta - 2.005\gamma_U\}$, and so $\pi(\tilde{f})(x) < \theta - \gamma_U$. However there are at least $m\,\epsilon(m, k, \delta)$ points $y \in \mathbf{y}$ such that $f(y) \geq \theta > r + 2\gamma$, so $\pi(\tilde{f})(y) > r + 2\gamma - \gamma_U > \max_j\{\pi(\tilde{f})(x_j)\}$. Since $\pi$ only reduces separation between output values, we conclude that the event $A_{\tilde{f}}(0)$ occurs. By the permutation argument, for fixed $\tilde{f}$ at most $2^{-\epsilon(m,k,\delta)m}$ of the sequences obtained by swapping corresponding points satisfy the conditions, since the $\epsilon m$ points with the largest $\tilde{f}$ values must remain on the right hand side for $A_{\tilde{f}}(0)$ to occur. Thus by the union bound

$$
\begin{aligned}
&P^{2m}\left\{\mathbf{xy} : \exists \gamma \in \mathbb{R}^+, \lfloor \log \mathcal{N}(\gamma'/4, \mathcal{F}, \mathbf{x}) \rfloor = U, \exists f \in \mathcal{F}, A_f(2\gamma_U)\right\} \\
&\leq E(|B_{\mathbf{xy}}|)2^{-\epsilon(m,k,\delta)m},
\end{aligned}
$$

where the expectation is over $\mathbf{xy}$ drawn according to $P^{2m}$. Hence, by Proposition 1 with probability at least $1 - \delta/2$

$$
\begin{aligned}
E(|B_{\mathbf{xy}}|) &\leq 2\mathcal{N}(\gamma_U, \mathcal{F}, \mathbf{x})2^{\alpha(U, \delta/2)U \log(17m) \log(5em/U)} \\
&\leq 2^{1 + U[\log(17m) \log(5em/U)\alpha(U,\delta/2) + 1]},
\end{aligned}
$$

and so $E(|B_{\mathbf{xy}}|)2^{-\epsilon(m,k,\delta)m} < \delta/2$ provided

$$
\epsilon(m, k, \delta) \geq \tfrac{1}{m}\left(U(1 + \log(5em/U)\log(17m)\alpha(U, \delta/2)) + \log \tfrac{4}{\delta}\right),
$$

as required. ∎

We define the mapping $\hat{\ } : \mathbb{R}^X \to \mathbb{R}^{X \times \{0,1\}}$ by

$$
\hat{\ } : f \mapsto \hat{f}(x, c) = f(x)(1 - c) + (2\theta - f(x))c,
$$

for some fixed real $\theta$. For a set of functions $\mathcal{F}$, we define $\hat{\mathcal{F}} = \hat{\mathcal{F}}_\theta = \{\hat{f} : f \in \mathcal{F}\}$. The idea behind this mapping is that for a function $f$, the corresponding $\hat{f}$ maps the input $x$ and it classification $c$ to an output value, which will be less than $\theta$ provided the classification obtained by thresholding $f(x)$ at $\theta$ is correct.

Let $T_\theta$ denote the threshold function at $\theta$: $T_\theta : \mathbb{R} \to \{0, 1\}$, $T_\theta(\alpha) = 1$ iff $\alpha > \theta$. For a class of functions $\mathcal{F}$, $T_\theta(\mathcal{F}) = \{T_\theta(f) : f \in \mathcal{F}\}$.

**Theorem 1.** *Consider a sturdy real valued function class $\mathcal{F}$. Fix $\theta \in \mathbb{R}$. If a learner correctly classifies $m$ independently generated examples $\mathbf{z}$ with $h = T_\theta(f) \in T_\theta(\mathcal{F})$ such that $\mathrm{Er}_{\mathbf{z}}(h) = 0$ and for all $\gamma$ such that $\gamma < \min |f(x_i) - \theta|$, then with confidence $1 - \delta$ the expected error of $h$ is bounded from above by*

$$
\epsilon(m, U, \delta) = \frac{2}{m}\left(U\left(1 + \alpha(U, \delta/2)\log\left(\frac{5em}{U}\right)\log(17m)\right) + \log\left(\frac{16m}{\delta}\right)\right),
$$

*where $U = \lfloor \log \mathcal{N}(\gamma/8, \mathcal{F}, \mathbf{x}) \rfloor$.*

**Proof**: Making use of lemma 3 we will move to the double sample and stratify by $U$. By the union bound, it thus suffices to show that $\sum_{U=1}^{2m} P^{2m}(J_U) < \delta/2$, where

$$J_U = \{\mathbf{xy} : \exists h = T_\theta(f) \in T_\theta(\mathcal{F}), \mathrm{Er}_\mathbf{x}(h) = 0, U = \lfloor \log \mathcal{N}(\gamma/8, \mathcal{F}, \mathbf{x}) \rfloor,$$
$$\gamma < \min |f(x_i) - \theta|, \mathrm{Er}_\mathbf{y}(h) \geq m\epsilon(m, U, \delta)/2\}.$$

(The largest value of $U$ we need consider is $2m$, since for larger values the bound will in any case be trivial). It is sufficient if $P^{2m}(J_U) \leq \frac{\delta}{4m} = \delta'$. Consider $\hat{\mathcal{F}} = \hat{\mathcal{F}}_\theta$. The probability distribution on $\hat{X} = X \times \{0, 1\}$ is given by $P$ on $X$ with the second component determined by the target value of the first component. Note that for a point $y \in \mathbf{y}$ to be misclassified, it must have $\hat{f}(\hat{y}) \geq \theta > \max\{\hat{f}(\hat{x}): \hat{x} \in \hat{\mathbf{x}}\} + \gamma$, so that

$$J_k \subseteq \Big\{ \hat{\mathbf{x}}\hat{\mathbf{y}} \in (X \times \{0, 1\})^{2m} : \exists \hat{f} \in \hat{\mathcal{F}}, r = \max\{\hat{f}(\hat{x}): \hat{x} \in \hat{\mathbf{x}}\}, \gamma < \theta - r,$$
$$U = \lfloor \log \mathcal{N}(\gamma/8, \mathcal{F}, \mathbf{x}) \rfloor, \Big| \{\hat{y} \in \hat{\mathbf{y}}: \hat{f}(\hat{y}) \geq \theta\} \Big| \geq m\epsilon(m, U, \delta)/2 \Big\}.$$

Replacing $\gamma$ by $\gamma/2$ in Lemma 4 and appealing to Lemma 3 we obtain $P^{2m}(J_U) \leq \delta'$ for

$$\epsilon(m, U, \delta) = \frac{2}{m} \left( U(1 + \alpha(U, \delta/2) \log(5em/U) \log(17m)) + \log(4/\delta') \right).$$

The condition of Lemma 3 is satisfied by this linking of $\epsilon$ and $m$. Substituting for $\delta'$ gives the result. ∎

Despite superficial appearances Theorem 1 is quite different from results obtained in [7]. For example, the bound involving the margin of a classifier given there relies on an *a priori* bound on the fat-shattering dimension for the whole class, not the fat-shattering dimension (or in our case the logarithm of the covering numbers) of the class restricted to the training set. The other result of [7] which is reminiscent of Theorem 1 involves bounding the generalization error in terms of the VC dimension of the set of hypotheses restricted to the training set. This result cannot take into account the margin of a large margin classifier, but refers to classical generalization bounds in terms of the VC dimension. The motivation for obtaining Theorem 1 is recent work computing the covering numbers for Support Vector Machines in terms of the eigenvalues of the kernel. These results will be described in the next section. They show that in many cases the bounds may be significantly smaller than could be obtained by a priori knowledge of the fat-shattering dimension. Thus even though the log covering numbers and fat shatterring dimension can only differ by $\log(m)$ factors, the *bounds one has* on the quantities can differ significantly; that is certainly the current situation with regard to support vector machines.

## 4    Generalization from Covering Numbers

This section will sketch how results can be obtained which combine Theorem 1 with bounds on covering numbers introduced in [10]. We will give one example of the type of bound that can be derived. We stress this is just one way to use the results; we will present others in a fuller version of this paper.

We first quote some results from the paper [10] that has developed the techniques for directly bounding the covering numbers of Support Vector Machines. In order to avoid introducing a large number of definitions we will summarise some of the results in the following theorem which combines Corollary 5 and Theorem 7 (assertion (12)) of [10]. The derivation of this result from the general theory derived in [10] requires restricting consideration of the input space to the training set. In this case the kernel function $k$ of the Support Vector Machine is completely defined by the inner product matrix $G_{ij} = k(x_i, x_j)$. We denote by $\lambda_s, s = 1, \ldots, m$ the eigenvalues of this matrix in decreasing order. The parameter $C_k$ of the kernel $k$ is the largest entry in the matrix of eigenvectors. For a vector $z$, let $\|z\|_{l^2} = \left(\sum_i z_i^2\right)^{1/2}$.

**Theorem 2.** *[10] Let $x \in X^m$ be an m-sample for a Support Vector Machine with kernel $k$, with $\lambda_s$ and $C_k$ defined as above. Let the maximal margin of the classifier be $\gamma$. Then the scale $\epsilon_N$ that can be achieved for a $d_x$ cover of size $N$ of the set of linear functions implemented by the SVM satisfies*

$$\epsilon_N \leq \inf_{(a_s)_s : a_s \neq 0} \frac{6C_k}{\gamma} \|(\sqrt{\lambda_s}/a_s)_s\|_{l^2} \max_{j \in N} N^{-1/j} (a_1 a_2 \ldots a_j)^{1/j}.$$

The above theorem can be used as follows. We have not attempted to provide a closed form formula for $\mathcal{N}(\gamma/8, \mathcal{F}, x)$ because the evaluation of the above bound depends very much on how the $\lambda_i$ decay. Specifically the $j$ for which the maximum occurs is difficult to determine precisely *a priori*. Since the whole point of using the result is to use empirical values which will necessitate a numerical computation in any case, we do not see this as a disadvantage.

Pick $a_s = \sqrt{\lambda_s}$. For any $N \in \mathbb{N}$ let $j^* = j^*(N) = \arg\max_j N^{-1/j} \prod_{s=1}^{j} \lambda_s^{1/2j}$. Thus

$$\epsilon_N \leq \frac{6C_k}{\gamma} \sqrt{m} N^{-1/j^*} \prod_{s=1}^{j^*} \lambda_s^{1/2j^*}.$$

Setting $\gamma/8 = \epsilon = \epsilon_N$ and solving for $N$, we obtain

$$\mathcal{N}(\gamma_N/8, \mathcal{F}, x)^{1/j^*} = N^{1/j^*} \leq \frac{48 C_k \sqrt{m} \prod_{s=1}^{j^*} \lambda_s^{1/2j^*}}{\gamma_N^2}$$

giving an effective VC dimension of $j^*$. One can readily make use of this numerically since $\gamma_N$ is monotonically decreasing in $N$ and hence a binary search can be used to find $N$ (and the relevant value of $j^*$) as a function of a given $\gamma$. The value of $\mathcal{N}(\gamma/8, \mathcal{F}, x)$ can be then used in Theorem 1.

In practical examples the eigenvalues of the inner product matrix frequently decay very fast. The above argument shows that such a decay can be translated into an "effective" VC dimension relevant to the achieved margin of the classifier.

# 5 Conclusions

This paper has presented a method by which recently achieved bounds [10] on the covering numbers of a function class on a training set can be used to bound the generalization error of the resulting classifier. In the previous section we have shown how this method can then be used to derive alternative bounds on the generalization error derived from observed properties of the margin and inner product matrix of a Support Vector Machine.

Improved bounds can be used to guide more refined Structural Risk Minimization over choices of different kernels for example. Hence, the approach developed here may well have applications in practical learning systems. Our hope is that these methods may also be able to give bounds that are more realistic than previous PAC estimates.

# References

1. N. Alon, S. Ben-David, N. Cesa-Bianchi and D. Haussler, "Scale-sensitive Dimensions, Uniform Convergence, and Learnability," *Journal of the ACM* **44**(4), 615–631, (1997).
2. Peter L. Bartlett, "The Sample Complexity of Pattern Classification with Neural Networks: The Size of the Weights is More Important than the Size of the Network," *IEEE Trans. Inf. Theory*, **44**(2), 525–536, (1998).
3. C. Cortes and V. Vapnik, "Support-Vector Networks," *Machine Learning*, **20**, 273–297 (1995).
4. Michael J. Kearns and Robert E. Schapire, "Efficient Distribution-free Learning of Probabilistic Concepts," pages 382–391 in *Proceedings of the 31st Symposium on the Foundations of Computer Science*, IEEE Computer Society Press, Los Alamitos, CA, 1990.
5. Gábor Lugosi and Márta Pintér, "A Data-dependent Skeleton Estimate for Learning," pages 51–56 in *Proceedings of the Ninth Annual Workshop on Computational Learning Theory*, Association for Computing Machinery, New York, 1996.
6. John Shawe-Taylor, Peter Bartlett, Robert Williamson and Martin Anthony, "A Framework for Structural Risk Minimization", pages 68–76 in *Proceedings of the 9th Annual Conference on Computational Learning Theory*, Association for Computing Machinery, New York, 1996.
7. John Shawe-Taylor, Peter Bartlett, Robert Williamson and Martin Anthony, "Structural Risk Minimization over Data-Dependent Hierarchies", *IEEE Transactions on Information Theory*, **44**(5), 1926–1940 (1998).
8. Vladimir N. Vapnik, *Estimation of Dependences Based on Empirical Data*, Springer-Verlag, New York, 1982.
9. Vladimir N. Vapnik and Aleksei Ja. Chervonenkis, "On the Uniform Convergence of Relative Frequencies of Events to their Probabilities," *Theory of Probability and Applications*, **16**, 264–280 (1971).
10. Robert C. Williamson, Alex J. Smola and Bernhard Schölkopf, "Entropy Numbers, Operators and Support Vector Kernels," EuroCOLT'99 (these proceedings). See also "Generalization Performance of Regularization Networks and Support Vector Machines *via* Entropy Numbers of Compact Operators," http://spigot.anu.edu.au/~williams/papers/P100.ps submitted to *IEEE Transactions on Information Theory*, July 1998.

# Entropy Numbers, Operators and Support Vector Kernels*

Robert C. Williamson[1], Alex J. Smola[2], and Bernhard Schölkopf[2]

[1] Department of Engineering,
Australian National University,
Canberra, ACT 0200, Australia
Bob.Williamson@anu.edu.au
[2] GMD FIRST, Rudower Chaussee 5,
12489 Berlin, Germany
{smola,bs}@first.gmd.de

**Abstract.** We derive new bounds for the generalization error of feature space machines, such as support vector machines and related regularization networks by obtaining new bounds on their covering numbers. The proofs are based on a viewpoint that is apparently novel in the field of statistical learning theory. The hypothesis class is described in terms of a linear operator mapping from a possibly infinite dimensional unit ball in feature space into a finite dimensional space. The covering numbers of the class are then determined via the entropy numbers of the operator. These numbers, which characterize the degree of compactness of the operator, can be bounded in terms of the eigenvalues of an integral operator induced by the kernel function used by the machine. As a consequence we are able to theoretically explain the effect of the choice of kernel functions on the generalization performance of support vector machines.

## 1 Introduction, Definitions and Notation

In this paper we give new bounds on the covering numbers for feature space machines. This leads to improved bounds on their generalization performance. Feature space machines perform a mapping from input space into a feature space construct regression functions or decision boundaries based on this mapping, and use constraints in feature space for capacity control. Support Vector (SV) machines, which have recently been proposed as a new class of learning algorithms solving problems of pattern recognition, regression estimation, and operator inversion [32] are a well known example of this class.

A key feature of the present paper is the manner in which we *directly* bound the covering numbers of interest rather than making use of a Combinatorial dimension (such as the VC-dimension or the fat-shattering dimension) and subsequent application of a general result relating such dimensions to covering numbers. We bound covering numbers by viewing the relevant class of functions as the image

---

* Supported by the Australian Research Council and the DFG (# Ja 379/71).

of a unit ball under a particular compact operator. The results can be applied to bound the generalization performance of SV regression machines, although we do not explictly indicate the results so obtained in this brief paper.

**Capacity control.** In order to perform pattern recognition using linear hyperplanes, often a maximum margin of separation between the classes is sought for, as this leads to good generalization ability independent of the dimensionality [28]. It can be shown that for separable training data $(\mathbf{x}_1, y_1), \ldots, (\mathbf{x}_m, y_m) \in \mathbb{R}^d \times \{\pm 1\}$, this is achieved by minimizing $\|\mathbf{w}\|_2$ subject to the constraints $y_j(\langle \mathbf{w}, \mathbf{x}_j \rangle + b) \geq 1$ for $j = 1, \ldots, m$, and some $b \in \mathbb{R}$. The decision function then takes the form $f(\mathbf{x}) = \text{sgn}(\langle \mathbf{w}, \mathbf{x} \rangle + b)$. Similarly, a linear regression $f(\mathbf{x}) = \langle \mathbf{w}, \mathbf{x} \rangle + b$ can be estimated from data $(\mathbf{x}_1, y_1), \ldots, (\mathbf{x}_m, y_m) \in \mathbb{R}^d \times \mathbb{R}$ by finding the flattest function which approximates the data within some margin of error: in this case, one minimizes $\|\mathbf{w}\|_2$ subject to $|f(\mathbf{x}_j) - y_j| \leq \varepsilon$, where the parameter $\varepsilon > 0$ plays the role of the margin, albeit not in the space of the inputs $\mathbf{x}$, but in that of the outputs $y$.

**Nonlinear kernels.** In order to apply the above reasoning to a rather general class of *nonlinear* functions, one can use kernels computing dot products in high-dimensional spaces nonlinearly related to input space [1, 7]. Under certain conditions on a kernel $k$, to be stated below (Theorem 1), there exists a nonlinear map $\Phi$ into a reproducing kernel Hilbert space $F$ such that $k$ computes the dot product in $F$, i.e. $k(\mathbf{x}, \mathbf{y}) = \langle \Phi(\mathbf{x}), \Phi(\mathbf{y}) \rangle_F$. Given any algorithm which can be expressed in terms of dot products exclusively, one can thus construct a nonlinear version of it by substituting a kernel for the dot product.

By using the kernel trick for SV machines, the maximum margin idea is thus extended to a large variety of nonlinear function classes (e.g. radial basis function networks, polynomial networks, neural networks), which in the case of regression estimation comprise functions written as kernel expansions $f(\mathbf{x}) = \sum_{j=1}^m \alpha_j k(\mathbf{x}_j, \mathbf{x}) + b$, with $\alpha_j \in \mathbb{R}$, $j = 1, \ldots, m$. It has been noticed that different kernels can be characterized by their regularization properties [30]. This provides insight into the regularization properties of SV kernels. However, it does not give us a comprehensive understanding of how to select a kernel for a given learning problem, and how using a specific kernel might influence the performance of a SV machine.

**Definitions and Notation** For $d \in \mathbb{N}$, $\mathbb{R}^d$ denotes the $d$-dimensional space of vectors $\mathbf{x} = (x_1, \ldots, x_d)$. We define spaces $\ell_p^d$ as follows: as vector spaces, they are identical to $\mathbb{R}^d$, in addition, they are endowed with $p$-norms: for $0 < p < \infty$, $\|\mathbf{x}\|_{\ell_p^d} := \|\mathbf{x}\|_p = \left( \sum_{j=1}^d |x_j|^p \right)^{1/p}$; for $p = \infty$, $\|\mathbf{x}\|_{\ell_\infty^d} := \|\mathbf{x}\|_\infty = \max_{j=1,\ldots,d} |x_j|$. Analogously $\ell_p$ is the space of infinite sequences with the obvious definition of the norm. Given $m$ points $\mathbf{x}_1, \ldots, \mathbf{x}_m \in \ell_p^d$, we use the shorthand $\mathbf{X}^m = (\mathbf{x}_1^T, \ldots, \mathbf{x}_m^T)$. Suppose $\mathcal{F}$ is a class of functions defined on $\mathbb{R}^d$. The $\ell_\infty^d$ norm *with respect to* $\mathbf{X}^m$ of $f \in \mathcal{F}$ is defined as $\|f\|_{\ell_\infty^{\mathbf{X}^m}} := \max_{i=1,\ldots,m} |f(\mathbf{x}_i)|$. Given some set $\mathcal{X}$, a measure $\mu$ on $\mathcal{X}$, some $1 \leq p < \infty$ and a function $f: \mathcal{X} \to \mathbb{R}$ we define $\|f\|_{L_p} := \left( \int |f(x)|^p d\mu(x) \right)^{1/p}$ if the integral exists and $\|f\|_{L_\infty} :=$ ess $\sup_{x \in \mathcal{X}} |f(x)|$. For $1 \leq p \leq \infty$, we let $L_p(\mathcal{X}) := \{f: \mathcal{X} \to \mathbb{R}: \|f\|_{L_p} < \infty\}$.

Let $\mathfrak{L}(E, F)$ be the set of all bounded linear operators $T$ between the normed spaces $(E, \|\cdot\|_E)$ and $(F, \|\cdot\|_F)$, i.e. operators such that the image of the (closed) unit ball $U_E := \{x \in E : \|x\|_E \leq 1\}$ is bounded. The smallest such bound is called the *operator norm*, $\|T\| := \sup_{x \in U_E} \|Tx\|_F$. The $n$th *entropy number of a set* $M \subset E$, for $n \in \mathbb{N}$, is

$$\epsilon_n(M) := \inf\{\epsilon > 0 : \exists \text{ an } \epsilon\text{-cover for } M \text{ in } E \text{ containing } n \text{ or fewer points}\}.$$

The *entropy numbers of an operator* $T \in \mathfrak{L}(E, F)$ are defined as $\epsilon_n(T) := \epsilon_n(T(U_E))$. Note that $\epsilon_1(T) = \|T\|$, and that $\epsilon_n(T)$ certainly is well defined for all $n \in \mathbb{N}$ if $T$ is a *compact operator*, i.e. if $\overline{T(U_E)}$ is compact. The *dyadic entropy numbers of an operator* are defined by $e_n(T) := \epsilon_{2^{n-1}}(T)$, $n \in \mathbb{N}$. A very nice introduction to entropy numbers of operators is [8]. The *$\epsilon$-covering number of $\mathcal{F}$ with respect to the metric $d$* denoted $\mathcal{N}(\epsilon, \mathcal{F}, d)$ is the size of the smallest $\epsilon$-cover for $\mathcal{F}$ using the metric $d$. By log and ln, we denote the logarithms to base 2 and $e$, respectively. By $i$, we denote the imaginary unit $i = \sqrt{-1}$, $k$ will always be a kernel, and $d$ and $m$ will be the input dimensionality and the number of examples $(\mathbf{x}_1, y_1), \ldots, (\mathbf{x}_m, y_m) \in \mathbb{R}^d \times \mathbb{R}$, respectively. We will map the input data into a feature space via a mapping $\Phi$. We let $\tilde{\mathbf{x}} := \Phi(\mathbf{x})$.

## 2 Operator Theory Methods for Entropy Numbers

In this section we briefly explain the new viewpoint implicit in the present paper. With reference to Figure 1, consider the traditional viewpoint in statistical learning theory. One is given a class of functions $\mathcal{F}$, and the generalization performance attainable using $\mathcal{F}$ is determined via the covering numbers of $\mathcal{F}$. More precisely, for some set $\mathcal{X}$, and $\mathbf{x}_i \in \mathcal{X}$ for $i = 1, \ldots, m$, define the *$\epsilon$-Growth function* of the function class $\mathcal{F}$ on $\mathcal{X}$ as

$$\mathcal{N}^m(\epsilon, \mathcal{F}) := \sup_{\mathbf{x}_1, \ldots, \mathbf{x}_m \in \mathcal{X}} \mathcal{N}(\epsilon, \mathcal{F}, \ell_\infty^{\mathbf{X}^m}), \tag{1}$$

where $\mathcal{N}(\epsilon, \mathcal{F}, \ell_\infty^{\mathbf{X}^m})$ is the $\epsilon$-covering number of $\mathcal{F}$ with respect to $\ell_\infty^{\mathbf{X}^m}$. Many generalization error bounds can be expressed in terms of $\mathcal{N}^m(\epsilon, \mathcal{F})$. An example is given in the following section.

The key novelty in the present work solely concerns the manner in which the covering numbers are computed. Traditionally, appeal has been made to a result such as the so-called Sauer's lemma (originally due to Vapnik and Chervonenkis). In the case of function learning, a generalization due to Pollard (called the pseudo-dimension), or Vapnik and Chervonenkis (called the VC-dimension of real valued functions), or a scale-sensitive generalization of that (called the fat-shattering dimension) is used to bound the covering numbers. These results reduce the computation of $\mathcal{N}^m(\epsilon, \mathcal{F})$ to the computation of a single "dimension-like" quantity. An overview of these various dimensions, some details of their history, and some examples of their computation can be found in [5].

In the present work, we view the class $\mathcal{F}$ as being induced by an operator $\bar{T}_k$ depending on some kernel function $k$. Thus $\mathcal{F}$ is the image of a "base class" $\mathcal{G}$

under $\bar{T}_k$. The analogy implicit in the picture is that the quantity that matters is the number of $\epsilon$-distinguishable messages obtainable at the information sink. (Recall the equivalence up to a constant factor of packing and covering numbers.) In a typical communications problem, one tries to maximize the number of distinguisable messages (per unit time), in order to maximize the information transmission rate. But from the point of view of the receiver, the job is made easier the *smaller* the number of distinct messages that one needs to be concerned with decoding. The significance of the picture is that the kernel in question is exactly the kernel that is used, for example, in support vector machines. As a consequence, the determination of $\mathcal{N}^m(\epsilon, \mathcal{F})$ can be done in terms of properties of the operator $\bar{T}_k$. The latter thus plays a constructive role in controlling the complexity of $\mathcal{F}$ and hence the difficulty of the learning task. We believe that the new viewpoint in itself is potentially very valuable, perhaps more so than the specific results in the paper. A further exploitation of the new viewpoint can be found in [36]. There are in fact a variety of ways to define exactly what is meant by $\bar{T}_k$, and we have deliberately not been explicit in the picture. We make use of one particular $\bar{T}_k$ in this paper. A slightly different approach is taken in [36].

We conclude this section with some brief historical remarks.

The concept of the metric entropy of a set has been around for some time. It seems to have been introduced by Pontriagin and Schnirelmann [24] and was studied in detail by Kolmogorov and others [19]. The use of metric entropy to say something about linear operators was developed independently by several people. Prosser [25] appears to have been the first to make the idea explicit. He determined the effect of an operator's spectrum on its entropy numbers. In particular, he proved a number of results concerning the asymptotic rate of decrease of the entropy numbers in terms of the asymptotic behaviour of the eigenvalues. A similar result is actually implicit in section 22 of Shannon's famous paper [27], where he considered the effect of different convolution operators on the entropy of an ensemble. Prosser's paper [25] led to a handful of papers (see e.g. [26, 15, 3, 21]) which studied various convolutional operators. A connection between Prosser's $\epsilon$-entropy of an operator and Kolmogorov's $\epsilon$-entropy of a stochastic process was shown in [2]. Independently, another group of mathematicians including Carl and Stephani [8] studied covering numbers [31] and later entropy numbers [23] in the context of operator ideals. (They seem to be unaware of Prosser's work — see e.g. [9, p. 136].)

Connections between the local theory of Banach spaces and uniform convergence of empirical means has been noted before (e.g. [22]). More recently Gurvits [14] has obtained a result relating the Rademacher type of a Banach space to the fat-shattering dimension of linear functionals on that space and hence via the key result in [4] to the covering numbers of the induced class. We will make further remarks concerning the relationship between Gurvits' approach and ours in [36]; for now let us just note that the equivalence of the type of an operator (or of the space it maps to), and the rate of decay of its entropy numbers has been (independently) shown by Kolchinskiĭ [17, 18] and Defant and Junge [12, 16]. Note that the exact formulation of their results differs. Kolchinskiĭ was motivated by probabilistic problems not unlike ours.

# 3 Generalization Bounds via Uniform Convergence

The generalization performance of learning machines can be bounded via uniform convergence results as in [34]. The key thing about these results is the role of the covering numbers of the hypothesis class — the focus of the present paper. Results for both classification and regression are now known. For the sake of concreteness, we quote below a result suitable for regression which was proved in [4]. Let $P_m(f) := \frac{1}{m} \sum_{j=1}^m f(\mathbf{x}_j)$ denote the *empirical mean* of $f$ on the sample $\mathbf{x}_1, \ldots, \mathbf{x}_m$.

**Lemma 1 (Alon, Ben–David, Cesa–Bianchi, and Haussler, 1997).** *Let $\mathcal{F}$ be a class of functions from $\mathcal{X}$ into $[0,1]$ and let $P$ be a distribution over $\mathcal{X}$. then, for all $\epsilon > 0$ and all $m \geq \frac{2}{\epsilon^2}$,*

$$\Pr\left\{\sup_{f \in \mathcal{F}} |P_m(f) - P(f)| > \epsilon\right\} \leq 12m \cdot \mathbf{E}\left[\mathcal{N}\left(\tfrac{\epsilon}{6}, \mathcal{F}, \ell_\infty^{\tilde{\mathbf{X}}^{2m}}\right)\right] e^{-\epsilon^2 m/36} \quad (2)$$

*where $\Pr$ denotes the probability w.r.t. the sample $\mathbf{x}_1, \ldots, \mathbf{x}_m$ drawn i.i.d. from $P$, and $\mathbf{E}$ the expectation w.r.t. a second sample $\tilde{\mathbf{X}}^m = (\tilde{\mathbf{x}}_1^T, \ldots, \tilde{\mathbf{x}}_{2m}^T)$ also drawn i.i.d. from $P$.*

In order to use this lemma one can make use of the fact that $\mathbf{E}\left[\mathcal{N}(\epsilon, \mathcal{F}, \ell_\infty^{\tilde{\mathbf{X}}^m})\right] \leq \mathcal{N}^m(\epsilon, \mathcal{F})$. The above result can be used to give a generalization error result by applying it to the loss-function induced class using standard techniques. Furthermore, one can obtain bounds on the generalization error of classifiers in terms of the margin achieved on a training sample in terms of these covering numbers — see [28].

# 4 Entropy Numbers for Kernel Machines

In the following we will mainly consider machines where the mapping into feature space is defined by Mercer kernels $k(\mathbf{x}, \mathbf{y})$ as they are easier to deal with using functional analytic methods. Such machines have become very popular due to the success of SV machines. Nonetheless in Subsection 4.3 we will show how a more direct approach could be taken towards upper–bounding entropy numbers.

## 4.1 Mercer's Theorem, Feature Spaces and Scaling

Our goal is to make statements about the shape of the image of the input space $\mathcal{X}$ under the feature map $\Phi(\cdot)$. We will make use of Mercer's theorem. The version stated below is a special case of the theorem proven in [20, p. 145]. In the following we will assume $(\mathcal{X}, \mu)$ to be a finite measure space, i.e. $\mu(\mathcal{X}) < \infty$. As usual, by "almost all" we mean for all elements of $\mathcal{X}^n$ except a set of $\mu^n$-measure zero.

**Theorem 1 (Mercer).** *Suppose $k \in L_\infty(\mathcal{X}^2)$ such that the integral operator $T_k : L_2(\mathcal{X}) \to L_2(\mathcal{X})$,*

$$T_k f(\cdot) := \int_{\mathcal{X}} k(\cdot, \mathbf{y}) f(\mathbf{y}) d\mu(\mathbf{y}) \tag{3}$$

*is positive. Let $\psi_j \in L_2(\mathcal{X})$ be the eigenfunction of $T_k$ associated with the eigenvalue $\lambda_j \neq 0$ and normalized such that $\|\psi_j\|_{L_2} = 1$ and let $\overline{\psi_j}$ denote its complex conjugate. Then*

*(a) $(\lambda_j(T))_j \in \ell_1$.*
*(b) $\psi_j \in L_\infty(\mathcal{X})$ and $\sup_j \|\psi_j\|_{L_\infty} < \infty$.*
*(c) $k(\mathbf{x}, \mathbf{y}) = \sum\limits_{j \in \mathbb{N}} \lambda_j \overline{\psi_j(\mathbf{x})} \psi_j(\mathbf{y})$ holds for almost all $(\mathbf{x}, \mathbf{y})$, where the series converges absolutely and uniformly for almost all $(\mathbf{x}, \mathbf{y})$.*

We will call a kernel satisfying the conditions of this theorem a *Mercer kernel*. From statement 2 of Mercer's theorem there exists some constant $C_k \in \mathbb{R}^+$ depending on $k(\cdot, \cdot)$ such that

$$|\psi_j(\mathbf{x})| \leq C_k \text{ for all } j \in \mathbb{N} \text{ and } \mathbf{x} \in \mathcal{X}. \tag{4}$$

(Actually (4) holds only for almost all $\mathbf{x} \in \mathcal{X}$, but from here on we gloss over these measure-theoretic niceties in the exposition.) Moreover from statement 3 it follows that $k(\mathbf{x}, \mathbf{y})$ corresponds to a dot product in $\ell_2$ i.e. $k(\mathbf{x}, \mathbf{y}) = \langle \Phi(\mathbf{x}), \Phi(\mathbf{y}) \rangle_{\ell_2}$ with

$$\begin{aligned} \Phi : \mathcal{X} &\to \ell_2 \\ \mathbf{x} &\mapsto (\phi_j(\mathbf{x}))_j := (\sqrt{\lambda_j} \psi_j(\mathbf{x}))_j \end{aligned} \tag{5}$$

for almost all $\mathbf{x} \in \mathcal{X}$. In the following we will (without loss of generality) assume the sequence of $(\lambda_j)_j$ be sorted in nonincreasing order. From the argument above one can see that $\Phi(\mathcal{X})$ lives not only in $\ell_2$ but in an axis parallel parallelepiped with lengths $2C_k\sqrt{\lambda_j}$.

It will be useful to consider maps that map $\Phi(\mathcal{X})$ into balls of some radius $R$ centered at the origin. The following proposition shows that the class of all these maps is determined by elements of $\ell_2$ and the sequence of eigenvalues $(\lambda_j)_j$.

**Proposition 1 (Mapping $\Phi(\mathbf{x})$ into $\ell_2$).** *Let $S$ be the diagonal map*

$$\begin{aligned} S : \mathbb{R}^{\mathbb{N}} &\to \mathbb{R}^{\mathbb{N}} \\ S : (x_j)_j &\mapsto S(x_j)_j = (s_j x_j)_j. \end{aligned} \tag{6}$$

*Then $S$ maps $\Phi(\mathcal{X})$ into a ball of finite radius $R_S$ centered at the origin if and only if $(\sqrt{\lambda_j} s_j)_j \in \ell_2$.*

PROOF.
($\Leftarrow$) Suppose $(s_j \sqrt{\lambda_j})_j \in \ell_2$ and let $R_S^2 := C_k^2 \|(s_j \sqrt{\lambda_j})_j\|_{\ell_2}^2 < \infty$. For any $\mathbf{x} \in \mathcal{X}$,

$$\|S\Phi(\mathbf{x})\|_{\ell_2}^2 = \sum_{j \in \mathbb{N}} s_j^2 \lambda_j |\psi_j(\mathbf{x})|^2 \leq \sum_{j \in \mathbb{N}} s_j^2 \lambda_j C_k^2 = R_S^2. \tag{7}$$

Hence $S\Phi(\mathcal{X}) \subseteq \ell_2$.

($\Rightarrow$) Suppose $(s_j\sqrt{\lambda_j})_j$ is not in $\ell_2$. Hence the sequence $(A_n)_n$ with $A_n := \sum_{j=1}^{n} s_j^2 \lambda_j$ is unbounded. Now define

$$a_n(\mathbf{x}) := \sum_{j=1}^{n} s_j^2 \lambda_j |\psi_j(\mathbf{x})|^2. \tag{8}$$

Then $\|a_n(\cdot)\|_{L_1(\mathcal{X})} = A_n$ due to the normalization condition on $\psi_j$. However, as $\mu(\mathcal{X}) < \infty$ there exists a set $\tilde{\mathcal{X}}$ of nonzero measure such that

$$a_n(\mathbf{x}) \geq \frac{A_n}{\mu(\mathcal{X})} \quad \text{for all } \mathbf{x} \in \tilde{\mathcal{X}}. \tag{9}$$

Combining the left side of (7) with (8) we obtain $\|S\Phi(\mathbf{x})\|_{\ell_2}^2 \geq a_n(\mathbf{x})$ for all $n \in \mathbb{N}$ and almost all $\mathbf{x}$. Since $a_n(\mathbf{x})$ is unbounded for a set $\tilde{\mathcal{X}}$ with nonzero measure in $\mathcal{X}$, we can see that $S\Phi(\mathcal{X}) \not\subseteq \ell_2$. $\blacksquare$

The consequence of this result is that there exists no *axis parallel* ellipsoid $\mathcal{E}$ not completely containing the (also) axis parallel parallelepiped $\mathcal{B}$ of sidelength $(2C_k\sqrt{\lambda_j})_j$, such that $\mathcal{E}$ would contain $\Phi(\mathcal{X})$. More formally

$$\mathcal{B} \subset \mathcal{E} \text{ if and only if } \Phi(\mathcal{X}) \subset \mathcal{E}.$$

Hence $\Phi(\mathcal{X})$ contains a set of nonzero measure of elements near the corners of the parallelepiped.

Once we know that $\Phi(\mathcal{X})$ "fills" the parallelepiped described above we can use this result to construct an inverse mapping $A$ from the unit ball in $\ell_2$ to an ellipsoid $\mathcal{E}$ such that $\Phi(\mathcal{X}) \subset \mathcal{E}$ as in the following diagram.

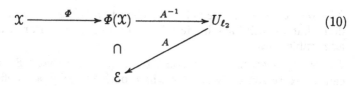

$$ \tag{10}$$

The operator $A$ will be useful for computing the entropy numbers of concatenations of operators. (Knowing the inverse will allow us to compute the forward operator, and that can be used to bound the covering numbers of the class of functions, as shown in the next subsection.) We thus seek an operator $A : \ell_2 \to \ell_2$ such that

$$A(U_{\ell_2}) \subseteq \mathcal{E}. \tag{11}$$

We can ensure this by constructing $A$ such that

$$A \colon (x_j)_j \mapsto (R_A a_j x_j)_j \tag{12}$$

with $R_A := C_k \|(\sqrt{\lambda_j}/a_j)_j\|_{\ell_2}$. From Proposition 1 it follows that all those operators $A$ for which $R_A < \infty$ will satisfy (11). We call such scaling (inverse) operators *admissible*.

## 4.2 Entropy Numbers

The next step is to compute the entropy numbers of the operator $A$ and use this to obtain bounds on the entropy numbers for kernel machines like SV machines. We will make use of the following theorem due to Gordon, König and Schütt [13, p. 226] (stated in the present form in [8, p. 17]).

**Theorem 2.** *Let $\sigma_1 \geq \sigma_2 \geq \cdots \geq \sigma_j \geq \cdots \geq 0$ be a non–increasing sequence of non–negative numbers and let*

$$D\mathbf{x} = (\sigma_1 x_1, \sigma_2 x_2, \ldots, \sigma_j x_j, \ldots) \tag{13}$$

*for $\mathbf{x} = (x_1, x_2, \ldots, x_j, \ldots) \in \ell_p$ be the diagonal operator from $\ell_p$ into itself, generated by the sequence $(\sigma_j)_j$, where $1 \leq p \leq \infty$. Then for all $n \in \mathbb{N}$,*

$$\sup_{j\in\mathbb{N}} n^{-\frac{1}{j}}(\sigma_1\sigma_2\cdots\sigma_j)^{\frac{1}{j}} \leq \epsilon_n(D) \leq 6\sup_{j\in\mathbb{N}} n^{-\frac{1}{j}}(\sigma_1\sigma_2\cdots\sigma_j)^{\frac{1}{j}}. \tag{14}$$

We can exploit the freedom in choosing $A$ to minimize an entropy number as the following corollary shows. This will be a key ingredient of our calculation of the covering numbers for SV classes, as shown below.

**Corollary 1 (Entropy numbers for $\Phi(\mathcal{X})$).** *Let $k\colon \mathcal{X} \times \mathcal{X} \to \mathbb{R}$ be a Mercer kernel and let $A$ be defined by (12). Then*

$$\epsilon_n(A\colon \ell_2 \to \ell_2) \leq \inf_{(a_s)_s \colon (\sqrt{\lambda_s}/a_s)_s \in \ell_2} \sup_{j\in\mathbb{N}} 6C_k \left\| \left(\sqrt{\lambda_s}/a_s\right)_s \right\|_{\ell_2} n^{-\frac{1}{j}}(a_1 a_2 \cdots a_j)^{\frac{1}{j}}. \tag{15}$$

This result follows immediately by identifying $D$ and $A$ and exploiting the freedom that we still have in choosing a particular operator $A$ among the class of admissible ones.

As already described in Section 1 the hypotheses that a SV machine generates can be expressed as $\langle \mathbf{w}, \tilde{\mathbf{x}} \rangle + b$ where both $\mathbf{w}$ and $\tilde{\mathbf{x}}$ are defined in the feature space $\mathcal{S} = \mathrm{span}(\Phi(\mathcal{X}))$ and $b \in \mathbb{R}$. The kernel trick as introduced by [1] was then successfully employed in [7] and [11] to extend the Optimal Margin Hyperplane classifier to what is now known as the SV machine. (The "$+b$" term is readily dealt with; we omit such considerations here though.) Consider the class

$$\mathcal{F}_{R_\mathbf{w}} := \{\langle \mathbf{w}, \tilde{\mathbf{x}} \rangle \colon \tilde{\mathbf{x}} \in \mathcal{S}, \|\mathbf{w}\| \leq R_\mathbf{w}\} \subseteq \mathbb{R}^{\mathcal{S}}.$$

Note that $\mathcal{F}_{R_\mathbf{w}}$ depends implicitly on $k$ since $\mathcal{S}$ does.

What we seek are the $\ell_\infty^m$ covering numbers for the class $\mathcal{F}_{R_\mathbf{w}}$ induced by the kernel in terms of the parameter $R_\mathbf{w}$ which is the inverse of the size of the margin in feature space, or equivalently, the size of the weight vector in feature space as defined by the dot product in $\mathcal{S}$ (see [33, 32] for details). In the following we will call such hypothesis classes with length constraint on the weight vectors in feature space *SV classes*. Let $T$ be the operator $T = S_{\tilde{\mathbf{X}}^m} R_{\mathbf{w}}$ where $R_{\mathbf{w}} \in \mathbb{R}$ and the operator $S_{\tilde{\mathbf{X}}^m}$ is defined by

$$
\begin{aligned}
S_{\tilde{\mathbf{X}}^m} &: \ell_2 \to \ell_\infty^m \\
S_{\tilde{\mathbf{X}}^m} &: \mathbf{w} \mapsto (\langle \tilde{\mathbf{x}}_1, \mathbf{w} \rangle, \dots, \langle \tilde{\mathbf{x}}_m, \mathbf{w} \rangle).
\end{aligned}
\tag{16}
$$

with $\tilde{\mathbf{x}}_j \in \Phi(\mathcal{X})$ for all $j$. The following theorem is useful when computing entropy numbers in terms of $T$ and $A$. It is originally due to Maurey, and was extended by Carl [10]. See [36] for some extensions and historical remarks.

**Theorem 3 (Carl and Stephani [8, p. 246]).** *Let $S \in \mathcal{L}(H, \ell_\infty^m)$ where $H$ is a Hilbert space. Then there exists a constant $c > 0$ such that for all $m \in \mathbb{N}$, and $1 \le j \le m$*

$$
e_n(S) \le c \|S\| \left( n^{-1} \log \left( 1 + \frac{m}{n} \right) \right)^{1/2}.
$$

The restatement of Theorem 3 in terms of $\epsilon_{2^{n-1}} = e_n$ will be useful in the following. Under the assumptions above we have

$$
\epsilon_n(S) \le c \|S\| \left( (\log n + 1)^{-1} \log \left( 1 + \frac{m}{\log n + 1} \right) \right)^{1/2}.
\tag{17}
$$

Now we can combine the bounds on entropy numbers of $A$ and $S_{\mathbf{X}^m}$ to obtain bounds for SV classes. First we need the following lemma.

**Lemma 2 (Carl and Stephani [8, p. 11]).** *Let $E, F, G$ be Banach spaces, $R \in \mathcal{L}(F, G)$, and $S \in \mathcal{L}(E, F)$. Then, for $n, t \in \mathbb{N}$,*

$$
\epsilon_{nt}(RS) \le \epsilon_n(R) \epsilon_t(S)
\tag{18}
$$
$$
\epsilon_n(RS) \le \epsilon_n(R) \|S\|
\tag{19}
$$
$$
\epsilon_n(RS) \le \epsilon_n(S) \|R\|.
\tag{20}
$$

*Note that the latter two inequalities follow directly from the fact that $\epsilon_1(R) = \|R\|$ for all $R \in \mathcal{L}(F, G)$.*

**Theorem 4 (Bounds for SV classes).** *Let $k$ be a Mercer kernel, let $\Phi$ be induced via (5) and let $T := S_{\tilde{\mathbf{X}}^m} R_{\mathbf{w}}$ where $S_{\tilde{\mathbf{X}}^m}$ is given by (16) and $R_{\mathbf{w}} \in \mathbb{R}^+$. Let $A$ be defined by (12) and suppose $\tilde{\mathbf{x}}_j = \Phi(\mathbf{x}_j)$ for $j = 1, \dots, m$. Then the entropy numbers of $T$ satisfy the following inequalities:*

$$
\epsilon_n(T) \le c \|A\| R_{\mathbf{w}} \log^{-1/2} n \log^{-1/2} \left( 1 + \frac{m}{\log n} \right)
\tag{21}
$$
$$
\epsilon_n(T) \le R_{\mathbf{w}} \epsilon_n(A)
\tag{22}
$$
$$
\epsilon_{nt}(T) \le c R_{\mathbf{w}} \log^{-1/2} n \log^{-1/2} \left( 1 + \frac{m}{\log n} \right) \epsilon_t(A)
$$

*where $C_k$ and $c$ are defined as in Corollary 1 and Lemma 3.*

This result gives several options for bounding $\epsilon_n(T)$. The reason for using $\epsilon_n$ instead of $e_n$ is that the index only may be integer in the former case (whereas it can be in $[1, \infty)$ in the latter), thus making it easier to obtain tighter bounds. We shall see in examples later that the best inequality to use depends on the rate of decay of the eigenvalues of $k$. The result gives effective bounds on $\mathcal{N}^m(\epsilon, \mathcal{F}_{R_w})$ since

$$\epsilon_n(T : \ell_2 \to \ell_\infty^m) \le \epsilon_0 \Rightarrow \mathcal{N}^m(\epsilon_0, \mathcal{F}_{R_w}) \le n.$$

PROOF. We will use the following factorization of $T$ to upper bound $\epsilon_n(T)$.

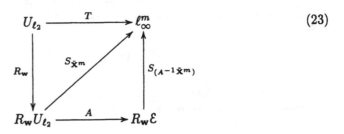

$$(23)$$

The top left part of the diagram follows from the definition of $T$. The fact that remainder commutes stems from the fact that since $A$ is diagonal, it is self-adjoint and so

$$\langle \mathbf{w}, \tilde{\mathbf{x}} \rangle = \langle \mathbf{w}, A A^{-1} \tilde{\mathbf{x}} \rangle = \langle A \mathbf{w}, A^{-1} \tilde{\mathbf{x}} \rangle. \tag{24}$$

Instead of computing the covering number of $T = S_{\tilde{\mathbf{x}}^m} R_{\mathbf{w}}$ directly, which is difficult or wasteful, as the the bound on $S_{\tilde{\mathbf{x}}^m}$ does not take into account that $\tilde{\mathbf{x}} \in \mathcal{E}$ but just makes the assumption of $\tilde{\mathbf{x}} \in \rho U_{\ell_2}$ for some $\rho > 0$, we will represent $T$ as $S_{(A^{-1}\tilde{\mathbf{x}}^m)} A R_{\mathbf{w}}$. This is more efficient as we constructed $A$ such that $\Phi(\mathcal{X}) A^{-1} \in U_{\ell_2}$ filling a larger proportion of it than just $\frac{1}{\rho} \Phi(\mathcal{X})$.

By construction of $A$ and the Cauchy-Schwarz inequality we have $\|S_{A^{-1}\tilde{\mathbf{x}}^m}\| = 1$. Thus applying lemma 2 to the factorization of $T$ and using Theorem 3 proves the theorem. ∎

One can give (see below) asymptotic rates of decay for $\epsilon_n(A)$. (In fact we can determine non-asymptotic results with explicitly evaluable constants.) It is thus of some interest to give overall asymptotic rates of decay of $\epsilon_n(T)$ in terms of the order of $\epsilon_n(A)$.

**Lemma 3 (Rate bounds on $\epsilon_n$).** *Let $k$ be a Mercer kernel and suppose $A$ is the scaling operator associated with it as defined by (12).*

*(a) If $\epsilon_n(A) = O(\log^{-\alpha} n)$ for some $\alpha > 0$ then $\epsilon_n(T) = O(\log^{-(\alpha+2)} n)$.*
*(b) If $\log \epsilon_n(A) = O(\log^{-\beta} n)$ for some $\beta > 0$ then $\log \epsilon_n(T) = O(\log^{-\beta} n)$.*

This Lemma (the proof of which is omitted; see [35]) shows that in the first case, Maurey's result (theorem 3) allows an improvement in the exponent of the entropy number of $T$, whereas in the second, it affords none (since the entropy numbers decay so fast anyway). The Maurey result may still help in that case though for nonasymptotic $n$. In a nutshell we can always obtain rates of convergence better than those due to Maurey's theorem because we are not dealing with *arbitrary* mappings into infinite dimensional spaces. In fact, for logarithmic dependency of $\epsilon_n(T)$ on $n$, the effect of the kernel is so strong that it completely dominates the $1/\epsilon^2$ behaviour for arbitrary Hilbert spaces. An example of such a kernel is $k(x,y) = \exp(-(x-y)^2)$.

### 4.3 Empirical Bounds

Instead of theoretically determining the shape of $\Phi(\mathcal{X})$ *a priori* one could use the training and/or test data to empirically estimate its shape and use this quantity to compute an operator $B_{\text{emp}}$ analogously to (10) which performs the mapping described above. We merely flag this here — the full development of these ideas requires considerable further work and will be deferred to a subsequent paper. There are some remarks in the full version of this paper [35]. Furthermore the statistical argument needed to exploit such techniques (bounding generalization error in terms of *empirical* covering numbers has now been developed — see [29].

## 5  Eigenvalue Decay Rates

The results presented above show that if one knows the eigenvalue sequence $(\lambda_i)_i$ of a compact operator, one can bound its entropy numbers. A commonly used kernel is $k(x,y) = e^{-(x-y)^2}$ which has noncompact support. The induced integral operator $(T_k f)(x) = \int_{-\infty}^{\infty} k(x,y)f(y)dy$ then has a continuous spectrum and thus $T_k$ is not compact [6, p.267]. The question arises: can we make use of such kernels in SV machines and still obtain generalization error bounds of the form developed above? This problem can be readily resolved by analysing the $v$-periodic extension of the kernel in question $k_v(x) := \sum_{j=-\infty}^{\infty} k(x-jv)$. A simple argument gives

**Lemma 4.** *Let* $k\colon \mathbb{R} \to \mathbb{R}$ *be a symmetric convolution kernel, let* $K(\omega) = F[k(x)](\omega)$ *denote the Fourier transform of* $k(\cdot)$ *and* $k_v$ *denote the* $v$-*periodic kernel derived from* $k$ *(also assume that* $k_v$ *exists). Then* $k_v$ *has a representation as a Fourier series with* $\omega_0 := \frac{2\pi}{v}$ *and* $k_v(x-y) = \sum_{j=-\infty}^{\infty} \frac{\sqrt{2\pi}}{v} K(j\omega_0)e^{ij\omega_0 x}$ *Moreover* $\lambda_j = \sqrt{2\pi}K(j\omega_0)$ *for* $j \in \mathbb{Z}$ *and* $C_k = \sqrt{\frac{2}{v}}$.

This lemma tells one how to compute the discrete eigenvalue sequence for kernels with infinite support; for more details see [35].

The above results show the overall covering numbers of a SV machine are controlled by the entropy numbers of the admissible scaling operator $A\colon \epsilon_n(A\colon \ell_2 \to \ell_2)$. One can work this out (with constants), although it is somewhat intricate to do so. Here we simply state how $\epsilon_n(A)$ depends asymptotically on the eigenvalues of $T_k$ for a certain class of kernels.

**Proposition 2 (Exponential–Polynomial decay).** *Suppose $k$ is a Mercer kernel with $\lambda_j = \beta^2 e^{-\alpha j^p}$ for some $\alpha, \beta, p > 0$. Then $\ln \epsilon_n^{-1}(A\colon \ell_2 \to \ell_2) = O(\ln^{\frac{p}{p+1}} n)$*

An example of such a kernel (for $p = 2$) is $k(x) = e^{-x^2}$. It can also be shown that the rate in the above proposition is asymptotically tight. For a proof, and related results, see [35].

## 6 The Missing Pieces and Some Conclusions

In this short version we have omitted many details and extensions such as

**Discretization** How should one choose $v$ in periodizing a non-compact kernel?

**Higher Dimensions** The results need to be extended to multi-dimensional kernels to be practically useful. Several additional technical complications arise in doing so.

**Glueing it all Together** We have given the ingredients but not baked the cake. Since the approach we have taken is new, and since there are a wide range of different uniform convergence results one may use we have refrained from putting it all together into "master generalization error theorem." It should be clear that it is *possible* to do so.

Combining all these pieces together does give an (albeit complicated) answer to the question "what is the effect of the kernel?" Different kernels, or even different widths of the same kernel, give rise to different covering numbers and hence different generalization performance. We hope eventually to be able to give simple rules of thumb concerning the overall effect. The mere fact that entropy number techniques provide a handle on the question is interesting in itself though.

In summary, we have shown how to connect properties known about mappings into feature spaces with bounds on the covering numbers. Our reasoning relied on the fact that this mapping exhibits certain decay properties to ensure rapid convergence and a constraint on the size of the weight vector in feature space. This means that the corresponding algorithms have to restrict exactly this quantity to ensure good generalization performance. This is exactly what is done in Support Vector machines. The method used to obtain the results (reasoning via entropy numbers of operators) would seem to be a nice new viewpoint and valuable for other problems.

## References

1. M. A. Aizerman, E. M. Braverman, and L. I. Rozonoér. Theoretical foundations of the potential function method in pattern recognition learning. *Automation and Remote Control*, 25:821–837, 1964.
2. S. Akashi. An operator theoretical characterization of $\epsilon$-entropy in gaussian processes. *Kodai Mathematical Journal*, 9:58–67, 1986.

3. S. Akashi. The asymptotic behaviour of $\varepsilon$-entropy of a compact positive operator. *Journal of Mathematical Analysis and Applications*, 153:250–257, 1990.

4. N. Alon, S. Ben-David, N. Cesa-Bianchi, and D. Haussler. Scale–sensitive Dimensions, Uniform Convergence, and Learnability. *Journal of the ACM*, 44(4):615–631, 1997.

5. M. Anthony. Probabilistic analysis of learning in artificial neural networks: The pac model and its variants. *Neural Computing Surveys*, 1:1–47, 1997. http://www.icsi.berkeley.edu/~jagota/NCS.

6. Robert Ash. *Information Theory*. Interscience Publishers, New York, 1965.

7. B. E. Boser, I. M. Guyon, and V. N. Vapnik. A training algorithm for optimal margin classifiers. In D. Haussler, editor, *5th Annual ACM Workshop on COLT*, pages 144–152, Pittsburgh, PA, 1992. ACM Press.

8. B. Carl and I. Stephani. *Entropy, compactness, and the approximation of operators*. Cambridge University Press, Cambridge, UK, 1990.

9. Bernd Carl. Entropy numbers of diagonal operators with an application to eigenvalue problems. *Journal of Approximation Theory*, 32:135–150, 1981.

10. Bernd Carl. Inequalities of Bernstein-Jackson-type and the degree of compactness of operators in Banach spaces. *Annales de l'Institut Fourier*, 35(3):79–118, 1985.

11. C. Cortes and V. Vapnik. Support vector networks. *Machine Learning*, 20:273 – 297, 1995.

12. Martin Defant and Marius Junge. Characterization of weak type by the entropy distribution of $r$-nuclear operators. *Studia Mathematica*, 107(1):1–14, 1993.

13. Y. Gordon, H. König, and C. Schütt. Geometric and probabilistic estimates for entropy and approximation numbers of operators. *Journal of Approximation Theory*, 49:219–239, 1987.

14. Leonid Gurvits. A note on a scale-sensitive dimension of linear bounded functionals in Banach spaces. Technical report, NEC Research Institute, 1997. To appear in ALT97 Proceedings.

15. D. Jagerman. $\varepsilon$-entropy and approximation of bandlimited functions. *SIAM Journal on Applied Mathematics*, 17(2):362–377, 1969.

16. Marius Junge and Martin Defant. Some estimates of entropy numbers. *Israel Journal of Mathematics*, 84:417–433, 1993.

17. V.I. Kolchinskiĭ. Operators of type $p$ and metric entropy. *Teoriya Veroyatnosteĭ Matematicheskaya Statistika*, 38:69–76, 135, 1988. (In Russian. MR 89j:60007).

18. V.I. Kolchinskiĭ. Entropic order of operators in banach spaces and the central limit theorem. *Theory of Probability and its Applications*, 36(2):303–315, 1991.

19. A.N. Kolmogorov and V.M. Tihomirov. $\varepsilon$-entropy and $\varepsilon$-capacity of sets in functional spaces. *American Mathematical Society Translations, Series 2*, 17:277–364, 1961.

20. H. König. *Eigenvalue Distribution of Compact Operators*. Birkhäuser Verlag, Basel, 1986.

21. T. Koski, L.-E. Persson, and J. Peetre. $\varepsilon$-entropy $\varepsilon$-rate, and interpolation spaces revisited with an application to linear communication channels. *Journal of Mathematical Analysis and Applications*, 186:265–276, 1994.

22. Alain Pajor. *Sous-espaces $\ell_n^1$ des espaces de Banach*. Hermann, Paris, 1985.

23. Albrecht Pietsch. *Operator ideals*. North-Holland, Amsterdam, 1980.

24. L.S. Pontriagin and L.G. Schnirelmann. Sur une propriété métrique de la dimension. *Annals of Mathematics*, 33:156–162, 1932.

25. R.T. Prosser. The $\varepsilon$-Entropy and $\varepsilon$-Capacity of Certain Time–Varying Channels. *Journal of Mathematical Analysis and Applications*, 16:553–573, 1966.

26. R.T. Prosser and W.L. Root. The $\varepsilon$-entropy and $\varepsilon$-capacity of certain time-invariant channels. *Journal of Mathematical Analysis and its Applications*, 21:233–241, 1968.

27. C.E. Shannon. A mathematical theory of communication. *Bell System Technical Journal*, 27:379–423, 623–656, 1948.

28. J. Shawe-Taylor, P.L. Bartlett, R.C. Williamson, and M. Anthony. Structural risk minimization over data-dependent hierarchies. *IEEE Transactions on Information Theory*, 44(5):1926–1940, 1998.

29. J. Shawe-Taylor and Robert C. Williamson. Generalization performance of classifiers in terms of observed covering numbers. 4th European Conference on Computational Learning Theory.

30. A. J. Smola, B. Schölkopf, and K.-R. Müller. The connection between regularization operators and support vector kernels. *Neural Networks*, 1998. in press.

31. H. Triebel. Interpolationseigenschaften von Entropie- und Durchmesseridealen kompackter Operatoren. *Studia Mathematica*, 34:89–107, 1970.

32. V. Vapnik. *The Nature of Statistical Learning Theory*. Springer Verlag, New York, 1995.

33. V. Vapnik and A. Chervonenkis. *Theory of Pattern Recognition [in Russian]*. Nauka, Moscow, 1974. (German Translation: W. Wapnik & A. Tscherwonenkis, *Theorie der Zeichenerkennung*, Akademie–Verlag, Berlin, 1979).

34. V.N. Vapnik and A.Ya. Chervonenkis. Necessary and sufficient conditions for the uniform convergence of means to their expectations. *Theory of Probability and its Applications*, 26(3):532–553, 1981.

35. R.C. Williamson, A. Smola, and B. Schölkopf. Generalization performance of regularization networks and support vector machines entropy numbers of compact operators. Technical report, Neurocolt Technical Report 1998-019, 1998. ftp://www.neurocolt.com/pub/neurocolt/tech_reports/1998/98019.ps.Z.

36. Robert C. Williamson, Bernhard Schölkopf, and Alex Smola. A Maximum Margin Miscellany. Typescript, March 1998.

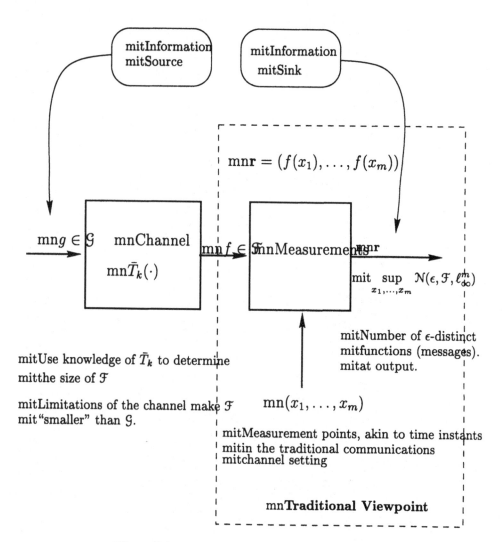

**Fig. 1.** Schematic picture of the new viewpoint.

# Author Index

# Springer
# and the
# environment

At Springer we firmly believe that an international science publisher has a special obligation to the environment, and our corporate policies consistently reflect this conviction.
We also expect our business partners – paper mills, printers, packaging manufacturers, etc. – to commit themselves to using materials and production processes that do not harm the environment. The paper in this book is made from low- or no-chlorine pulp and is acid free, in conformance with international standards for paper permanency.

 Springer

# Lecture Notes in Artificial Intelligence (LNAI)

# Lecture Notes in Computer Science